WRITING IN POLITICAL SCIENCE
A PRACTICAL GUIDE

THIRD EDITION

Diane E. Schmidt
California State University, Chico

PEARSON
Longman

New York   Boston   San Francisco
London   Toronto   Sydney   Tokyo   Singapore   Madrid
Mexico City   Munich   Paris   Cape Town   Hong Kong   Montreal

Vice President and Publisher: Priscilla McGeehon
Executive Editor: Eric Stano
Senior Marketing Manager: Elizabeth Fogarty
Media and Supplements Editor: Kristi Olson
Cover Design Manager: Wendy Ann Fredericks
Cover Designer: Maria Ilardi
Cover Photo: © Jonathan Kirn/ Stock Connection/PictureQuest
Manufacturing Buyer: Lucy Hebard
Printer and Binder: Courier Corporation/Westford
Cover Printer: Lehigh Press, Inc.

Please visit our website at http://www.ablongman.com

ISBN 0-321-21735-7

3 4 5 6 7 8 9 10—CRW—07 06 05 04

Dedication

To Alan, Casey, Jonathan, and Margie
and
in memory of Margaret and Ausby

Contents

Preface

As political scientists, we are rarely directly involved in politics; instead, we write about it the same way sports commentators report on baseball games. We theorize and conjecture but rarely play the game. Some of us keep statistics about our players, some of us just provide the color commentary while the players are in the arena, and some of us analyze the actions of the players to see how the winners won and the losers lost. Mostly, we study and learn by observing and providing a reasoned perspective about political activities.

What political scientists do best is write. Part of what this book is about is writing in political science. It is not a formal book of style nor is it a tome on what it means to think critically about politics or to be a political scientist. It is a practical, sometimes irreverent, and usually serious guide to becoming a color commentator, armchair quarterback, or an expert on politics. It is about becoming a professional in political science and communicating with a community of students and scholars of government and policy. In other words, this book is a guide to communicating about political events, about political ideas, about political passions, and about political agendas. It is not just about writing; it is about *thinking* about politics, *reading* about politics, and *arguing* about politics.

There are many reasons why I wrote this book. I noticed early in my teaching career that students in my courses, regardless of their major or class standing or grade point average, exhibited a general confusion about what and how to communicate in political science assignments. My first response was to condemn the public high school system and the English department for not training students to write coherently. But that was too easy. Upon investigation, I found that there was a different approach to writing among political science, English composition, and the hard sciences. Approximately at the same time I discovered the Writing Across the Curriculum approach, I received the best, most instructive assessment of the problem from a retiring English composition professor. She said, "I'm not surprised that your students are having problems. We teach them to write for us. If you want them to write well in political science, teach them to write for political science." That, in a nutshell, is what Writing Across the Curriculum promotes. That, in a nutshell, is what this book is intended to accomplish.

I wrote this book for political science majors and for students who are passing through the discipline as an elected activity. But this guide is more than an abridged writer's guide with explicit references to political science writing assignments. In addition to outlining the standard form for student assignments, the guide provides practical information and advice about criteria used to evaluate student assignments. It provides and uses the vocabulary of the political science discourse community while keeping the directions and formats simple enough to understand and execute without guidance from an instructor. Anyone who can follow a recipe in a cookbook, read an auto repair manual, or use an automatic teller machine at a bank, can follow the instructions in this book and turn out a professional level, high quality manuscript concerning politics.

Unfortunately, this book is not a jump-start for writing and the directions must be followed closely. The advice in this book cannot compensate for poor effort or preparation. Although many parts of this guide mirror sections of general stylebooks and English composition textbooks, it is not a substitute for a comprehensive style guide or a course in composition. This guide stresses the application of general principles of expository writing to common projects and assignments given to students in political science classes. The style and composition sections are designed to enhance and refresh skills already acquired through introductory composition coursework. These sections build on standard writing forms while applying them to the kind of study and investigation conducted in the discipline of political science.

In many ways, this guide is an extended information sheet, not unlike those given to students by their professors. In addition to stating criteria for assignments, it includes gentle reminders about critical thinking, research habits, and general formatting of manuscripts. The guide provides the instruction and examples of political science writing assignments that help students begin and end in the right direction for meeting the instructor's expectations.

More importantly, the guide provides examples, yes, examples of actual student manuscripts written for the sole purpose of getting a grade. None of the student papers was written expressly for the book. Some were written before I ever conceived the idea of writing the book. With a few exceptions, the papers were written by students in my courses and reflect some of the best examples of papers produced by following the format and structure directions for the particular type of writing assignment required in those courses.

In fact, the examples in this guide are some of its most distinguishing and beneficial aspects. Unlike standard guides for writing research papers or even guides to writing in political science, this guide provides, in exhaustive detail, an explanation about the difference between writing an analysis of legislation or an analysis of a public policy *and* how to write them both. Because it is important for students to see, and not to be just told, that different courses and different subfields in political science have different forms and expectations for written research, there is an example for every exercise and every assignment listed in the book.

Because the book includes both the directions concerning form and examples that exhibit an application of such forms, students will, with or without an instructor's help, be able to choose and narrow a topic, formulate a research agenda, execute a study, write about the findings, and learn something about politics at the same time. The examples in this guide, though very good, are not necessarily the most spectacular work performed concerning the topic or assignment requirements. Those standards are difficult and almost impossible for most people to achieve. No, the examples reflect the efforts of good, hardworking, conscientious students who followed directions, researched their topics earnestly, and produced fine manuscripts which encompass a reasoned perspective on their topics. With the instructor's help, students can use the advice and examples as templates for classroom work. Without the instructor, students may reasonably assume that some approximation of an example related to the course focus will be a good approach.

There is one aspect of this book that may not seem obvious at first that I should explain. The examples in this guide are particularly skewed toward American government, public policy, public law, and public administration. There are several reasons for this. Although I am cross-trained in all these areas, I teach American government and public policy. The examples come from my students because I know their potential. I set the goals, structured the incentives for achieving them, and measured how closely they were achieved. The examples are testimony to the utility of providing the students a clear statement of goals, of expectations, and of standards for assignments. I know these techniques work because they have worked for me at every course level from introductory to graduate classes.

Because the techniques used in this guide are based on a Writing Across the Curriculum perspective, they have also worked for colleagues and students in several sub-fields, several disciplines, and several institutions who adopted this book in draft form. In fact my book was used to help train Lithuanian masters students in a Master's in Public Administration program in Lithuania! From freshman to graduate level, from history to anthropology, this guide has been helpful for instructors and students alike. Just like a recipe for cheesecake or barbecue, the application of these techniques varies between users. Instructors put in their own personal touches, accents, and emphasis. In contrast, my students sent copies to friends and siblings and have taken the guide along to law or graduate school because of its versatility and straightforward, understandable advice.

Nonetheless, the principles and advice in the guide can be applied to political theory, comparative government, and international relations. Wherever possible and appropriate, I have provided instruction and advice about using the materials in these fields. The topic section has examples of choosing subfield specific topics for all subfields. The sections on enhancing comprehension and synthesis as well as the section on handling and processing class materials are standard. The section on conventional papers includes a short discussion of how such papers are used in other subfields. The advice concerning assignments requiring special analytical techniques and assignments in applied political science can be utilized for any institutional level regardless of the country on which or in which it was performed. Finally, the section on managing and preserving achievements for career development is not subfield specific.

Thus, what this guide lacks in discipline breadth, it makes up for in depth and comprehensiveness related to instructing on the discourse, the professional standards, and the method of discovery in political science as a profession. The examples were taken from a cross-section of student writing styles and issues of interest to many students. While each paper exhibits a unique perspective, the thread that ties them together is the salient and controversial nature of each topic. As with any work, some gross errors were made by students and thus corrected. Some typographical errors are my fault. I have never been a good copy editor for my own work. For the most part, the papers clearly reflect the students' efforts. Small mistakes in logic, as well as some usage errors, were preserved to maintain the personality and spirit of the writers. As teaching tools, they are instructive. As statements on political events, they are interesting and well reasoned. As examples, they set standards that are attainable. This combination makes these student papers assets to the guide and makes the goals of the guide attainable.

For the second and third editions, I added material and expanded sections on Internet research, Internet source evaluation, reading tables and graphs, creating tables and graphs, writing editorials, writing case studies, and referencing. The section on Internet research was co-authored by a political science librarian according to the American Library Association's standards for research literacy. Unlike other Internet guides that are written by technicians or scholars in the field, this section provides practical techniques *actually used by students* for student research. So much of the available advice is written for users who actually enjoy "surfing" the net. I have found that my students prefer direct practical advice for locating information fast. This section provides the minimum information on Internet terminology while focusing the student's attention on efficient Internet use.

I also added an expanded section on research methods and statistical research. Because the Internet provides a dearth of data, and because spreadsheet technology is so user-friendly, I added a section about locating and using data. I included a section on primary research for conducting interviews, creating surveys, and analyzing surveys. Included in this section is advice on reading and constructing tables, graphs, and figures. I also included a section on finding secondary sources and data on the Internet. Finally, I provided Web site addresses and advice for using Web-based information.

I also expanded and improved the referencing section. I added formats for Internet citations both in the text as well as in the bibliography. I also provided comparative formats for *MLA*, *Chicago Manual of Style*, and *APA styles*. For each type of source, I provided an example from each of the three styles.

In addition, I added editorials and case studies. Editorial writing is a skill that helps students participate in the process after leaving their educational institutions. Furthermore, unlike concept or position papers, the case study approach to the study of politics provides opportunities for students to apply what they learned in class to a specific agency or entity. I included two types of case studies. The first type is an academic case study approach where students learn to evaluate analysis problems in organizations. The second type is a problem solving case study where the student chooses a particular problem, researches it, and provides a recommendation for resolving the problem.

Finally, I added new examples of writing assignments in the third edition. I added new examples of proposals, legislative analysis, policy evaluation, policy proposals, and clipping files. These new examples highlight the changes in researching in these fields, particularly given the wealth of information available through government and private organizational Web sites.

In sum, this is not just another writing guide. It is a complete guide for being or becoming a professional in political science. It can be used from freshman to graduate level coursework, from entering a student career to graduating and pursuing a professional career after graduation. It is a style guide, a class handout, a writing manual, an organizing guide, and a resume guide. It is everything students need to begin their research, their writing, and their careers. Enjoy!

Acknowledgments

I wish to express my appreciation to the many people who encouraged me and helped me in the preparation of the first, second, or third edition of this book, including Bruce Appleby, Bob Lorinskas, Terry Plain, Sari Ramsey, Jerry Hostetler, Amy Andrews, Leila Niehuser, Cecilia Lause, Mark Toews, Beth McMillin, David Phihour, Jon Ebeling, Kathi Fountain, Rich Meade, Chris Trowbridge, Steffan Winkler, Judy Bordin, Eric Stano, and Rick Ruddel. I am also indebted to my students who have been complementary and supportive of my efforts in this third edition to help them develop professionally.

Finally, I am indebted to friends and family for their unconditional support of this project including Kay Heidbreder, Marji Morgan, Suzy Parker, Teresa Murphy, Cindy McKinney, Cindy McGee, Jim Mallien, Joan Brown, Bonnie Hallman, Nicole Thompson, Don McBride, and Donna Kemp. They have been friends when I needed them. I also want to thank my family, especially my mother Margie Brown and my sisters Sharon Rankin and Karon Houck, for their support and pride in my accomplishments. Last, but not least, I wish to thank my sons Casey and Jonathan for being patient during my never-ending string of projects and my husband, Alan, for his contributions to the text and his support and understanding when I was too involved in this project to worry about less pressing matters. These are the people I cherish most and who have been my greatest inspiration. Thank you.

Diane E. Schmidt

CHAPTER 1

Political Inquiry

Introduction

This writing guide is designed to help students sharpen, reinforce, and develop good writing and research habits in political science. Writing is a process through which we learn to communicate with others. No one expects students to be perfect writers. We all learn and help each other learn. Through organization, writing and re-writing drafts, and logical presentation of our ideas, we engage in an intellectual process which helps us grow and be a part of the discourse community of political science.

What the guide is supposed to do:

1. Sharpen writing skills particular to political science.
2. Provide information to students about standards and expectations concerning political science writing.
3. Help students differentiate between writing for political science and other disciplines.

What the guide cannot do:

1. This material does not teach primary writing skills.
2. This material is not intended to be a substitute for a formal class in writing.
3. This material will not teach grammar, spelling, or punctuation.
4. This material cannot substitute for poor preparation.

The Art of Political Inquiry Defined

Many students are unaware that writing assignments for political science classes requires different skills from those required for English composition, creative writing, and journalism courses. Although the basic skills are the same, political scientists, as members of a discipline:

1. Ask different questions and seek different answers to questions than those of the humanities and physical sciences.
2. Are interested in more than a description of what happened, where something happened, or when something happened.
3. Are interested in the political process or the causal connections between political events.

An event or a phenomenon must be politically relevant for it to be of interest to political science scholars. Of course, the standard definition of what is politically relevant is often in the eye of the beholder! A general rule for writing in political science classes is to always ask yourself, before you write anything: What are the politics or power relationships existing in a political event?

Professional Level Research

Professional research in political science is based on the acquisition of scientific knowledge. Locating scientific knowledge requires developing or applying theories either through induction (based on observations) or deduction (based on prior expectations). According to Jones and Olson (1996), such theories include:

1. *Systems theory:* this theory explains political activities as part of a process or system. Researchers using this theory explain political phenomena by examining elements in the political environment (citizen activism, parties, interest groups, etc.).
2. *Power theory:* this theory explains political activities by examining the power relationship between individuals or groups.
3. *Goals theory:* this theory explains political activities by examining the purpose or goals of political phenomena.
4. *Rational Choice theory:* this theory explains political activities as a result of individuals' preferences and self-interest.

Professional Methods of Investigation

There are a variety of approaches to examining political phenomena.

1. *Philosophical Method:* those using this approach examine the scope, purpose, and values of government activity. Often, those using this method ask how government *should* act.
2. *Historical Method:* those using this approach examine what conditions contributed to the occurrence of government activity.
3. *Comparative Method:* those using this approach compare and contrast experiences of governments, states, and other political entities.
4. *Juridical Method:* those using this approach examine the legal basis for government activities.
5. *Behavioral Method:* those using this approach study the behavior of political actors by examining data collected on actual political occurrences.
6. *Post-behavioral Method:* those using this approach examine, usually with mathematical models, not only observed behavior but values associated with the behavior.

For more information on political inquiry in political science, see Laurence F. Jones and Edwards C. Olson. 1996. *Political Science Research: A Handbook of Scope and Method.* NY: HarperCollins.

Types of Student Writing

Although professional level research is rarely expected of students, political science assignments often emulate professional research. The following is a list of common types of writing assignments required in political science classes.

Analysis: these assignments usually ask students to examine the relationships between the parts of a political document or some political events. Typically, these assignments require the student to provide a perspective or reasoned opinion about the significance of an event or a document. For example, students may be required to assert and defend an opinion about the most important features in the Bill of Rights.

Argument: these assignments often require the student to prove or debate a point. Typically, these assignments ask for normative assertions supported by evidence and examples. For instance, instructors may ask students to provide an argument supporting (or not) automatic voter registration, random drug testing, or a constitutional amendment protecting the flag.

Cause and Effect: these assignments typically require the student to speculate about the reasons why some political event has occurred. For example, students may be asked why people vote, why members of Congress worry about their images, what caused the civil war, or why some people are disillusioned with government.

Classify: these assignments usually ask the student to identify a pattern or system of classifying objects such as types of voters, types of political systems, or types of committees in Congress.

Compare or Contrast: these assignments usually ask the student to identify the differences and similarities between political roles, political systems, or political events.

Definition: these assignments usually ask the student to define a political concept, term, or phrase such as democracy, socialism, or capitalism. Students must provide examples of distinguishing features and differentiate the topic from others in its functional class.

Process: these assignments usually ask the student to describe how some political phenomena relate functionally to other political phenomena. For example, students may be asked to describe how media influence voting behavior or how decisions are made in committees.

The Process of Political Inquiry

Professional political scientists, as part of a discourse community, engage in a process of political inquiry that involves using research techniques, critical thinking skills, and theory building. In general, political inquiry involves posing a question (a hypothesis), collecting data, analyzing the data, and drawing conclusions about whether the data support the hypothesis.

Understanding the nature of evidence and uses of data to support an assertion or hypothesis is critical to the inquiry process. The process functionally relates questions to evidence to conclusions to knowledge.

Hypothesis

Evidence

Conclusions

Knowledge

A **hypothesis** is a generalization that can be tested. Hypotheses state **expected** relationships between the *dependant variable* (the event being explained) and the *independent variables* (occurrences that caused or are associated with causing the event). Most importantly, hypotheses assert precisely how a change in the independent variable(s) change(s) the dependent variable.

Data are **evidence**. There are two kinds of data:

Quantitative evidence: objective or numerical data usually from surveys, polls, tests, or experiments.

Qualitative evidence: subjective or authoritative data usually from interviews, first-hand observations, inference, or expert opinions.

Conclusions are assertions made by the author concerning the relationship between the hypothesis and the evidence.

Knowledge is what we have learned from political inquiry. The goal of all political inquiry is to contribute to a universal body of knowledge. As scholars, we are obliged to learn and contribute to this body of knowledge.

The Author's Argument: The Nature of Assertions

Sometimes, in conversation with friends and colleagues, we take for granted that assertions or statements are true or are reasonably close to being correct. Sometimes we even switch from opinions to beliefs to facts as though they were of the same class of statements. These terms, however, have specific meanings and, as critical thinkers, we need to distinguish clearly between statements of fact, of opinion, of belief, and of prejudice.

Beliefs are convictions based on personal faith, values, perceptions of morality, and cultural experiences. They are not based on fact or evidence. Like facts, they cannot be disproved and are not subject to argument.

Facts are verifiable information. They do not make good assertions because the truth of a fact is not debatable.

Opinions are judgments based on facts. A thesis sentence of an argument is an opinion. Opinions are testable and arguable because they are viewpoints arrived at through the examination of facts and evidence. Opinions are not arguments—arguments with supporting evidence are used to support opinions.

Prejudices are opinions that have been formed on insufficient or unexamined evidence. They are often thoughtless oversimplifications and typically reflect a narrow-minded view of the world. They are testable and easily refutable by the presentation of facts and evidence.

The Author's Evidence: Supporting an Argument with Data

The strength of an argument rises and falls based on the evidence or data presented by the writer to support an assertion. Specificity and breadth are the main characteristics of good supporting evidence. To convince readers of the correctness of an assertion, writers must provide readers with evidence that is accurate and relevant (relating directly to the point).

Data and evidence are essentially the same thing. We typically use the word "data" to refer to numerical evidence. This, however, need not be the case. Whatever we use to support our arguments can be seen as data. We use our own observations or those of others to back up our assertions. Evidence varies in strength based on its individual properties and the contexts of its use. Whether these data are facts, expert opinions, examples, or statistics, we use them, in combination, to support our arguments.

Examples are specific references or instances of the point being made and are typically referred to as anecdotal evidence. The strength of anecdotal evidence is found in its generalizability and representativeness.

Expert opinions are judgments made by authorities based on their experiences with evidence and assessment of the facts. When facts are unavailable, expert opinions are the next strongest evidence a writer can supply to support an argument. Expert opinions are some of the strongest kinds of evidence a writer can use.

Facts are statements that can be verified. They are the strongest proof or evidence a writer can supply to support an assertion. They are also the most difficult kind of evidence to obtain.

Statistics are often called probabilistic evidence because they are based on probabilities of correctness and depend on strict adherence to representative sampling techniques. Statistics are not facts: they are the next best things to facts when facts are unavailable. Unfortunately, statistics alone provide weak support for an argument. Together with expert opinion and examples, statistics can provide powerful support for arguments.

CHAPTER 2

Critical Thinking About Politics

Critical Thinking: The Cornerstone of Political Inquiry

If we as political scholars are obliged to contribute to a body of knowledge, then we must learn to ask questions that are politically interesting. Critical thinking skills separate students who are information sponges from those who are information filters.

- **Sponges** indiscriminately, unquestioningly absorb information.
- **Filters** sort information and ask questions not only about the information provided but also about the validity of the evidence and assumptions used to produce the information.
- **Filters** sort the politically relevant from the irrelevant. Not all information is worth analyzing.

Critical Thinkers

- Define problems, examine evidence, and analyze the assumptions leading to a conclusion.
- Question arguments, causal theories, evidence, broad generalizations, and simple correlation.
- Are open to both sides of an argument.
- Are prepared to examine and poke holes in all arguments, even their own.

Critical Thinking Defined

When listening to a speaker or reading a document, essay, article, or book, students must first identify the structure of the author's argument. A good argument usually identifies an issue, provides reasons, and concludes something. Second, the student must examine the structure of the author's conclusion. Within each structure, we can ask questions about the validity of the evidence and assumptions.

How to Think Critically

The first step in obtaining critical thinking skills is identifying what to look for in a written work (Schmidt et al., 1989; Fowler and Aaron, 1989, 128–158).

First: Identify the author's argument or hypothesis.

- Ask yourself, what is the author's point?

8

- Look for the thesis statement.
- Know what an argument is and is not.
  - An argument is not a fact, a definition, an example, or descriptive information.
  - An argument or a hypothesis poses a testable question.

Second: Identify what the author uses as evidence.
- Find out how the author supports the point made in the work.
- Look for data.
- Identify what kind of data or types of evidence are used.
  - Is it qualitative or quantitative?
  - If it is statistical data, examine the method used to collect it.
  - If it is qualitative data, examine the context in which it is being used.
- Know what evidence is and what it is not.
  - Evidence is facts, survey results, authoritative opinion, and examples.
  - Evidence is not hearsay, the author's personal opinion, speculation, or values espoused by the author.

Third: Identify the author's conclusion.
- What does the author say about the relationship between the hypothesis and the evidence?
- Know what a conclusion is and is not.
  - A conclusion is not a fact, a definition, an example, or descriptive information.
  - A conclusion asserts that the question posed is either supported or not by the evidence.
- Look for identifying or indicator words to locate the conclusion: Words such as, *thus, therefore, in fact, it follows that, as a result, the point is,* and *it has been shown* indicate a concluding statement.

Critical Thinking and Reasoning

Learning to think and write critically means commanding a sense of what properties a well-reasoned argument should possess. Reasoning is essential to the writing process. In fact, sound reasoning is more important in political science writing than creativity and eloquence. Political science writing depends heavily on arguments about the structure of political or power relationships. Because of this, communicating a point about an issue is dependent on a clear, well-reasoned exposition of the evidence.

   Much of the work of political scientists is based on a scientific method of inquiry. The scientific method is based on inductive and deductive reasoning as well as inference and generalization. Here are some brief definitions of these terms (Fowler and Aaron 1989, 132–137).

Inductive reasoning: generalizing from observations or attributing a cause to a set of observed circumstances.

Deductive reasoning: applying generalizations or conclusions that are accepted as true to slightly different but similar situations or issues.

Inference: a conclusion based on evidence. This is based on inductive reasoning.

Generalization: a characterization based on the assumption that what applies in one set of circumstances also applies in similar circumstances.

Political Inquiry and Inductive Reasoning

Inductive reasoning involves a process of collecting enough data or evidence to make a confident assertion about political or power relationships. We can infer a conclusion after examining and collecting information about what an author thinks about an issue.

- Inference and inductive reasoning are important steps in the process used by political scientists to identify the causal relationships between political phenomena.
- Inference and inductive reasoning provide the mechanism by which political scientists use data to increase the body of political knowledge.
- Inference and inductive reasoning promote sound conclusions based on sound evidence.

Most of what we know or think we know about politics and political behavior is based on inductive reasoning. Conclusions in voting studies, for example, are primarily based on inductive reasoning from empirical evidence. If we want to know what factors influence the voting turnout of the elderly, we would need to observe some behavior:

Observation: After conducting a survey based on a representative random sample of the elderly, we observe that most of the elderly say that they vote only when social security is in jeopardy.

Observation: We find that exit polls show that when social security is an issue a large number of the elderly vote.

Conclusion: Based on these two pieces of evidence, we can reasonably conclude, through inductive reasoning, that most of the elderly are motivated to vote when their interests are threatened.

Political Inquiry and Deductive Reasoning

Political scientists also use deductive reasoning but it is less obvious than the use of inductive reasoning. Deductive reasoning underlies many of the arguments used in political science writing. Through deductive reasoning, we can use the generalizations we asserted through inference to make an argument about specific cases.

Deductive reasoning is composed of at least two factual statements (premises) and a conclusion. This constitutes a syllogism. A syllogism is simply two premises stating facts or judgments that together lead to a conclusion. The conclusion must derive from the premises.

Example of Deductive Reasoning

Premise: Most elderly citizens vote when their interests are threatened.

Premise: Many of the elderly are worried about the stability of the social security system.

Conclusion: Many of the elderly will vote in the next election.

Unfortunately, not all deductive arguments are presented clearly. Some deductive arguments will rely on either unstated (implied) premises or will overstate a premise.

Example of Implied Premise

"Many of the elderly are worried about the stability of the social security system, so they will vote in the next election."

The premise, that the elderly vote when their interests are threatened, is left unstated.

Example of Overstated Premise

"The elderly always vote when their interests are threatened. Many of the elderly are worried about the stability of the social security system, so they will vote in the next election."

The first premise overstates the generalization because it would be hard to apply it to all circumstances. Absolute words such as all, no one, never, or always force the generalization to apply strictly to every case and circumstance. Premises that cannot be applied to every case use limiting words such as *some*, *many*, and *often*.

Common Problems in Critical Thinking

Once an argument is offered, the author is obligated to address the argument directly with evidence, and then reach a reasonable conclusion. There are, however, common problems in logical exposition of an argument, which influence the reasonableness and validity of an author's point (Fowler and Aaron 1989, 137–143).

Examine the lists of common problems in critical thinking located below. After the definition of each problem is an example. These examples were taken from student answers to an essay question concerning the desirability of requiring poor women with small children to work in order to receive public aid.

BEGGING THE QUESTION

An argument begs the question when the author treats a debatable opinion as a proven fact.

Example: Welfare mothers should have to work for their money because they only have children to collect free money.

Problem: This author assumes that receiving money without working for it causes women to have babies, which is a highly questionable generalization at best.

IGNORING THE QUESTION

An argument ignores the question when the author appeals to the reader with reasons that have nothing to do with the issues raised. The most common occurrence of these errors is found in political campaign slogans and commercial advertising. Authors ignore or evade the question when they engage in one or more of the following:

Emotional appeals—appeals to the reader's sense of decency, fear, or pity.

Example: "Any self-respecting woman would not take money she did not earn, even from the government."

Problem: The author suggests that poor women are not good, decent people but provides no proof of that assertion. The author is appealing to the reader's sense of decency.

Snob appeal—appealing to the reader's desire to be like someone they admire.

Example: "Pioneer women were able to raise families without government aid while their husbands were off on cattle drives or fighting wars."

Problem: The author is appealing to a glorified image of rugged women settlers. The author is suggesting that women who are able to take care of their families alone are like pioneer women and those who cannot take care of their families are not living up to their potential. While the assertion itself is debatable, the example of pioneer women is inappropriate because it is based on a stereotypical image, not reality.

Bandwagon approach—appealing to the reader's desire to be like everyone else.

Example: "Every hard-working American resents giving money to people who do not work for it."

Problem: The author creates an impossible situation for the reader. Because many people like to think of themselves as hard workers, to be part of this group the reader must adopt the same attitude toward cash assistance for poor women. The assertion is debatable and presents an inappropriate reason for being against cash assistance.

Flattery—projecting qualities on the reader.

Example: "As an intelligent and hard-working person, you should resent giving people money for doing nothing."

Problem: The author is projecting the qualities of being intelligent and hard working onto the reader. The statement implies that disagreeing with the author is tantamount to admitting that the reader does not exhibit these qualities.

Ad hominem—personalizing the issue by concentrating on the real or imagined negative characteristics of those who hold different or opposing views.

Example: "Because most people work hard for their money, the only people who continue to support free money to lazy women are old, drugged-out hippies and know-it-all liberal scholars."

Problem: The author projects the negative, currently and socially unacceptable images of old hippies and overbearing liberals on to the supporters of cash assistance to poor women. The author is counting on the reader to reject cash assistance for poor women based on its association with those unpopular stereotypical images.

FAULTY REASONING

Fallacies, or errors in reasoning, are problems because they weaken the author's argument.

Hasty generalizations—a generalization that is based on very little evidence or which overstates the facts.

Example: "Welfare mothers are just lazy. I know of two welfare mothers who do nothing but watch television all day."

Problem: The author is generalizing about all poor women receiving public assistance on the basis of two such women he or she has observed. A selection of two observations is much too small a sample to make a generalization about an entire class of people.

Oversimplification—stating that one event caused another when there is either no relationship or where other causes exist.

Example: "Providing free money to mothers may actually cause more harm than good for their children. Children of welfare mothers rarely excel in school."

Problem: The author suggests that cash assistance to mothers discourages their children from achieving in school. There is no reason to believe that cash assistance causes poor scholastic achievement. There are a host of other causes, however, which contribute to low achievement among children in general. Cash-poor schools, overcrowding, malnutrition, and poor health care are but just a few alternative causal variables in poor scholastic achievement, regardless of the source of the child's family income.

Post hoc fallacy—jumping to the conclusion that event A caused event B just because event A occurred earlier.

Example: "The availability of free money to poor families causes these families to break up. Fathers leave so that their families can collect welfare."

Problem: The author suggests that the only reason fathers leave their families is the availability of cash assistance. Application for public aid is a response to families in trouble; it does not necessarily follow that public aid causes families to break up. Fathers leaving their families is not a necessary or sufficient condition for receiving public aid.

False dilemma—stating that a complex question has only two answers that are both good, both bad, or one good and one bad.

Example: "By continuing to provide free money to poor mothers, we can expect only a continuation of poverty or an erosion of the American work ethic."

Problem: The author suggests that continuing public aid to poor mothers can only result in two undesirable conditions. The author neglects to identify other possible resulting conditions that are desirable, such as a reduction in the number of children who are malnourished, from continuing public aid.

Non sequitur—when two ideas are presented with no logical connection.

Example: "Providing free money has done nothing to improve the quality of life among the poor. Wealthy and middle-class citizens continue to take tax deductions for charitable contributions."

Problem: The author is suggesting that because people still make contributions to charity, no change in the situation of the poor has resulted from public assistance to poor mothers. There is no logical connection between public assistance and tax deductions for charity. The contribution need not be for the poor to be deductible.

False analogy—assuming that things that are alike in one respect are alike in other respects.

> **Example**: "In general, welfare mothers are characterized by poor work skills and little work experience. Few will take the initiative to acquire new skills or work at low-skilled jobs without a coercive incentive, such as working for their welfare checks."
>
> **Problem:** While the author's assertion about the skills and experience of welfare mothers may be valid, there is no logical reason to accept that all welfare mothers will resist acquiring training unless coerced. If given the opportunity to acquire job skills and experience, some may do so and some may not. We cannot predict, based on receiving public aid, whether or not a person will seek to improve his or her marketability.

Tips for Critical Thinking

Below is a summary checklist followed by a detailed set of questions that students should ask themselves as they read a book, an article, or an essay. There are two classes of questions. One set examines the author's argument and evidence. The other set of questions examines the author's conclusions. (The summary and the detailed questions are based on material from *Critical Thinking*, Fowler and Aaron 1989, and Schmidt et al 1989.)

Summary Checklist for Reading or Writing Critically

Below is a checklist for students to use in checking their arguments as well as those of other authors.

1. Has the author stated the central point or assertion of the essay, article, or book in a thesis sentence?
2. Does the body of the work demonstrate the validity of the thesis sentence by breaking it down into other statements or assertions?
3. Has the author reasoned inductively or deductively?
4. Is the evidence provided varied, representative, relevant, and inclusive of facts, examples, and expert opinion?
5. Are there areas where the argument exhibits problems of faulty reasoning or where the author did not face the question posed?

Detailed Set of Questions to Ask About the Author's Argument and Evidence

(Adapted from *Critical Thinking ...*, Ruggiero 1991, 54–64, 149–157)

Issues

A. Look for an explicit reference to the issue. Often authors will use subjective language to introduce the issue and their point of view. For example, here is a statement: "Should flag desecration be a crime?"

1. Students should ask what the author's definition of flag desecration is and which forms of flag desecration the author is concerned about.

2. Students should ask under what conditions misuse of the flag would be considered punishable or not punishable, according to the author.

B. Look for implicit references to the issue.

1. This may involve examining the closing or concluding remarks of the author.

2. Authors will often use words that sum up or suggest relationships in the conclusion that imply what issue has been examined in the work.

Reasons

A. Authors are obligated to give readers reasons why their points are true or valid.

B. Students should look for clues in the literature to identify the evidence.

1. Look for identifying words such as because, since, for one thing, also.

2. Look for ordered paragraphs starting with first, second, third, finally.

3. Look for statistics, graphs, or tables.

Ambiguity

A. Look for words or phrases which may seem obvious, but have multiple meanings.

B. Look for ambiguous or abstract words.

1. Words such as liberal, conservative, freedom, equality, and Justice are abstract and lack specificity.

2. Be sure you know how such words are being used. Look for qualifying references and definitions.

C. Understand all the terms, concepts, and phrases used, including professional jargon.

D. Beware of tautologies or truisms.

1. Tautologies or truisms are statements that are always true and cannot be disproved by any evidence or data.

2. One example of a truism is that people will either vote or they will not. Whether people vote or do not vote does not matter because either way the statement remains true.

Value Assumptions

A. Look for the author's stated ideas or beliefs about what influences behavior or choices.

1. Does the author base points and arguments upon values concerning the desirability of competition, Justice, freedom of speech?

2. Does the author make assumptions about behavior or choices that are generally true?

B. Look for the author's unstated beliefs about what influences behavior or choices. Read between the lines.

C. Realize what your personal values and biases are and be prepared to accept defeat in light of a well-reasoned, factually-based argument made by someone else.

1. Identify the stated and unstated value assumptions that are consistent with your own.

2. Identify the stated and unstated value assumptions that conflict with your own.

Evidence

A. If empirical (quantitative) data are used as evidence then examine the data fully.

    1. Are the data representative (in size, breadth, and randomness) of the target population being studied?

    2. Look for misleading use of percentages: comparisons of percentages and reporting, especially large percentages, are often suspect.

    3. Be sure you know the size on which the percentages were based. Small sample sizes often produce misleading results.

    4. Remember that correlation is not the same thing as causation. When two things are correlated (occurring at the same time) they may not necessarily be causally related (one thing causing the occurrence of the other thing).

B. If the evidence is qualitative then examine the context of the evidence.

    1. Be sure that the evidence is from an objective and respected authority.

    2. For example, a recommendation by the American Medical Association for action concerning a disease would be an appropriate piece of evidence. However, a recommendation by the American Medical Association concerning National Health Insurance is suspect because that organization has a personal stake in the outcome and cannot be considered an objective authority.

    3. Be cautious of one compelling example used as evidence. Remember, as data, the example would be a non-representative sample composed of one data point.

Logical Errors

A. Be sure that the evidence fits the conclusions.

    1. Form your own conclusions from the data and check them against the author's conclusion.

    2. If the author's conclusion differs from your own conclusion, go back and check the author's reasoning, value assumptions, and qualifying terms and definitions.

B. Reject evidence when it exhibits the following flaws:

    1. Attacks an individual's character rather than the issue.

    2. Creates a false dilemma by oversimplifying the choices or alternatives.

    3. Diverts the reader's attention by changing subjects within the argument.

    4. Begs the question by using a reason that repeats the conclusion in different words.

Omissions

A. Has more than one viewpoint been presented?

    1. Have credible contrary views been acknowledged?

    2. Have the contrary views been explained and reasons given why they are not acceptable?

B. Is the evidence supporting the argument or thesis overwhelming? Can you think of anything that has been left out?

C. Has the author examined the underlying reasons concerning an issue?

D. Has the author gone beyond his or her argument and added a normative idea?

1. A positive argument deals with an issue, provides reasons, and concludes based on those reasons.
2. A normative argument goes beyond the reasons presented and prescribes a solution about what should be done. This prescription is based on value assumptions and biases that require a separate analysis.

Reading Critically to Write Critically

So far, we have examined specific examples of arguments and evidence used to support an opinion. Rarely are arguments so contrived to fit the evidence or is the evidence clearly presented. In the following pages is an example of an editorial concerning the controversy over funding art that is politically unacceptable to a political majority of citizens. Read the essay; mark the text to find the critical point made by the author using the suggestions presented on this and the previous pages. Then look at the annotated examination of the essay immediately following the essay. By reading the annotations of the essay, you should have a better understanding of the elements of expository writing in political science.

In particular, reading critically simply means asking questions as you are reading and noting where the arguments, evidence, and conclusions are weakest or strongest. Not all information must be remembered verbatim or memorized. Use shorthand symbols to mark in the margins of personal copies of books, articles, and essays for easy retrieval of information. You should be able to identify at least the important points, the hypothesis, the evidence, and the conclusion in a piece of literature.

Here are some suggestions for identifying critical points in a piece of literature:

1. Use a "T" to identify the theory, hypothesis, or thesis sentence.
2. Use a star (°) to identify an important point. The more important the point, the more stars you put in the margin.
3. Use an "E" to identify quantitative evidence and information that is proven or known to be true.
4. Use an "S" to identify suggestive or qualitative evidence.
5. Use a "V" to indicate where the author has used a value assumption to make a point.
6. Use a question mark (?) to indicate where the author's reasoning is unclear or use of evidence is suspect.
7. Use an "X" to indicate where the author's evidence or point is not valid.
8. Use a "C" to identify a conclusion based on an assertion about the relationship between the author's hypothesis and the evidence presented.

FEDERAL FUNDING FOR NEA
AND
THE ROLE OF THE ARTS IN A DEMOCRACY

By Alan G. Schmidt

The controversy over federal funding for the arts has moved to center stage again, as Congress—faced in an election year with the possibility of having to raise taxes—considers the budget for the National Endowment for the Arts (NEA). Emotions run high on both sides of the issue, and there are valid arguments to support both sides. On the one hand, it can be argued that culture is something that rises naturally out of the common values of a community and not something that can be dictated from a centralized bureaucratic source. It follows from that argument that America would not suddenly be without culture if a budget cut forced a trim in the NEA's funds. On the other hand, when artists are subsidized, they should not be subjected to political censorship and denied their First Amendment rights as a condition for public funding. Although public funding of the arts is not a cultural necessity, denial of funding for artists who express politically unpopular views erodes the value of important constitutional guarantees of equal protection, free speech, and minority rights.

One of the important issues in the debate over funding politically offensive art is whether public funds should support undesirable activities. This issue, however, obscures a hidden problem of equal protection. Public funds have been and are used to support undesirable activities. For example, tobacco farmers are given public subsidies to produce a crop that will kill half a million people every year. These tobacco farmers are given subsidies in spite of acknowledged government and public support for banning smoking as an undesirable, socially unacceptable activity.

Another important issue in the debate over public funding targets is not socially undesirable activities but politically oriented activities that may or may not be politically unacceptable. The crux of this argument stems from a desire to prevent tax dollars from being spent by individuals engaging in political debate. Unfortunately, this argument is flawed and inconsistent with standard tax subsidies provided to non-profit organizations. For example, according to this argument, the tax-exempt status for churches should be abolished. The Catholic Church spends over a million dollars a year on political lobbying against abortion and yet it pays no taxes. A tax exemption has the same effect as a tax subsidy—money from taxes which could be used for other public purposes is given (not collected) to churches for private use. No one seems to be asking Cardinal O'Connor or Jerry Falwell or Pat Robertson to stop engaging in politics as a condition of their organizations' tax-exempt status. Political expression, even that which is espoused by leaders of tax-exempt churches, is protected by the First Amendment.

At the very least, it seems that some consistency in what is considered protected rights and obligations is in order for examining public funding for the arts. There is one argument against funding the NEA, however, that could prove dangerous for all Americans, no matter what their feelings about the current controversy. Jonathan Yardley of *The Washington Post* has argued that public funds should not be granted to artists who engage in political expression. Although it was not clear who would judge an artist's work as political or apolitical and because assessing the content of a work is a subjective process, what Yardley apparently meant was that funding should be withheld for artists whose political agendas do not agree with his political agenda.

Again, constitutional provisions establishing equal protection and minority rights which inhibit arbitrary and subjective government activities help diffuse, but not disarm, this argument. Yardley's idea is disturbing because he expects artists who live in an open, democratic society to produce work totally devoid of democratic ideas. Much, if not all American art—from the poetry of Walt Whitman to the films of Frank Capra to the music of Elvis Presley—is inherently political. If American arts do not reflect the ideals and the conflicts in society, what purpose would they serve in society? Tolerance of statements about government and society, as promulgated by political philosopher J.S. Mill, is necessary for the maintenance of a democratic society and is at the very heart of the American experiment with democracy.

The basic artistic values and ideals of American culture were inherited from the ancient Greeks, for whom art (along with politics and good citizenship) was considered an essential act of public service. To refuse to fund works by artists for budgetary reasons is vastly different from refusing to fund works because they reflect political values. An artist has just as much right to express political ideas as anyone else. How can Americans promote their experiment to the world as an exemplary model of democratic government if they refuse to allow political discourse in the publicly funded arts?

The debate over tax-supported arts is one that may be on the public agenda for a long time. It is difficult to predict how it will resolve. Judging from Yardley's arguments, the debate will be centered on confusing rhetoric and a manipulation of emotions. Nonetheless, artists have just as much right to use their skills to influence political outcomes as anyone else. Public funding for NEA has helped to secure the right to political expression for artists whose activities are not often valued monetarily. Some federally funded art may indeed be offensive and objectionable to the majority of Americans, but to deny funding to the arts because of their political nature should be offensive and objectionable to all Americans.

AN ANNOTATED ANALYSIS OF A POLITICAL ARGUMENT

The following material is an annotation of the political argument immediately preceding this page. The essay has been critically reviewed based on the validity of the arguments and evidence presented below. Although a diagram of the reasoning would help to evaluate questionable parts of the argument, I have only concentrated on those problems or errors which correspond to the material discussed in Chapters One and Two. The author of the essay uses many kinds of evidence discussed in Chapter One and types of arguments examined in Chapter Two. The essay is broken down into logical development of the argument, uses of evidence, and conclusions based on induction or deduction.

Analysis of *Federal Funding for NEA and the Role of the Arts in a Democracy*

Introduction to the Problem

"The controversy over federal funding for the arts has moved to center stage again, as Congress—faced in an election year with the possibility of having to raise taxes—considers the budget for the National Endowment for the Arts (NEA)."

- The introduction quickly identifies the issue of federal funding for the arts as controversial.
- As a critical thinker, you should be wondering what the controversy is about and why it is important.

Context of the Problem

"Emotions run high on both sides of the issue, and there are valid arguments to support both sides. On the one hand, it can be argued that culture is something that rises naturally out of the common values of a community and not something that can be dictated from a centralized bureaucratic source. It follows from that argument that America would not suddenly be without culture if a budget cut forced a trim in the NEA's funds. On the other hand, when artists are subsidized, they should not be subjected to political censorship and denied their First Amendment rights as a condition for public funding."

- The author explains what the controversy concerns. He does this in two ways. He begins with deductive reasoning; he establishes the first part of the argument in the following way. Conclusion B is one part of the controversy, yet Premise 1 is overstated. The word "all" makes this statement apply to all cases. It is an unstated value assumption that all art is culture. Because Premise 1 is weak, this weakens conclusions A and B.

Premise 1:	(*implied*) All art is culture.
Premise 2:	Culture arises from common values of the community.
Conclusion A:	(*implied*) All art arises from common values of the community.
Premise 3:	Common values cannot be dictated from government.
Premise 4:	Culture exists without public funding.
Conclusion B:	(*implied*) All art will exist without public funding.

- The author also sets up the second part of the argument. Unlike the first part of the controversy, the second part is mostly implied. The author now has established the second view, that denial of public funding is unlawful.

(all implied)

Premise 1:	Art that conforms to politically correct values receives funding.
Premise 2:	Art that does not conform to politically correct values does not receive funding.
Premise 3:	Denying funds for political reasons is censorship.
Premise 4:	Censorship is a violation of First Amendment Rights.
Premise 5:	Violating First Amendment Rights is unlawful.
Conclusion:	Denying funds to artists for political reasons is unlawful.

Thesis

"Although public funding of the arts is not a cultural necessity, denial of funding for artists who express politically unpopular views erodes the value of important constitutional guarantees of equal protection, free speech, and minority rights."

- The author establishes his perspective on the issues.
- He is implying that although the first view has some validity, it misses the point. The real problem is that denial of funding for political reasons violates the constitution.

Assertion 1: An Expressed Opinion

"One of the important issues in the debate over funding politically offensive art is whether public funds should support undesirable activities. This issue, however, obscures a hidden problem of equal protection. Public funds have been and are used to support undesirable activities."

- In this first assertion, the author begins his defense of his thesis and a further examination of the important issues in the controversy.
- He presents one issue and proceeds to show, through inductive reasoning, that the objection to public funding is inconsistent with other kinds of public funding.

Evidence Supporting Assertion 1: A Statistic

"For example, tobacco farmers are given public subsidies to produce a crop that will kill half a million people every year."

- The author is supplying a statistic to support the implied assertion that tobacco consumption is an undesirable activity.
- As a critical thinker, you should be asking, where did this figure come from? Is it a fact that tobacco kills people? Could this be a case of begging the question by treating a debatable theory as a fact? Could this be a case of a false analogy between politically offensive art and tobacco consumption?

Evidence Supporting Assertion 1: An Example

"These tobacco farmers are given subsidies in spite of acknowledged government and public support for banning smoking as an undesirable, socially unacceptable activity."

- The author argues that the public objects to tobacco consumption. But is this valid?
- He implies that all of the public objects to smoking. Is this true? Is this a case of a hasty generalization? Who acknowledges this support?

Assertion 2: An Expressed Opinion

"Another important issue in the debate over public funding targets is not socially undesirable activities but politically oriented activities that may or may not be politically unacceptable."

- In this assertion, the author expresses an opinion about what issues he believes contribute to the controversy.
- He is suggesting that the issue is not social, but political activities, that are defined as problems.

Assertion 3: Assertion 2 Interpreted

"The crux of this argument stems from a desire to prevent tax dollars from being spent by individuals engaging in political debate. Unfortunately, this argument is flawed and inconsistent with standard tax subsidies provided to non-profit organizations."

- Without actually explaining the difference between social activities and political activities, the author re-defines the issue to focus on political activities. Is there a difference? Does differentiating between social and political debate create a false dilemma?

- He concludes that the issue is the use of public money to fund political activities. But who are the people who do not desire this? The author's reference to "desire" is vague.
- Nonetheless, the author proceeds to show that such a desire is inconsistent with other policies.

Evidence Supporting Assertion 3: A Factual Example

"For example, according to this argument, the tax-exempt status for churches should be abolished. The Catholic Church spends over a million dollars a year on political lobbying against abortion and yet it pays no taxes. A tax exemption has the same effect as a tax subsidy—money from taxes which could be used for other public purposes is given (not collected) to churches for private use."

- Using a conclusion resulting from deductive reasoning, the author argues that subsidizing church organizations that engage in political activities makes the separation between subsidizing only social activities and not subsidizing political activities invalid.

Evidence Supporting Assertion 3: An Example

"No one seems to be asking Cardinal O'Connor or Jerry Falwell or Pat Robertson to stop engaging in politics as a condition of their organizations' tax-exempt status."

- The author is using an appeal to emotions here.
- For an appeal to be effective, the reader must know that the individuals referenced here are highly controversial, politically outspoken religious leaders.

Evidence Supporting Assertion 3: A Fact and an Example

"Political expression, even that which is espoused by leaders of tax-exempt churches, is protected by the First Amendment."

- The author uses a fact to establish the credibility of his assertion that protection of political expression is applied to politically questionable people who receive public subsidies.
- If readers accept the previous evidence, then they accept assertion 3.
- By accepting assertion 3, readers concede acceptance of assertion 2.

Assertion 4: An Expressed Opinion

"At the very least, it seems that some consistency in what is considered protected rights and obligations is in order for examining public funding for the arts. There is one argument against funding the NEA, however, that could prove dangerous for all Americans, no matter what their feelings about the current controversy."

- Having set up his argument so that he has invalidated objections to public funding in principle and in particular instances where political expression is concerned, the author then questions the credibility of the key opponents asserting that one of them has ideas that are dangerous to the public.
- He then begins to present an example.

Evidence Supporting Assertion 4: An Example

"Jonathan Yardley of *The Washington Post* has argued that public funds should not be granted to artists who engage in political expression. Although it was not clear who would judge an artist's work as political or apolitical and because assessing the content of a work is a subjective process, what Yardley apparently meant was that funding should be withheld for artists whose political agendas do not agree with his political agenda."

- The author restates the opposition's case and identifies a problem with the opponent's position.
- The author implies that the danger is using subjective measures of political activity.
- He implies that this subjectivity could be abusive and self-interested.
- But who is Yardley anyway? Is his opinion worth noting? Can he act in any effective way on his opinion?
- As critical thinkers, we first need to be certain that Yardley's view is representative of the opposition to public funding.
- Second, we need to decide whether we trust the author to interpret the opposition's intentions correctly.
- In this matter, the author personalizes the issue—ad hominem—by concentrating on imagined negative characteristics.

Assertion 5: An Expressed Opinion

"Again, constitutional provisions establishing equal protection and minority rights which inhibit arbitrary and subjective government activities help diffuse, but not disarm, this argument. Yardley's idea is disturbing because he expects artists who live in an open, democratic society to produce work totally devoid of democratic ideas."

- The author builds on the reader's acceptance of assertion 4 to continue interpreting the opposition's view as being unacceptable.
- He implies that Yardley's commitment to or understanding of democratic society is questionable.
- The author is attempting to cast doubt on the credibility of the opponent's view by suggesting that the opponent is not knowledgeable about the issue.
- Again, the author is appealing to the negative characteristics—ad hominem—of his opponent.
- To accept this as valid evidence, we must trust that the author is fairly representing the opponent's credentials.

Evidence to Support Assertion 5: An Example

"Much, if not all American art—from the poetry of Walt Whitman to the films of Frank Capra to the music of Elvis Presley—is inherently political. If American arts do not reflect the ideals and the conflicts in society, what purpose would they serve in society?"

- The author is using a set of examples to show that the distinction between social and political activities is not valid when applied generally to art.
- He is implying that to reflect societal values is by definition a reflection of political values in society.
- The author supports this, however, by using what appears to be the beginning of a non-sequitur form of reasoning.

- He presents two ideas that have no obvious connection. The first idea questions what thing art reflects. The second idea is what purpose art serves in society.
- He is hoping to induce the reader to accept that art serves a role in society that is to reflect its ideals and conflicts. Yet, he did not say how reflecting an ideal relates to serving society.

Evidence to Support Assertion 5: An Expert Opinion

"Tolerance of statements about government and society, as promulgated by political philosopher J.S. Mill, is necessary for the maintenance of a democratic society and is at the very heart of the American experiment with democracy."

- Now the author makes the connection for us by paraphrasing a famous political philosopher and commentator.
- Historical accounts of the early days of the framing of our constitution tell us that the framers were highly influenced by the teachings of Mill.
- The author is using an appeal to authority to convince the reader that tolerance of political statements serve to preserve democratic society.

Evidence Supporting Assertion 5: A Fact

"The basic artistic values and ideals of American culture were inherited from the ancient Greeks, for whom art (along with politics and good citizenship) was considered an essential act of public service."

- This piece of evidence is being used as additional support for the connection between art, societal ideals, and preservation of democracy. It is also setting up the next assertion by appealing to the emotions—to the romanticism and reverence held for those ancient cultures who were among the first to experiment with democratic government. It implies that to be against political art is to deny America's ancient and sacred cultural heritage.

Assertion 6: An Opinion

"To refuse to fund works by artists for budgetary reasons is a vastly different matter than refusing to fund works because they reflect political values. An artist has just as much right to express political ideas as anyone else."

- The author is now granting that for non-political, civic, or objective reasons, refusing to fund the arts could be acceptable. It is the act of refusing funding for political reasons that is a denial of rights.
- The author is using a bandwagon approach akin to "everybody does it, so why can't they?"
- He implies that political expression should not come with a political cost. Does everyone have the right to freely express himself or herself and be guaranteed protection from political costs?

Evidence Supporting Assertion 6: An Example

"How can Americans promote their experiment to the world as an exemplary model of democratic government if they refuse to allow political discourse in the publicly funded arts?"

- The author expresses a belief here and uses it as evidence supporting the notion that the American democratic experiment holds special historical significance in the preservation of democratic ideals.

- Again, the author appeals to the emotions, especially to patriotism, to induce support from the reader.
- There is no question, by now, about the author's understanding of democracy. Is this true? He has firmly established his appreciation of and commitment to democratic values. Or has he?

Conclusion 1

"The debate over tax-supported arts is one that may be on the public agenda for a long time. It is difficult to predict how it will resolve. Judging from Yardley's arguments, the debate will be centered on confusing rhetoric and a manipulation of emotions."

- The author now restates the problem and identifies the causes more clearly.
- By referring to Yardley, his first conclusion implies that emotional, not rational reasons, are used by opponents as evidence against public funding as a way of censoring views held by artists who are in the political minority.

Conclusion 2

"Nonetheless, artists have just as much right to use their skills to influence political outcomes as anyone else."

- The author re-asserts his contention that the problem with denying public funding to the arts is a matter of equal protection.

Conclusion 3

"Public funding for NEA has helped secure the right to political expression for artists whose activities are not often valued monetarily."

- The author re-asserts his position that public funding helps ensure minority rights and free speech.
- This is implied by the reference to artists who do not profit from their activities related to political expression and may not be able to pay the costs of expressing unpopular views.

Knowledge

"Some federally funded art may indeed be offensive and objectionable to the majority of Americans, but to deny funding to the arts because of their political nature should be offensive and objectionable to all Americans."

- What have we learned from this argument?
- In essence, the author has shown us that to be against funding art, especially if it is political in nature, is (at best) to be ignorant of American values or is (at worst) un-American!
- Are you convinced that this is true?
- If readers accept all the assertions made and evidence presented as valid, then they must accept this conclusion.

CHAPTER 3

Topic Selection

Choosing a Topic

Students should view open-ended writing assignments as opportunities to develop their long-term professional interests. Each subdiscipline in political science offers a set of rich and varied subjects for students to explore. Students may wish to combine one or more types of topics to limit the scope of their research. They can also limit the scope of their research by examining a characteristic of an object associated with a concept. The combinations are limited only by the nature of the course and constraints set by the instructor.

Objects: Things That Can Be Seen Physically

Players: these are people who are politically important. Presidents, members of Congress, interest group leaders, bureaucrats, and judges are examples of political players.

Institutions: these are any body that engages in routinized patterns of interaction. Affiliations, associations, alliances, and political organizations such as Congress, bureaucracies, political parties, interest groups, and even families are institutions.

Events: these are occurrences or situations that led to political outcomes or consequences or are political outcomes. The Kent State Massacre, political assassinations, campaigns, the Great Depression, and the Nixon resignation are examples of events.

Policies: these are or can be any decision made by any public official in any branch of government which has the force of law. Policies also include custom as well as non-decisions on problems. Congressional legislation, bureaucratic regulations, presidential orders, judicial decisions, and common law are policies.

Concepts: Things That Are Believed, Acknowledged

Dilemmas: these are undesirable situations or problems that seem to be difficult to resolve. They are often associated with unwanted and unsatisfactory conditions. They can also be related to a difficulty in achieving some preferred outcome. Political apathy, political intolerance, providing for social welfare during a recession, providing for cleaner air without devastating the coal industry, and reconciling individual liberties with the public good are examples of dilemmas.

Processes: refers to observable patterns of political behavior in people and groups. They are associated with procedures and mechanisms for using, acquiring and distributing political power. The methods and structure of congressional, judicial, and bureaucratic decision-making are examples of processes. Democracy, federalism, confederation, oligarchy, monarchy, feudalism, socialism, and communism are all different processes for organizing government.

Values: these are outlooks, perspectives, and subjective or biased opinions. Values are often associated with irrational, moral, or ethical judgments. A value is a sentiment that may or may not be socially acceptable. For example, support for a political party or for racial supremacy are values which sustain vastly different levels of public support. Patriotism, individualism, collectivism, racism, and loyalty are examples of values.

Beliefs: These are a state of mind related to a conviction or unconscious trust in a statement which is not fact-based or based on objective evidence. They are often associated with faith or custom. Natural rights, liberty, justice, freedom, and self-sufficiency are examples of beliefs.

Principles: these are doctrines or codes of conduct that are usually held in high esteem. Self-determination, limited government, constitutionalism, rule of law, and legitimacy are examples of principles.

Ideologies: these each have an integrated body of ideas, values, beliefs, and aspirations that constitute a socio-political program. They are associated with a desire, a need, a moral obligation, or a utopian vision. The ideas, beliefs, or values need not be socially acceptable; all that is needed is that the ideas, beliefs, and values are linked coherently. Liberalism, Conservatism, anarchism, authoritarianism, pacifism, imperialism, Marxism, fascism, Nazism, libertarianism, and nationalism are examples of ideologies.

Theories: are sets of plausible statements or general principles offered to explain phenomena or events. Theories offer testable hypotheses or speculations about the causes of political outcomes. Theories are often modified or constrained by ideological perspectives. Democratic theory, corporatism, the Downesian model of party competition, egalitarianism, the American voter model, the domino theory, feminism, elitism, and pluralism are all theories.

Tips for Choosing a Topic

When choosing a topic, students must keep in mind that whatever they have chosen to write about must relate to the course material, be interesting to study, and adhere explicitly to the instructions and limitations set by the instructor. Failing to keep these three criteria in mind when choosing a topic will, in most instances, result in an undesirable grade. There are a number of ways that students can assure that their topics contain these characteristics.

Look at the table of contents in your course textbooks.

1. Make a list of the people, institutions, or other objects that seem interesting to you.
2. Make a list of any theories, ideologies, or other concepts that seem interesting to you.
   - Do not waste time worrying about whether a concept fits into a particular category.
   - If the thing is something that cannot be touched, then it is a concept.
3. Combine the list of objects and concepts in different ways.

4. Choose the combination that most piques your curiosity.

5. Use verbs and qualifiers to transform the combination of objects into a question.

Check the handout, syllabus, or whatever the instructor gave you that states the requirements for the assignment.

1. Note any special information or questions that must be addressed in the written assignments.

2. Use these in combination with the abstract and concrete topics you listed as interesting from your textbooks to pose your topic question.

3. Focus the topic so that it clearly addresses the requirements of the instructor.

4. Follow up on an interesting comment or idea presented in a class, seminar, or workshop you attended.

Limit the time frame so that the topic can be addressed within the page limits set by the instructor.

1. A five-page paper can support only a very narrow topic. Combine an abstraction and a concrete topic and specify a short time frame to narrow the topic.

2. A ten-page paper can support a focused, but very specific topic. Combine two concepts or combine a concept and an object, but limit the period to no more than a decade.

3. A fifteen-page paper can support a complex topic. Combine two or more objects with a concept, but be careful that the period or scope does not become all encompassing or historical.

4. A twenty-page paper or longer can support a complex topic and endure some description of historical context. Combine several objects with one or more concepts and keep the period manageable.

Example of Combining Objects and Concepts

AMERICAN GOVERNMENT

OBJECTS		CONCEPTS	
PLAYERS:	Jesse Jackson	**DILEMMAS**:	Reconciling government aid with balanced budget
INSTITUTIONS:	Presidency		
EVENTS:	Scandal		
POLICIES:	Job Training		
		PROCESSES:	Congressional voting
		VALUES:	Individualism
		BELIEFS:	Justice
		PRINCIPLES:	Limited government
		IDEOLOGIES:	Libertarianism
		THEORIES:	Egalitarianism

POSSIBLE COMBINATIONS

Combination One:	Jesse Jackson and Social Justice
Combination Two:	Reconciling Government Aid with a Balanced Budget and Congressional Voting in Urban Areas
Combination Three:	Job Training and Limited Government
Combination Four:	Scandal and the Presidency
Combination Five:	The Presidency, Libertarianism, and Justice
Combination Six:	Jesse Jackson and the Presidency
Combination Seven:	Libertarianism and Limited Government
Combination Eight:	Scandal and Congressional Voting
Combination Nine:	Job Training and Reconciling Government Aid with a Balanced Budget
Combination Ten:	Jesse Jackson, Egalitarianism, and Individualism

Example of Combining Objects and Concepts

INTERNATIONAL RELATIONS

OBJECTS		CONCEPTS	
PLAYERS:	Saudis	**DILEMMAS**:	Presidential authority to deploy troops in peacetime
INSTITUTIONS:	United Nations		
EVENTS:	Mideast crisis		
POLICIES:	War Powers Act		
		PROCESSES:	Communism
		VALUES:	Patriotism
		BELIEFS:	Liberty
		PRINCIPLES:	Rule of Law
		IDEOLOGIES:	Nationalism
		THEORIES:	Democratic theory

POSSIBLE COMBINATIONS

Combination One: Mideast Crisis, the United Nations, and Presidential Authority to Deploy Troops in Peacetime

Combination Two: Communism and Patriotism

Combination Three: The United Nations and Nationalism

Combination Four: The War Powers Act and Rule of Law

Combination Five: The Saudis and the United Nations

Combination Six: Communism and Democratic Theory

Combination Seven: Liberty and the Mideast Crisis

Combination Eight: Patriotism and Liberty

Combination Nine: Presidential Authority to Deploy Troops in Peacetime and the United Nations

Combination Ten: Nationalism and Patriotism

Example of Combining Objects and Concepts

COMPARATIVE POLITICS

OBJECTS		CONCEPTS	
PLAYERS:	M. Thatcher	**DILEMMAS**:	Political intolerance
INSTITUTIONS:	Parliament		
EVENTS:	Falklands War	**PROCESSES**:	Parliamentary decision-making
POLICIES:	G.B. Poll Tax		
		VALUES:	Patriotism
		BELIEFS:	Natural Rights
		PRINCIPLES:	Legitimacy
		IDEOLOGIES:	Conservatism
		THEORIES:	Elitism

POSSIBLE COMBINATIONS

Combination One: Margaret Thatcher and the Growth of Political Intolerance

Combination Two: Parliament, the Falklands War, and Natural Rights

Combination Three: Margaret Thatcher, Poll Tax, and Elitism

Combination Four: Parliamentary Decision-Making, Margaret Thatcher, and Legitimacy

Combination Five: The Falklands War and Patriotism

Combination Six: Political Intolerance, Natural Rights, and Parliament

Combination Seven: Conservatism, Elitism, and Margaret Thatcher

Combination Eight: Britain's Poll Tax, Legitimacy, and Parliament

Combination Nine: Parliament and Parliamentary Decision-Making

Combination Ten: Poll Tax and Political Intolerance

Example of Combining Objects and Concepts

CRIMINAL JUSTICE

OBJECTS		CONCEPTS	
PLAYERS:	John Ashcroft	**DILEMMAS**:	Protecting civil liberties and anti-terrorism restrictions
INSTITUTIONS:	FBI		
EVENTS:	Terrorist attack		
POLICIES:	Patriot Act 2001		
		PROCESSES:	Democracy
		VALUES:	Patriotism
		BELIEFS:	Justice
		PRINCIPLES:	Rule of law
		IDEOLOGIES:	Authoritarianism
		THEORIES:	Rehabilitation

POSSIBLE COMBINATIONS

Combination One:	John Ashcroft and the Patriot Act
Combination Two:	John Ashcroft, FBI, and Patriotism
Combination Three:	Terrorist Attacks and Rule of Law
Combination Four:	FBI, Patriot Act, and Authoritarianism
Combination Five:	John Ashcroft, Terrorist Attacks, and Democracy
Combination Six:	FBI, Civil Liberties, and Anti-Terrorism Regulations
Combination Seven:	Rehabilitation, Democracy, and Justice
Combination Eight:	Patriot Act, Individual Liberty, and Rule of Law
Combination Nine:	John Ashcroft, Authoritarianism, and Rule of Law
Combination Ten:	Rule of Law, Justice, and the Patriot Act

PUBLIC ADMINISTRATION

OBJECTS		CONCEPTS	
PLAYERS:	Jack Kemp	**DILEMMAS**:	Reconciling bureaucratic discretion with accountability
INSTITUTIONS:	Congress		
EVENTS:	HUD scandal		
POLICIES:	Revenue sharing		
		PROCESSES:	Bureaucratic decision-making
		VALUES:	Loyalty
		BELIEFS:	Liberty
		PRINCIPLES:	Legitimacy
		IDEOLOGIES:	Liberalism
		THEORIES:	Elitism

POSSIBLE COMBINATIONS

Combination One:	Congress and Reconciling Bureaucratic Discretion with Accountability
Combination Two:	Jack Kemp, Congress, and the HUD Scandal
Combination Three:	Revenue Sharing and Reconciling Bureaucratic Discretion with Accountability
Combination Four:	Congress, Revenue Sharing, and Bureaucratic Decision-Making
Combination Five:	Jack Kemp, Loyalty, and Legitimacy
Combination Six:	Congress, Loyalty, and Bureaucratic Decision-Making
Combination Seven:	Jack Kemp, HUD Scandal, and Bureaucratic Decision-Making
Combination Eight:	Revenue Sharing, Liberty, and Liberalism
Combination Nine:	Congress, Loyalty, and the HUD Scandal
Combination Ten:	Congress, Elitism, and Bureaucratic Decision-Making

Example of Combining Objects and Concepts

PUBLIC LAW

OBJECTS		CONCEPTS	
PLAYERS:	Earl Warren	**DILEMMAS**:	Political intolerance
INSTITUTIONS:	The Family		
EVENTS:	Civil Rights March	**PROCESSES**:	Judicial decision-making
POLICIES:	Abortion		
		VALUES:	Racism
		BELIEFS:	Liberty
		PRINCIPLES:	Limited Government
		IDEOLOGIES:	Conservatism
		THEORIES:	Egalitarianism

POSSIBLE COMBINATIONS

Combination One: Justice Warren and Egalitarianism

Combination Two: Justice Warren, Racism, and Limited Government

Combination Three: Civil Rights Marches, Political Intolerance, and Liberty

Combination Four: Abortion, The Family, and Limited Government

Combination Five: Judicial Decision-Making, The Family, and Abortion

Combination Six: Political Intolerance, Abortion, and Conservatism

Combination Seven: Civil Rights Marches, Racism, and Justice Warren

Combination Eight: Racism, Limited Government, and Civil Rights Marches

Combination Nine: Abortion, Conservatism, and Liberty

Combination Ten: Judicial Decision-Making and Racism

Example of Combining Objects and Concepts

POLITICAL THEORY

OBJECTS		CONCEPTS	
PLAYERS:	Thomas Jefferson	**DILEMMAS**:	Reconciling liberties with the public good
INSTITUTIONS:	Congress		
EVENTS:	American Revolution	**PROCESSES**:	Democracy
POLICIES:	Bill of Rights	**VALUES**:	Individualism
		BELIEFS:	Freedom
		PRINCIPLES:	Self-Determination
		IDEOLOGIES:	Nationalism
		THEORIES:	Corporatism

POSSIBLE COMBINATIONS

Combination One:	Thomas Jefferson and Democracy
Combination Two:	Congress and Reconciling Individual Liberties with the Public Good
Combination Three:	Bill of Rights and Reconciling Individual Liberties with the Public Good
Combination Four:	Thomas Jefferson, Bill of Rights, and Self-Determination
Combination Five:	Bill of Rights/Corporatism
Combination Six:	The American Revolution: Thomas Jefferson and Self-Determination
Combination Seven:	Corporatism and Freedom
Combination Eight:	Congress, Bill of Rights, and Democracy
Combination Nine:	Democracy, Reconciling Individual Liberties with the Public Good, and Congress
Combination Ten:	Congress, Reconciling Individual Liberties with the Public Good, and Freedom

CHAPTER 4

Locating Research Materials
Using Indexes, Databases,
and the Internet

Coauthored by Kathleen Carlisle Fountain
Reference/Political Science and Social Work Librarian
California State University, Chico

Introduction

Thorough, well-documented research is the basis for all good writing. This chapter provides students with the basic tools to engage in professional-level, high-quality research. Regardless of the scope of a research assignment, students need to master the search and retrieval skills for locating high-quality information to learn about a topic as well as support their arguments or perspectives about the topic. The suggestions in this chapter are written in compliance with standards developed by the Association of College and Research Libraries in *Information Literacy Competency Standards for Higher Education* (Association of College and Research Libraries 2000). Using the information in this chapter should provide students with the opportunity to demonstrate information literacy in their writing projects.

Characteristics of Sources Used in Research Papers

A well-written paper is only part of what determines whether a manuscript is a good scholarly effort. Scholarly research requires professionalism in the choice of resources used for locating information about the relationship between concepts and objects involved in the research topic. Professionalism is determined by the care and thoughtfulness invested in the collection of resources in different resource formats that fit the scope of the research effort. The sources used in a well-documented research paper are characterized as being clearly relevant, of high quality, and exhibiting depth, breadth, and variety.

Relevance

Students should remember that identifying and sorting information is an important part of the research process. To support their hypotheses and arguments in the paper, students will have to locate supporting arguments, perspectives, qualitative data and/or quantitative data as evidence. To provide balance, students must also locate similar information that does not support their views and explain how such information changes (or not) the types of assertions that students can make about their topics.

Quality

Students should remember that the quality of their work depends on the quality of the materials they used in their research. Different types of research projects require a different mix of evidence. There are a variety of types of information available to students to provide background information, discussions of the issues involved in their topics, and evidence to support their assertions. Sources that have been produced by scholars, reputable professionals in the field, research organizations, and/or government reports provide the foundations and evidence for a high-quality, well-researched paper.

Depth and Breadth

A well-researched paper has, at minimum, a blend of existing information from different resources that are organized by the student's original thoughts about the topic. Students must learn to synthesize (blend) historical and current information to provide a new perspective on a topic or issue when writing a research paper. Both recent and older information sources exist and serve valuable purposes for informing and supporting student research.

Current sources: As in all disciplines, it is important in political science research to find and cite the most current research available on the topic. Not only is it necessary to read recent scholarship to understand the latest arguments made about a topic, but many topics require references to the latest related laws, regulations, or data. When searching for information students should pay close attention to *when* (the time period) the author or publisher produced the information. Students must make a special attempt to ensure that the information used is the most current and relevant for their research topics.

Historical sources: The necessity of current scholarship does not imply that historical scholarship, that is older articles or books or data, is useless or invalid for student research. In fact, graduate students of political science spend a great deal of time learning the foundational literature of the discipline, some of which are considered classics in the field. Academic research is essentially a conversation among scholars, and authors of new articles will reference past contributions to the conversation on their topic. Conducting a research project allows the student to enter into this longstanding scholarly conversation with their own insights. To do so, it may be necessary to make references to the same landmark literature as other scholars do.

Variety

Students should use a variety of information from different types of resources to support their research questions. It is **never** appropriate to base the entire research paper on a single resource such as one book, one article, Web sites, or mass media such as newspapers. *A well-researched political science paper should include, at minimum, references to books, scholarly journal articles, and government documents* as the foundation for most of the research. Additional references may include Web sites, mass media, personal interviews, or secondary analyses of text or data.

Distinguishing Between Types of Information

Not only is it important to know that information is available in a variety of resource formats such as books, journal articles, videos, audio tapes, CDs, or DVDs, it is important to understand the purpose and content of those sources as they relate to the unit of analysis and scope of the research investigation. There are two kinds of information, qualitative (descriptive) and quantitative (numerical) information, that are available in primary or secondary sources.

Primary Sources

Primary sources are evidence gathered in the form of archival documents (qualitative information) or raw data (quantitative information) that are analyzed by the researcher. Projects that attempt to determine causal relationships will likely require some primary sources. Including primary sources within the scope of the research project takes more time and often requires information searches outside of the services offered through university or college libraries. See Chapter Five for a description of the types of archival and raw data, and for strategies and techniques used for creating evidence from such primary sources.

Secondary Resources

A secondary source contains arguments and information gathered by other researchers and *is not created by student researchers*. In particular, secondary sources are *published* reports, discussions, or data based on primary research. The quality and currency of the information contained in secondary sources depend on whether the material is intended for a mass market (popular) or academic (scholarly) audience. Both popular and scholarly source literature are available through university or college libraries services. Popular materials tend to be better sources of current event reporting for the average person while scholarly sources tend to be better sources for informed or expert opinion and professional analysis used by researchers in the field. While the *content* of secondary sources can be analyzed to create primary raw data, the *information* provided in secondary sources is primarily used to locate facts for research projects. For example, a student may analyze the content of newspapers to create *primary raw data* about the tone and amount of political candidate news coverage or a student may use newspaper articles to gather *secondary data* such as facts about positions or polling numbers associated with a candidate.

Popular or Mass Media

These types of materials are intended for the average adult. This material appeals to mass audiences and typically covers current news events. Examples include any newsstand magazines like *Newsweek* and *Time*, newspapers such as the *New York Times* and *Washington Post*, television programs on *CNN* or other networks, or webzines like *Slate*. (The novel *Primary Colors*, which spoofed President Clinton's campaign, could also be considered popular literature.) These types of materials are available through libraries, Web sites, or commercial publishers and distributors. Many newspapers and magazines are available through microfilm, microform, and/or online services. The purpose of these sources is to provide general information about current events. While popular literature provides information, they generally do not include the detailed analysis and historical context offered by scholarly literature. The characteristics of popular literature include:

Authors: The information is written by staff writers employed by the magazine, newspaper, or television show. Although the authors are generally given credit, in some formats they are not provided. The authors are rarely scholars or experts in the field or on the topic of the work. Decisions to publish the information is based on decisions by media owners and editors.

Cited Sources: These materials rarely have direct citations. While the author may mention sources within the text of the work, print documents will not include footnotes with complete citation information.

Language: The language used to provide the information is generally simple and easy to understand.

Graphics: There is generally substantial advertising and extensive photographs provided to accompany mass media information.

Quality Professional Publications and Law Reviews

These types of materials are intended for professionals and knowledgeable individuals in the field. Quality professional publications generally cover current events, controversies, and phenomena. Examples include *Congressional Quarterly Weekly Reports*, *National Journal*, *Congressional Digest*, *Monthly Labor Review*, and *Clement's International Report*. Law reviews, however, are articles about various aspects of local, state, and federal law that are often written by practitioners or legal experts but edited by law students. The purpose of these sources is to provide information about, and thoughtful analysis of, current political and legal activities and events for professionals in the field. These sources may provide historical context. The characteristics of quality publications and law reviews include:

Authors: The information is written by and for skilled professionals in their field. Although the authors may not be scholars, they are respected as specialists.

Cited Sources: Direct citation of sources may occur in quality professional publications but is sporadic throughout the text. Law review articles, however, include frequent citations to relevant laws, cases, and other literature. When citations are made, the text will include footnotes or endnotes with complete citation information.

Language: The language used to provide the information is generally professional and geared toward a specialized and educated audience.

Graphics: There is generally very little advertising and the graphics are professionally presented and discussed in the text.

Government Documents

For the most part, government documents are *official records* of the public activities of individuals working either a legislative or executive office. At the federal level, government documents are published by the Government Printing Office or placed on the Internet by individual agencies. Government documents include agency reports, congressional hearings, the *Congressional Record*, congressional reports, and reports of the president.

Authors: The information is written by skilled professionals in their institutions. The authors may be highly trained, may or may not be named directly, and may or may not work in the institution full time. Some documents may also be direct transcripts of the statements made to and by government officials.

Cited Sources: The authors may make references to sources. If references are used they are typically infrequent and the text will include footnotes or endnotes with complete citation information.

Language: The language used to provide the information is generally professional and geared toward a professional or educated audience.

Graphics: There is no advertising and the graphics are professionally presented and discussed in the text.

Legal Documents

These documents are laws, regulations, and court opinions that govern the activities of individuals and groups. These publications are *official documents* of the legislature, regulatory agencies, and courts. Examples include the *United States Supreme Court Reports*, *Federal Reporter*, *United States Code*, and *Code of Federal Regulations*.

Authors: The information is carefully written by skilled legal professionals including legislators, federal bureaucrats, and judges.

Cited Sources: The authors often use references to support their assertions. When references exist, the text will include footnotes or endnotes with complete citation information.

Language: The language used is specialized for a legal audience.

Graphics: There is no advertising or graphics.

Scholarly Materials

Most scholarly literature appears in the form of journal articles and books. Some professors may refer to it as "academic," "peer reviewed," or "refereed." Regardless of what it is called, scholarly literature exists to inform an educated audience of fellow researchers in a particular discipline. It analyzes specific academic topics, provides historical context, and makes conclusions based on in-depth research.

Authors: The literature is written by scholars, usually professors working for universities, and the article or book should mention the author's credentials. The decision to publish the material is generally based on recommendations by experts in the field (peers) through a blind review process.

Cited Sources: The information sources are cited with footnotes, endnotes, or parenthetical references. The document will include complete citation information. A list of references or bibliography should appear at the end of the piece unless they are provided in footnotes or endnotes.

Language: The authors will use professional language, jargon, or terms understood by scholars in the field. For example, scholars may mention Latin legal terms, political theories, or work by other scholars without significant explanation because it is expected that the readers will know these commonly used discipline-specific concepts.

Graphics: Scholarly literature most commonly includes charts or graphs directly related to the content of the writing. Photographs are rarely included in scholarly publications. Some advertising may appear, but the products marketed are more likely to be books or other academic products rather than commercial consumer products such as beauty aids or automobiles.

Secondary Raw Data

Secondary raw data are generally original data that were gathered by other researchers, used in their research, and then made available to other researchers for re-analysis. These "raw" data may be available to students free of charge, through subscriptions services, and/or for a fee. The advantage of using data collected by others is that students save time and, in some cases, money. The disadvantage of using existing data sources is a loss of control over content and method of collection. See Chapter Five for a discussion of these data sources.

Retrieval Systems for Locating Sources

Print indexes, databases, and the Internet are the three main retrieval systems for locating both primary and secondary sources. In the past, students depended on printed materials such as indexes and card catalogs to locate information in their libraries. The advent of personal computers created opportunities for providing alternative systems for locating materials including computerized library catalogs, databases on CDs, and online databases. Some libraries continue to rely on printed indexes but most libraries provide databases that are accessed directly or indirectly via the Internet. The research identified by the indexes, databases, and the Internet bear no relationship to the holdings of individual libraries. They, instead, serve the purpose of making students and other researchers aware of the scholarship published and information available from all over the world.

In general, these systems differ by organization, subject coverage (single or multiple), and search term language. Single subject systems focus on information from specific disciplines or sources. Multidisciplinary systems compile references to information from many subjects.

The methods used to search print indexes, databases, and the Internet also varies because of the way those systems are constructed. Printed indexes use *controlled vocabulary* whereas databases and the Internet primarily use *keyword searching*. Controlled vocabulary searching involves using specially selected words from an established list of terms to find information. Keyword searching, however, involves using any relevant word or set of words that matches those from the author, title, subject, or text of a document to locate information.

Printed Indexes

Printed indexes organize published literature (books and articles) into annual volumes. Like online databases, indexes provide references (including author, title, journal, date, etc.) to scholarship related to a particular topic. In fact, many online databases simply provide electronic access to the information contained in a printed index. For example, *PAIS* initially existed as a printed index to public policy literature, but the publisher migrated the content into an electronic version called the *PAIS* Database and sold it to libraries across the country.

Printed indexes continue to serve a valuable purpose in library research. Because they pre-date databases, scholars may often need to use them to identify scholarship before the development of the database counterpart. Also, some libraries are unable to afford the cost of a database and thus choose to continue subscribing only to the print version of an index.

Organization

Before using a printed index, students need to determine how the index is organized. Fortunately, each individual index offers a description in the beginning of the volume that tells the researcher the index's organization (e.g., by subject headings, category, or author). Nonetheless, reference librarians are an important source of aid/help in interpreting how to use these indexes. In general, the indexes are organized by author and/or by subject in annual volumes. Each volume contains a list of bibliographic citations by author or subject for approximately one year of scholarship. To ensure students find all relevant material for their research topics over time, the same topic or author must be looked up in multiple volumes. Some print indexes will have a cumulative index that provides references to literature covering several volumes. Because of this, these cumulative indexes make it easier to search across many years at a time.

For most indexes, students look up a subject or author in the cumulative index and that will usually refer to a description of an article on a particular page or section of the index. The description should include the author, article title, journal title, volume, issue, number, date of publication, and abstract. After finding a reference to an article, students must determine if the journal is available in the library or online.

Subject Coverage

Subject coverage in print indexes can be single subject or multidisciplinary. Individual indexes exist for political science, law, criminal justice, and public administration. In addition, some printed indexes cover a wide variety of sources either by type of information or by topic. For example, a printed index may cover the stories published in a particular newspaper (i.e., the *New York Times*), or it may reference only social science literature from journals. Some of the more common single subject print indexes include *ABC Political Science*, *International Political Science Abstracts*, and *Index to Legal Periodicals & Books*. Some of the more common multidisciplinary print indexes include *Social Science Citation Index*, *Social Science Index*, *Book Review Digest*, and *Readers' Guide to Periodical Literature*.

Search Term Language

Students may locate information in print indexes either by using controlled vocabulary or by the author's name. Controlled vocabulary means that all topics covered by the index are grouped into *subject headings* and those subjects then describe all related articles. This allows similar articles to be grouped into one section of the index, although students must determine which term the index uses to describe their topic.

The language, or controlled vocabulary, used to describe particular topics will vary from publisher to publisher. For example, for items in library catalogs, the Library of Congress produces a list of terms in its *Library of Congress Subject Headings* that dictates how libraries can describe the books they own. This controlled vocabulary, then, sets the protocol for selecting search terms. Because every index has its own controlled vocabulary and a limited number of subjects listed, it is important to search for the subject in the way the index describes it. In the *Library of Congress Subject Headings*, World War II, for example, is described as "World War, 1939–1945," so a student looking for World War II books should look up "World War, 1939–1945." Further, single subject indexes may use professional language and jargon to organize their subjects while multidisciplinary indexes generally use simpler, more common terms as their subject headings. Reference librarians can advise students on what kind of search language terms to use with each index. Students may also consult a thesaurus for the index if the publisher issues one.

> ### Example of Controlled Vocabulary in Indexes
>
> For the topic "regulation of garbage services," search for:
> "Waste Management" in *ABC Political Science*
> "Solid Waste Management" in *Index to Legal Periodicals & Books*
> "Refuse and Refuse Disposal" in *Readers' Guide to Periodical Literature*

Databases

Databases are often the *online* versions of printed indexes. They may provide the student with only descriptions of articles or with direct, full text access to the document. The quality of information retrieved from databases is more reliable than information from the Internet because databases are purposefully constructed collections of material. While they are accessed through the Internet via the World Wide Web, databases are not part of what most people consider the Internet nor are they organized or searched the same way as the Internet. Importantly, use of databases is not free and open to the public; database access is *purchased* by libraries for use by patrons and accessed through library facilities.

Organization

Unlike searches using printed indexes, databases allow students to search and retrieve references to and/or copies of published documents for more than one year at a time. In one search attempt, students may retrieve references to related research from the most recent journals or to articles published as many as 15 years earlier. The time period limit for searching is determined by the publishers of the database and the journal publishers with whom they do business. A good rule of thumb is to expect databases to provide references to literature written beginning in the late-1980s. Databases typically provide a list of publications included in the collection with the dates of coverage.

At a minimum, databases offer a *search box* that allows the user to type in a keyword or words related to their research topic. Many offer more advanced searches where the user may limit the search to a particular time period, publication, full text availability, and scholarly (refereed) documents. Many databases also allow the user to expand the search beyond the title, author, or abstract to include searches of the text of the document or words related to the keyword typed in by the user. Depending on the type of database, the search results generally include complete bibliographic information (author, article title, journal title, volume, issue, number, date, pages, etc.) for published materials. Databases most often direct researchers to journal and magazine articles, but some also include books, government documents, and newspapers.

With the exception of database searches for books, most databases provide opportunities to download, email, or print copies of most types of documents free of charge either as PDF full text or HTML full text versions. PDF full text documents are essentially *pictures* of the pages of the document as it was originally published whereas HTML versions are documents that have been reformatted by the database publisher. This is an important distinction for two reasons.

The information provided in the two documents may not be the same: While PDF versions are identical to the published version of the document, HTML versions may or may not include the charts, tables, graphs, or photos from the original article. They rarely identify page breaks in the article. If given a choice, always print or save the PDF version.

Referencing a PDF article in a research paper is easier than citing an HTML version: Because the PDF is identical to the original publication, the original page numbers are preserved. This allows students to cite specific page numbers. HTML versions, however, tend to eliminate any mention of the original pagination. For that reason, references to HTML versions **must** include the name of the database and/or subscription service where the article was obtained online. Citations may need to include a section heading instead of a page number to indicate the source of a particular quote in the article. For example, as shown below, if a student referenced an article from the *ABA Journal* retrieved in PDF format from the *Academic Search* database (sometimes referred to as EBSCOhost or epnet.com), the student may use the page numbers of the original article in the citation. In general, if the student retrieved the same article in HTML format, the student should cite page numbers if possible and must reference the name of database and the date the document was retrieved from the database in the reference citation. Although most styles leave the date of access as optional, we recommend that students provide these dates. (For examples of other citation styles, students should see Chapter Eight.)

CITING DATABASE ARTICLES IN *CHICAGO MANUAL OF STYLE*

PDF reference format:
Chanen, Jill Schachner. 2000. Daddy's home. *ABA Journal*. 86 (11): 90–91.

HTML reference format:
Chanen, Jill Schachner. 2000. Daddy's home. *ABA Journal* 86 (11): 90.
http://www.epnet.com (accessed August 27, 2003).

Subject Coverage

Individual databases exist for political science, law, criminal Justice, and public administration. Because databases are often online versions of print indexes, they may cover a single subject or may be multidisciplinary. Currently, the two most important online databases for general political science research are *Worldwide Political Science Abstracts* and *International Political Science Abstracts*.

Search Term Language

The subscription services also organize their subjects with their own controlled vocabulary, but the flexibility of searching online allows researchers to use a broader range of language for searching. Students should always refer to the "help" option for specific searching recommendations in each database. Single subject databases may use professional language and jargon, but multidisciplinary databases often use simpler terms as their subject headings. Besides searching using controlled vocabulary, databases also allow for *keyword searching* of subject headings, abstracts, or even full text articles. Most databases allow for three different types of searching using keywords:

Field searching: This function allows the student to search a particular field. A "field" is a segment of the item description and commonly includes author, article title, journal title, subject headings, and abstract. Specialized databases may also include specialized fields, which will be described in the database itself. Author field searching can be particularly useful to find literature written by known experts of a subject.

Phrase searching: This function allows the user to search for a particular title or a particular phrase. Most databases automatically search multiple word strings as phrases. For example, a search using the phrase *chewing tobacco* as search terms produces articles only with both words in that exact order. Phrase searching may be combined with *field searching* and *Boolean searching* (see below) to further limit the number of results.

Boolean searching: Unlike print indexes, databases operate with sophisticated searching capabilities, called Boolean, that allow researchers to limit their search results to the most useful items. Boolean operators are terms (*AND, OR, NOT*, etc.) placed between keywords. These terms control the relationships between the keywords and determine the results retrieved. In general, database searches will yield fewer yet more relevant results when the keyword search includes more combinations and narrow concepts and/or objects. Database keyword searches will yield a larger number of results yet these results tend to be more irrelevant because they are searched with broad, less precise terminology.

COMMONLY USED DATABASE SEARCH OPERATORS

AND   Reduces the number of results by requiring both words in the same article. The more words included, the fewer results. Example: *smoking AND regulation AND advertisements*.

OR   Expands the number of results by allowing one or the other word to appear. Example: *smoking OR tobacco*.

NOT   Reduces the number of results by eliminating unwanted references. This is best used after a first search found too many articles or documents about an unrelated topic. Example: *tobacco NOT chewing*.

*   Use at the end of the word to find a root word and all its variations. Particularly useful for finding singular and plural forms of the same word. Users must check to see if the database employs the exclamation point (!) or the question mark (?) instead of an asterisk (*). Example: *advertis** finds *advertisements, advertising, AND advertise*.

( )   Parentheses group search terms together to create more complex searches. Example: *(smok* OR tobacco) AND (regulation* OR rule*)*

Internet   (Written with the assistance of Leila Niehuser)

The Internet has become a useful tool when searching for research sources. When used correctly, the Internet can reduce research time. When used incorrectly, the Internet can be at best a waste of time and, at worst, can provide students with false or misleading information. Because it is unregulated, information provided through an Internet source (Web site) can be as reliable as information found in government documents or as unreliable as information provided in terrorist propaganda—and just as dangerous. To use the Internet efficiently, students must first understand how it is organized. Second, students must become proficient in Internet search techniques. Third, students must learn how to evaluate Internet sources for quality and reliability.

Organization

The Internet (also called the World Wide Web or Web) is not like any other known information providing or processing entity. The Internet links users to freely available content from companies, universities, governments, and organizations. As a worldwide system of computer networks linked together, the Internet provides a forum for sharing information and resources. It is not free. There are real costs and implicit costs. The real costs are the costs to set up an Internet account and any fee the information provider wishes to charge. The implicit costs are found in how the information is collected and the time it takes to retrieve information.

When students retrieve material from a Web site, they must reference the entire Web address for the document as well as the author, title, subtitles, date of creation or last updated (day-month-year), and date of access in the bibliographic citation. It is not acceptable for students to use the date of access in place of the date of creation (or last updated). It is the student's responsibility to locate this information. Quality Web sites generally provide the information. For all others, students may have to search the document or seek the information from any links or menus available in the Web site. (For examples of citation styles, students should see Chapter Eight or http://www.bedfordstmartins.com/online/citex.html.)

INTERNET REFERENCES IN *CHICAGO MANUAL OF STYLE* FORMAT

With an Author:

Galinsky, Ellen, Stacy Kim, and James Bond. 2001. *Feeling overworked: When work becomes too much*. Families & Work Institute. http://www.familiesandwork.org/announce/workforce.html (accessed May 21, 2003).

Without an Author:

Center for Work and Family. 2000. *Workplace flexibility: A powerful strategy for today's dynamic marketplace*. http://www.bc.edu/centers/cwf/research/highlights/ (accessed May 21, 2003).

Because no one authority controls Internet information, each network is free to set its own standards and rules. Although the Web path or address is fairly standardized, other important information about the Web site, such as author, title, and date of publication, is not standardized across domains. Some will be authored by individuals and others will be authored by the sponsoring organization. Some Web sites will include a month-date-year for the creation or date the Web site was updated that is clearly stated, while such information in other Web sites will not be easy to find. Although no one controls the Internet content, there are some common requirements.

COMMON REQUIREMENTS FOR THE INTERNET

Web Access: All Internet connections require software providing protocols, an Internet service provider, and a modem to provide the connection to the computer. Access to the World Wide Web is gained through a browser such as *Netscape Navigator* or Microsoft's *Internet Explorer*.

Resource Characteristics: Information on Web sites is stored in files often referred to as Web pages or home pages. These Web pages are structured by HTML, or Hypertext Markup Language.

URL: In addition, each information source has a unique electronic mail address called a Uniform Resource Locator (URL). The URL is sensitive to errors and must be typed in precisely as given, including any capitalization, punctuation marks, underlining, and characters. A simple URL format is generally as follows:

protocol://domain.name/directory/subdirectory/filename.ext

Protocol: Each URL contains a protocol (type of link) or service made. Each service requires a different piece of software. The most commonly used protocols include:

World Wide Web service is *http://*

Email service is *mailto://*

Telnet service is *telnet://*

FTP for file transfer service is *ftp://*

Network News Transfer Protocol *usenet://*

Domain.name: Each URL contains a domain name that identifies the owner of the Web site. The domain name has at least two parts separated by a "dot." The word before the dot is called the second-level domain and the word after the dot is called the top-level domain. Some URLs will contain third and fourth level domains as well. The most important is the top-level domain which tells the user the type of organization that owns the domain. These include but are not limited to:

.edu for colleges and universities

.gov for government institutions

.org for nonprofit organizations

.com for commercial organizations

.net for networking services

.mil for military sites

.us for United States (or any other two-letter Internet country code)

Directory: Some URLs contain a path (directory and subdirectories) to the information on the Web site. The directories are simple organizing mechanisms for the stored information. These directories are separated in the URL by a "/" or forward slash. Some paths also may include a "~" (tilde) that often indicates who in the organization is assigned that particular directory.

Filename.ext: The filename and extension, which are separated by a dot, are the most specific reference to information in a file. The filename can be brief or lengthy. The extension is generally, for most Web pages, *.htm* or *.html* for text material. Some material will have a *.pdf* extension which is read by *Adobe Acrobat Reader*. Some material is still readable as ASCII text as indicated by the *txt* extension.

Subject Coverage

Subject coverage on the Internet may include single subject or multidisciplinary directories. Students can usually find Web sites by using a search engine or a meta-search engine to surf (explore, search) for information if they do not know the URL for a Web site.

While the difference between directories and search engines has become increasingly blurred over time, there are some quality differences in the way that information about Web sites is classified and retrieved.

Subject Directories: Subject directories (also called subject guides or Web directories) provide links to Internet sources by subject. The links in the subject directories are specially selected and organized hierarchically from most general to most specific key words in "layers" or levels of information. In general, most subject directories are searchable by keywords as well. There are two basic types of directories. **Commercial** directories, such as *Yahoo!* are created to serve the general public and are not appropriate for scholarly research. **Professional** directories, such as *INFOMINE*, are generally created by subject experts to serve as research tools. Students should use professional subject directories when they have a broad topic and/or wish to locate high quality information. The links in these directories are generally chosen for their relevance and quality for academics and professionals in the field. While some professional subject directories provide a broad range of searchable materials, others are narrowly tailored to **political science**. Some of the more common professional subject directories include:

Professional General Subject Directories	Political Science Subject Directories
INFOMINE [http://infomine.ucr.edu]	National Politics Index [http://www.politicalindex.com]
AcademicInfo [http://www.academicinfo.net]	Political Science Resources on the Web [http://www.lib.umich.edu/govdocs/polisci.html]
WWW Virtual Library [http://www.vlib.org]	International Affairs Resources on the World Wide Web [http://www.etown.edu/vl/]
BUBL LINK [http://bubl.ac.uk/link]	Library of Congress Resources [http://www.loc.gov/]
Librarian's Index to the Internet [http://lii.org]	Political Resources on the Net [http://www.agora.stm.it/politic]

Search Engines: A search engine is a database of Internet sources. Search engines use "spiders" or "robots" to retrieve individual Web pages or documents, either because the author of the engine prefers to list the Web site, or because the Web site owner has asked to be listed. Search engines tend to "index" (record by word) all of the terms on a given Web document. Alternatively, they may index all of the terms within the first few sentences, the Web site title, or the document metatags.

There are two types of search engines. **Individual search engines** retrieve information for their indexes using their own spiders. Older or first generation search engines retrieve information that contains some or all of the search terms requested. Second generation search engines rank the results based on the quality of the Web page links. **Meta-search engines** combine several search engines simultaneously. Often referred to as parallel search tools, these meta-search engines do not build their own databases. These tools use the search engines and directories created by others. The best way to find information fast is to conduct a meta-search. The meta-search tools identify the most relevant sites across numerous individual search indexes for the information requested. Most of these search engines retrieve documents that have been set up to be accessed from Web pages. Some of the more sophisticated search engines may also search the databases and non-text files (graphics, etc.) in the "deep Web" (sometimes referred to as the invisible Web). *Google, ProFusion*, and *Lycos* will search the deep Web. For an excellent list and discussion of the deep Web, see *http://library.albany.edu/internet/deepweb.html*. Here is a list of some of the search engines currently being used on the Internet for scholarly research that are considered award winning, top choice, or popular by *SearchEngineWatch.com*:

Individual Search Engines	Meta-Search Engines
Google [http://www.google.com]	Vivisimo [http://www.vivisimo.com]
All the Web	Fazzle [http://www.fazzle.com]
[http://www.alltheweb.com]	Ixquick [http://www.ixquick.com]
AltaVista	ProFusion [http://www.profusion.com]
[http://www.altavista.com]	Dogpile [http://www.dogpile.com]
MSN Search	Excite [http://www.excite.com]
[http://search.msn.com]	MetaCrawler [http://www.metacrawler.com]
HotBot [http://www.hotbot.com]	The Invisible Web [http://www.invisibleweb.com]
Lycos [http://www.lycos.com]	Invisible-web.net [http://www.invisible-web.net]

Search Term Language

Unlike indexes and databases, Internet search engines rely on natural language searches to retrieve results. In plain English, this means that databases return results based on the words searched that match the words on the Web page. Subject directories and search engines generally operate on the same basis as database searching using Boolean logic. Students should refer to the "help" menu for specific details on the type of search operators or terms the search subject directory and search engine uses. Some will use the Boolean "AND" and "OR" operators (see examples **Commonly Used Database Search Operators**) and some will use implied Boolean symbols for these such as "+" or "–".

INTERNET SEARCH OPERATORS

" "   Requires that more than one word be found as a phrase. ***Example***: "*tobacco man-ufacturer.*"

+   The plus sign next to or placed directly in front of the keyword will assure that the search will result in documents that include that keyword. By placing additional plus signs in between a list of keywords, students may further limit the search to documents that contain only the terms listed. This works like the Boolean term "and." ***Example***: *+child +sex +abuse.*

-    The minus sign next to or placed directly in front of the keyword will assure that the search will result in documents that do not include the keyword. Using the minus sign in conjunction with the plus sign will remove unwanted documents from the hit list. This works like the Boolean term "not." **Example**: +child -sex -abuse.

Saving Materials from the Web: It is important for students to save and/or print any materials they plan to use in their research project and ***record the date that the material was accessed on the Internet.*** Internet materials, unlike any other sources available, are subject to frequent revisions (minute by minute, daily, weekly, monthly, annually) that make George Orwell's *1984* an easier world for research than ours! In Orwellian fashion, not only are Web sites updated, they can be re-written with new information that is different, even contrary, to that which was posted earlier. "Here today, gone tomorrow" is common for Web sites. Unlike books and articles that are available through interlibrary loan if not available at the school library, Web sites removed temporarily or permanently cannot be reconstructed on demand. ***Because Internet information is so unstable, students should print or save the material to a disk to preserve it and note the date on which the Web site was accessed in addition to the URL for that Web page.*** For the purposes of their research, students must be able to produce the materials they used for instructors who ask for them. Many instructors randomly check student sources or subscribe to software services that search for evidence of plagiarism. For books and articles, instructors can check the library. For Web materials it is not always possible to find the materials when the source of the materials has been discontinued or changed. It is the student's responsibility to provide evidence of the validity and reliability of the Web materials.

TO SAVE THE ENTIRE WEB PAGE

- Insert a floppy disk into the computer
- Select *File* then select *Save As* then select the drive the floppy is in
- Give the file a name
- Select *Plain Text* (.txt) or *Web Page* (.htm or .html)
- Select *OK*

TO SAVE PART OF A WEB PAGE

- Click and hold the left mouse button at the beginning of the text
- Drag the cursor over the range of text to be saved. Release the button.
- From the menu bar, select *Edit* then select *Copy*
- Open a word processing application
- From the menu bar of the word processing application, select *Edit* then select *Paste*
- Put quotes around any part of the document that you copied directly from the Web
- Type the name of the Web page, the address, and the time you found the document online
- Save the file with a filename

TO SAVE A WEB ADDRESS WITH A TITLE

- Click and hold the left mouse button at the beginning of the address in the box marked Netsite
- Drag the cursor over the range of text to be saved. Release the button.
- From the menu bar, select *Edit* then select *Copy*

- Open a word processing application
- From the menu bar of the word processing application, select *Edit* then select *Paste*
- Repeat the process for the title of the Web page
- Edit and change the font of the text, if necessary.
- Annotate (write about) the site with any other descriptive information or notes about the site.
- Do not forget to record the date of creation or date the Web site was last updated.
- Save the file with a filename

Selecting the Right Search Tools for Locating Research Materials

For nearly every topic researched by students of political science, one can find information in a range of resources. News articles, journal articles, laws, or books may provide arguments and facts to help a student prepare a research paper. Because students often research current events and issues, they should understand how the information industry affects the availability of research sources over time. After determining what might be available, students should then choose the appropriate tool for retrieving that information.

The Information Timeline

As current events and issues unfold in the public eye, writers and scholars begin to generate research sources. Depending on the format of the source, however, information *may not* be available shortly after a significant political event. The availability and type of sources for research is highly determined by the time period. For example, if a student chooses to research the attacks against the World Trade Center in New York City and the Pentagon in Washington, DC on September 11, 2001, the information available the day after the event would be limited to newspaper articles, video from broadcast or cable sources, and news on Web sites. It would be difficult to find the variety of sources necessary to write a thoroughly researched 10-page paper using only information from September 12, 2001. Scholars and government officials may have begun research about the event, but September 12 would have been too early to have any of their research published. In sum, locating information requires a clear understanding of what purpose the source serves and how each type of source fits into the research process. Each provides information in different formats and time periods. The following chart describes the availability of resources available over time. Use this chart to determine what source will provide the type of information needed.

The Information Timeline

Time Period	Source(s)	Type of Information	Authors	Audience
Day of the event	Non-print news reports: radio, television, & Internet news services	General: who, what, and where (not necessarily why)	Journalists	General public
1–3 Days	Print & non-print news: newspapers, radio, television, Internet news services	Varies: some articles include analysis, statistics, photographs, editorial opinions	Journalists	General public
Week	Popular & mass market magazines (i.e., *Time* & *Newsweek*)	Still in reporting stage (who, what, where, & why); general; editorial & opinions; statistics; photographs; usually no bibliography available	Journalists (usually not specialists in the field)	General public to educated layperson
Months	Scholarly journal articles	Research results, detailed & theoretical discussion; bibliography available	Specialists & scholars in the field	Scholars, specialists, & students
Two years	Books & conference proceedings	In-depth coverage of a topic; edited compilations of scholarly articles related to a topic; bibliography available	Specialists & scholars in the field	General public to scholars
Ten years	Reference sources (i.e., specialized encyclopedias)	General overview giving factual information; bibliography available	Specialists & scholars in the field	Scholars, students, laypersons

Source: Chart based on UCLA College Library's "Flow of Information" tutorial located at: http://wwwtest.library.ucla.edu/libraries/college/help/flow/index.htm (Johnson and Blakselee 2004).

Search Tools by Format

Each type of source format (i.e., books and articles) has a set of efficient search tools. The availability of tools such as indexes and databases varies for each library so students should determine what sources their libraries offer by checking their library's Web site.

Books

Every library offers a library catalog (a database) to find books owned by the library. The catalog should also include all other items in the library including journals, videos, CDs, maps, and government documents. Searching in multi-library catalogs, databases that include the holdings of many libraries, allows students to identify items owned in libraries around the world and request them via the library's Interlibrary Loan services.

Important Book Search Tools

Source	Indexes	Databases	Web sites
Single library	Card Catalog (if available)	Local Library's online catalog	Internet Public Library [http://www.ipl.org/div/books/]
		Library of Congress [http://catalog.loc.gov/]	Online Books Page [http://onlinebooks.library.upenn.edu]
Multi-library		Melvyl [http://melvyl.cdlib.org]	Project Gutenberg [http://promo.net/pg]
		WorldCat	
Commercial	Books in Print	Located on any publisher's Web site	AllDirect.com [http://www.alldirect.com]
		Books in Print	Amazon.com [http://www.amazon.com]

Scholarly Journal Literature

Scholarly, peer reviewed, and law review articles are found in journal databases or printed indexes. If searched by subject, the database or index provides information about published journal articles matching the subject. Online databases may even include the complete text of the article, so it may be emailed or printed directly. Printed indexes, however, offer only a citation and require the student to identify if the journal mentioned is available in the local library. Databases and indexes may be multidisciplinary, covering a wide variety of academic subjects, or single subject, representing the literature of a single discipline like law or political science. While Web sites are generally poor sources for locating scholarly journal publications, there are e-journals that publish scholarly, peer reviewed articles. The e-journals are often not included in searchable databases, so locating them is sometimes difficult. Also, e-journals may charge a fee for access to materials on their Web sites.

Important Journal Search Tools

Discipline	Indexes	Databases	Web sites
Social Science	Readers' Guide to Periodical Literature	Academic Search	Directory of Open Access Journals [http://www.doaj.org/]
	Social Science Citation Index	Expanded Academic	Electronic Journal Miner [http://ejournal.coalliance.org//]
	Social Sciences Abstracts	JSTOR	All Academic [http://www.allacademic.com/index.html]
	Social Sciences Index	Social Sciences Abstracts	Social Science Online Periodicals [http://www.unesco.org/shs/shsdc/journals/shsjournals.html]
			INFOMINE [http://infomine.ucr.edu]
Political Science	ABC Political Science	International Political Science Abstracts	Social Science Online Periodicals [http://www.unesco.org/shs/shsdc/journals/shsjournals.html]
	CSA Political Science & Government	Political Science Abstracts	Directory Political Science Journals [http://dir.yahoo.com/Social_Science/Political_Science/Journals/]
	International Political Science Abstracts	Worldwide Political Science Abstracts	Politifo.com [http://www.politinfo.com/search/]
Criminal Justice	Criminal Justice Periodicals Index	Criminal Justice Periodicals Index	National Criminal Justice Reference Service [http://www.ncjrs.org]
International Relations	International Periodical Index	Columbia International Affairs Online	Directory Political Science Journals [http://dir.yahoo.com/Social_Science/Political_Science/International_Relations/Journals/]
Public Administration	Public Administration Abstracts	ABI/Inform	Center for Accountability and Performance [http://www.aspanet.org/cap/index.html]
		PAIS	Directory of Journals in Public Affairs [http//:www.chatpress.com/directory_of_journals_in_public_.htm]
		Business Source	Electronic Hallway [http://www.hallway.org/journal/]
Public Policy	Encyclopedia of American Public Policy	PAIS	Directory Political Science Journals [http://dir.yahoo.com/Social_Science/Political_Science/Public_Policy/Journals/]
		ABI/Inform	Electronic Hallway [http://www.hallway.org/journal/]

Quality Professional Publications (for Law Reviews, see *Law* below)

Industry experts often consider these publications "trade publications" because they are articles written by experts for experts. Many libraries subscribe to such trade magazines and journals, and they can often be searched through journal databases (see the above section on Scholarly Journal Literature). Government issued magazines, like *FBI Law Enforcement Bulletin* or the *Monthly Labor Review*, can be searched in sources that focus on U.S. government reports.

Important Quality Publication Search Tools

Indexes	Databases	Web sites
PAIS	CQ Weekly	Electronic Journal Miner [http://ejournal.coalliance.org]
CSA Political Science and Government	CQ Public Affairs Collection	Ejournals [http://nnlm.gov/libinfo/ejournals/]
Social Sciences Abstract	LexisNexis Government Periodicals Index	Index Morganagus [http://sunsite.berkeley.edu/ ~emorgan/morganagus/index.html]
	National Journal's Policy Central	FindArticles.com [http://www.findarticles.com/PI/index.jhtm]
	PAIS	
	ABI/Inform	

Law

Academic libraries, especially those that support pre-law programs or law schools, buy legal documents including state and federal codes, opinions, and regulations. Increasingly, this same information can be found online for free, though access may be limited to recent information. Databases purchased by libraries for their students generally include a broad range of historical and current legal documents.

Important Court Decisions, Laws, and Regulations Search Tools

Indexes	Databases	Web sites
U. S. Supreme Court Digest	LexisNexis Academic	Findlaw [http://www.findlaw.com]
West's Federal Practice Digest	Westlaw	Legal Information Institute [http://www.law.cornell.edu]
		LexisOne [http://www.lexisone.com]

Important Law Review Articles Search Tools

Indexes	Databases	Web sites
Index to Legal Periodicals and Books	LexisNexis Academic (Law Reviews)	E-Journals Coalition [http://law.richmond.edu/jolt/e-journals]
		Findlaw [http://www.findlaw.com]

Government Reports

The federal government issues an array of official information in the form of statistical data, reports, or law. This information is not protected by copyright and is, thus, often packaged in for-profit databases by enterprising businesses or found for free online from the government directly. Many libraries also hold collections of government documents, which can be found by searching the library catalog. In addition, state and local governments also issue an array of official information in the form of statistical data, reports, or law. Much of this information can be found for free online from the governments directly. Many libraries also hold collections of state documents, which can be found by searching the library catalog. Some libraries have special collections housing local documents.

Important U.S. Government Search Tools

Indexes	Databases	Web sites
American Statistics Index	LexisNexis Congressional	FirstGov [http://www.firstgov.gov]
Monthly Catalog of Government Publications	Government Periodicals Index	Google Uncle Sam [http://www.google.com/unclesam/]
	PAIS	GPO Access [http://www.gpoaccess.gov]
	LexisNexis Statistical	Public Policy Process [http://www.csuchico.edu/~kcfount/bills/]

Important State and Local Government Search Tools

Indexes	Databases	Web sites
Statistical Reference Index	LexisNexis Statistical	FirstGov [http://www.firstgov.gov]
Monthly Checklist of State Publications	PAIS	State & Local Government on the Net [http://www.statelocalgov.net/index.cfm]

International Reports

The United Nations and its auxiliary organizations produce a substantial number of important documents related to individual countries and international issues. A select number of large universities serve as depositories for U.N. documents, and much like other libraries, are U.S. depositories. Access to their publications can also be found through databases and the U.N. Web site.

Important International Report Search Tools

Indexes	Databases	Web sites
Index to International Statistics	AccessUN	United Nations [http://www.un.org]
Index to United Nations Documents and Publications	LexisNexis Statistical	

Popular or Mass Media (News)

Newspaper and magazine articles may be searched in a variety of locations including databases, on the Internet, or on microfilm. Databases allow students to search the full text of articles from around the world over a long period of time. The Internet provides recent articles, audio and video clips, though online news sources may charge fees to view some articles and video. Microfilm preserves very old issues of newspapers and magazines, which helps when researching historical topics.

Important Popular or Mass Media Search Tools

Indexes	Databases	Web sites
New York Times Index	Factiva	Newslink [http://newslink.org/menu.html]
Readers' Guide to Periodical Literature	Lexis/Nexis Academic	E&P Media Links [http://www.editorandpublisher.com/editorandpublisher/business_resources/medialinks.jsp]
	Newstand	NewsTrawler [http://www.newstrawler.com/]

Private Reports

Businesses, interest groups, educational institutions, or think tanks may issue private reports. As mentioned earlier, this information is typically difficult to find. The reference sections of most libraries carry a variety of organizational directories that can lead students to published addresses for these private organizations and sometimes provide Web site addresses as well. A growing number of databases and Internet sites, however, provide access to information disseminated to the public. Effective searching through Internet search engines may identify useful reports.

Important Private Report Search Tools		
Organizational Directories	**Databases**	**Web sites**
Encyclopedia of Business Information Sources	PolicyFile	Public Agenda Online [http://www.publicagenda.org]
Gale's Encyclopedia of Associations		Political Advocacy Group [http://www.csuchico.edu/kcfount/]

Research Strategies for Locating Sources: A Simulation

Students should be aware that there is a hard way and an easy way to locate source material for a research paper. **THE HARD WAY:** Read everything you can find that is connected to your topic in two weeks or less. This means that interlibrary loan materials, books, journal articles, and government reports will probably not be available in time for finishing the research paper. **THE EASY WAY:** Let the experts guide you. This section illustrates the process by which a student investigates and locates resources for a project examining tobacco regulation for a paper in a policy evaluation course.

Step One: Review Expectations of Assignment & Choose a Topic

Students should have a clear idea of what their professor expects for the assignment. If students are unsure they should check with the instructor for clarification on the assignment's requirements and the appropriateness of the chosen topic. See Chapter Three for more information on choosing a topic. For this example, the topic *"Regulation of Tobacco and the Protection of Minors"* combines two objects and a concept (policy players, and values).

Set up a research folder with expectations and topic options prominently displayed.

Chapter Fourteen describes the process of setting up a project folder. Essentially, students should keep notes, copies of information, bibliographies, etc., in a folder or binder that is specific to the project. Students should also keep a copy or list the specific research requirements and expectations that the instructor provided as part of the class assignment in this folder.

Keep careful records.

Students should plan to save all relevant citation information of sources as they engage in the research process. This is essential for anything students plan to cite in their papers.

Journal article (printed or PDF copy): author, article title, journal title, date of publication, volume, issue or number, pages.

Journal article (HTML copy): author, article title, journal title, date of publication, volume, issue or number, pages, database name, date of retrieval.

Government report: author (a person or an agency name), title of the report, place and date of publication, and publisher. If retrieved online, include Web address and date of retrieval.

Book: author, title, place and year of publication, and publisher.

Law: title of the law, title of the book, volume number, section number and date.

Case: party names, case citation including volume, book title abbreviation, pages, and year.

Web page: author, title, date of last update, date of retrieval, Web address.

Step Two: Find Background Information

Gathering background information will provide students with knowledge that will help them *identify* leading authors in a research area, *focus* the research on a manageable topic, and *evaluate* the information collected from secondary sources. To research a project involving tobacco regulation, students should be looking for information about the history of government regulation of tobacco and the smoking rates of young people to determine the nature of the problem. To find this information, students should:

Look in the assigned textbook for the course.

Read essays, sections, or chapters that relate to the topic. Not only will this provide course specific information, but it will be presented in a context that is relevant for the class. Students should take special note of any authors, issues, examples, or relevant facts mentioned.

Look in reference books related to the topic.

The most useful books will be encyclopedias with brief essays (about 3–5 pages). These typically summarize the recent research and identify some of the most influential scholars and current areas of debate. Specialized dictionaries may also help by defining theories or concepts central to the research topic. To find reference books:

- Ask a reference librarian for relevant recommendations.
- Browse the "J" (for Political Science) or "K" (for Law) call number area of the Reference collection in the library.
- Browse the school library's Web site to see if there are any links to useful sources. Many libraries organize research tools by subject. Look for recommendations for political science, law, public administration and related fields.

For example, for the topic *"Regulation of Tobacco and the Protection of Minors,"* reference books, including *Statistical Abstract of the United States*, *Encyclopedia of American Public Policy*, and *CQ Researcher* contain the following important facts:

- In 1985, 29.4% of youths aged 12–17 considered themselves current users of cigarettes. By 1999, that percentage dropped to 15.9%.
- Congress passed several laws regulating the marketing and distribution of cigarettes. Among them are the Cigarette Labeling and Advertising Act (1965) and the Public Health Cigarette Smoking Act of 1969.
- Cigarette companies recently faced public criticism for targeting their advertisements to young people in order to create loyal, lifelong smokers.

Browse government Web sites or government documents.

With few exceptions, most topics involving government and/or politics are addressed in some way in government documents. Policy evaluations, for example, should always begin with locating the public law and the legislative history of the policy. For example, using the database *Lexis/Nexis Congressional*, a search of U.S. Codes using the keywords *Public Health Cigarette Smoking Act AND (child OR children OR minors)* locates a document that identifies and/or links to current amendments, the legislative history, the controlling bureaucratic agency, court decisions, and the parts of the legislation that relate to regulation of smoking by minors.

Step Three: Write a Preliminary Research Hypothesis or Question

After doing some preliminary investigation about a topic, the variety of available primary and secondary sources of research will emerge. The brief articles in reference sources will highlight issues of legitimate inquiry. Use this information to develop an initial research hypothesis or question. For example, preliminary research into tobacco regulation and children suggests that the target of the policy is tobacco advertising. As a result, the research question could be "how has the regulation of tobacco advertising affected teen smoking?" or the hypothesis could be "regulation of tobacco advertising has reduced teen smoking." Either way, the focus and purpose of the research is to evaluate the effectiveness of regulating advertising as a means of reducing teenage smoking.

Step Four: Identify Types of Sources Needed for the Project

Different tools, such as databases or catalogs, find different sets of material. For a thoroughly researched political science paper and depending on the scope of the assignment, students generally need:

Sources required for all political science papers:
- Research or scholarly articles that examine objects and/or concepts related to the topic
- Books that examine objects and/or concepts related to the topic

Sources that may be available or required involving the objects and/or concepts related to the topic:
- Government documents (reports, hearings, and/or debates)
- Federal, state, or local laws
- Federal, state, or local court cases
- Quality publications (especially law review articles and professional publications)

- Relevant mass media (especially editorials or investigative reports/analysis)
- Expert analysis (especially provided by think tanks, scholarly institutes, reputable organizations)
- Quantitative data (primary or secondary)

For example, to research the topic *"Regulation of Tobacco and the Protection of Minors,"* the student must find scholarly articles, government sources, books, and some quality publications. In particular, the student will benefit from locating books or an edited book with a summary article on the history of tobacco regulation.

Step Five: Build a Set of Search Terms

The preliminary research of the topic should provide the student with a set of words or terms and synonyms for those terms that can be used as keywords for locating additional sources. Once they locate additional sources, students will find additional terms they can use to locate even more additional sources. As the student's knowledge and familiarity with the topic increases, the quality, relevance, and usefulness of search results increases as well. To do this:

Create keywords from the hypothesis or research question.

For example, the keywords for the research question, "How has the regulation of tobacco advertising affected teen smoking?" are: *tobacco, advertising, regulations, teen,* and *smoking.*

Develop synonyms based on these keywords.

List synonyms for the keywords identified in the research question or hypothesis. Students can use a thesaurus to identify synonyms. Many word processing programs have a built-in thesaurus. Importantly, students should use the information from their preliminary research to note different terms or ways of expressing/describing the same things. For example, to research tobacco regulations and use by minors, a student would list the following terms and their synonyms as keywords:

- Tobacco, cigarettes, nicotine, smoking
- Advertising, commercials, billboards, advertisements, infomercial, ads
- Regulations, rules, restrictions, control, limitations, limits, policies
- Teen, adolescent, young adult, underage, kid, teenager, children
- Smoking—same as "tobacco"
- Philip Morris, manufacturer, company (to describe the major tobacco industry players)
- Public Health Cigarette Smoking Act (to find information about a particular law)
- Department of Health, Education, and Welfare, Food and Drug Administration, Alcohol Tobacco and Firearms, and agencies (to find information on federal agencies and their role in tobacco regulation)

Step Six: Searching in Relevant Indexes, Databases, & Internet Sites

Remember that indexes, databases, and search engines use different searching technology, and that searches should be structured to reflect these differences.

There *should not* be a "perfect" article that covers the entire topic exactly as stated in the research question.

Students should be telling their own stories and supporting their own arguments based on the unique combination of secondary and/or primary sources they have collected in the research process. No single article, book, or report will be or should be identical to the focus, purpose, justification, hypothesis, method of inquiry, or the results of the student's efforts.

Students should begin a search for secondary sources using all available resources.

Indexes: Look up different terms from the keywords list in an index. One of them will direct the student to relevant literature. For example, a student may look up "tobacco" in:

- The school library's *Online Catalog* to see if there are books on any aspect of the topic
- *ABC Political Science* and find a reference to "see smoking." The heading for "smoking," then, will list a number of interesting articles.

Databases: Search some of the keywords in combination with Boolean operators. Choose no more than one term for each concept or object, and combine them to find articles that address the topic. *Importantly, in most databases, unless a student specifically requests a search of the full text of the article or document, the database search will be limited to titles and abstracts/summaries of the article. For a thorough search for secondary sources of research on the topic, students should indicate (often by marking the box "search within text") that they want the entire document searched for their keywords.* By doing this, students will find more documents that address the objects and concepts related to their topic that, although directly address the topic, did not contain the specific keywords they used in their keyword search. As an added bonus, most database programs will identify the keyword in bold each time it appears in the text. For example, the students seeking documents related to tobacco regulation and minors may use:

- *LexisNexis Congressional* for information about Congress' role in regulating tobacco
- *LexisNexis Academic-Law Reviews* for law review articles related to regulating tobacco
- *PAIS* to find articles and government reports about public policies
- *Academic Search* to find scholarly articles from many different fields (such as political science and medical journals)
- *CQ Weekly* to find quality articles written by professionals covering Congress

To locate documents with these databases, a student may use the following keywords related to tobacco regulation and minors:

- *Tobacco AND regulation AND advertising*
- *Smoking AND policies AND teens*
- *Tobacco AND regulat° AND advertis°*
- *Smok° AND polic° AND teen°*

Search engines: Visit Web sites recommended for each type of resource format (reports, laws, etc.). Search within these sites, particularly if they have directories or a search option before moving on to more general search engines like *Google* or *MetaCrawler*. In particular, because *FirstGov* searches only government Web pages, it automatically filters results so that the documents retrieved will generally be useful and relevant. For example, the students seeking documents related to tobacco regulation and minors may use:

- *FirstGov Web site* for reports and statistics from the federal government
- Web sites for the American Lung Association and the American Cancer Association for high-quality nongovernmental reports and data regarding tobacco consumption and regulation

To locate documents with these search engines, a student may use the following keywords related to tobacco regulation and minors:

- *Tobacco regulation "Food and Drug Administration"*
- *Cigarette +advertisements +Teens +smoking*

Modify keywords and search terms based on search results.

Because computers try to match the words typed to the words in a database or on a Web page, students may need to use different terms to find more information. Are there words appearing in results that can be added to the original keyword list? Do the indexes and databases offer subject headings that could be searched? If so, students should modify their list of keywords with these new terms.

For example, after searching using the keyword list derived from the student's research question, the student discovers that a legal settlement reached between the states and the tobacco industry companies affected the way in which tobacco products could be marketed. Because of this new information, the student begins searching for more information about the settlement. The new keywords are:

- *settlement, lawsuit, case, litigation, class action*
- *prevention, public health, health policy*

These new keywords can be combined with the original keywords. For example:

- *Tobacco AND settlement AND advertisements*
- *Smoking AND prevention AND settlement°*
- *Smoking AND teen° and prevent° AND lawsuit°*
- *Lawsuit AND market° AND cigarette°*

Try searching in many indexes, databases, and search engines.

This ensures that students find the most current, relevant, and important information for their topic. In addition, the diverse sources provide a range of perspectives on the topic. For example, while searching *PAIS* for articles on tobacco regulation the student discovered a particularly relevant court case. To search the court case, the student moves the search from the *PAIS* database to *LexisNexis Academic* to conduct research for legal information regarding the case and its impact on tobacco regulation.

Step Seven: Examine the Bibliographies of Materials Retrieved

Once students have located reference texts, books, and articles, they should review the bibliographies, references, footnotes, endnotes, and/or works cited pages of those sources. The references listed by the authors of these documents provide a rich supply of additional research sources that may have been untapped by searches in indexes, databases, and/or the Internet.

Remember: All document retrieval systems have source and time limits.

Students should remember that indexes, databases, and Internet search engines are limited to the document sources that *their sponsors choose to include* in the search criteria. All of these document retrieval systems have time limits as well. Research documents that exist before the index was published, the database was compiled, or not accessible to the Internet are left unacknowledged. There is no universal source of all research. Yet, there is a wealth of creditable research that is left out of searches using these retrieval systems that are known to scholars in the field. Identifying these scholars and their publications provides students with access to more documents.

Locate references to the same authors in several of the documents.

Authors who are knowledgeable, credible, respected, and renowned for their expertise tend, with a few exceptions, to be considered experts in the field. Although not all scholars in the field may agree with these author's viewpoints or perspectives, their published research in scholarly books and articles have been peer-reviewed (evaluated by other scholars) and deemed significant contributions to the field. Students need to acknowledge the work of these authors and locate relevant research published by such experts. Often the work of these authors is referenced in many publications. To find work by these authors, students should do the following:

Identify authors referenced in textbooks and/or reference books. When an author or a particular document by an author is listed or referenced in the student's textbook and/or reference books, it is usually because the author is considered to have made an important contribution to the field related to the student's topic.

Identify authors referenced in several documents. If an author is listed in the references of several books and/or articles, it is very likely that this author is considered a highly recognized scholar or authority in the field related to the student's research topic. Students should make a list of authors of books and articles that are related to their topic and list the titles of the referenced documents under each of these author's names.

Search for more articles by these expert authors.

Return to appropriate indexes, databases, and Web sites for the topic. Search for the expert authors identified in textbooks, reference books, and listed in many sources. Most databases are particularly useful for locating these publications because searches can be limited to author's name, the title of the book or monograph, the title of the article and/or the title of the publication. To find publications by these authors, student should do the following:

Do full text searches by author's name. Students should do a full text search by the author's name. The full text search will find documents written by the author as well as documents by other authors who referenced that author in their research. This activity will provide students with additional sources as well as provide an indication of how important this author is to the field.

Do full text searches by document title. Students should also do a full text search in databases using the exact title of the author's publication in quotations or mark the *"phrase search"* box (whichever applies to the database) so that every available document that references the article or book is retrieved in the search. Again, this provides the student with additional sources as well as an indication of how important the document is in the field.

Do an Internet search by author's name. Often, leading scholars in the field will publish research results on academic and nonacademic institutional Web sites. Indexes and databases do not search these sources, but Internet search engines often do. This is especially true of the search engines that search the "invisible Web."

Evaluating the Quality and Reliability of Sources

All materials retrieved for a research project must be evaluated before they can be used. Regardless of whether students are using books, articles, or Web materials, each item should be evaluated based on the author's credentials, accuracy of the information, objectivity, timeliness, focus, audience, and origins of the evidence. Students may want to access the "Web Evaluation Menu" from Widener University at *http://www.widener.edu/ ?pageId=857*. For an evaluation of a site, read *Web Wisdom: How to Evaluate and Create Information Quality on the Web* by Jan Alexander and Marsha Ann Tate (Lawrence Erlbaum Assoc. 1999) or use the guidelines below.

Examine the Author's or Source's Credentials

Students should be wary of any source that does not have an identifiable author. Sometimes the author is listed as an organization, sometimes as a series of individuals, and sometimes as a single individual. Some of the questions students should ask about the author of the materials include:

General Guidelines

- If the author is an individual, what are the author's credentials and educational background? Academic scholars, those authors who are listed as faculty at a university, typically produce more scientifically based research.
- Are there multiple sources written by the same author? If so, they may be leading authors in the field.
- Who published the sources—a government agency, a nonprofit institution, a university, etc.? For example, sources in Web sites with a domain name ending in *.gov*, *.us*, or *.edu* have higher credibility than unknown individuals or some obscure organization. Books published by university presses have a higher reputation than those published by commercial (mass market) publishers and non-academic associations.

Web Guidelines

- Read Web sources carefully. Some Web sites will try to confuse the researcher by using domain names that sound like governmental or university organizations but are really owned and maintained by individuals. Look for a statement that the content has been approved by the organization or that the organization holds the copyright. If it is not clear that the organization is responsible for the contents of the page, the Web site may not be credible.

- If there is any doubt about the origins of the Web site, find out who operates it by going to *http://www.internic.net/*. Click on the "Whois" search database of registered domain names. Type in the domain name of the Web site. Another way to locate this same information is through another Web site supported by *Network Solutions*. *Network Solutions* maintains the central database for domain registration on the domain name central server. See *http://www.networksolutions.com/en_US/whois/index.jhtml*.
- A tilde (~) in the Web site address generally means that it is an individual's home page. Be very careful of these types of home pages. Even some *.gov* and *.edu* Web sites will include these. Remember that an individual home page regardless of the domain still represents just the individual's viewpoint.
- Web sites with long complicated addresses are also suspect. Such Web sites are generally so imbedded and distant from the Web site owners that the researcher cannot easily find out who the owner of the site is. For such sites, start by deleting parts of the address from right to left until the domain name and home page appear. This is like peeling an onion; the purpose of this is to get to the owner of the Web site.

Assess the Accuracy of the Information

Just because it is published does not make information true or accurate. All information needs verification.

General Guidelines

- Look for references to other sources for any factual information. One way to assess the accuracy of the information is to find it in two different sources. If it can be found in two places, preferably at least one government, academic, or university source, the information is probably accurate.
- Another way to assess a resource is to look for relative balance in the information presented. Does the author present alternative views? Is the author associated with an organization with an interest in the outcome?

Web Guidelines

- Web sites with hyperlinks (links to sites) that only link the user to the same author or server are also suspect. Hyperlinks in Web sites should direct the user to additional information and corroborating sources not authored or provided by the same server.
- Just because a credible Web site lists additional sites does not mean those sites are equally credible.
- Web sites that refer users to resources in print form (books and journals, for example) have a higher credibility than those that refer users to nothing else or to their own servers.
- Web sites with frequent grammatical and spelling errors are also suspect. Credible servers/authors professionally maintain their Web pages.

Does the Source Demonstrate Objectivity?

Assessing objectivity is difficult if the researcher is unfamiliar with general information about the topic. Until the researcher is better informed about the topic, using verbal clues and cues will help determine the value of the information. Value laden, manipulative, belief driven, baseless information is of very little value in academic research. Other than being used as an example of a type of opinion or perspective, the information contained in such sources is often tainted by the author's biases. Assess the information using the following questions:

- Is the language used in the document neutral or persuasive?
- Are the terms used value neutral or value laden?
- Are the author's assertions based on beliefs or quantifiable, reliable data?
- Does the author express opinions with or without factual evidence?

Identify the Timeliness of the Source or Data Used in the Source

Timeliness is an important characteristic if the research project requires current information or data. All data and facts in the source should contain a date collected and/or some indicator of the context in which it was collected.

General Guidelines

- Check statistics and any numerical facts for a date collected or compiled. If there is no indication of when the data were collected, do not use the data.
- Check statistics and any numerical facts for the context of the time period. Any numbers that are used as indicators should have a reference or footnote stating time period or year to which they are indexed or referenced.

Web Guidelines

- Make sure to record the date the material was accessed on the Web. Web sites are frequently changed, updated, corrected for errors, removed, etc.
- Examine when the Web site was last updated. Assertions about current trends based on Web information that has not been updated for years will not be valid.

Identify the Focus of the Source

The focus of the information is important. Searches identify any source that has a word matching the keyword requested. Such searches result in sources that have the research topic as the focus as well as sources that may mention the keyword in a footnote or as an aside. The better sources are those that have the research topic as the focus of the information.

- Does the source have the keyword in the title?
- Does the source include material unrelated to the keyword?
- Does the source discuss the topic in depth?

What Is the Purpose of the Content?

The best sources are those that are compiled for educational, scholarly, academic, and informational purposes. Expectations for such sources are high. If the purpose of the content is popular, entertaining, recreational, or promotional, the value of this source diminishes and it is not appropriate for student research.

- Does the content include data professionally presented in charts and graphs or with glitzy icons, music, flashing characters, etc.? Scholarly information rarely incorporates glitzy presentations.
- Does the content provide references in the form of parenthetical citations, footnotes, or endnotes? Scholarly material, as a rule, provides full disclosure of where and how evidence used was collected.
- Does the content include a request for money, product offerings, advertising, membership invitations, or other inducements? Scholarly material rarely includes any such inducements or advertisements.

What Are the Origins of the Data?

The source's content may include primary or secondary data or evidence. If the source uses primary (original) data or resources, students must examine how, when, where, and why the data or resources were collected. While for primary data or resources the researcher must investigate the methods of collecting the information, for secondary data or resources the researcher must investigate how the material has been used or manipulated from its intended purpose.

- Does the author discuss the methods of data or resource collection? Are the methods reasonable, understandable, and conform to generally accepted practices?
- Does the author reference work by other researchers without discussing the context of the work? If so, look at the original work before referencing or using any assertions by the author about that work.

CHAPTER 5

**Creating Evidence with
Primary and Secondary Data**

Introduction

Students should identify the information (data) they need for their research early in the research process. If it is not available in secondary form, students must then determine if it is feasible within their research project's time frame to use primary data to produce the information they need for their project. Primary data are produced either by locating raw data or creating the data. To produce primary data as evidence, students must collect it either from original documents, a questionnaire, or personal interviews. If such research is being done on human beings and in conjunction with coursework or campus activities, students generally must obtain permission to do the research from their campuses' Human Subjects Committee. Once collected, primary data must be processed through one or more methods of data reduction. This chapter begins with an overview of secondary data sources and then progresses to a discussion of primary data collection. To assist students in deciding how to use such data as evidence, this chapter also provides a primer on data reduction methods.

Secondary Sources of Quantitative Data

A secondary data source is a set of data that is not collected by the student. Students who do not have the time or the need for primary data collection may analyze existing sources of data to provide evidence for their research papers. Such data is often collected by public agencies, private organizations, and scholars for particular purposes. The data collected by others and used to create their analyses may be available to students free of charge, through subscription services, and/or for a fee.

Secondary data can be used in a variety of ways. It can be used in its raw form, through data reduction methods, or merged with primary data. The advantage of using data collected by others is that students save time and in some cases money. The disadvantage of using existing data sources is that students do not control content and method of collection.

Public Data

Unless classified, public institutions are required by law to make data available to the public that they use as the basis of their government reports. Many federal and state data sets are available by request. Some data sets are available on government Web sites. For information not available locally or on a Web site, students may have to file a Freedom of Information Act (FOIA) request to obtain the data they need for their project. Students should be aware that FOIA requests may take as long as three months from request to delivery; using data acquired through FOIA requires significant pre-planning and knowledge of precisely what the data are and where they are held or collected. Some of the most common data sources used in political research include:

Federal Data

Census Bureau Data: The Department of Commerce, Bureau of the Census, compiles data on many topics in addition to demographic data about the population. The census is taken every 10 years (since 1790); however, various kinds of data are collected every five years. The *Census of Governments* and *USA Counties* provides information on local governments. In addition, the *Current Population Survey* includes demographics and employment data also collected once a month. The *County and City Data Book* provides demographic characteristics and services of counties and cities. A simplified version of these data can often be found in the *Statistical Abstract of the United States*.

Other Bureaucratic Agency Data: The U.S. Departments of Commerce, Education, Health and Human Services, Justice, Labor, and State, as well as independent agencies (e.g., Environmental Protection Agency) and independent commissions or boards (e.g., SEC, NLRB, EEOC, OSHA) routinely collect data on services, spending, enforcement activities (e.g., OSHA citations, number of small business loans granted, cases processed), and current conditions of clientele and jurisdictions (statistics on labor, economy, business, land use, etc.). Many of these types of statistics are compiled into yearbooks such as the *Statistical Abstract of the United States, Sourcebook of Criminal Justice Statistics, United States Health, Digest of Education Statistics, Handbook of Labor Statistics,* and *Vital Statistics on American Politics*.

Federal Records

National Archives: This archive includes a collection of historical data collected by the U.S. government.

State and Local Data

The Book of the States: This data book provides information about state governments in the U.S. including state services, laws, and finances.

Federal Agencies: Federal agencies collect and disseminate extensive data on state and local regions. Check census and other federal data sources for information about cities, counties, and states.

International and Comparative Nations Data

United Nations: The UN publishes a variety of data sources including the *Statistical Yearbook, Demographic Yearbook,* and the *Yearbook of the United Nations* that provides data on production, population, employment, health, death rates, birth rates, etc.

Europa Publications: This publisher offers specialty handbooks on international issues and data including the *Europa World Year Book* and the *International Yearbook*.

Private Data

Unless the material is related to publicly regulated activities, private and non-profit organizations are under no obligation to make their data available to the public. Organizational

Web sites provide data authorized for public dissemination. For information not available on Web sites or in public documents, students may have to request information directly from the organization's staff. Most moderate to large-scale private and non-profit organizations employ public relations staffs who handle public requests for information.

Professional and Special Interest Organizations

American Lung Association, American Cancer Society, Sierra Club, National Rifle Association, National Organization of Women, AFL-CIO, and the American Bar Association are examples of organizations that conduct studies and collect data. Some of these data are made available through their publications and some are available by request.

Think Tanks

Organizations such as The Brookings Institution, The Urban Institute, Hubert H. Humphrey Institute of Public Affairs, RAND, and the Organization for Economic Co-operation and Development (OECD) collect data and provide some public access to their collections.

Corporations

R.J. Reynolds Tobacco Company, General Motors, and many other large corporations collect industry data and provide some data through press releases. Other data are available to the public by request.

Commercial Data

There are numerous organizations that collect information for a fee. Some of this data is available in raw form through subscription services and some are available for purchase. Subscription services are generally offered to organizations and institutions, but not to students as individuals. Here are some examples of data sources:

ICPSR

The Inter-University Consortium for Political and Social Research (ICPSR) provides access to the world's largest compilation of computerized data on human behavior. ICPSR provides user support to assist identifying relevant data. The holdings include collections of a wide variety of data on populations, wars, education, public opinion, elections, and more, compiled at the national, state, local, and international levels.

Gallup Poll

The Gallup Organization routinely compiles polling data including demographic, opinion, and behavioral data, usually by contract, to client organizations. It has expanded to collect comparative data overseas, as well. The data are collected by professionals, provided to the client, and later made available to the public either in publications or for a fee.

Field Poll

Field Research Corporation is a national consumer marketing and public opinion survey research firm that collects data for business, industry, and government. The Field

Poll is the most prestigious state level poll in the U.S. It is generally administered four times a year during non-presidential election years and six times during presidential election years. It is also administered for special occasions, such as the California recall of the governor.

NORC

The National Opinion Research Center conducts an annual General Social Survey (GSS) for the National Science Foundation. This survey is done annually to collect data opinions, beliefs, and behavior related to contemporary social and political issues in the U.S. It is considered one of the finest data collection sites in the U.S.

Roper

The Roper Center for Public Opinion Research collects opinion data on political and social issues in the U.S. and numerous other nations.

Creating Primary Data

Primary (raw) data are *created by the student researcher* through qualitative research techniques. Most primary data are created through the use of survey research question-naires or are collected directly from a source. Creating evidence using primary sources involves a two-step process. Qualitative data are first created by researching specific infor-mation found in sources, such as original text documents, observations, and/or by con-ducting interviews. Once the qualitative data are collected, the student must then engage in data reduction by conducting a content analysis, creating a quantitative data set from the qualitative data, or writing a descriptive analysis of the results.

Creating Qualititative Data from Original Text Documents

Original text documents (often referred to as archival or historical documents) can be used to gather descriptive or evaluative information. Original text documents may provide the foundation for descriptive evidence about events and attitudes over time. Students may want to analyze newspaper coverage over a period of years or evaluate a set of historical documents (such as presidential letters or congressional hearing reports) to describe changes in attitudes or treatment of events. To research in original text documents, stu-dents must formulate a research question and hypothesis that identifies the nature and variety of information needed from the documents. This requires prior research, not only on the topic of the student's research, but also on the availability of the materials for the research time frame. While newspapers and magazines may be available on microform or online for a long time period, some documents, such as local government meeting min-utes, may be available only for a short time period.

In general, there are several types of archival materials available for analysis. Students may use **public documents**, such as government proceedings, hearings, reports pro-duced by any institution of government to document events, political positions, or any other political phenomena for historical research. Students may also use **private docu-ments**, such as annual reports, news releases, letters, writings, and public relations materials, for documenting events or changes in the organizations' or an individual's political, economic, or social position. Finally, students may analyze *media*, such as the content of books, newspapers, broadcast or cable news media (CNN, ABC, PBS, NPR, etc.), magazines, videos, DVDs, or CDs to discover conceptual patterns in the attitudes and substances of the materials. Many newspapers and magazines are available through microfilm, microform, and/or online services. To create data from original text documents, students must:

1. **Determine the information needed.** Students must formulate a research question and hypothesis that identifies the nature and variety of information needed from a set of documents. This requires prior research on the topic of the student's research. Students need to know what kind of information (descriptive, evaluative, or both) they need as evidence in their research project. Students also need to know if they need to use a complete set of documents for the time frame of the research project or if a random sample of documents is sufficient to support their research.

2. **Locate the copies of the original text documents for the entire scope of the study.** Prior to committing to a study that includes information gathered from historical or archival documents, students should make sure that copies of these documents are available for research. Although securing personal copies of such materials is best, it is not always possible because of restrictions on the document's use or because it may be costly to produce copies. Students should obtain permission to use and conduct research in advance for original text documents that are not public documents or readily available to the public.

3. **Construct a set of research questions.** Students should have a set of research questions they intend to answer using original text documents. Ordinarily, student researchers choose to formulate their research questions based on testing theories related to issues involving their topics. Using these theories, students should construct a set of variables that they expect to find information about in the text documents.

4. **Engage in data reduction.** Students must read and evaluate each text document individually. Using their research questions and the identified set of variables, students should then engage in classifying and analyzing the text document. Students may use either descriptive analysis or content analysis techniques for the data reduction. (See the discussion below for a description of data reduction techniques.)

5. **Write about the results.** Once students have collected the information and analyzed it, through either a descriptive or content analysis, they can then use the data as evidence in their research papers. Students must report the documents they used to collect the data (with full citations for each document), the method of selecting the documents (complete set or random sample), any problems involving the validity or accuracy of the documents, and how they reduced the data for analysis (descriptive or content analysis).

Creating Qualitative Data from Direct Observation/Field Research

Observational or field research involves student researchers directly in the subject of their research. Data created through this technique are based on information that researchers collect while participating in and/or observing activities or events. Student researchers can be either directly involved by participating in events, they can be direct observers, or some combination of participant and observer. Collecting information as a ***participant observer*** requires that the student participate in the activities they are observing. For example, a student may want to volunteer as a campaign worker to collect information on how a candidate's campaign headquarters is organized. (Students should see Chapter Thirteen for an example of this type of research combined with an internship.) Alternatively, collecting information as a ***nonparticipating observer*** requires that the student remain detached from the activities they are observing. For example, a student may attend court hearings once a week for two months to observe and identify patterns in the types of people and issues brought before the court over that time period. (Students should see Chapter Thirteen for an example of this type of research using event observation and keeping a journal.)

This type of data collection is perhaps the most flexible and experiential for students studying any topic. Field research can be highly focused and theory based where students formulate a hypothesis, and through observation of and/or participation in events, find evidence that supports a theory or hypothesis. Alternatively, students may also simply participate in events or observe behavior and formulate their own impressions. Because the student researcher is physically "in the field," field research is also one of the least objective and generalizable techniques of gathering qualitative data. While other forms of data collection can be replicated, field research cannot be reproduced because it is conducted on a unique population and at a specific point in time. Furthermore, even though field research is rarely completely unbiased, it is especially useful for validating theories or assertions about human behavior. Students must make a special effort to prevent or minimize their personal biases in how they record and analyze the data they collected from their experiences. Students should also understand that by being involved, either actively through participation, or passively through observation, they may influence the nature and quality of the information they are collecting. This is especially true if the population involved in the event knows the student is collecting information and the subjects being observed alter their behavior.

Although there are no particular rules for conducting field research, there are a number of expectations that students must address in conducting their research projects:

1. **Determine the information needed.** Develop a set of clear-cut objectives for the field research. Although students need not have a thesis or hypothesis, they should have a reason for conducting field research. Students may want to conduct field research to learn about how people interact within a particular context and use that information to focus and inform their library research. Alternatively, students may have a well-developed set of theories or hypotheses that they wish to validate or test by observing people or events. In addition, if students are engaged in collecting information at a non-public event that involves particular people, students should obtain permission to do the research from their campus Human Subjects Committee.

2. **Choose the context and time frame.** Prior to committing to the research, students should be informed about the events and the population they are observing. Based on this information, students must choose the events and the time frame of the field research. Depending on what students want to observe, they may either choose to engage in continuous monitoring or randomly select the set of events they plan to observe. For example, observing court proceedings by one judge every Tuesday for a month does not provide as much diversity and validity as observing on a randomly

selected day in different court rooms for two months, or observing such court proceedings every day for two months. Students should not, however, switch back and forth from continuous monitoring to random selection.

3. **Choose a role to play.** Students must decide before beginning their research how they are observing and who knows about their research. Students may not change their roles after they have begun their research. Students must decide whether they are fully participating or strictly observing; students may not switch their level of participation during the data collection activity. Students must also decide whether or not to fully inform the population that they are the subjects of a research project. If the subjects who are not informed about being observed discover, during the observation period, that the student is collecting information, the research project must be stopped at that point.

4. **Choose a level of depth and breadth of the field notes.** Students must be willing to regularly record (usually through journals or logs) both objective information, as well as their subjective impressions. Students should describe what they see, hear, and feel. They should identify in their notes which information is objective (just describing) and which information is the student's reaction or impressions of the events observed. Students should never tape record, take pictures, or video tape any activities without getting permission from the subjects of the observations. Students should carefully describe what they observed and note their reactions to the following:

   • ***Context***: Log the contexts of the place in which the event is being held.

   • ***Demographics***: Log the characteristics of the population involved in the activities.

   • ***Activities***: Log how people interact, how they behave, how they react, and what they do. If you are a participant, and not just an observer, describe your interactions and what you contributed. Ask questions where possible and appropriate.

   • ***Distinguish between expected and unexpected events***: Log the routine activities and be sure to note which activities were unexpected.

   • ***Collect documentation***: Secure copies of free public information. Students should not take documents that are private or public documents without permission.

5. **Analyze the results through data reduction.** Students should transcribe their notes as soon as possible. Students must then engage in classifying and analyzing their notes through descriptive data reduction techniques.

6. **Write about the experience.** All observation information related to individuals must be kept confidential, unless the student has the individual's permission to use identifying characteristics in the analysis. Students should report complete information about when and where observations were conducted in the text, footnotes/endnotes, or reference section of their analysis.

Creating Primary Qualitative Data from Personal Interviews

Data created through this technique are based on information that researchers collect by interviewing an individual. The source of this data originates from face-to-face, unstructured interviews with specific people. Personal interviews are valuable for providing background information, individual perspective, and insider information about political events. To conduct a personal interview, students must:

1. **Determine the information needed.** Students must formulate a research question and hypothesis that identifies the nature and variety of information needed from a particular person (respondent). This requires prior research, not only on the topic of the student's research, but on the respondent as well. Students should contact their Human Subjects Committee for approval of their projects. The information may include facts that cannot be otherwise found in public documents. The information may also include the respondent's opinions about trends, events, or remedies for problems related to the subject of the student's research. Finally, this information could also provide context or background information known only to insiders in the organization the respondent represents.

2. **Contact the person.** Always call or write for permission to do the interview. Tell the respondent about the purpose and focus of the interview. Arrange a date and time for the interview.

3. **Construct a set of interview questions.** Students should have questions written down and in order from vague to specific questions. The vague or more general questions should be asked first, and then progress to the most specific questions. Students should be prepared to ask follow-up or explanatory questions based on the respondent's answer to the question asked. More detail is better than less detail! All responses should be recorded either by a tape recorder or through student note-taking. Students must get permission from the respondent to tape record the interview.

Example of Interview Questions

Question 1:	Please describe the process through which you were hired for the director's position in the National Labor Relations Board Regional Office in St. Louis, Missouri.
Follow-up:	What credentials were most helpful in securing this position?
Question 2:	Since taking the position, describe the kinds of organizational problems you have addressed most frequently.
Follow-up:	How would you describe the relationship between the national office and your regional office staff?
Follow-up:	Do you sense antagonism between the national office and your staff?
Follow-up:	Do you sense antagonism between your legal and nonlegal staff?

4. **Attend the interview.** Students should arrive at the interview shortly before the pre-arranged time, dress professionally, and be prepared to begin on time.

5. **Thank the persons interviewed.** Students should write a thank-you note to each of the respondents.

6. **Clean and analyze the results through data reduction.** Students should transcribe their notes or recordings as soon as possible. Students must then engage in classifying and analyzing the responses through data reduction.

7. **Write about the results.** All interview information is to be kept confidential unless the student has the respondent's permission to report the source. In their research

papers, students should include information about when the interviews were conducted and a list of the questions in an appendix. If the respondent permits the student to identify the source, then the respondent's name, position, and date of interview should be listed in the reference page and the source cited in the text.

Creating Primary Qualitative Data from Focus Groups

Data created through this technique are based on information that researchers collect while facilitating discussions between and among pre-arranged small groups of individuals. Focus groups are valuable for providing background information, individual perspectives, and group perspectives about political events. The purpose of a focus group is to explore feelings, attitudes, and perceptions of a set of individuals. Often, focus groups are used in exploratory research to identify a range of opinions or issues involving a particular topic. Although focus groups are used to generate an understanding of the issues, the results cannot be generalized or applied to the general population. To conduct a focus group:

1. **Determine the information needed.** Develop a set of clear objectives for the focus group. Students should prepare a set of questions based on their research topic and hypothesis that identifies the nature and variety of information needed from the group. This requires prior research and identification of what information is available without a focus group and what kind of information is available only through a focus group. Students should acquire Human Subjects Committee approval of their project and questions before beginning their focus group research.

2. **Determine the population sample.** Identify and recruit a set of individuals that represent a range of opinions about the research topic, while also exhibiting diversity of demographic characteristics (e.g., education, occupation). Focus groups are generally as small as six or as large as twelve individuals. Professionals often provide incentives for participating in the focus group. Depending on the topic and range of opinions needed for the study, participants may be identified through membership lists, referrals, or random sampling. Regardless of how the participants are determined, each participant must be contacted (usually by telephone) to request participation and provide details about the purpose of the study, their role in the study, the place, as well as the duration of the study.

3. **Plan the meeting and recruit assistants.** To conduct the focus group, students will need a staff, a location, refreshments, and equipment. The staff includes a moderator, an assistant moderator, and note-takers. The location should be a room with comfortable chairs. The refreshments and amenities should be available to all participants. The equipment should include tape recorders, flip charts with markers, and notepads.

4. **Prepare a set of focus group questions.** Prepare ten to twelve questions to stimulate group discussion. The moderator should be prepared with follow-up questions for each question asked. To do so, the moderator must be knowledgeable about the topic. If demographic characteristics (age, gender, occupation, income, etc.) are important to the study, students should be sure to collect this information separately from the focus group meeting.

5. **Convene the participants.** Once the group is convened, the moderator should first set up the ground rules for the discussion (one person talking at a time, raising hands, etc.) and assure participants of the confidentiality of the recording. After a

brief introduction, the moderator asks the first question followed by comments that encourage responses from each participant. Based on the responses, if all comments are about the positive aspects of the issue, then the moderator should follow up with the questions about the negative aspects of the issue. This continues until the questions and/or time allotted for the discussion have been exhausted.

6. **Thank the participants.** Students should thank each participant and follow up with a thank-you note the next day after the focus group. Any inducements to participate should be delivered as promised.

7. **Clean and analyze the results.** Students must then engage in classifying and analyzing the responses through data reduction.

8. **Write about the results.** All responses are to be kept confidential unless the student has written permission to report their source. In their research paper, students should include information about when the focus group was conducted, recruitment methods, the demographic characteristics of the focus groups, and a list of the questions in an appendix.

Creating Primary Data from Questionnaires or Surveys

Data created through this technique are based on information that students collect from a structured interview or survey of a sub-set of the public. Questionnaires or surveys create quantitative data from qualitative or opinion assessments. Questionnaires are just structured interviews or surveys of public opinion. Students should remember that, unless sampling a target population specifically designed to include respondents that are knowledgeable about the topic, survey opinion is not necessarily informed opinion. To conduct such a survey:

1. **Determine the information needed.** Students must formulate a research question and hypothesis that identifies the nature and variety of information needed to study political problems, political actors, and/or public policies. Students must decide what kind of factual and/or attitudinal data must be obtained.
   - *Factual information* generally consists of demographic data about the respondent (occupation, age, sex, education, income, etc.).
   - *Attitudinal information* includes how people think or feel about public policies or societal problems.

2. **Determine the population sample.** Students must identify the target population for the survey. A target population is the portion (sample) of the public whose attitudes are important to the study. The individuals in the sample being asked the questions are called respondents. There are various ways to gather a sample.
   - *Representative sample* is a random selection of the target population, where the types of respondents included in the sample are reasonably close to their proportions in the general population. For example, if women comprise 52 percent of the target population, the sample should contain approximately 52 percent women. The result is a relatively objective survey of respondents that represent the target population. Under these conditions, the sample results can be used to describe attitudes in the target population.
   - *Nonrandom sample* is an approach where the respondents are not selected randomly and/or the sample does not include respondents in the same proportion as

they occur in the general population. One example of this is to sample the first 100 people you see in a shopping center. The result is a biased survey. Such a survey may be used only to describe the sample population and cannot be used to describe the attitudes in the target population.

3. **Determine the method of contact.** Students must decide on how the respondents are to be contacted. Surveys may be mailed, conducted door-to-door (face-to-face), contacted by telephone, or through email or the Internet. The costs and the response rates (percentage of survey responses completed of all respondents contacted) are lower for mailed surveys than they are for the other door-to-door or telephone formats. The expected response rate for mailed surveys is less than 50 percent. For telephone surveys, the expected response rate is less than 75 percent. For face-to-face surveys, it is less than 90 percent. Email and Internet survey response rates vary by the currency of the respondent lists, but are generally expected to be lower than mailed surveys.

4. **Decide whether to use existing survey questions or create the survey questions.** Students may use questions written by professional survey research designers (from published studies, for example) or write their own questions. A pre-test of the questionnaire before distributing to the target population can help identify problems in the construction of the questionnaire. Good surveys are short, clear, and direct.

   - **Short.** The total questionnaire should be fewer than six pages. The questions should use about 20 words or less per question.

   - **Clear.** Questions should address one issue at a time. Questions requiring a reference to a time period should be clearly stated with the time frame in the question. For example, "Did you vote in the 2000 presidential election?" The responses should be mutually exclusive (fit in only one category) and exhaustive (all possible responses are provided as choices). Professionals often include an "other, please specify" category in case the respondent has an answer that was unanticipated by the researcher.

   - **Direct**. The questions and responses use value-neutral and simple language. This means using words that are as objective as possible; students should avoid using words with strong emotional or value connotations. Students should also avoid using jargon or technical terms with sample populations drawn from the general public. Broad, less controversial questions should be placed at the beginning of the questionnaire, while personal questions should be placed at the end of the questionnaire.

5. **Decide on question format.** Students must decide whether the survey will provide an opportunity for the respondents to answer the questions as they wish, with open-ended questions, or constrain the respondents to a choice of predetermined answers with close-ended questions. Open-ended questions are best used in surveys that also include close-ended questions.

   - **Open-ended**. Some questionnaires are designed with questions that are open-ended (with space for the respondent's own words). Open-ended questions require a content analysis and a coding scheme for data reduction and analysis. An open-ended question does not provide a list of choices, so respondents are free to answer with any information they wish to provide, regardless of its relevance to the question. Questions such as, *"What do you think your local government should do about homeless people in your community?"* provide the respondent with an opportunity to offer an opinion without being constrained to a fixed set of choices. Open-ended questions provide the researcher with an opportunity to discover unanticipated ideas and perspectives.

- *Close-ended.* Some questionnaires are designed with questions that are close-ended (with fixed answer choices). Close-ended questions are generally characterized as providing multiple choice answers with fixed choices within those answers.

6. **Decide answer format for close-ended questions.** Students should consider whether the close-ended questions must elicit nominal, ratio, ordinal, or interval data in the answers. Regardless of the answer format, the answer choices should include an option for "don't know," "no opinion," or "refused." This allows the researcher to identify those respondents who do not know how they feel about the subject or do not want to answer the question.

- *Nominal.* These questions ask for information with close-ended answers of two or more choices that may be *"yes"* or *"no,"* *1=Democrat, 2=Republican, 3=Other (specify)*. These are often referred to as categorical data because the choices provided are in categories. The numbers attached to the choices have no numerical value other than identifying the choice. For example, a *Republican* is not valued twice as much as a *Democrat.*

- *Ratio.* These questions ask for information where the answers are ordered, measurable, and of equal distance. It is also possible for the answer to be an absolute zero. They are often associated with questions asking for income, number of children, etc., because it is possible that someone can have zero income or zero children.

- *Interval.* The answers to these questions have exact and constant values. The responses are ordered and continuous, but have no absolute zero point. IQ scores are an example of interval data.

- *Ordinal.* These questions ask for information where the close-ended answers are scaled or rank-ordered to measure the direction and intensity of the opinion. They generally progress from highest to lowest or from lowest to highest values.

7. **For ordinal answer formats, choose a scale such as Likert or Guttman scales.** Ordinal answer formats are frequently used to measure the intensity of opinions across a set of questions.

- **Likert scale**: This format provides a choice of options from *Strongly Agree* to *Strongly Disagree* or from *Very Poor* to *Excellent* with usually no more than seven responses for a series of questions.

Example of a Likert scale

Would you strongly support, somewhat support, neither oppose nor support, somewhat oppose, or strongly oppose rules that would restrict smoking on campus?					
1	**2**	**3**	**4**	**5**	**DK**
Strongly Oppose	Somewhat Oppose	Neither Oppose nor Support	Somewhat Support	Strongly Support	Don't Know

- **Guttman scale**: This format provides options, such as *"Agree or Disagree, Yes or No, Check all that you agree with,"* for a series of statements arranged from the most general to the most specific. Each question item is assigned a value based on the intensity of the item content. The respondent is then asked to check statements they agree with in the list. Agreement with the last item in the list implies agreement with the statements preceding it. The respondent's answers are then summed across these questions to create a score.

Example of a Guttman Scale

People have different opinions about smoking tobacco products in public. Read each statement below. Circle either the answer *Yes* or the answer *No*.

People should refrain from smoking tobacco products in public places. (Yes No)

People should not smoke tobacco products in public places. (Yes No)

People should not be permitted to smoke tobacco products in public places. (Yes No)

People should be fined for smoking in public places. (Yes No)

People should be arrested for smoking in public places. (Yes No)

8. **Clean and analyze the results through data reduction**. Once the survey is conducted and the questionnaires completed, students should describe and analyze the data. All the open-ended questions and the "other, please specify" categories in close-ended questions must be examined through a content analysis and coded into categories of responses. Once these data are coded, the data should first be reported by examining the frequency of answers chosen per question. Students may want to compare responses based on demographic characteristics, such as gender, age, income, party affiliation, or occupation. These summary results (often referred to as descriptive statistics) can then be presented graphically or in table form. For more sophisticated analysis of answers chosen by different types of respondents (cross-tabulation), students should use a statistical processing program to calculate the mean, standard deviation, adjusted error, and significance tests for the cross-tabulations. Many computer spreadsheets are capable of calculating these statistics, creating tables, and graphing data.

9. **Write about the results**. When writing about the data results, students should report the total number of respondents in the sample, the response rate, and when, where, and how the sample was administered. Students should report the mean, standard deviation, error, and significance tests if they were calculated.

A Primer on Qualitative Data Reduction Methods

Researchers engage in data reduction to convert text and comment information by summarizing the information with a descriptive analysis or by creating quantitative data using a content analysis of information, once it is collected.

Descriptive Analysis

Descriptive Analysis is a method of describing patterns and tendencies in the information collected through evaluating documents. This is a particularly important type of analysis for communicating information created through interviews and observation. To do so, students must do the following:

1. **Summarize the fundamental nature of the information**. Generalize across all discussions, observations, and/or coded information about what the data suggest concerning the hypothesized relationships.

2. **Look for trends and patterns**. Report any trends and patterns that appear to exist from the examination. Group similar responses or events by demographic characteristics (supportive comments by gender, etc).

3. **Record frequency**. Identify and discuss the value of information that is frequently found in the document.

4. **Report observed behavior**. For interviews (both face-to-face and focus groups) and observation notes, report and indicate the significance of body language observed during the data collection.

5. **Identify meaningful statements**. Students should identify and report verbatim quotes from their source documents or interviews to illustrate the validity of their generalized assertions about their findings. Students should use names of people only if granted permission to do so prior to writing the report. Otherwise, all references to individuals should be referred to by a non-descriptive characteristic (Defendant 1; Legislator 2, etc.).

6. **Keep information confidential**. All information is to be kept confidential unless the student has permission to report the source. In their research papers, students should include information about when and where the data were collected.

Content Analysis

Content Analysis is a system for defining categories of information and coding the basic units of each category. A content analysis can be used to summarize information taken from original documents, journal entries, notes recorded during observations, or comments recorded in focus groups. To do so, students must do the following:

1. **Select a sample**. For original text documents, students must select a sample of the documents. Students must formulate a research question and hypothesis prior to the examination of the documents. The collection of documents should be manageable for the period of the student's coursework.

2. **Identify information**. For all types of documents, students must identify the kind of information that they are looking for in the text.
   - *Subject matter* that relates to the student's hypothesis about the relationship between the objects and concepts in their research project.
   - *Frequency of occurrence* of the subject matter.

3. **Define categories**. Based on the kind of information they need, students must define categories of the subject matter and expected characteristics of each category as indicators of hypothesized relationships. The list of categories and characteristics comprise the **coding scheme** for the study. The coding scheme must include categories, and the characteristics must be exhaustive and mutually exclusive.
   - *Exhaustive*: The characteristics include all known characteristics.
   - *Mutually exclusive*: The characteristics in each category must not overlap.

For example, for party membership, the categories and characteristics may be *Democrat-registered, Democrat-not registered, Republican-registered, Republican-not registered, Other-registered (specify), Other-not registered (specify)*.

4. **Pre-test**. Students should pre-test the list of categories and characteristics on a small sample of the documents to make sure the categories exhibit validity, reliability, and objectivity.

  • *Validity* is determined by whether the category measures what it is supposed to measure.

  • *Reliability* is determined by the ability to reproduce the results.

  • *Objectivity* is determined by whether the results are unbiased.

  One way to do this is to have two or more people examine a small sample of the documents (10 each) using the list of categories and characteristics. If each reviewer finds the same information, or very nearly the same information, then the categories and characteristics will exhibit validity, reliability, and objectivity. Professionals calculate and report an *intercoder reliability* score. To calculate the score for two coders, count the number of times the coders agree, multiply that number by two (the number of coders), and then divide that number by the total number of codings by each. For example, if each person coded 10 documents, and they agreed on 8 out of 10 codings, then the calculation would be:

  Intercoder reliability score: $(8 \times 2) / (10+10) = 16/20$ *or 80%*

  The result should be 80 percent or greater; any score less than 80 percent means the coding scheme needs clarification and revision.

5. **Code all documents**. Once the coding scheme is pre-tested, students should read and code all the documents on data sheets organized by the coding scheme. To code the documents, students generally record an identifying characteristic (e.g. date and page number of the newspaper, observation date and journal page, respondent number and note-page) and then record the characteristic. For instance, suppose a student wants to study support for recreational use of public lands in California. To learn more on decisions about public land use, the student may examine the California Bureau of Labor Management Resource Advisory Council meeting minutes regarding off highway vehicle (OHV) use of public lands. The example below shows how the first three lines of data from a content analysis coding sheet may look for such a study:

Example (Abridged Content Analysis Coding Sheet)

MEETING DATE	RAC MEMBER COMMENTS 1=*Pro use* 2=*Against use*	TOPIC 1=*OHV use on public lands* 2=*OHV designated areas* 9=*other (specify)*
3/30/2000	1	1
3/31/2000	1	9 (grants to build more trails)
7/13/2000	2	2

6. **Count frequency per characteristic**. Students must count the frequency of the occurrences of each characteristic in each category (e.g., the number of times each characteristic of each category was found in the text). For example, the following table could be the result from analyzing a content analysis on the RAC meeting minutes.

Example: Content Analysis of California RAC Meeting Minutes 2000

RAC Member Comments Support OHV Use	Frequency	RAC Member Comments Limit/Oppose OHV Use	Frequency
OHV use on public lands	12	OHV designated areas	6
More demand of OHV use	6	Limit OHV access	6
More demand for recreational opportunities	3	Stop inappropriate OHV use	1
Outdated land use plans related to OHV access	2	Management/Guidelines for OHV trails	11
Need for more OHV trails	4	Limit OHV trails	10
Need more OHV grant funds/ more OHV trails	2	Conserve natural resources, protect plants, animals	13

Data source: http://www.ca.blm.gov/news/rac.html RAC Meeting Dates: March 30, March 31, June 28, June 29, July 13, July 14, and August 29, 2000. Adapted from *Policy Implementation and the Collaborative Management Process* by Gilbert Peña Dueñas (Chico, CA: California State University, Chico. 2003), Table 1, p. 39.

7. **Summarize and interpret**. Finally, students should make an interpretation of the findings as they relate to their hypothesis. Use tables, graphs, or models to illustrate the findings. Students may reduce the data further by collapsing the main categories into one or several main themes as the example below demonstrates:

Example: Interpretation of California RAC Meeting Minutes 2000

RAC Member Comments Support OHV Use	Frequency	RAC Member Comments Limit/Oppose OHV Use	Frequency
Need more OHV trails/access	8	Limit/Stop proliferation of OHV trails/access	30
Promote OHV use as recreation	21	Discourage OHV because of environmental problems	13
Total Support for OHV	*29*	*Total Opposition for OHV*	*43*

Data source: http://www.ca.blm.gov/news/rac.html RAC Meeting Dates: March 30, March 31, June 28, June 29, July 13, July 14, and August 29, 2000. Adapted from *Policy Implementation and the Collaborative Management Process* by Gilbert Peña Dueñas (Chico, CA: California State University, Chico. 2003), Table 2, p. 40.

8. **Discuss the results**. Students should discuss each illustration fully and describe how the illustrations support or do not support their assertions or assertions made by others. Students should also include information about the source of the text analyzed

by the content analysis with the illustrations, as well as in their reference pages. They should also include a copy of the coding sheet in an appendix.

A Primer on Quantitative Data Reduction Methods

Regardless of whether students collected primary data from a source, created data through a content analysis, or are using databases created by others, the data are essentially "raw" or are lists of numbers. Raw data can be used as evidence in a number of ways. Raw data can be converted into statistics, tables, figures, and graphs. Raw data can also be used in statistical models.

Tables

Tables can be composed of either raw data or data that has been transformed into statistics. According to Cuzzort and Vrettos (1996), the format and information in a table should be self-supporting and presented simply.

Format for Constructing a Table

A good table should, by itself, contain all the relevant information needed to read and interpret the data.

Title: The title should tell the reader what the data refer to, where the data were collected, when the data were collected, what kind of data are listed, source of the data, and categories in the table. The information can be listed in the title or footnoted at the bottom of the table.

Amount of Data: The data listed in the columns and rows should not exceed 12 rows and columns for most tables. Of course, the number of rows (horizontal) and columns (vertical) depends on what data are being presented. Obviously, listing grades for a class of thirty violates this rule of thumb; the point is to keep the presentation simple.

Labels: Each row and each column must be labeled. In general, whatever is being explained is usually listed on the left-hand side and whatever is being used to explain it is listed across the top of the table.

Data Presented: Data in raw form (absolute values) should accompany percentages (relative values).

Legible Spacing: Each row and column should be spaced so that the table is easy to read. Vertical lines and bold horizontal lines can be used to separate important divisions in tables.

Cells Complete: Each space (cell) in the table should include information. If no data are available for that cell, it should tell the reader by indicating *not available* or *N/A*. Even data that are zero or near zero should be displayed. Data that are near zero should be displayed in decimals (.003).

Interpreting a Table

1. **Take a little bit at a time!** Identify the items that are interesting and relevant to your paper.

2. **Identify the outliers (extreme values):** Look for values that are much higher or lower than the most common values. Are they reasonable and fit with reality? If not, there might be an error in the data set.

3. **Examine the context:** Identify information that challenges theories or contradicts what is generally known and assumed.

4. **Be conservative:** Do not overstate the importance of the data results.

Example of a Table Using Primary Data

In the following example, the authors use a table to exhibit the association between party dominance in each chamber of Congress and confirmation of presidential appointees. At first glance, the table appears as just a set of numbers. Now, notice the outliers. The large values in President Kennedy's and President Clinton's first administration **number of withdrawn nominees** are different than those of the rest of the presidents. Why? Kennedy and Clinton both faced a Democratic Congress, so why did they withdraw so many more of their nominees than other presidents? Does this contradict or confirm what is known or assumed? How important are these results? Why did Presidents Carter, Bush, and Clinton have so many nominees left unconfirmed? What does this say about their presidencies or their abilities to work with Congress?

PRESIDENTIAL NOMINATIONS AND SENATE ACTION BY POLITICAL DIVISION SINCE 1960[a]

Congress	President	Democrats in the Senate	Republicans in the Senate	Number of Confirmed Nominees	Number of Withdrawn Nominees	Number of Rejected Nominees	Number of Unconfirmed Nominees
87th	Kennedy	64	36	100741	1279	0	829
88th	Johnson	67	33	120201	0	6	1953
89th	Johnson	68	32	120865	0	173	1981
90th	Johnson	64	36	118231	0	4	1966
91st	Nixon	58	42#	133797	2	487	178
92nd	Nixon	54	44#	114909	11	0	2133
93rd	Nixon	56	42#	131254	15	0	3069
94th	Ford	61	37	131378	6	0	3801
95th	Carter	61	38	124730	66	0	12713
96th	Carter	58	41	154665	18	0	1458
97th	Reagan	46	53°	184844	55	7	1346
98th	Reagan	46	54°	97262	4	0	610
99th	Reagan	47	53°	95811	16	0	3787
100th	Reagan	55	45#	88721	23	1	5933
101st	Bush	55	45#	88078	48	1	7951
102nd	Bush	56	44#	75349	24	0	756
103rd	Clinton	57	43#	76122	1080	0	2741
104th	Clinton	48	52°	73711	22	0	8472

[a] Data taken from History of Congressional Elections (http://clerweb.house.gov/histrecs.../elections/political/divisions.html); Kurian 1994; Mackenzie 1996; Stanley and Niemi 1998. Table created by Diane Schmidt and Shelly Tall (1999).

[b] ° indicates Republican dominance.

[c] # indicates close Republican margin

Graphical Displays

Graphical displays, often referred to as graphs, figures, diagrams, and charts, are dramatic visual illustrations of data. Like tables, graphic displays may be used with raw or statistically-transformed data.

Types of Graphic Displays

- *Bar Graph*. This displays ordinal or nominal data either horizontally or vertically by category. The height or length of the bar represents the frequency of occurrences for each category.
- *Histogram*. This displays interval data using bars. The height and width of the bars relate to the size of the interval. The area of the bar represents the frequency of the occurrences.
- *Pie Charts*. This displays the proportion of each part of a nominal or ordinal category. The circle represents the entire category (for example, voters) and the divisions show the different parts to the category (for example, the proportion of Democrats, Republicans, and Independents).
- *Pictograms*. These are another way of presenting pie charts. The only difference is that an icon or picture is used to represent the proportion of each category.
- *Line Diagram*. This displays interval data by connecting all the cases with a continuous line. These graphs show how the data change over time.

Format of Graphic Displays

- *Title*. The title should tell the reader what the data refer to, where the data were collected, when the data were collected, what kind of data are listed, source of the data, and categories in the graphical display. The information can be listed in the title or footnoted at the bottom of the illustration.
- *Amount of Data*. The data listed in illustrations should be presented simply. All data presented should exhaust the category—that is, include all parts of the category.
- *Labels*. Each part of the illustration must be labeled. For line graphs, whatever is being explained is usually listed on the left-hand side and whatever is being used to explain it is listed across the bottom of the graph. For figures, charts, and pictures, each division must be labeled clearly. Distinctions are generally made by color coding, creating a legend, or using shading.
- *Cells Complete*. Each space (cell) in the illustration should include information. The illustration should make complex data and ideas simpler to understand.

Interpreting Graphic Displays

A good graphical display should communicate concepts and ideas with precision and efficiency. The illustration should show the reader visually the nature of the relationship between two or more events.

1. *Size Matters*. Notice the size of the bars, proportions, or "peaks and valleys" in the illustration. Identify the events that are interesting and relevant to the research topic.
2. *Identify Dramatic Shifts in Values*. Look for values that are much higher or lower than the other values. What does this say about the relationship between the events?

3. *Examine the Relative Proportions*: Identify relative relationships that challenge theories or contradict what is generally known and assumed.

Example of Two Types of Graphs

Look at the two illustrations below. Both use data from the table of presidential nominations shown earlier, however, the data presented in the graphs below are from only one category and one part of the data. Which one is easier to read? Which one best illustrates the relationship between presidential administration and number of nominees left unconfirmed?

Figure 1: Presidential Nominations Left Unconfirmed by Senate from Carter to Clinton.

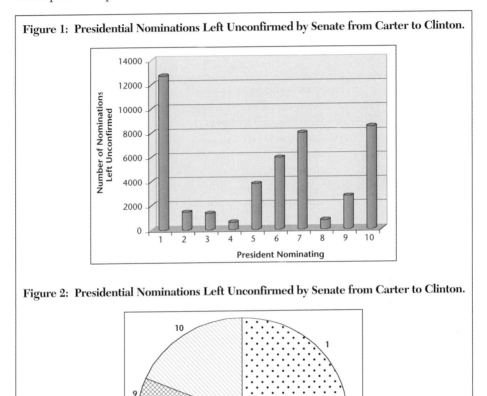

Figure 2: Presidential Nominations Left Unconfirmed by Senate from Carter to Clinton.

Legend: 1=Carter (95th), 2=Carter (96th), 3=Reagan (97th), 4=Reagan (98th), 5=Reagan (99th), 6=Reagan (100th), 7=Bush (101st), 8=Bush (102nd), 9=Clinton (103rd), 10=Clinton (104th)

Source: Data taken from *History of Congressional Elections* (http://clerweb.house.gov/histrecs.../elections/political/divisions.html); Kurian 1994; Mackenzie 1996; Stanley and Niemi 1998.

A Primer on Data Analysis

In more advanced political science courses, instructors may give students the opportunity to include quantitative evidence that has been produced or summarized through data analysis. Whether students have collected the data themselves (primary data collected through a content analysis, survey, or directly from the source) or used a data bank produced by someone else (secondary data), it is likely that the data are in "raw" form. This means that the data are in the form of lists of numbers. To make these data meaningful, it is often necessary to summarize the data.

Data Reduction with Simple Descriptive Statistics

Analysts use simple descriptive statistics in mass media, advertisements, political speeches, and informal conversation to summarize or reduce data into manageable, understandable forms. Data used in descriptive analysis include frequencies, means, modes, percentages, and ratios. Analysts use these measures to describe the current state or level of things. Frequencies indicate the absolute value of variables while means, modes, percentages, and ratios specify the relative value of variables. In particular, means, modes, and percentages describe the central tendency (typical values) of a variable in different ways and, because of this, can lead the researcher to different conclusions depending on which statistic they use. As such, each type of descriptive statistic has a different use, purpose, and meaning for summarizing or describing data. Many computerized statistical programs can calculate each statistic.

Frequency: A frequency is how many different items are in a group or category. Find this by counting the number of each item in a category. For example, there are three categories for a variable measuring political party affiliation. Of the 125 people who were asked their party affiliation, 60 said they were Democrats, 45 said they were Republicans, and 20 said they were Independent.

The frequency of Democrats is 60, of Republicans is 45, and of Independents is 20.

Mean: A mean is an average. In other words, a mean indicates the typical value found in the data. This is only true if the data do not have some unusual extreme values (often referred to as outliers). When the data include a limited number of very high or very low values compared to the other values in the data, a mean will misrepresent the typical value. Where the data include comparatively few very high values, the mean will be higher than it should be. Where the data include comparatively few very low values relative to the other values, the mean will be lower than the typical value. To address this, sometimes researchers will exclude an outlier from the mean and simply note the exclusion and a reason why they excluded the value. To find a mean, add all the numerical values in one category together to find the sum (total). Next, divide the sum by the number of items in the category. If students prefer a whole number as a result, they should round the number to the nearest preferred value. For example, the test grade for student A is 99, student B is 85, student C is 71, student D is 60, and student F is 52. To find the mean:

> *Add: 99 + 85 + 71 + 60 + 52 = 367*
> *Divide: 367 / 5 = 73.4*
> *Round to 73. This is the average grade.*

Median: The median is often used in place of a mean when the data contain outliers which cannot or should not be dropped from the dataset. The median is the middle value when the data values are listed from smallest to largest. (If there is an even number of data values, then the two middle values in the list should be added together, then divided by 2. The result is the median for a list of data values when there is an even number of values.) For example, the test grade for student A is 99, student B is 85, student C is 71, student D is 60, and student F is 52. To find the median:

> *Add:* 99 + 85 + 71 + 60 + 52 = 367
> *Locate the value in the middle of the list of these five numbers.*
> *The median is 71.*

Percentages: Percentages are proportions of the total of the variable. To find a percentage, divide the number of a specific type of thing by the total number of all items in a category and multiply by 100. For example, in a survey of 125 people, 60 people identified themselves as Democrats. To find the percentage of people in the study who identified themselves as Democrats:

> *Percentage voting:* 60/125 = .48 x 100 = 48%

Percentage Change: A percentage change measures the change in the frequency of an event over time. It is calculated by examining the amount of change in two frequencies of the same variable from one period to the next. To calculate this, subtract the frequency of the earlier event from the frequency of the later event and divide by the frequency of the earlier event. Then, transform the result into a percentage by multiplying by 100. The formula is [(Event in time 2) – (Event in time 1)/(Event in time 1)] × 100. For example, a county had 2800 people in 1988 and 3500 people in 1998. To find the percentage change in population:

> *Calculate (3500–2800)/2800 = .25*
> *Change the figure into a percentage .25 × 100 = 25% increase in population*

Mode: A mode is the category with the greatest number of cases. Find this by looking for repeated values. For example, the grade for student A is 75, student B is 75, student C is 64, and student D is 56.

> *Two students received 75 and one student each received 64 and 56. The mode is 75.*

Ratios: Ratios show a relative proportion. It is used to compare the proportion of one number to another for relative value. Find this by creating a fraction out of the two numbers. Reduce the fraction until it cannot be reduced any further. The ratio is the larger number compared to the smaller number in the fraction. In a group of 4500 women and men public administrators, there are 3000 men and 1500 women. To find the ratio of men to women:

> *Create a fraction. 3000/1500*
> *Reduce it. 30/15 = 2/1*
> *The ratio of men to women is 2 to 1.*

Rates: Rates compare the number of occurrences of an event in a jurisdiction to the total population of that jurisdiction. This is done by dividing the frequency of the occurrence by the total population in the jurisdiction. Because the denominator (total population) is so much larger than the numerator (the frequency of occurrence), it is necessary to multiply them by a base number (such as 100 or 1000 or 10,000) to convert the small decimal number into a whole number. The formula is (Events/Population)×(Base Number). For example, a county of 15,600 people had 32 accidents last year. To find the accident rate per 1000 people:

> *Do the following: 32/15,600 = .00202*
> *Multiply .00202 by a base of 1000: (.00202) × 1000 = 2.02*
> *The rate is 2.02 per 1000 of population.*

Data Reduction Using Statistical Methods

Data reduction using statistical methods provides the researcher with opportunities to examine relationships between variables in a structured and systematic way. Some of the statistical techniques are simple and others are quite complicated. The best way to approach data analysis is through a social science statistics course. Students who have already taken a statistics course may wish to refresh their memories by obtaining a copy of *Essential Statistics for Public Managers and Policy Analysis* by Evan M. Berman (Washington, DC: Congressional Quarterly Press, 2002), a copy of *Interpreting Basic Statistics: A Guide and Workbook Based on Excerpts from Journal Articles, 3rd edition,* by Zealure C. Holcomb (Los Angeles, CA: Pyrczak Publishing, 2002), and/or a copy of *The Research Methods Knowledge Base, 2nd edition,* by William Trochim (Cincinnati, OH: Atomicdog Publishing, 2001, or online at http://www.atomicdog.com). These books have just about everything a student needs to know about data analysis. They are written without jargon in a readable and simple format. Without burdening the reader with details, the authors describe and provide examples of simple elementary statistical analysis, as well as techniques that are more sophisticated. Together they are handy reference guides for looking up statistical terms and explanations of significance tests that are frequently used in scholarly political science materials as evidence of a theory's validity.

Another way to learn about statistical techniques for data analysis is to view a Public Broadcasting Service (PBS) series entitled *Against All Odds: Inside Statistics.* This is available on VHS videocassettes. There are twenty-six individual half-hour programs which demystify statistical methods by providing living examples of using mathematical formulas to measure social phenomena. The series appeared on PBS television stations in fall 1989 and was produced for a mass audience. Check the college or university tape and film library to see if it contains a copy of this series. If not, obtain a copy through an inter-library loan. The programs examine everything from a definition of statistics, to time series analysis, to conducting a case study.

Finally, another way to learn about statistical methods for social science is to browse through or study the many books produced by Sage Publications, Inc. The *Quantitative Applications in the Social Sciences Series* and the *Applied Social Research Methods Series* together contain over seventy books on methodology in social science. Students can view a list of books in these series at http://www.sagepub.com.

Even if students are not conducting a statistical analysis for their research projects, they should be aware of how other researchers use statistical evidence to support their assertions or conclusions. Researchers use a set of terms and measures to support their assertions about political relationships. Listed below are common terms used in data analysis to describe research methods.

Hypothesis: This is a term to describe researchers' theories about how events or conditions relate to each other. Researchers pose a hypothesis about the structure of these relationships. They also pose a null hypothesis that the relationships do not exist or are a result of coincidence or chance. Using evidence to test the strength and structure of these relationships, researchers either reject or accept the null hypothesis. In other words, researchers test whether the evidence supports their theories about how things relate or not.

Variables: These are things such as attitudes, characteristics, policies, etc., usually measured by numbers that vary (change) in the frequency (how often) or level in which they occur. Employment rates or the percentage of people voting in an election will differ from one time to the next. They are variables because neither occurs at a constant rate. There are different kinds of variables:

Dependent Variable: A dependent variable is a measure of what researchers are interested in explaining. For example, if students want to learn about public support for smoking regulation, their dependent variable could be data gathered on public opinion about smoking regulation. If they want to study college student support for smoking regulations at their school, their dependent variable could be data gathered regarding college student opinions about regulating campus smoking.

Independent Variable: Independent variables are measures of things researchers believe cause or influence the dependent variable. For example, if students are interested in investigating what kind of individual characteristics are associated with support for smoking regulations, they may collect data on individuals' age, gender, smoking habits, family smoking habits, peer smoking habits, etc. Each of these characteristics exist for each individual regardless of whether he or she supports regulation or not. A person who is 60 years old, male, smokes a pack a day, has family and friends who smoke, lives in Kentucky, and works for tobacco growers is not likely to support tobacco regulation. A person who is 25 years old, female, never smoked, has no family or friends who smoke, lives in California, and works for a hospital is likely to support tobacco regulation.

Dummy Variable: A dummy, or control variable, is a special kind of measure that is created as a way to indicate (or control for) whether a condition or an event has or has not occurred. The data for dummy variables are usually coded into zeros and ones, where zero is the absence of the condition or event and one indicates the presence of the condition or event. For example, a student may create a dummy variable to indicate whether an individual lives in a tobacco producing state. In this case, the researcher would create a dummy variable called *Tobacco-State* and enter a one (1) for each of the respondents who live in a tobacco producing state and a zero (0) for each of the respondents who do not live in such a state. By comparing this variable and a person's support for regulation, a student could examine whether those who live in states that do not produce tobacco have more support for smoking regulations than those who live in tobacco producing states.

Constant: This is a term to describe a characteristic that is common to all the data. For example, if a researcher is studying roll call voting in the Senate, then Senate membership is a constant because all subjects of the study are members of the Senate.

Causal Relationship: This term describes the relationship between variables; where one or more variables (independent) cause another variable (dependent) to move either *positively* (as the independent variable increases, the dependent variable increases), *negatively* (as the independent variable decreases, the dependent variable decreases), or *inversely* (as the independent variable increases, the dependent variable decreases or as the independent variable decreases, the dependent variable increases). For a causal relationship to exist, the change in one variable must be plausibly related to the change in another variable. For example, there may be a positive causal relationship between smoking a pack a day and a person's lack of support for tobacco regulation. This is plausible (believable) because it would be illogical for smokers to want constraints on their ability to smoke.

Crosstabulation: Crosstabulation allows the researcher to examine the relationship between two (bivariate) categorical variables or sometimes three (multivariate) categorical variables. A crosstabulation is a process where the frequency in which categories of one variable occurs with the categories of another categorical variable. This is best conducted by using a statistical program. For example, if a dataset on college smoking habits included a variable which measured the amount of smoking (none, less than a pack a day, at least a pack a day) and a variable recording the respondent's gender, the student researcher could crosstabulate the amount of smoking variable with the gender variable. The result would show how many male respondents do not smoke, how many male respondents smoke less than a pack a day, and how many male respondents smoke more than a pack a day. The same kind of results would be available for female respondents.

Contingency Tables: Contingency tables record the frequency for each combination between two variables. Where there is a causal relationship hypothesized, the dependent variable is listed horizontally (in rows) and the independent is listed vertically (in columns); otherwise it does not matter which variable is placed on the row or column. The table usually has row and column totals. For example, to examine the relationship between college smoking habits and gender, the labels for the row variable would be the different categories for the variable measuring smoking habits. The labels for the column variable would be the different categories of the gender variable. The table would then contain the numerical frequency of each combination of characteristics.

Correlation: This term describes how characteristics or variables vary together. They can be correlated in the same direction (positive) or in opposite directions (negative). Correlation suggests that variables only change in these directions, not that one variable causes another's movement. For example, personal smoking habits may correlate positively with family smoking habits (i.e. increases in amount of smoking are correlated with increases in number of family members who smoke), yet personal smoking habits cannot be said to cause family smoking habits or vice versa. Something else could be causing both variables to increase. If something else is causing both variables to vary together, then that is considered a *spurious* (coincidental or accidental) correlation.

Standard Deviation: This is one of the most often used measures of volatility in the variation or change in a variable. The standard deviation measures the degree to which a value of a variable differs from the mean (average) of the entire set of data on that variable. Most computer applications will calculate this measure. For variables such as age, the values could be widely dispersed (18, 39, 72) or narrowly dispersed (18, 22, 23). The standard deviation indicates how widely or narrowly the data are dispersed in the data set. Discussions of trends in data are generally more meaningful where most of the data are more narrowly dispersed around the mean of the data.

Significance: This is a term used to indicate whether the results from data analysis used to measure relationships between variables is reasonable or valid. Often researchers will refer to a measure as significant at a probability level of .05 or .01. These are probabilities (the odds) that the researchers are wrong about the nature of the relationship between variables or items. In other words, a significance level of .05 (reported as P=.05) indicates that there is a 5 percent chance that the researchers' hypothesis about the relationship between the dependent variable and independent variables is false, when they claim it is true. This means the data results can be used as evidence that the hypothesized relationships are probably valid. While most computer applications can produce a variety of statistics for testing significance (especially Chi-square, t-tests, R-square), researchers specify which types of tests they want conducted on their data analysis results. Most computerized statistical programs will calculate both a test statistic and the significance level for each type of test requested.

Chi-square (χ^2) *test:* This is a statistical test used to measure the existence and strength of the relationship between two categorical variables. This test is a mathematical formula that basically compares the expected value (usually the mean) to the actual values (observed frequency) for the two variables while controlling for the size (often referred to as N) of the dataset. When the actual values deviate from the expected value in a pattern, then the results suggest that the relationship in that pattern is not coincidental.

Student's t-distribution (t-test): This is a statistical test used to measure the existence and strength of the relationship between a continuous and a group variable. Using a mathematical formula, a statistical computer program can calculate whether the means for each group differ in a discernible pattern. For example, a t-test can be used to test whether smoking habits differ by gender.

R-square (R^2)*:* This is a statistical measure of the amount of variance in the dependent variable that is explained by the variance of independent variables. It is more often used in multivariate analysis. The mathematical formula for this measure also controls for the size of the dataset and the number of independent variables associated with the dependent variable. For example, an R^2 can be used to suggest how the combination of variables such as smoking habits, gender, and age will determine attitudes toward smoking regulation. To measure the strength of the relationships, the formula creates a statistical result between 1 and 0; the closer the number is to 1, the "tighter" or stronger the relationship is between the dependent variable and the independent variables.

CHAPTER 6

Properties of Essays and Research Papers

Properties of a Good Essay or Research Paper

A well-written, well-documented essay or research paper has three basic parts: an introduction, a body, and a conclusion. The **introduction** must include a thesis sentence that structures and focuses the paper on an assertion or a hypothesis about the relationship between concrete and/or abstract political objects. The **body** of the paper must include arguments, assertions, or points that provide reasons why the thesis sentence is true and counter-arguments against the thesis. The body also includes evidence to back up each reason or assertion. There is no absolute number of reasons required for supporting a thesis. The diagram below shows the thesis supported by three arguments with evidence for illustrative purposes only. The **conclusion** generally summarizes the main supporting points and clarifies the functional or logical relationships between the evidence and the inferences made by the author.

PROPERTIES OF AN ESSAY OR PAPER

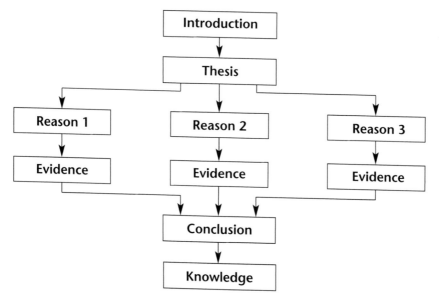

Recognizing and Writing a Good Thesis Sentence

Functions of a Thesis Sentence

- A thesis sentence sums up the main ideas that the writer wants to make.
- A thesis sentence asserts something about the topic.
- A thesis sentence conveys the writer's purpose.
- A thesis sentence acts as a working guide to organize the writer's points.
- A thesis sentence provides a concise preview of the major subtopics addressed in the written work.

Requirements of a Thesis Sentence

- Does it make an assertion about your topic?
- Does it convey a purpose?
- Is it limited to an assertion of only one main point?
- Is the assertion specific?
- Does it suggest a plan for the paper or essay?

Writing a Thesis Sentence for an Essay or Essay Test

Essay exams are designed to demonstrate the student's specific knowledge of a subject. Students are responsible for choosing the right facts and organizing them coherently to demonstrate what they know.

Definition of Terms

An essential element in constructing a thesis sentence is to understand the question being asked. Students must first read the question thoroughly and identify the key words that determine the meaning of the question. Very often, the verb determines the meaning of the question and the nature of the answer. Here is a list of important terms and definitions that are commonly used in political science essays (Corder and Ruszkiewicz, 1998, 631).

Analyze: give main divisions or elements

Classify: arrange into main divisions

Compare: point out the likenesses

Contrast: point out the differences

Criticize: give your perspective on good and bad features

Describe: name the features of or identify the steps

Discuss: examine in detail

Evaluate: give your perspective on the value or validity

Explain: make clear, give reasons for

Illustrate: give one or more examples of

Interpret: give an explanation or clarify the meaning of

Justify: defend, show to be right

Review: examine on a broad scale

Significance: show why something is meaningful

Summarize: briefly go over the essentials

Common Problems in Answering Essay Questions

Here are some common problems that students have experienced in writing opinion essays or essays for exams. An instructor may use an acronym to signify these problems. An example of each problem follows each explanation based on the following question:

Essay Question: Describe the important changes which would occur in the structure of power relationships in Congress if the outcomes of the House and Senate elections resulted in a change in party dominance.

Good Answer: If the Republicans were to recapture control of either chamber, the changes would not be nearly as radical in the Senate as they would be in the House because the Democrats have dominated the House leadership positions for a very long time.

Reason: This sentence answers the question directly by describing the changes as radical in the House and less radical in the Senate. In particular, it provides reasons why this would be true.

Begs the Question (BQ)

These types of thesis sentences do not answer the question asked. They typically make assertions about some small aspect of the question without really answering the question at all.

BQ Answer: There would be a dramatic change in the structure of power relationships in Congress if the outcome of the Senate elections resulted in a change in party dominance.

Reason: This sentence begs the question by answering only a small part of the question. It does not address the comparison between the House changes and the Senate changes.

Ambiguous or Vague (AV)

These types of thesis sentences typically need clarification and/or limiting. They usually lack specific detail about the topic. Such thesis sentences result in the reader asking such questions as, "So what? So why should we worry about that?"

AV Answer: If the outcome of the elections resulted in a switch from one party to another, some say it would have little impact.

Reason: This sentence is vague. It does not tell the reader why such a change would not have much of an impact. In addition, it does not say who says that a change in party dominance would not have much of an impact.

Descriptive or Historical (DH)

These types of answers are typically factually correct but do not provide a critical or analytical response to the question. Very often, these thesis sentences prepare the reader for a chronology of events without addressing the controversy associated with the events or relationships.

DH Answer: Party dominance has changed from one party to another in both chambers and has changed the structure of power relationships in them many times, yet Congress continues to function.

Reason: This sentence, while it may appear to answer the question, actually prepares the reader for a chronology of elections where the party dominance has changed in one or both chambers. It does not address the comparative intent of the question.

Writing a Thesis Sentence for a Research Paper

Research paper assignments help students demonstrate their ability to organize their thoughts about a topic or subject. Such assignments help students clarify their understanding about political phenomena. A research paper requires students, more than any other assignment, to synthesize and integrate information and opinions.

- Research papers require students to organize material coherently to support an argument or statement.
- Research papers are most often assigned without any particular question to answer.
- Research papers require students to think critically and formulate an opinion or a perspective about their topics that is both interesting and supportable within the scope of the assignment.

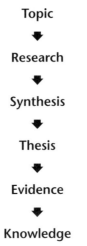

Topic

⬇

Research

⬇

Synthesis

⬇

Thesis

⬇

Evidence

⬇

Knowledge

Understanding the Function of the Thesis Sentence in a Research Paper

Students often have trouble understanding the reason for having a clearly stated thesis sentence for their papers. The thesis sentence is usually found in the first paragraph. This thesis lays out the plan for the paper by incorporating the major subtopics or points within the statement. The function of the thesis sentence is to provide a preview of the main supporting ideas and the order in which the writer will address these ideas. One way to think of the function of a thesis sentence for a research paper is to:

1. **Visualize the thesis as a defendant in a murder case.**
2. **Visualize yourself as Clarence Darrow presenting a classic legal defense.**
3. **In your opening statement to the jury, after presenting some background information, you declare a thesis sentence. For example, your client is not guilty because of the following reasons:**
   - He has exhibited a lifetime commitment to nonviolence.
   - He had no motive.
   - He was with someone else at the time of the murder.
4. **The thesis sentence is on trial for being a false statement. It is up to you to defend it through:**
   - Sound reasoning.
   - Presenting material and evidence supporting your position.
   - Defending your position against contrary evidence.
5. **The jury can reasonably expect the summary:**
   - To summarize every valid point asserted in the thesis.
   - To summarize every point refuted but asserted in the thesis.

Formulating a Thesis Sentence for a Research Paper

1. **Once students have picked out their topics, they must do some preliminary research to narrow and limit the focus of their papers**.
   - Only after students do this preliminary research can they begin to develop a preliminary thesis sentence or hypothesis.
   - This hypothesis is a statement which can be tested and confirmed (or disconfirmed) through the presentation of empirical evidence.
   - Here is one *example* of a hypothesis that is testable through the presentation of information and data. "Women's issues have a greater chance of getting on to the congressional agenda when Democrats control the White House and the Congress."
2. **Once students have formulated their preliminary thesis, subsequent research should either lend support or disprove their assertion**.
   - Students should expect to refine and revise their thesis sentences many times throughout the course of their research.
   - As the thesis is narrowed and focused, it takes on a more controversial tone.
   - An increasing knowledge base allows students to ask more sophisticated and critical questions about the topic.
   - The more knowledgeable students become about their topics, the more focused they should become with their assertions about the topic.

3. **For most student papers, a thesis statement with one main idea supported by three subtopics is usually sufficient and preferable to more complex and complicated thesis sentences**.
   - The rule of thumb is to keep the thesis sentence simple, narrow, and specific.
   - The best way to do this is to capsulize and state succinctly the causal relationships between the main point and the subtopics.
   - *A word of caution*: The length of the manuscript and the nature of the topic will influence the structure and desirability of having more or less than three subtopics in the thesis statement.

Example of Narrowing and Refining a Thesis

To give students a better idea of how a thesis can be revised over time, the following are examples of revisions, from start to finish, of one thesis sentence. As you read each revision, notice how each statement further refines and focuses the main idea. Each subsequent statement also reflects a greater and greater sophistication and mastery of the material.

1. **Labor union leaders, during the past decade, have been less effective than business leaders in mobilizing worker or political support**.
   - This thesis sentence, though narrow enough, is vague.
   - What does effectiveness mean? Political support from whom? Why have they been less effective?
2. **Lane Kirkland is not the leader Walter Reuther was in safeguarding his union against economic blackmail upheld by the NLRB, market fluctuations, and a union-busting president**.
   - This thesis sentence is focused too narrowly on one person and one union and is vague about the causal relationship between the variables.
   - The thesis does not specify what economic blackmail is, nor does it refer to any specific time period.
3. **Labor unions, as political-economic groups, have fallen onto hard times in the past decade due to a hostile presidential administration, the recession, and new techniques in union busting**.
   - This thesis sentence is more specific about the causal relationship between the variables.
   - The thesis does not identify the important political actors or the intervening relationships that helped produce this political problem.
4. **Next to management's advanced, state-of-the-art techniques for busting unions with the support of the Reagan administration appointees to the NLRB, efforts by union leaders such as Lane Kirkland dwarfed in comparison when conducting organizing campaigns during the worst U.S. recession since the Great Depression**.
   - This thesis sentence, while quite complex, fully describes the context, the players, and the variables associated with problems in union organizing.
   - This thesis is testable.

Tips for Writing a Thesis Sentence for Papers with Specific Requirements

Sometimes students are given a paper assignment for which the instructor has provided the reading materials, a question to be answered, and/or that requires certain types of questions to be answered within the text of the paper. This should not alter the student's ability to construct an effective thesis statement. It does, however, limit the range of ideas and points that can be made in the paper.

1. **To construct a thesis sentence for a paper assignment in which the instructor has provided the reading materials and a specific question to answer:**
   - Use the essay test thesis sentence format.
   - Answer the question directly and reference the reading material to support the main points of the thesis.

2. **To construct a thesis sentence for a research paper that must answer specific questions within the text:**
   - Reflect the paper's main idea in the thesis sentence and subdivide the paper so that it reflects the answers to the questions.
   - Structure the paper's main arguments to comply with the requirements of the assignment.

Common Problems in Constructing a Thesis

Here are some common problems that students have experienced in writing a thesis sentence for a research paper. An instructor may use an acronym to signify these problems.

Ambiguous or Vague (AV)

These types of thesis sentences are usually worded very generally and typically need clarification and/or limiting. They often lack specific detail about the topic.

Example 1: *"Labor union members have different voting patterns than non-union workers."*

- Such thesis sentences result in the reader asking questions like "How are they different and why is this information important to know?"

Example 2: *"Many men and women do not fully participate in the political system."*

- These types of statements result in the reader asking questions such as, "So what? So, why should we worry about that? How many? What is considered full participation? Which political system?"

Not Unified (NU)

These types of thesis sentences typically attempt to link two different ideas without suggesting how they are related.

Example: *"Workplace participation can help reinforce democratic values even if people do not vote."*

- Such thesis sentences result in the reader asking questions like "What does this mean? Does one part cause the other?"

Too Factual or Obvious (TF)

These types of thesis sentences typically declare or assert some opinion or perspective that is not controversial.

> **Example:** *"Automatic voting registration would require the government to spend money."*

- Such thesis sentences result in the reader asking questions like "What will the rest of the paper be about? So, tell me something I do not know!"

Recognizing and Writing a Good Paragraph

Paragraph construction in expository or argumentative writing is both similar to and different from other kinds of writing, such as technical or creative writing styles. They both use the same grammatical rules for sentence and paragraph structure. Nevertheless, the paragraphs and the sentences in a paragraph constructed for expository writing must logically and functionally relate to one another. This is not always the case for creative or even technical writing.

Functions of a Paragraph

All paragraphs do not function in the same way nor do they have the same properties.

There are three types of paragraphs:
- Introductory paragraphs
- Supporting or explanatory paragraphs in the body
- Concluding or summary paragraphs

Each of these types of paragraphs has a special job to do in communicating the writer's goals and ideas to the reader. There is no absolute number of paragraphs required for supporting an introductory paragraph. The diagram below shows the introductory thesis paragraph supported by three explanatory paragraphs for illustrative purposes only.

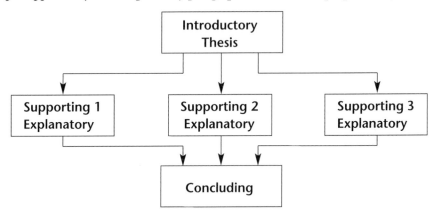

Properties of an Introductory or Opening Paragraph

An opening paragraph should capture the reader's attention and interest in the topic, specify what the writer will be discussing, and set the tone, direction, scope, and content of the essay or paper.

An opening paragraph should contain at least three sentences which include:

- A general statement (a topic or thesis sentence).
- A clarifying sentence.
- An explanatory sentence.

The best opening paragraph begins with a general statement, followed by a clarifying statement or two, and ends with the thesis sentence.

Advice for Constructing Introductory Paragraphs

Try one of these ways of constructing the first paragraph:

- State the subject.
- Use a meaningful or thought-provoking quotation.
- Ask a question.
- Make a historical comparison or contrast.
- State an important fact.

DO NOT use these methods in an introductory paragraph

- Do not use vague generalities.
- Do not use "The purpose of…" in the first line.
- Do not use the title of the paper in the first line.
- Do not use "According to…" in the first line.
- Do not use truisms and statements of the obvious.

Example of an Introductory Paragraph (Sullivan 1988)

The political dynasty, in the American context, is an organization usually centered on a family that transcends traditional norms in campaign and voter perception. By transcending these norms, the dynasty develops the image of American "royalty." The Kennedy and Rockefeller families have evolved as the most dominant examples of political dynasties in the twentieth century. The phenomena, as evidenced in these examples, appear to center around one individual and build from there. Once established, this mutation of American politics becomes its own organization, nearly independent of their respective parties in power and strategy (Salmore 1989, 39). Even though the later elements of the dynasty benefit from their link to the overall public perception, they are, at times, mistakenly associated and credited with the dynasty's accomplishments as well (Granberg 1985, 504–516).

Properties of a Concluding Paragraph

A concluding paragraph is not just the last paragraph; it concludes or summarizes the author's main points, completes the writer's thoughts about the topic, and ties the ending to the beginning of the paper or essay. The concluding paragraph must contain at least three sentences:

- A general statement.

- A clarifying sentence.
- An explanatory sentence.

The best concluding paragraph restates the thesis and summarizes the evidence.

Advice for Constructing Concluding or Closing Paragraphs

Use these methods to construct a closing paragraph:

- Summarize the paper's main assertions or points.
- Clarify, qualify, and restate the main issues.
- Answer the question asked in the introduction.
- Suggest a course of action based on your evidence.

DO NOT use these methods to construct a closing paragraph:

- Do not provide new arguments or information.
- Do not restate your introduction.
- Do not conclude more than you reasonably can from the material and arguments you presented in the paper.
- Do not apologize for materials or views presented.

Example of a Concluding Paragraph (Sullivan 1988)

The success of the Kennedy and the Rockefeller families, as two prime examples of American dynasties, exemplifies the primary political dynamics that are essential to being part of American political life. These dynamics are instant name recognition for family members, instant empathy from the electorate for the family member's position on issues, nonrational voting based on residual biases associated with the family, and ability to exhibit independence from party politics. The practical effect of establishing a political dynasty is political survival. The societal effect is much less noticeable; political dynasties package political change as familial continuity and thus provide for the survival of their family's influence as well as goals for society. Because of this, political dynasties built in the past shape present political life and have uncommon influence over the America's destiny.

Properties of a Paragraph in the Body of the Paper

The paragraphs in the body of the written work function to support the thesis sentence and explain the writer's perspective on the topic in detail.

- The paragraphs in the body of the work help to break down the thesis sentence into subtopics and ideas.
- The paragraphs in the body of the work break down the central point or thesis into manageable parts, discuss each part, and relate each part to each other.
- Because the writer makes a commitment to the reader in the thesis sentence, paragraphs that follow must inform readers by filling in details, supporting claims, and giving examples.

Each Paragraph Must Contain Three Types of Sentences:
- A general statement or topic sentence.
- A specific or clarifying and limiting sentence.
- A sentence which provides details or examples.

Example of a Paragraph for the Body of the Paper (Sullivan 1988)

> Each political dynasty, however, is different; each dynasty has its own dynamics that separates it from the rest of the political community. The Kennedys, for example, are a nationally recognized political family even though the family center or core is in Massachusetts. The Rockefellers, while equally nationally known, have spread their political dominance over the governor mansions in New York, Arkansas, and West Virginia (Salmore 1989, 125). While both families exhibited a drive for dominance, the political bases of their influence span the spectrum from highly centralized to decentralized (Clinch 1973, x).

Properties of a Topic Sentence

Every paragraph needs a topic sentence, except the paragraph that holds the thesis sentence. Like a thesis sentence, a topic sentence states the central idea and the writer's perspective about it. Topic sentences, however, elaborate on parts of the thesis sentence in the body of the paper. In particular, the topic sentence states the main idea of the paragraph and every sentence following it supports that one idea.

Where to Place the Topic Sentence

Most of the time the topic sentence is placed at the beginning of the paragraph. Sometimes, writers put the topic sentence at the end of the paragraph. The structure of the rest of the paragraph depends on where the topic sentence is placed.

Try thinking of a paragraph as a car, a stick shift vehicle to get your idea or point to the reader. If you place the topic sentence at the beginning, you would downshift. If you place it at the end, you would shift up. If you know anything about cars with stick shifts, you know that upshifting without enough speed results in the car losing power. Downshifting too fast results in grinding the gears and may damage the transmission.

A Visual of the Two Patterns of Paragraph Construction

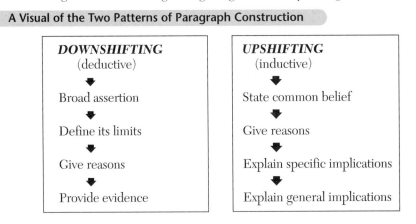

DOWNSHIFTING (deductive)	**UPSHIFTING** (inductive)
Broad assertion	State common belief
Define its limits	Give reasons
Give reasons	Explain specific implications
Provide evidence	Explain general implications

Writing a good explanatory paragraph takes as much skill and attention as shifting a car. Just as a car's transmission can be damaged by improper shifting, the "transmission" of your argument from your head to your reader can be equally damaged by improper shifting from idea to evidence to conclusion. Clearly state your idea in a topic sentence, support the topic sentence with explanatory and supporting sentences (at least one), and resolve the paragraph with a sentence.

Be careful! If you shift from an idea or belief to your resolution without explaining your point clearly, you will weaken your assertion and your general argument will lose power. If you shift from a broad assertion to a resolution without limiting your assertion and backing it up with evidence, you may bring your argument to a grinding halt. Political scientists are in the business of communicating and evaluating information. As a writer, you must be careful that ideas or points are not lost in the transmission due to poor explanatory paragraph development.

Tips for Reasoning Once the Topic Sentence Has Been Placed in a Paragraph

When It Is Placed at the Beginning of a Paragraph:

- It is the first sentence when it introduces a general point or idea.
- It is the second sentence when the author has made a transition from one point to the next. The first sentence in this case is a transition sentence.
- Writers must use deductive reasoning for constructing the rest of the paragraph.
- This means that the topic sentence will make a broad statement that is then supported, enriched, and expanded by other sentences.

Example of a Topic Sentence at the Beginning of the Paragraph (Sullivan 1988)

Although political dynasties may benefit similarly from the same sources of power, the political bases of their influence span the spectrum from highly centralized to decentralized (Clinch 1989, x). Each political dynasty is different. Each dynasty has its own dynamics that separates it from the rest of the political community. The Kennedys, for example, are a nationally recognized political family even though the family center or core is in Massachusetts. The Rockefellers, while equally nationally known, have spread their political dominance over the governor mansions in New York, Arkansas, and West Virginia (Salmore 1989, 125).

When It Is Placed at the End of a Paragraph:

- It is the last sentence when it makes a general statement about the implications of an idea or point.
- Writers must use inductive reasoning for constructing the rest of the paragraph.
- This means that the topic sentence will make an assertion about how some specific idea applies generally.
- This method requires a climactic order, from least important to most important, from most familiar to least familiar, or from simplest to complex supporting reasons or examples.

Example of a Topic Sentence at the End of a Paragraph (Sullivan 1988)

> Each political dynasty, however, is different. Each dynasty has its own dynamics that separates it from the rest of the political community. The Kennedys, for example, are a nationally recognized political family even though the family center or core is in Massachusetts. The Rockefellers, while equally nationally known, have spread their political dominance over the governor mansions in New York, Arkansas, and West Virginia (Salmore 1989, 125). While both families exhibited a drive for dominance, the political bases of their influence, however, span the spectrum from highly centralized to decentralized (Clinch 1989, x).

Advice for Constructing Paragraphs

Use a commitment and response pattern for your paragraphs.

1. Make a commitment in your topic sentence to a main idea.
2. Then, make sure each sentence in the paragraph contributes to explaining and supporting that idea.
3. DOWNSHIFT!!!! When all else fails, start general and get specific.

ALWAYS ALWAYS ALWAYS Use a Topic Sentence

1. Make a point in one sentence and stick to it.
2. In the draft copy of your paper, highlight what you think is your topic sentence in every paragraph.
3. Then make sure each sentence says something about the point you made in the topic sentence in each paragraph.

Use Transitions

Use transition sentences and transitional words or phrases to keep the paragraph unified and coherent. These link ideas together between sentences or between paragraphs. (See List of Transitional Expressions.)

1. **Use varying sentence structures and styles by using transitional words and phrases to keep the ideas in the paragraph coherently linked together.**
   - Repeat important words; use synonyms.
   - Use connecting words such as *however, for example.*
   - Use pointer words such as *first, second,* and *finally* to keep track of supporting ideas.
2. **Transitional sentences provide a bridge between the current paragraph and the previous paragraph.**
   - Transitional sentences help the writer make a change in direction without losing the reader.
   - Transitional sentences point back to the previous idea and forward to the new one at the same time.

- For a major change in direction, it may take more than one transitional sentence.
- The topic sentence then comes after the transitional sentence.
- All supporting information comes after the transitional sentences.

List of Transitional Expressions

The terms listed below should be used to link sentences together within a paragraph. Most are used at the beginning of sentences. Some terms, such as "however," should be used only within a sentence. For example, "This policy, however, failed to remedy the problem of malnutrition." (Adapted from Fowler and Aaron 1989, 95–96.)

To add or show sequence: again, also, and, and then, besides, equally important, finally, first, further, furthermore, in addition, in the first place, last, moreover, next, second, still, too

To compare: also, in the same way, likewise, similarly

To contrast: although, and yet, but, but at the same time, despite, even so, even though, for all that, however, in contrast, in spite of, nevertheless, notwithstanding, on the contrary, on the other hand, regardless, still, though, yet

To give examples or intensify: after all, an illustration of, even, for example, for instance, indeed, in fact, it is true, of course, specifically, that is, to illustrate, truly

To indicate place: above, adjacent to, below, elsewhere, farther on, here, near, nearby, on the other side, there, opposite to, to the east, to the left

To indicate time: after a while, afterward, as long as, as soon as, at last, at length, at that time, before, earlier, formerly, immediately, in the meantime, in the past, lately, later, meanwhile, now, presently, shortly, simultaneously, since, so far, soon, subsequently, then, thereafter, until, until now, when

To repeat, summarize, or conclude: all in all, altogether, as has been said, in brief, in conclusion, in other words, in particular, in short, in simpler terms, in summary, on the whole, that is, therefore, to put it differently, to summarize

To show cause or effect: accordingly, as a result, because, consequently, for this purpose, hence, otherwise, then, therefore, thereupon, thus, to this end, with this object

Common Problems in Constructing Paragraphs

Here are some common problems that students have experienced with paragraphs. An instructor may use an acronym to signify these problems.

Not Unified (NU)

Paragraphs exhibiting this problem usually include an idea or point that is unrelated to the topic sentence.

- These paragraphs are not focused on a central point.
- The reader will typically ask the question, "How does this contribute to the central point (topic sentence)?"

NU Example: *The structure of our federalist government has influenced the ways* *people act in society today. It helps to set the standards that influence people's lifestyles. It is not only one person who enforces these rules but a set of institutions. In our socie-ty, the people elect representatives to these institutions that shape and enforce the rules of the government.*

Problem: It includes points and ideas that are unrelated to the topic sentence.

Solution: Take out all sentences and information which does not directly contribute to the central point made in the topic sentence. In this case, that is everything after the second sentence.

Incoherent (IC)

Paragraphs exhibiting this problem usually have sentences that do not establish a clear relationship between ideas or points.

- These paragraphs are generally confusing because the author has not linked the sen-tences together logically or functionally.
- The reader will typically ask the question, "How do the sentences relate to the main topic or to one another?"

IC Example: *The goal of regulating national powers became mandatory for the framers. The national government, like the state and local government, has three law-making bodies: the executive, the legislative, and judicial branches of government. The president makes up the executive branch. Congress makes up the legislative branch, and the Supreme Court makes up the judicial branch.*

Problem: The sentences do not establish a clear relationship between the ideas or points.

Solution: Use transitional expressions to link important ideas and sentences togeth-er. In this case, we could say "that one way the framers sought to achieve this goal was to divide....For example...."

Too Long in Length (LG)

Paragraphs exhibiting this problem usually encompass more than one idea in a paragraph.

- The writer will fail to communicate the main point of the paragraph clearly and will confuse the reader.
- The reader will generally ask the question, "Which point does the information sup-port?"

LG Example: *The U.S. constitution and tradition provide the office of the presidency with many powers and responsibilities. His role represents a fusion of the stature of a king and the power of a prime minister. While his role as the symbolic leader of the nation provides him societal support, the president's veto power also gives him much influence over the congressional agenda. The persuasive ability of the individual hold-ing the office of the presidency also contributes to the president's power. The ability of the president to harness and focus competing groups inside and outside of the govern-ment, especially in Congress, greatly influences his effectiveness in promoting his agen-da. To be effective, the president must be able to persuade others to follow his lead.*

Problem: It tries to cover more than one main idea in a paragraph.

Solution: Break up the paragraph where the sentences change in time, place, direction, focus, or emphasis. In this case, break the paragraph before the sentence concerning the president's persuasive abilities.

Too Short in Length (ST)

Paragraphs exhibiting this problem fragment an idea among two or more paragraphs. Often these paragraphs are only one or two lines long.

- The writer will fail to establish the main point of the paragraph and/or will not support the point with sufficient evidence or limiting information.
- The reader will generally ask the question, "What is the point of giving me this information?"

ST Example: *Media, interest groups, and political parties become important political influences on mass attitudes. Even if at times they are criticized, our political system would not work as well without them.*

Problem: The paragraph is too short. It does not make a point, nor does it follow through with evidence and supporting information.

Solution: Expand on the central idea expressed in the topic sentence by including additional limiting information, evidence, or examples. In this case, expand on the desirable and undesirable ways that media, interest groups, and political parties similarly influence mass attitudes.

First Aid for Bad Paragraphs

Break up long paragraphs wherever the sentences in the paragraph shift in time, place, direction, focus, or emphasis.

1. **Remember: use only one main point or idea per paragraph.**
2. **A unified, coherent paragraph is usually no longer than half of a typed, double-spaced page with one-inch margins.**
3. **A quick way to tell visually if your paragraphs are too long:**
   - Measure—if a paragraph is longer than five inches of the page, then it is too long. Keep an 8" by 5" index card handy to use as a template to measure as you revise.
   - There should not be less than two paragraphs on a typed, double-spaced page.

Develop the ideas in a short paragraph or combine the paragraph with adjacent paragraphs.

1. **If the paragraph makes a point which is different from those of previous and following paragraphs then:**
   - Develop the idea sufficiently by narrowing your assertion.
   - Provide evidence to support the topic sentence.
2. **If the paragraph does not make a point that is different from those of previous and following paragraphs then:**
   - Identify the topic sentence in each of the previous and following paragraphs.
   - Identify which topic sentence would be best supported by the information provided in the short paragraph.

- Merge the short paragraph with that paragraph.

3. A quick way to tell visually if your paragraphs are too short:

- If a paragraph is smaller than the width of two fingers placed side by side, then it is too short.
- There should not be more than three paragraphs on a typed, double-spaced page.
- If a paragraph is only three lines long, then it is too short.
- If a paragraph does not contain at least three sentences (a topic, a specific, and an explanatory sentence), then it is too short.

CHAPTER 7

Common Problems with Writing

Common Stylistic Problems

Although some stylistic problems are particular to the writer, many are common to even some of the best writers. Good writing requires diligence and persistence in learning to recognize functional errors. While stylistic problems are not the primary cause of poor communication of ideas, they interfere in the relationship between the author and the reader. Stylistic problems create confusion at best, and at their worst, they reflect negatively on the writer's credibility.

Misinterpreting the Audience for the Student's Work

Students must define their audience before writing even one word on a page. Letters written to a friend, a senator, a parent, and a judge differ in tone, content, and mutual expectations. This is true of academic writing as well.

Students should avoid the following in written assignments:
- Students should not assume that the audience is composed of their friends or relatives. This encourages familiar, informal, and pedestrian writing.
- Students should not write for themselves. This encourages incomplete thought and shallow explanations.

Students should target the following audiences when writing a paper for a class:
- Students should write for scholars in the field. This encourages students to approach the assignment in a professional way.
- Students should write for the professor and keep in mind what his or her expectations and objectives are for the assignment.
- Students should write for the class as well as for the professor. This will keep the student's approach at a less pompous level than it might be if written for the professor alone.

Using the Wrong Voice

Students should approach their assignments in a serious, thoughtful, respectful, and professional way. The voice for an assignment should be formal, unless the professor directs the student otherwise.

Students should avoid the following in written assignments:

- Students should not use colloquial language, such as "The senator gave the majority leader the slip on that piece of legislation."
- Students should not address their opinions or assertions by using a first person reference. Statements such as "It is my opinion that…," or "I believe that…," or "I can only conclude that…" are inappropriate and weaken the student's arguments.
- Students should not use contractions in their written work. Such words as *don't*, *won't*, *didn't*, *she'd*, and *can't*, while technically correct, reduce a student's writing to an informal or pedestrian level.
- Students must never use vulgar, profane, or obscene language or references in their written work. Statements such as "The senator really kicked butt on the floor" have no place in professional writing. This type of language weakens the credibility of the author as well as the argument.

Linguistic Bias

Race, class, and sexual stereotyping have no place in academic writing. These kinds of linguistic biases demean individuals and weaken the author's arguments. Unfortunately, it is difficult to break old habits. Although linguistic biases may not be intentional, students should carefully edit their work to avoid linguistic biases which are most obvious (see Ward 1990, 1–5, 29–32, and her Appendix 4).

Students can avoid problems with linguistic bias if they:

1. **Refer to race by a socially acceptable reference**.
   - Attach the word "American" to the reference of an individual's heritage. For example, use African American to refer to U.S. citizens of African heritage.
   - Black is still an acceptable reference to people of African heritage.
   - "Minorities and people of color" are acceptable references to people who are not of Caucasian heritage residing in the United States.

2. **Refer to the problems of the poor or disadvantaged as a problem of society, not as a character flaw in individuals belonging to that class**.
   - Avoid overgeneralizing about preferences and characteristics of individuals classified based on social or economic criteria.
   - Avoid attributing problems experienced by one set of people as a class problem.

3. **Change the structure of sentences and terminology to reflect gender neutral language**.
   - Substitute a plural for a gender pronoun or alternate between female and male pronouns.
   - Substitute the words *someone, anyone, person*, or *people* for references to men and women in general (such as "people who become police officers…").
   - Refer to people by occupation or role only (such as "parents are concerned about child care…").
   - Use more specific terms rather than using the suffix of "man" to refer to people's occupations (such as members of Congress rather than Congressmen).

- Avoid using the term "man" as a catch-all term to refer to a group (such as all men were created equal).
- Avoid descriptions that imply stereotypical behavior (such as rugged men and delicate women).

Punctuation

Issues of punctuation plague us all. The best way to properly punctuate is to keep your sentences simple. Long, complex sentences are difficult to read and comprehend. Sometimes it is necessary, though, to create complex sentences. Punctuation, then, provides the mechanism for helping the reader absorb the complexities of the thought the sentence represents.

Capitalization: Capitalize proper nouns (names of people, places, and things, i.e., *Alabama*) and proper adjectives (adjectives created from proper nouns (i.e., *American flag*). In general, capitalize titles of anything, any geographic location, names of organizations, names of types of people (race, ethnicity).

Colon: Use a colon in a sentence after which you list or describe items. Whenever possible, students should make the list or description using a complete sentence.

Semicolon: Use a semicolon in a sentence whenever you wish to connect two complete thoughts directly. Both parts of the sentence must be complete sentences as well.

Commas: Use a comma to break up complex sentences that either have descriptive clauses or a series of information.

Apostrophes: An apostrophe is used for two reasons: Either to show possession for a noun (i.e., *dog's* bone) or to indicate a contraction (i.e., *won't*). Pronouns (such as *she* or *it*) never have apostrophes showing possession. The only time a pronoun has an apostrophe is to indicate a contraction (*she's* for *she is*, *it's* for *it is*).

Common Errors: Proofreading the Manuscript

Proofreading manuscripts is essential for catching typographical, spelling, usage, and grammatical errors. But proofreading can also catch omissions and errors related to the standards and requirements set by the instructor.

1. Complying with the specific requests of the instructor is important for receiving full credit for the students' research and writing efforts.
2. Good writing skills and good presentation skills are not the same things.
   - Writing is a creative activity.
   - Good presentation is a mechanical activity—it is simple compliance and attention to detail.
3. Poor presentation of the written material diminishes the quality of the manuscript as a product of the author.
   - A poorly proofed manuscript impinges on the credibility of the author.
   - A sloppy manuscript implies sloppy research as well.
   - Attention to detail implies that the author is thoughtful and thorough.

Tips on Proofing Papers

Choose someone, preferably from class, to be a draft partner.
- Make a common list of the requirements for the assignment.
- Trade drafts of manuscripts and read them in the presence of one another.
- Check for compliance to the minimum requirements.
- Check the logical development of arguments and presentation of evidence.
- Discuss inconsistencies with each other.

Re-read your own manuscript for the above as well.
- Address all criticisms by your draft partner.
- Ask the instructor for clarification of requirements and issues on which you and your partner disagree.

Once the minimum requirements are met, proofread for typographical, spelling, usage, and grammatical errors.

1. *Read the corrected draft aloud.* Typographical, spelling, usage, and grammatical errors are more noticeable when you read the text aloud. Reading the text aloud and from the last sentence to the first sentence (if you can stand it!) allows students to disconnect from the substance of the paper and focus on proper usage, spelling, and grammar.

2. *Spelling is a talent, not a skill.* Those less talented in spelling should take heart in the following quotation from Mark Twain and then do the following:

   > "To spell correctly is a talent, not an acquirement. There is some dignity about an acquirement, because it is a product of your own labor…[To] do a thing merely by [grace] where possibly it is a matter of pride and satisfaction,…leaves you naked and bankrupt" (Twain 1961, 27).

   Spell Checker: When using a word processor, use the spell checker. Spell checkers identify typographical or spelling errors as long as the error is not a real word. Spell checkers are not fool proof but generally keep you from making a fool of yourself with typographical and spelling errors!

   "I" before "e": The most common spelling error is found in words containing "ei" or "ie." Remember that the letter "i" comes before the letter "e" except when these letters follow the letter "c." The word is spelled with an "ei" when the letter "c" precedes this vowel combination.

   Keep a list of your most common spelling errors: Search the text for these words and double-check the spelling.

   Keep a dictionary and a thesaurus handy: If you cannot find the word in the dictionary, look up a synonym (a word that has a similar meaning) in a thesaurus. Usually, the word will be listed in the thesaurus.

   Spelling Aids: For students who have great difficulty with spelling but cannot use a spell checker, there are several handy spelling aids. Buy the following inexpensive tools:

- A *Bad Speller's* or *Misspeller's Dictionary*. These dictionaries list the words as they are commonly pronounced (or mispronounced) phonetically, or as they are most commonly misspelled; then they provide the correct spelling.
- A *Word Book* or *Expression Locator*. A *Word Book* is simply a list of words spelled and divided. An *Expression Locator* has the words spelled, divided, and in the context in which they are frequently used.

Ask for help: If none of these tools are available or useful, either ask someone or choose a synonym to replace the word! Do not purposely leave a spelling error uncorrected.

3. *Usage problems are different from spelling problems.* These are errors in word choice.

Since: For example, students often use the word "since" to suggest a reason and as a substitute for "because." This is incorrect.

- The word "since" is used to designate a time dependent or temporal relationship.
- The word "because" is used to designate a causal relationship.

Affect or Effect: For example, students often use the word "affect" and "effect" interchangeably. This is incorrect.

- The word "affect" is a verb that means "to influence."
- The word "effect," as a verb, means "to bring about, accomplish."
- The word "effect," as a noun, means "result."

Usage Guides: Students who are unsure of the correct usage of a word should do the following:

- Buy a copy of *The Elements of Style* by William Strunk Jr. and E.B. White. This book is a short but thorough guide to usage.
- Many publishers have desk reference materials that include a usage glossary. Buy one that is concise. For example, Houghton Mifflin publishers has one entitled *The Written Word*.
- Avoid fancy, big words when small common words express your ideas as clearly. Usage problems are common with words that are not used frequently in communication.
- Use an expression locator to match the context in which you want to use the word with the most common context in which it is used.

4. *Clean up questionable grammar.* Good grammar is an acquired skill. It is acquired through careful attention to placement of commas, tense agreement, and verb-noun agreement.

Grammar Checker: When using a word processing program, use the grammar checker. Grammar checkers identify usage errors in sentence structure. They are not fool proof but they identify long sentences, wordiness, sentence fragments, improper punctuation, improper word use, and verb-noun disagreements.

- Caution: not every error identified by these programs is really an error. Students must know what proper usage is and what is not.
- In general, even when the program identifies a problem in a sentence that is

not really a problem, usually some awkward, vague, or ambiguous language triggered the program's response. Take a serious look at any sentence targeted by the program and find a way to re-write the sentence so that it does not trigger an error anymore.

Commas: Commas are required between two or more words modifying a noun, lists of items in a series, compound sentences, transitional words, and descriptive phrases.

- A rule of thumb when reading the text aloud: if you paused in reading the sentence, the sentence probably needs a comma wherever you paused.
- Usage guides typically have sections on punctuation rules for commas, periods, and other forms of punctuation. When in doubt, look it up.

Tense: A common problem in writing is switching from the present to the past or future tense in the middle of a sentence or paragraph.

- Make the usage of verbs such as *was, is, were, have, had,* and *has* agree with the tense chosen for the paragraph or paper.
- Make sure words ending in "ed" agree with the tense of the paragraph or paper.

Verb-noun Agreement: Verb-noun agreement is essential to clarity of expression. Verb-noun agreement occurs where the activity associated with the noun is clearly one that can be done by the noun.

- For example, students often write that "our government makes policies..." or "the institution produced...." This is incorrect. Governments and institutions are things that are acted upon; they cannot act. People make policies but policies are made in government institutions.
- A rule of thumb: people act; things and places are acted upon. If the noun is a thing or place, then avoid language that suggests that things and places are responsible for some action.

How to Use a Writing Center

Most universities have a writing center or lab for students who need assistance in completing their writing assignments. Knowing what the writing center can do and what it cannot do helps students use the resource efficiently (Leahy 1990).

What Writing Centers Do

- Writing centers offer limited assistance for students who need help in picking topics and structuring papers.
- Writing centers can help students prepare for research by showing them ways to organize their thoughts.
- Writing centers assist students in the writing process.

What Writing Centers Will Not Do

- Writing center staffs are not proofreaders. They can show a student how to proofread but they do not proofread papers.
- Writing centers typically do not offer remedial help for students who lack basic skills. Students with severe writing problems should take remedial classes in basic skills.

Using the Writing Center

All students should use the Writing Center at least once during the writing process. Professors are often too busy or too close to the assignment to give sufficient attention to students' individual writing problems. Students can best benefit when the Writing Center staff is seen as a partner in a collaborative learning process.

1. Visit the Writing Center when you are in the discovery phase of your research project. Ask the Writing Center to give you suggestions on how to work through an idea or freewrite about a topic.

2. Construct your thesis sentence. Ask the Writing Center tutor to critique it for focus and specificity.

3. Construct your topic outline. Ask the Writing Center tutor to critique it for logical development.

4. Write a first draft. Ask the Writing Center tutor to critique it for logical development, coherence, and unity.

On-line Writing Lab/Centers (OWL)

The Internet hosts numerous sites on writing research papers. While many of these sites are useful for quick information about referencing, usage, grammar, and style, some are not much more than *fronts* for term and research paper sales.

There are numerous sites offering term and research papers for "free" or for sale. **Do not use these**. To acquire a paper from the Internet is inviting a poor grade at best and trouble for plagiarism at worst.

Generic Papers: These are generic papers and will be easily spotted by the instructor. Most instructors have specific guidelines and topics for the assignments.

Custom Ordered: Even those supposedly "custom ordered" are easy to spot because the context of the research materials and resulting paper do not reflect the instructor's course specific context. Because students have been taught the course material within the context of the instructor's individual style and perspective, students' written papers generally unwittingly reflect such a style and perspective.

Plagiarism Software: Many instructors are now acquiring software specifically designed for identifying Internet plagiarism (cheating). Not only can the software detect plagiarism in commercially produced papers, but it can also detect material that has been taken in whole or in part from the Internet.

There are numerous sites offering *ideas* for term and research papers. Be very careful using these. If you decide to use an idea, ask the instructor *before you do any research* if the topic or idea is appropriate for the assignment. There is nothing wrong with getting ideas from others.

Here are some useful sites for information about writing and editing:

Indispensable Writing Resources: This site provides information about resources on the Net that will help you write or research a paper. It includes links to reference materials, writing labs, and related sites. http://www.stetson.edu/~rhansen/writing.html

OWL Handouts (listed by topic): OWL handouts are indexed by topic. They include one useful topic on general writing concerns. They also have information on planning/starting to write, effective writing revising/editing/proofreading, and types/genres of writing sentences. http://owl.english.purdue.edu/handouts/index2.html

Paradigm Online Writing Assistant: This site provides information about discovering, organizing, revising, and editing. http://www.powa.org/

The Writing Center: This site provides information on writing literature, research, and reviews. http://www.wisc.edu/writing/index.html

What to Do About Writer's Block

Writers of every variety, at one time or another, experience trouble getting started on their manuscripts. Starting the manuscript, with those first few words on the page, is often a frustrating experience. Here are a few tips for breaking your writer's block.

1. **Work with your research materials.**
   - Talk about your research and your topic with a friend.
   - Freewrite about your topic. Do not worry about organization, grammar, punctuation, or style. Write in a stream of consciousness style—write anything that comes to mind about your topic.
   - Examine the result of your freewriting. Using a cut and paste method, group ideas, arguments, and evidence together into broadly defined categories. Try to find at least three categories. Often two categories are too broad and more than four are too narrow.

2. **There is no substitute for good research organization.**
   - Using the three or four broadly defined categories from your freewriting exercise, write a scratch outline, then a topic outline, and then a sentence outline.
   - On your sentence outline, match your research notes to your ideas, arguments, and evidence. Write the citation next to each of these.
   - By the time you are done you will have reviewed, organized, integrated, and synthesized your materials to coordinate with your ideas and arguments.

3. **Now you are ready to write.**
   - Use your first paragraph to quickly sketch a framework for your thesis sentence.
   - Do not linger on the first paragraph. If necessary, skip it altogether. Write your thesis sentence and begin a new paragraph with the first explanatory paragraph for the body of the work. You can and should always return to the introduction and rewrite it after you have completed the conclusion.
   - Write without editing and critiquing your work as you go along. Forget about grammar, structure, usage, and spelling. Concentrate on expressing your ideas.

- Work as though you are writing a timed, in-class essay. Do not stop to mull over a point. If you are stuck on expressing a point, write a note to yourself in the text to address this issue later and continue with the next point.
- Continue working until you have completed a draft with a conclusion.
- If there is enough time between the date you finished the draft and the date the assignment is due, put the assignment away for at least a day.
- Examine your research materials and supplement them, if necessary, to address the issues, arguments, and evidence you had problems addressing.
- Examine your draft for logical development of ideas, be sure your paragraphs exhibit a commitment and response pattern, expand paragraphs which are too short, break up paragraphs which are too long, and then write your introduction.
- Now correct your grammar, usage, and spelling.
- Now, using your draft checklist, make sure you have complied with the instructor's requirements.
- You should be ready now to re-write and revise the second draft copy.

4. **Using the second draft, proofread for the final copy using the tips for proofreading to correct for common errors described in the preceding pages.**

CHAPTER 8

Manuscript Format and
Referencing Styles

Standard Manuscript Presentation

Although professors have their own preferences about how a paper should be presented, students should observe a few standards. Students should check their syllabus or handout concerning their written assignments for specific details.

Presentation of an Assignment

Text: Assignments should be typed, double-spaced, with one-inch margins.
- Do not justify the right-hand margin. It is difficult to read and distracting.
- Do not double space between the lines in your bibliography, only between references, unless instructed to do so.
- Each page should be numbered, except the title page, the abstract pages, and the executive summary.

Printing: The paper should look presentable.
- The paper should be printed or typed on white bond or computer paper with the edges clean and smooth.
- Do not use erasable bond paper. Erasable bond smears easily and the assignment could be destroyed.
- Tear off all tractor edges and separate each page of a manuscript printed on computer paper.
- Use a new or dark ribbon in your typewriter or set your printer on near-letter quality or best quality.
- Never purposely turn in an assignment in which the type is barely readable.

Binding: The paper should be bound sensibly.
- The simplest and best method of binding the paper is with a staple in the left-hand corner.
- Unless the instructor tells students otherwise, do not use paper clips, folders, multiple staples along the edge, or binders of any kind.

Good habits:
- **Always always always** make a photocopy of your paper or print an extra copy. Store your computer file on two forms of media (hard drive and floppy disk, for example)—papers get lost.

- Re-write your work at least once before you turn in your paper.
- Learn to use a word processing program and type your draft; then revising is easy.
- **Never never never** wait until the night before to type your paper. Typewriter ribbons that break and computer files that get lost at the stroke of midnight are common and unconvincing excuses for late papers.
- Avoid overquoting. A rule of thumb: do not use more than two quotes for every ten pages of text.
- Make sure that your work is well documented. A rule of thumb: make sure every paragraph of substantive secondary information has at least two references.

Ethical Considerations and Plagiarism

Ethically, all information obtained through the research process must be referenced. While most students realize that direct quotations from a source or a fact taken from a table must be referenced, students often do not realize that paraphrasing someone else's work or their own work must be referenced as well. Each writer has a stylistic contribution to the communication of ideas and information. Paraphrasing without acknowledging the author of the idea or information, and/or without acknowledging the author's unique contribution, is considered plagiarism. In general, cautious students should include at least two references per paragraph in the body of their papers and make sure all terminology, phrasing, or ideas are referenced frequently and directly. Introductions and conclusions generally do not need references unless the phrasing of the information is particular to someone else. (The information for some of the discussion below has been adapted or based on Babbie 1998; OWL 1995–2004; University of California, Davis 2001; Standler 2000; Indiana University, Bloomington 2004.)

Controversies About Plagiarism

The controversy about plagiarism is about using other people's ideas and data without acknowledging how they were used. Researchers are expected to build on other people's work; they are not supposed to take credit for other people's work. When researchers take credit for words, ideas, or facts created by others, they commit an act of plagiarism.

What Is Plagiarism?

Plagiarism is the intentional or unintentional use of someone else's ideas, phrasing, terminology, or words without providing an acknowledgment in the form of a footnote, endnote, parenthetical reference, or direct comment in the text.

Text Plagiarism. Copying text word for word where either the words are identical to the original text, the tone or style is nearly identical to the original text, or the structure of the words is nearly identical to the original text is plagiarism if a student does not acknowledge the relationship between the words they used in their papers and the original author of those words.

- Plagiarism is using someone else's exact words without quotation marks and a reference. This includes paragraphs, sentences, and unique phrasing of words. For example, Robert Salisbury published an article in 1968 where he wrote on page 151 the words *Public policy consists in authoritative or sanctioned decisions by governmental actors*. To use these words, a student must put quotation marks in front of the word *Public* and after the period in the sentence. The student must then report the author's name, the publication year, and the page number where the words can be found.

- Plagiarism is using someone else's words from a text and re-writing them by substituting synonyms (words that mean the same thing) without a reference and without stating that you have changed the words. For example, a student who changes Robert Salisbury's words *Public policy consists in authoritative or sanctioned decisions by governmental actors* to *Public policy is made up of official decisions by people in government* is plagiarizing unless they preface the statement by saying "To paraphrase Salisbury (1968, 151), public policy is made up of official decisions by people in government."

- Plagiarism is using someone else's words from a text and re-writing them by shifting the order of the words without referencing the author and without stating that you have changed the order of the words from the original text. For example, a student who shortens and/or rearranges Robert Salisbury's words *Public policy consists in authoritative or sanctioned decisions by governmental actors* by writing *Government actors create public policy through authoritative or sanctioned decisions*, is plagiarizing unless they preface the statement by saying "To paraphrase Salisbury (1968, 151), *government actors create public policy through authoritative or sanctioned decisions.*"

Idea Plagiarism. Adopting or adapting ideas, models, theories, hypotheses, arguments, assertions, perspectives, and/or opinions without acknowledging that they are someone else's original thoughts is plagiarism if the student does not reference the source from which they took the information. Plagiarism is using someone else's ideas, etc., without referencing the author of these ideas. This includes any and all ideas expressed in writing or orally. For example, a student who wishes to use Robert Salisbury's ideas communicated in the sentence *Public policy consists in authoritative or sanctioned decisions by governmental actors (1968, 151)* by writing a paraphrase such as *Public policy is defined by actions taken by government officials* is plagiarizing Salisbury's idea unless the statement is accompanied by a reference at the end of the sentence that paraphrased Salisbury's idea that includes the name of the author, the year of publication, and the page number where the idea can be found.

Fact Plagiarism. Using facts, data, statistics, figures, charts, graphs, tables, pictures, findings, research results that were gathered and reported by someone else without referencing the source of these "facts" is plagiarism.

- Any number or numerical information taken from a source must be referenced by the author's name, the year of publication, and the page number where the number can be found. The reference should be placed at the end of the sentence where the fact is reported.

- If students use a graph, chart, etc., from someone else's original work, they are plagiarizing unless the graph, chart, etc., is copied exactly as reported by the original author and fully referenced (usually at the bottom of the graph, chart, etc.) with a author's name, the title of the publication, the place of publication (for books) or the source (for articles and electronic media), the year of publication, and the page number where the source can be located (or in the case of electronic sources, the full URL and accessed date).

- If students use data created by someone else to create an illustration (chart, graph, etc.), they are plagiarizing unless the data used to create these illustrations are recorded exactly as they are reported by the author. Students must provide a complete reference at the bottom of the illustration including the author's name, the title of the publication, the place of publication (for books) or the source (for articles and electronic media), the year of publication, and the page number where the source can be located (or in the case of electronic sources, the full URL and accessed date).

Why Is Plagiarism Wrong?

Plagiarism is wrong because it infringes on property rights and perpetuates academic dishonesty. Just as stealing a car is wrong, using someone else's intellectual property without permission or outside of fair use provisions is against the law. Along with cheating on tests, plagiarism is an act of academic dishonesty at best, and fraud at worst.

Property Rights Violations: Plagiarism violates the intellectual property rights of individuals. Protecting intellectual property is one of the first protections of private property created by the framers of the U.S. Constitution. In the U.S. Constitution, Article I, Section 8, Clause 8 grants exclusive rights to authors. To further define and support these rights, the Copyright Act of 1790 (and many amendments, revisions, and court interpretations to this law as well) implements and sets constraints on use of other people's work (Association of Research Libraries 2002). Under fair use policies, researchers are allowed to reference and use the intellectual properties of others as long as the owners of the property are acknowledged and/or compensated according to the conditions set by these regulations.

Dishonesty: Plagiarism impedes intellectual growth because those who plagiarize take credit for ideas and information that are not a product of their intellectual investment. Essentially plagiarism is lying by misrepresenting one's intellectual investment. In this sense, plagiarism is a form of cheating and academic dishonesty. Plagiarism further perpetuates intellectual property crimes because those who do so are stealing the property of others. In serious cases, especially where an entire source has been copied (an article, a purchased term paper, etc.), the act of plagiarism can be prosecuted as a crime.

Why Plagiarism Happens

There are a variety of reasons why people plagiarize the work of others. The most disturbing perception is that people deliberately steal other people's work. The most generous perspective on plagiarism is that it is accidental or based on poor training.

Deliberate Misrepresentation: Some people cheat; while the reasons are generally personal, sometimes plagiarism is a choice people make when they are ignorant, poorly organized, or lazy. Sometimes students are unsure about how to perform a task required by an instructor so they simply copy somebody else's work so that they can comply with the requirements of the course. Sometimes students misjudge how long or difficult an assignment is and run out of time to finish the work. To finish an assignment, they resort to cutting and pasting the work of others without synthesizing (merging ideas together) and putting the ideas into their own words. Finally, some students are just lazy. For them, it is easier to purchase or copy material and represent it as their own work. Using work performed by others without acknowledgment, even if it is purchased, is deliberate misrepresentation and fraud.

Mistakes: Some people are disorganized or poorly trained for research. Sometimes students accidentally plagiarize material created by others because they did not organize their research efforts. Without good organization and note-taking skills, students often forget where they found information. This often happens when students have used cut and paste software tools for taking notes from electronic resources. In addition, poorly trained students may not know how or understand when they must acknowledge the source of their information. While students often know they must provide a source for their materials, they may not understand the difference between quoting, paraphrasing, and summarizing information.

Confusion: Some people are confused about how to write a paper that is creative and based on their own work when their work is based on the intellectual property of others. Students sometimes fail to differentiate *writing creatively* with *writing something that is unique* or original. Creative writing and research using secondary research sources (other people's work) is based on *how the intellectual properties of others are used as evidence* to support the students' ideas and perspectives on the topic. It is the synthesis, organization, variety, depth, and breadth of the secondary sources students use for writing about the topic that generates a research paper that becomes their intellectual property.

What Sources Must Be Referenced or Acknowledged?

Students must reference all secondary sources of information that are taken directly or rephrased from someone's or something's intellectual property. Compliance with this requirement is important because experts on the topic (such as professors) recognized not only the origins of such secondary source information but are also familiar with the unique phrasings and style of the sources' authors. Shifts in style and language in a student's paper are strong indicators of plagiarism, especially when such shifts in the language and presentation of information have no references or acknowledgments. Students also should be aware that many educational institutions are acquiring software programs designed to flag or identify plagiarism. Thus, all electronic sources of information of any type must be referenced directly and accurately as well as all secondary sources of information in more traditional formats.

Secondary Sources of Information

A secondary source is a set of information created by someone or something other than the researcher or writer of the research paper. When using some other person's, organizations', or entity's creative work from any communication source, students must reference the source.

- This includes writings and findings from all books, journals, pamphlets, electronic media, billboards, broadcast media, entertainment media, conversations, graphs, tables, etc. that you have not personally created.

- Anything written, observed, visually presented, spoken, and/or heard in any form or format not created by the student for the research paper or project.

Unique or Distinctive Words or Sets of Words

When using some other person's, organization's, or entity's unique or distinctive words, wording, phrasing, or conceptualization (model), students must reference the source. This includes direct (word for word) quotes, paraphrasing (modified wording), or summarizing (condensing).

Electronic Sources of All Types

Plagiarism software generally uses one or more databases to search for text that is copied verbatim or paraphrased. Students should be careful when taking notes, especially when those notes have been cut and pasted from electronic sources, that they attribute that information to the source if they use it in their research papers. This is because plagiarism software programs identify suspect words or phrases (usually underlined or highlighted) and the original source is usually linked to these words or phrases. If a student has cut and pasted a document from an electronic source, the software will identify material as possible plagiarism. A well-documented research paper should have no trouble being processed through plagiarism software.

Student Researcher's Manuscripts

Students must reference themselves when they are using research findings and/or text from manuscripts that they created for other research projects regardless of whether these manuscripts have been published or not. It is common for researchers to build on their previous studies, but once they produce a manuscript, use of any part of the manuscript should be referenced. For students, this means that if they write a paper for one class, they should not use any part of that paper for any other class without referencing the original and/or asking permission of the professor of the class they wrote the paper for and the professor of the class for which they are writing the new paper.

What Sources Do Not Have to Be Referenced or Acknowledged?

There is no information or communication that does not have to be acknowledged in some way. Yet, the burden of reference is lighter for personal experiences, common knowledge, and conclusionary statements. The decision to reference or not to reference in these instances must be made on a case by case basis.

Personal Experiences

Students' personal experiences do not have to be referenced, although students must identify the context (where, when, how, and why) of such experiences. As such, even personal experiences have references.

Original Research

Students' findings from primary data research do not have to be referenced, although students must identify and reprint the methodological process for creating original or primary data. As such, results from primary or original research are referenced by the methodological process through which the student collected the data or findings.

Common Knowledge

Students do not need to reference common knowledge, although what is considered common knowledge is contextually determined by culture, profession, and time. Common knowledge differs by generations, political or social cultures, and fields or sub-fields within a professional area of study. Unless the information is *obviously* part of the traditions and socialization of the audience (i.e., Thomas Jefferson wrote the *Declaration of Independence* is common knowledge in America), even common knowledge should have references.

Personal Conclusions

Students generally do not need to reference in the conclusion sections of their papers, although the conclusions must be a product of the students' own analysis and efforts. If students use unique or distinctive words, wording, phrasing, or anything else that is *not* based on the students' own thoughts or insights and/or if the conclusions are *not* clearly based on the analysis in the body of the paper, then students should reference this information.

How to Avoid Plagiarizing Due to Mistakes and Confusion

Students can minimize and/or prevent problems with plagiarizing or being accused of plagiarizing by being organized and informed about the use of intellectual property. By organizing their research methodically around attributing information as it is collected in the research process, students may avoid plagiarism that results from mistakes and confusion. By improving their skills and strategies for referencing in the writing process, students may avoid plagiarism problems, especially ones that arise from their manuscripts being processed through plagiarism software, that are a result of mistakes and confusion about how to reference secondary sources.

Avoiding Plagiarism in the Research Process

Set up a binder: Put a reference for every source of communication (books, articles, etc.) into a binder.

- Before reading anything, write the complete bibliographic information of the source on paper; one sheet of paper per source.
- If the source is electronic, then while you are still in the file, copy the URL (and as much other bibliographic information available from the source) using cut and paste tools. Paste these items into a word processing file and save it for creating your reference page. Print out the source reference and put it into the binder.
- Record, on paper, the author, date, and place where you heard, saw, experienced, or observed information.
- Keep the references in the binder in alphabetical order.

Organize notes: When taking notes on a source place the name of the author (person, organization, entity) and year of publication at the top of your first note page and every page of notes you make on that reference. When there is no author, use an abbreviated title (just as you would for your citation in the paper) that is clearly identified to the bibliographic page you created for the binder.

Annotate quotes: If you are copying the author's information to your notes word for word, write the word **QUOTE** first, then the page number(s), and finally, put quotation marks around the words.

- Quotes can be any text in the source.
- Quotes are quantitative or concrete information such as numbers or facts unique to the source.
- Quotes can be abstract or qualitative information such as opinions or concepts.

Annotate paraphrases: If you are paraphrasing in the notes, then underline the words that you used that are modified or similar to the author's exact words. Write the **PARA-PHRASE** and the page number(s).

- Using a thesaurus to change the author's words is paraphrasing.
- Using different forms of the words such as using past or present tense of verbs or different pronouns to modify the nouns is paraphrasing.

Annotate summaries: If you are summarizing an author's work, you may or may not have to use page numbers in the reference, although students must remember that using a thesaurus to change the author's words is not summarizing. Summarized information *should not be* similar in form, style, cadence, phrasing, personality, or wording to the original author's wording. The summary should reflect the students' writing style and personality.

- If you are summarizing a distinct set of ideas or information from an author's work, write the word **SUMMARY**, the page numbers over which you are summarizing the information, and then put the information in your own words.
- If you are summarizing the entire contents of an author's work, as is often done for annotated bibliographies, then write the words **SUMMARY-PURPOSE** and then summarize the purpose of the work in a few short sentences. Then write the words **SUMMARY-SIGNIFICANCE**, and summarize the conclusions of the author and state the importance of the findings to the field and/or your research topic in a few short sentences.

Avoiding Plagiarism in the Writing Process

Quotes: *Acknowledge exact or modified quotes (information taken word for word from a author's text) by attributing the words to the author directly before or after the quote.* All quotes must be introduced by using words and phrases such as *said, says, according to, argued, stated*, etc. The quotation marks are placed before the words from the author's text begin and after the words from the author's text ends. Students must identify any modifications to the author's exact phrasing using brackets for information changed, or ellipsis (three periods) for indicating information excluded.

Quoting Techniques

For example, to acknowledge Robert Salisbury's work on public policy, students may quote and reference using any of the following techniques. (These examples are in *The Chicago Manual of Style* parenthetical citation format).

Technique 1:
Salisbury (1968, 151) says, "Public policy consists in authoritative or sanctioned deci-sions by governmental actors. It refers to the *substance* of what government does and is to be distinguished from the processes by which decisions are made."

Technique 2:
According to Salisbury, "Public policy consists in authoritative or sanctioned decisions by governmental actors. It refers to the *substance* of what government does and is to be distinguished from the processes by which decisions are made" (1968, 151).

Technique 3:
Many scholars have argued about the definition of public policy, yet Salisbury states clearly that "[p]ublic policy... refers to the *substance* of what government does and is to be distinguished from the processes by which decisions are made" (1968, 151).

Technique 4:
For this research paper, public policy is defined as "the *substance* of what govern-ment does" (Salisbury 1968, 151).

Technique 5:
Public policy is not defined by the "processes by which decisions are made"; it is "the *substance* of what government does" (Salisbury 1968, 151).

Paraphrase: Acknowledge modified or similar wording by attributing the informa-tion to the author by using phrases such as *according to, suggested, argued, found, dis-cussed, reasoned, intimated,* etc.

Paraphrasing Technique

For example, in a discussion of Robert Salisbury's work on public policy, students may attribute **paraphrased** ideas by using the following techniques. (These examples are in *The Chicago Manual of Style* parenthetical citation format.)

Technique 1:
According to Salisbury (1968, 151) public policy is defined by government actions and not the decision processes.

Technique 2:
Policy, as suggested by Salisbury (1968, 151), is not about decision-making processes; it is about what the essence of what governments do in society.

Technique 3:
Yet, Salisbury (1968, 151) indicated that public policy is not defined by government processes but by government actions.

Technique 4:
Salisbury (1968, 151), in his article defining the meaning of public policy, explained that it is what governments *do* that defines policy.

Technique 5:
Salisbury (1968, 151) elaborates as well as disagrees with other scholars' definition of public policy; he argues that policy is what governments do.

Summaries: Acknowledge summarized information by attributing the information to the author using a reference to the author at the end of the sentence or set of sentences you used to summarize the author's contribution to knowledge. If the information is summarized from a unique portion of the author's work, then use page numbers in the citation. If the information is a summary of the purpose and/or the contributions and findings of the author's work, then the reference need not have page numbers included in the citation.

Summarizing Techniques

For example, in a discussion of Robert Salisbury's contribution to the field of public policy analysis, students may attribute a **summary** of his work by the following techniques. (These examples are in *The Chicago Manual of Style* parenthetical citation format.)

> *Technique 1:*
> Public policy analysis, as a field, has been the subject of intense academic debate. Policy scholars disagree on whether policy is best understood by case studies of policy outcomes or by examining the ways in which decisions are made and implemented within a society (Salisbury 1968, 151–153).
>
> *Technique 2:*
> Public policy is more than a process; it is defined by the characteristics of policy outcomes. How those outcomes are distributed, particularly when there are implications of zero-sum results, is important to defining and understanding constraints on political behavior (Salisbury 1968).

Format and Placement of Items in the Paper or Essay

A description of each of the items below can be found in the following pages. The descriptions of the format and placement of each item reflect the standard form across style guides. Check the style guide preferred or required by the instructor to verify that these suggestions conform to the standards set by your guide.

> THE MANUSCRIPT SHOULD INCLUDE:
> - a title page
> - an abstract or executive summary
> - Table of Contents (for long papers)
> - List of Tables and Figures (rarely necessary for short papers)
> - headings and subheadings
> - an appendix (when necessary)
> - tables and figures (when necessary)
> - parenthetical, footnote, or endnote citations
> - explanatory notes (when necessary)
> - quotations (only when absolutely necessary)
> - a bibliography or reference page

PLACEMENT OF ITEMS IN THE MANUSCRIPT:

1. Title Page
2. Abstract Page or Executive Summary (if required)
3. Table of Contents and/or List of Tables and Figures
4. Text: (Identify parts of text by using subheadings)
   - Introduction
   - Explanation or Background or Literature Review
   - Method or Test of Argument or Reasons
   - Results or Linking of Argument with Evidence
   - Conclusion or Summary
5. Appendix (after last sentence of the body)
6. Explanatory Notes
7. References
8. Tables
9. Figures

Format for the Title Page

1. The title of the paper should be centered and two inches above the middle of the page (the title should not be longer than 12 words).
2. The student's name should be two inches from the bottom of the page.
3. The course number and professor's name should be under the student's name.
4. The date should be under the professor's name.

Example

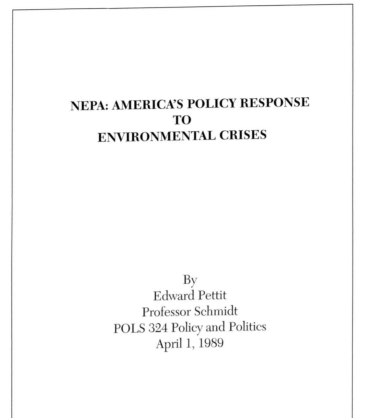

NEPA: AMERICA'S POLICY RESPONSE
TO
ENVIRONMENTAL CRISES

By
Edward Pettit
Professor Schmidt
POLS 324 Policy and Politics
April 1, 1989

Format for an Abstract

1. The abstract should be on a separate page following the title page.
2. Do not number the abstract page.
3. There are only two parts to an abstract: the title and the text.
4. The word **Abstract** is used as a title and is centered at the top of the page. Double space before writing the text of the abstract.
5. The abstract should summarize the paper in 150 words or less in one paragraph that is at least four sentences long. (See Chapter 11 for examples.)
6. The abstract is not an introduction. It should include, in order:
   - A description of the nature of the problem

- A description of the major points and thesis
- A description of the methods or evidence used
- A description of the major conclusions reached

7. The abstract should not contain direct quotations from the text.
8. The abstract must use proper sentence structure and grammar.
9. Keep the ideas and main points identified in the abstract in the same order as they are presented in the paper.
10. The abstract may be double- or single-spaced.

Tips for Writing an Abstract

- Read your paper carefully.
- Summarize the focus of the introductory paragraph in one sentence.
- Write down the main points.
- For each point, write down the evidence used to support the point.
- Summarize the focus of the concluding paragraph in one sentence.
- Use this information to write the abstract.
- Use transitions to link the ideas together.

Format for an Executive Summary

1. The executive summary should be on a separate page following the title page.
2. Do not number the executive summary page.
3. There are only four components to an executive summary: the title, the purpose, the methodology, and the findings. (See Chapter 12 for examples.)
4. The words **Executive Summary** are used as a title and are centered at the top of the page. Double space before writing the descriptions of purpose, methodology, and findings sections.
5. The executive summary is not an introduction. For a short, simple study, the executive summary should summarize the paper in about a single-spaced page for a short paper. For a short paper, it should include:
   - A description of the purpose of the study—about one paragraph.
   - A description of how the study was conducted—about two paragraphs.
   - A description of the major findings—a one to two sentence generalization with the specific findings *listed with bullets or numbering*.
6. For more in-depth studies, the executive summary should be longer and include headings and subheadings to indicate the different parts of the analysis. Use bullets or numbering to summarize main points and findings in the analysis.
7. The executive summary should not contain direct quotations from the text.
8. The executive summary must use proper sentence structure and grammar.
9. Keep the ideas and main points identified in the executive summary in the same order as they are presented in the paper.
10. The executive summary may be double- or single-spaced. Usually, it is single-spaced.

- Read your paper carefully.
- Summarize the focus of the introductory paragraph in one sentence.
- Write down how the study was conducted.
- For each finding, list the evidence used.
- Summarize the focus of the concluding paragraph in one sentence.
- Use this information to write an executive summary.
- Use transitions to link the ideas together.

Format for Headings and Subheadings

1. Use headings and subheadings when assignments call for specific information and questions to be answered, or when the paper topic is complex. (See Chapter 12: Example of a Policy Recommendation.)

2. There are three kinds:

- **Major** headings: A major heading should be centered or left justified (to the left margin), in bold and capital letters. These are generally used to identify the major parts of the paper such as the introduction and conclusion.
- **Primary** subheadings: A primary heading should be left justified, in bold letters, and the first letter in each word capitalized. These are used to identify transitions between points or arguments within major parts of the paper.
- **Secondary** subheadings: A secondary heading should be left justified and in bold italic letters or bold and underlined. They are generally the first words in the paragraph, they are usually phrases (not complete sentences) that end in a period. These are used to distinguish between subsections of one of the primary parts of the paper.

3. Double space between the major heading or primary subheading and the following paragraph.

4. For papers that are twenty pages or less, only major headings and primary headings are used.

5. Major headings should be used when the paper is longer than five pages and develops identifiable points and arguments.

Format for the Table of Contents or List of Tables and Figures

Most students will never use a Table of Contents or need a List of Tables and Figures. The Table of Contents is generally produced for papers longer than 25 pages, with several parts or chapters. The List of Tables and Figures are usually only used when the paper is produced with many figures and/or tables embedded in the text of the paper.

1. The Table of Contents and the List of Tables and Figures are placed on separate pages after the abstract or executive summary and before the introduction.

2. On a page by itself, the Table of Contents lists all the headings used in the paper and provides a page number for each heading and subheading used. The headings are left justified and listed in the order they appear in the text. The page numbers where the

headings can be found are right justified.

3. On a page by itself, the List of Tables and Figures lists all the tables and figures used in the paper and provides a page number for where each can be found. The table/figure numbers and names are left justified and listed in the order they appear in the text. The page numbers where the table/figure numbers and names can be found are right justified.

4. Do not number the Table of Contents or List of Tables pages.

Format for the Appendix

1. If the paper has an appendix, put it after the last page of text and before the endnotes (if any), the reference page, and any tables or figures.

2. The appendix must be on a separate page.

3. An appendix is used mostly to present background information not presented in tables or figures.

4. An appendix should be identified in the text with a parenthetical reference such as (*see Appendix*).

5. If there is more than one appendix, identify them as Appendix A, Appendix B, and so on.

Format for Tables and Figures

1. Place the tables, if any, after the references. (See Chapter 12: Example of a Policy Recommendation.)

2. Place the figures, if any, after the tables or after the reference page when there is no table.

3. Tables and figures should be numbered separately, placed on separate pages, and fully referenced with a complete citation.

4. The writer should address information found in the table or figure in the text by phrases, such as "as seen in Figure 1…" or "as the data in Table 1 shows…."

5. After the table or figure has been mentioned in the text, a direct reference to the table or figure is placed on a centered, separate line.

Example of Referencing a Table in the Text

Importantly, as seen in Table 1, most of his nominees were confirmed.

(Table 1 About Here)

The data in the table show that the Democrat's large majorities, ranging from 57 percent to 75 percent in the 73rd–77th Senate, combined with Roosevelt's adherence to traditional selection methods, resulted in very few unconfirmed or rejected nominees.

Format and Placement for Quotations

1. Quotations are sets of information which have been copied verbatim from a source.
2. Quotations should be used very very very sparingly and only when absolutely necessary.
   - **Rule of thumb:** avoid quotes altogether.
   - **Rule of thumb:** do not use more than two quotations for every ten pages of text.
3. Quotations must be cited with an exact page number.
4. Quotations that are shorter than three lines long should be placed between quotation marks (at the beginning and the end) and the citation placed after the ending quotation mark.
5. Quotations that are longer than four lines long should be single-spaced and indented 10 spaces on the left and right margins. The citation is placed after the last sentence of the quotation.
6. Quotations should never be used as a substitute for writing or synthesizing information.
7. Quotations must be introduced or framed into the text in some way.
   - One way is to identify the author or work directly or indirectly.
   - Another way is to explain why the words that are being quoted are significant.
8. Use quotes:
   - When the exact wording of a statement or point is crucial to the meaning of it.
   - To preserve distinctive phrasing or eloquence of a point.

Example of a Short Quote

Media influence on political behavior has been argued to be minimal until recently.[1] Some scholars argue that news coverage shapes people's attitudes about important political actors as well as people's perspectives on political events. For example, Lipset and Schneider (1987) found that "…interest group leaders had an incentive to maintain a high level of criticism…" in the media to justify their positions (405). Lipset and Schneider conclude that people have lost confidence in big government, big business, and big labor due to exploitative news coverage about each of them.

---

[1] The major point of debate over how media influences political behavior is over how information is processed. Some studies show that people read selectively and absorb very little of the news. See Graber 1984.

Media influence on political behavior has been argued to be minimal until recently.[1] Studies show that media is the major source of political information. Lipset and Schneider (1987) suggest that television carries with it a special consideration and influence in providing information to the public.

> The special impact of television is that it delivers the news to a much larger and "inadvertent" audience than was the case before television, when only a limited segment of the population chose to follow news about politics and government. When people read newspapers and magazines, they edit the information by skipping over articles about subjects they are not interested in. Television watchers, however, are exposed to everything. (Lipset and Schneider 1987, 405).

They conclude that people's attitudes have changed toward big government, big business, and big labor due to exploitative news coverage about them.

---

[1]The major point of debate over how media influences political behavior is over how information is processed. Some studies show that people read selectively and absorb very little of the news. See Graber 1984.

Format and Placement for Explanatory Notes

1. Explanatory notes are put in the same place as footnotes or endnotes.
2. These are typically used to comment on the context of a fact or opinion, to explain a source, to elaborate on an idea, to define a term, or to provide background on an idea or methodology used.
3. Explanatory notes can be used in papers that have parenthetical citations.
4. If explanations are needed when the paper has footnote or endnote citations, explanatory information can be added after the citation or can stand alone with its own raised number.
5. All endnotes or footnotes must be identified with a raised number in ascending order regardless of whether they are explanatory or merely reference a source.

Media influence on political behavior has become increasingly noticeable.[1] For example, by analyzing a set of opinion polls, Lipset and Schneider show that news coverage shapes peoples attitudes about important political actors as well as people's perspectives on political events. The poll results suggest that people have lost confidence in big government, big business, and big labor due to exploitative news coverage about each (Lipset and Schneider 1987).

---

[1]The major point of debate over how media influences political behavior is over how information is processed. Some studies show that people read selectively and absorb very little of the news. See Graber 1984.

Format and Placement for Citations or References

Styles of Citing or Referencing Materials

1. Research papers may include footnotes, endnotes, or parenthetical (author-date) references to sources. Unless otherwise directed by the instructor, students should choose one form of citation and stick with it.

2. Parenthetical (author-date), endnote, or footnote citations should be used to identify the source of quotations and all controversial, obscure, or significant facts.
   - *Rule of thumb*: each paragraph in the body of the paper which deals with evidence or ideas borrowed from others should contain **at least two citations**.
   - *Rule of thumb*: when in doubt, reference the information.

3. All forms of citations must include a specific page number when quoting directly or paraphrasing a fact or data from a source.

4. There are three referencing style guides that are commonly used when writing a research paper: the *MLA*, the *APA*, and *The Chicago Manual of Style*.
   - *The Chicago Manual of Style*. 15th ed. Revised and Expanded. Chicago: University of Chicago Press. 2003.
   - Gibaldi, Joseph. *MLA Handbook for Writers of Research Papers*. 6th ed. NY: Modern Language Association of America. 2003.
   - *Publication Manual of the American Psychological Association*. 5th ed. Washington, DC: American Psychological Association. 2001.

5. Each referencing system varies slightly in format from the other. The specifics of each system are explained in detail in the appropriate reference guide book. There are two accepted methods for referencing research materials within the body of a research paper.
   - The first involves using *endnotes* or *footnotes* in combination with a bibliography (see below for examples).
   - The other is referred to as the *"author-date"* system, which involves in-text parenthetical documentation and a reference page. In political science, *The Chicago Manual of Style (Chicago Manual)* and the author-date system is the preferred reference guide and style. Sections 16.90–16.107 of the *Chicago Manual* detail the author-date system (see below for examples).

Structure for Endnote and Footnote Citations

The footnote and endnote system of referencing has a particular style and format.

Usage: Endnotes and footnotes are substitutes for each other and cannot be used together. They differ from each other only by where they are placed.

- Footnotes are placed at the bottom of the page in which they were referenced.
- Endnotes are listed on a page by themselves entitled with the word "Notes" centered on the first line of the page. Double space between the title and the first citation.
- The endnote page is placed after the appendix or last page of text if there is no appendix.

Text Format: The text format for footnotes and endnotes is the same and should be indicated in the text by a raised number.

- They should be listed in ascending order.
- The endnote or footnote contains all reference information the first time a source is cited.
- Subsequent citations to the same source immediately following the first citation can be designated by the term "ibid." Some styles guide rules suggest that the source of the citation referenced after the first time include the last name of the author and the year and no other indicator such as "ibid" (check with your instructor or the required style guide).
- Ideas attributed to more than one author are identified by listing the authors together separated by semicolons.

Reference Format: The reference format for footnotes and endnotes should be left justified except for the first line, which should be indented by five spaces.

Titles: The title of the book, journal, or Internet site must be formatted differently than the rest of the text. Most often the title is placed in italics.

No Works Cited or Reference Page: Because footnotes and endnotes must contain, at least in the first citation of the source, complete citation information, they are generally not accompanied by a bibliography, reference page, or works cited page. There are occasions when a bibliography is required. If a bibliography is requested, then the information for the bibliography is basically the same as the information included in the footnotes or endnotes in the first citation of the source. The format is different. The bibliographic citation begins with the last name, then the first name of the author. The information is separated by periods. The entire list of sources are listed on the bibliography page in alphabetical order (See *The Chicago Manual of Style* 2003: Section 16.71–16.89).

Content and Punctuation for Footnotes and Endnotes

Footnotes and Endnotes should include the following information ***separated by commas*** (adapted from Kalvelage et al. 1984; Harnack and Kleppinger 1998; *The Chicago Manual of Style* 2003: Sections 17.17, 17.148, 17.234):

Book Footnote or Endnote Information

- the raised number
- the author's full name, first name first
- the complete title (in italics)
- the editor's name (if any)
- the edition (if it is not the first)
- the name and number of the series (if any)
- the place of publication
- the name of the publisher
- the date of publication
- URL for Internet sources
- date of access for Internet sources (Month Day, Year)

Article Footnote or Endnote Information

- the raised number
- the author's full name, first name first
- the title of the article (in quotation marks)
- the name of the periodical (in italics)
- the volume number of the periodical
- the date of the periodical
- the page numbers of the article
- URL for Internet sources
- date of access for Internet sources (Month Day, Year)

Internet Footnote or Endnote Information

- author's name (if available)
- title of the document (in quotation marks)
- title of the complete site (in italics)
- date of the posting or last revision
- volume number (if any)
- URL for Internet sources
- date of access for Internet sources (Month Day, Year)

Examples of Footnotes and Endnotes Used for Reference Citations

Here is a sample of footnote/endnote style formats based on *The Chicago Manual of Style*. The information is separated by commas until the end of the sentence.

Book:

[1]Jay M. Shafritz, *The Dictionary of American Government and Politics* (Chicago, IL: Dorsey Press, 1988).

Journal article paginated by volume (page numbers begin at 1 for the first issue and continue in the next issue with the ending page number from the first issue):

[2]Edmond Costantini, "Political Women and Political Ambition: Closing the Gender Gap," *American Journal of Political Science* 34 (August 1990): 741–70.

Journal article paginated by issue (page numbers begin at 1 for each issue):

[3] James Coast, "Environmentally Safe Insecticides," *Consumer Digest* 23, no. 2 (1974): 25–32.

Article in an edited book:

[4]Hugh Heclo, "Issue Networks and the Executive Establishment," in *The New American Political System*, ed. Anthony King (Washington, DC: American Enterprise Institute for Policy Research, 1978), 34.

Book with multiple authors:

[5] Schweller, John, Christopher Jones, and Timothy Fuller, *Principles of Ecological Wisdom* (New York: Simon and Schuster, 2002), 42.

Multiple works by an author:

[6]John E. Chubb, "Politics, Markets, and the Organization of Schools," *American Political Science Review* 82 (September 1988), 87–1065.

[7]John E. Chubb, *Politics, Markets, and America's Schools* (Washington, DC: Brookings, 1990), 70–80.

Government document:

[8]U.S. Congress. House. Committee on Foreign Relations. *Report on Aid to South Africa*, 98th Cong., 2nd sess. (Washington, DC: Government Printing Office, 1985), 1.

Newspaper or magazine article:

[9]Robert S. Greenberger, "Hottest Labor Consultant in Washington Adopts New Right Techniques to Bolster Union's Image," *The Wall Street Journal*, October 23, 1981.

Source with no author:

[10]"Dr. King's Widow Testifies in a Civil Trial," *New York Times*, sec. A17, November 17, 1999.

Internet source:

General Web site Internet source:

[11]Raymond Agius, "Quality and Audit in Occupational Health," *Health, Environment and Work*, May 1999, http://www.med.ed.ac.uk.HEW/quality.html (accessed June 8, 1999).

Organizational Web site Internet source:

[13]AFL-CIO, *Working Families Need a Voice: Who's Behind It?*, 14 January 1999, http://www.aflcio.org/silence/behind.html (accessed July 19, 1999).

Electronic Journal Web site Internet source:

[14]"Clinton Proposes Increased Child Care Subsidies," *Amarillo Business Journal*, 3, no. 2 (1999), http://businessjournal.net/stories/020698/child.html (accessed August 25, 1999).

Electronic Magazine Web site Internet source:

[15]Debra Rosenberg, "More Than Just a Kiss: Hillary's Conflicted Life as First Lady and Candidate," *Newsweek*, November 22, 1999, http://www.newsweek.com/nw-srv/printed/us/na/a55101-1999nov14.html (accessed November 17, 1999).

Government site Internet source:

[16]National Labor Relations Board, "National Labor Relations Board Members", February 17, 1999, http://www.nlrb.gov/members.html (accessed July 14, 1999).

Personal site Internet source:

[17]Jon Brown. "Homepage," October 24, 1998, http://www.polsci.swms.edu/brown/personal.html (accessed July 8, 1999).

Electronic news and journal databases:

[18]Jill SchachnerChanen, "Daddy's Home," *ABA Journal* 86, no. 11 (2000): 90, http://www.epnet.com (accessed August 27, 2003).

Personal interviews:

[19]Paul Simon, Personal Interview, 12 August 1998.

Structure for Parenthetical Author-Date Citations System

Styles of parenthetical referencing have a common set of characteristics. (See *The Chicago Manual* 2003: Sections 16.107–120.)

Format: Parenthetical citations are references to sources that appear in the text between parentheses. This citation system uses a reference that is place directly into the text, usually after the writer reports information, paraphrases, or directly quotes another writer's material. When the writer is summarizing a conclusion or the work of someone else's work, the reference includes the author's last name and the year the work was published. For example (Jones 2001).

Page numbers: If the information includes specific information or a direct quote from someone else's material, then the reference must include the author's last name, the year the work was published, and then the page number where the information can be found. Although *The Chicago Manual of Style* suggests using a comma to separate the year and the page number, some professions prefer using a colon. For example (Jones 2001, 46) or (Jones 2001: 46).

Placement: The parenthetical citation is generally placed before the period at the end of a sentence.

Reference to same author: Multiple references to the same author are indicated with the same format regardless of how many times the author is cited.

Reference to several works: Ideas attributed to more than one author are identified by listing the references together. The references are separated by semicolons and enclosed together by parentheses. For example (Jones 2001; Brown 1990, 42).

Multiple authors: References to works with multiple authors are listed the first time with all the authors' last names, but the second time only the first author's name followed by a comma and "et al." For example (Smith et al. 1990).

References with no author: References with titles only should be referenced with an abbreviated title followed by three periods and year of publication. For example ("How Environments..." 2000).

An Example of a Parenthetical Citation

> The public is primarily exposed to new information about labor unions through the media. Media are generally seen as agenda setters and in some cases actually shape public opinions (Graber 1984; Iyengar 1987). While the citizens' views may come from their considerations of the political environment, the meaning of events tends to be defined for them by the media. In this sense, media act as agenda setters when pre-existing attitudes are strong and may change attitudes when pre-existing attitudes are weak (Iyengar 1987, 815–20).

Format for the Author-Date Citation System Reference Page

Placement

Place the reference page (entitled **References** or **Works Cited**) after explanatory endnotes or after the last page of text in the absence of an appendix or endnotes.

- A reference page is required for author-date citation systems.
- All sources used for the assignment must be listed on the reference page.

Format

All the sources listed should be typed using a hanging paragraph.

- A hanging paragraph has the first line flush with the margin (left justified) and all remaining lines indented five spaces.

- *Microsoft Word* has an autoformatting function for this type of paragraph in the *Format, Paragraph* menu. (Highlight the reference, then use the *Format, Paragraph menu* and look for *Special* and then click the arrow until *Hanging* appears in the box.)

Alphabetical Order

Do not separate the books from the articles or Web references.

- All references should be listed together in *alphabetical* order by the last name of the author.

- *Microsoft Word* has an autoformatting function in the *Table, Sort* menu to alphabetize a list of information. (Highlight all the references, then use the *Table, Sort* menu, and click *OK*.)

Content and Punctuation for Author-Date Reference Page

Stylebooks differ on the order and punctuation of the source information, so check with the instructor for suggestions on which stylebook to use.

- For multiple sources by one author, use a line five spaces in length or a 3-em dash (often available in the *Insert, Symbol, Special Character* menu in *Microsoft Word*) instead of the author's name on the subsequent entry. Some professions prefer to repeat the name in the reference list. Both types of entries are acceptable.

- Citations listed on a reference page must have the following information separated by periods (adapted from Kalvelage, et al. 1984; Harnack and Kleppinger 1998; *The Chicago Manual of Style 2003:* Sections 16.90–106, 17.12, 17.17, 17.148, 17.234, 17.359).

  Book Reference Page Information
  - the author's full name, last name first
  - the complete title (in italics)
  - the editor's name (if any)
  - the edition (if it is not the first)
  - the name and number of the series (if any)
  - the place of publication
  - the name of the publisher
  - the date of publication
  - URL for Internet sources
  - date of access for Internet sources (Month Day, Year)

Article Reference Page Information
- the author's full name, last name first
- the title of the article
- the name of the periodical (in italics)
- the volume number of the periodical
- the date of the periodical
- the page numbers of the article
- URL for Internet sources
- date of access for Internet sources (Month Day, Year)

Internet Material Reference Page Information
- author's name (if available)
- title of the document
- title of the complete site (in italics)
- date of the posting or last revision
- volume number (if any)
- date of access
- URL for Internet sources
- date of access for Internet sources (Month Day, Year)

Examples of Common Author-Date References Page

Here is a comparison of reference page style formats for three popular style guides: these guides are *The Chicago Manual of Style* which is used by the American Political Science Association, *Publication Manual of the American Psychological Association,* and *MLA Handbook for Writers of Research Papers*. **Once a format is chosen**, **students must use the same format throughout the references**. For formatting information concerning document types not listed below, please refer to the style guides or see the following Web sites or books.

Chicago Manual
Chicago manual of style FAQ, http://www.press.uchicago.edu/Misc/Chicago/cmosfaq.html
Chicago manual of style. 2003. 15th ed. Chicago: University of Chicago Press.

APA
American Psychological Association. <http://www.apa.org/journals/faq.html>
Publication manual of the American Psychological Association. 2001. 5th edition. Washington, DC: American Psychological Association.

MLA
Modern Language Association (MLA). *Publication Manual FAQ* <http://www.mla.org/main.stl.htm>
Modern Language Association. *How to cite information from the World Wide Web.* (MLA) http://www.apa.org/journals/webref.html.
Gibaldi, Joseph. 2003. *MLA handbook for writers of research papers.* 6th ed. New York: The Modern Language Association of America.

Book:

Chicago Manual

Shafritz, Jay M. 1988. *The dictionary of American government and politics*. Chicago, IL: Dorsey Press.

APA

Shafritz, Jay M. (1988). *The dictionary of American government and politics*. Chicago, IL: Dorsey Press.

MLA

Shafritz, Jay M. The Dictionary of American Government and Politics. Chicago, IL: Dorsey P, 1988.

Book with two authors:

Chicago Manual

Wilson, Ian, and Stuart I. Morse. 2003. *Law and social change: Civil rights and their consequences*. San Francisco, CA: Munner Press

APA

Wilson, Ian, & Morse, Stuart I. (2003). *Law and social change: Civil rights and their consequences*. San Francisco, CA: Munner Press

MLA

Wilson, Ian, and Stuart I. Morse. Law and Social Change: Civil Rights and Their Consequences. San Francisco, CA: Munner, 2003.

Book with three or more authors:

(Editors Note: By convention if a book has more than six authors only list the first six followed by "et al." Style guides differ on the specifics of this policy so check the appropriate style guide.)

Chicago Manual

Schweller, John, Christopher Jones, and Timothy Fuller. 2002. *Principles of ecological wisdom*. New York: Simon and Schuster.

APA

Schweller, John, Jones Christopher, & Fuller, Timothy. (2002) *Principles of ecological wisdom*. New York: Simon and Schuster.

MLA

Schweller, John, Christopher Jones, and Timothy Fuller. Principles of Ecological Wisdom. New York: Simon, 2002.

Multiple works by an author:

(Editor's Note: Multiple works by the same author are listed and organized by year of publication. If the author and the year are the same then the publications for the same author are alphabetized by title and then the year is distinguished by placing an a, b, or c, etc., behind it.)

Chicago Manual *(Editor's Note: While* The Chicago Manual *encourages the use of the 3-em dash, students may use a line five spaces long ending with a period to simulate a 3-em dash. It is also acceptable to repeat the author's name instead of either the line or the dash.)*

Chubb, John E. 1988. Politics, markets, and the organization of schools. *American Political Science Review* 82:1065–87.

————. 1990. *Politics, markets, and America's schools*. Washington, DC: Brookings.

APA

Chubb, John E. (1988). Politics, markets, and the organization of schools. *American Political Science Review, 82,* 1065–87.

Chubb, John E. (1990). *Politics, markets, and America's schools.* Washington, DC: Brookings.

MLA

Chubb, John E. "Politics, Markets, and the Organization of Schools." American Political Science Review 82 (1988): 1065–87.

——. Politics, Markets, and America's Schools. Washington, DC: Brookings, 1990.

> ### Article in an edited book:

Chicago Manual

Heclo, Hugh. 1978. Issue networks and the executive establishment. In *The New American Political System,* edited by Anthony King, 51–84. Washington, DC: American Enterprise Institute for Policy Research.

APA

Heclo, Hugh. (1978). Issue networks and the executive establishment. In Anthony King (Ed.), *The new American political system* (pp. 51–84). Washington, DC: American Enterprise Institute for Policy Research.

MLA

Heclo, Hugh. "Issue Networks and the Executive Establishment." The New American Political System. Ed. Anthony King. Washington, DC: American Enterprise Inst. for Policy Research, 1978. 51-84.

> ### Journal article paginated by volume:

(Page numbers begin at 1 for the first issue and continue in the next issue with the ending page number from the first issue.)

Chicago Manual

Costantini, Edmond. 1990. Political women and political ambition: Closing the gender gap. *American Journal of Political Science* 34:741–70.

APA

Costantini, Edmond. (1990). Political women and political ambition: Closing the gender gap. *American Journal of Political Science, 34,* 741–770.

MLA

Costantini, Edmond. "Political Women and Political Ambition: Closing the Gender Gap." American Journal of Political Science 34 (1990): 741–70.

Journal article paginated by issue:

(Page numbers begin at 1 for each issue.)

Chicago Manual

Coast, James. 1974. Environmentally safe insecticides. *Consumer Digest* 23 (2): 25–32.

APA

Coast, James. (1974). Environmentally safe insecticides. *Consumer Digest, 23*(2), 25–32.

MLA

Coast, James. "Environmentally Safe Insecticides." <u>Consumer Digest</u> 23.2 (1974): 25–32.

Government document:

Chicago Manual

U.S. Congress. 1985. House. Committee on Foreign Relations. *Report on aid to South Africa*. 98th Cong., 2nd sess. Washington, DC: Government Printing Office.

APA

U.S. Congress. House. Committee on Foreign Relations. (1985). *Report on aid to South Africa*. 98th Cong. 2nd Sess. Washington, DC: U.S. Government Printing Office.

MLA

United States. Cong. House. Committee on Foreign Relations. <u>Report on Aid to South Africa</u>. 98th Cong., 2nd sess. Washington: GPO, 1985.

Legal Citations:

Chicago Manual *(Editor's note:* The Chicago Manual of Style *provides little guidance for legal citations used in nonlegal writing or general works. It is important that the reference include case names, the year, volume number of the reporter series, the abbreviated name of the court, and page number. See sections 17:283-17.289 for more examples and details.)*

Washington v. Davis. 1976. 96 S.Ct. 2040.

APA

Washington v. Davis. 96 S.Ct. 2040. (1976).

MLA

Washington v. Davis. 96 S.Ct. 2040. 1976.

Newspaper or magazine article:

Chicago Manual *(Editor's Note: While* The Chicago Manual of Style *recommends against including the page number for a newspaper, it is good practice in academics to include the page number. See Section 17.188).*

Greenberger, Robert S. 1981. Hottest labor consultant in Washington adopts new right techniques to bolster union's image. *The Wall Street Journal*, October 23, sec. B3.

APA

Greenberger, Robert S. (1981, October 23). Hottest labor consultant in Washington adopts new right techniques to bolster union's image. *The Wall Street Journal*, p. B3.

MLA

Greenberger, Robert S. "Hottest Labor Consultant in Washington Adopts New Right Techniques to Bolster Union's Image." <u>The Wall Street Journal</u> 23 October 1981: B3.

Newspaper article with no author:

Chicago Manual *(Editor's Note:* The Chicago Manual of Style *prefers that the reference for newspaper articles begins with the source, not the title of the work. See Section 17:192.)*

New York Times. 1999. Dr. King's widow testifies in a civil trial, November 17, sec. A16.

APA

Dr. King's widow testifies in a civil trial. (1999, November 17). *New York Times,* p. A16.

MLA

"Dr. King's Widow Testifies in a Civil Trial," <u>New York Times</u> 17 November 1999: A16.

Source without an author (except for newspapers):

Chicago Manual

SAS user's guide. 1992. Cary, NC: SAS Institute.

APA

SAS user's guide. (1992). Cary, NC: SAS Institute.

MLA

<u>SAS User's Guide</u>. Cary, NC: SAS Institute. 1992.

Personal interviews:

Chicago Manual

Simon, Paul. 1998. Personal interview. August 12.

APA

Simon, Paul. (1998, August 12). Personal interview.

MLA

Simon, Paul. Personal Interview. 12 August 1998.

Online Database:

Editor's Note: Online databases often provide the user with an option for viewing a PDF or HTML version of the document. A PDF document should be referenced as though it were viewed in its original format because it is just a picture of that material. An HTML version of the material has been reformatted. Because it has been reformatted, it must be referenced as a product of the online service. For most styles, the HTML reference should include the citation of the main directory of the database. Although some styles do not require a date of access, it is good practice to include it in the citation for HTML versions of a document.

Chicago Manual (*See section 17.359*)

Chanen, Jill Schachner. 2000. Daddy's home. *ABA Journal* 86(11): 90. http://www.epnet.com (accessed August 27, 2003).

APA

Chanen, Jill Schachner. (2000). Daddy's home. *ABA Journal, 86* (11), 90. Retrieved August 27, 2003, from Academic Search database.

MLA

Chanen, Jill Schachner. "Daddy's Home." <u>ABA Journal</u> 86.11 (2000): 90. <u>Academic Search</u>. 27 Aug. 2003 <http://www.epnet.com>.

For an Internet Source:

(Editor's Note: When the Internet source does not have a date of publication, the date the site was last updated or created is sufficient. Occasionally, a Internet source will not have any date. In this event, use the abbreviation for no date—"n.d."—in place of the year.)

Organizational Web Site Internet Source:

Chicago Manual

AFL-CIO. 1999. Working families need a voice: Who's behind it? 14 January. http://www.aflcio.org/silence/behind.html (accessed July 19, 1999).

APA

AFL-CIO. (1999, January 14). *Working families need a voice: Who's behind it?* Retrieved July 19, 1999, from http://www.aflcio.org/silence/behind.html

MLA

AFL-CIO. <u>Working Families Need a Voice: Who's Behind It?</u> 14 January 1999. 19 July 1999 <http://www.aflcio.org/silence/behind.html>.

Electronic Journal Web Site Internet Source:

Chicago Manual

Harris, J., 1999. Clinton proposes increased child care subsidies. *Amarillo Business Journal* 3 (2). http://businessjournal.net/stories/020698/child.html (accessed August 25, 1999).

APA

Harris, J. (1999). Clinton proposes increased childcare subsidies. *Amarillo Business Journal, 3*(2). Retrieved August 25, 1999, from http://businessjournal.net/stories/020698/child.html

MLA

Harris, J., "Clinton Proposes Increased Child Care Subsidies." <u>Amarillo Business Journal</u>, 3.2 (1999). 25 August 1999 <http://businessjournal.net/stories/020698/child.html>.

Electronic Magazine Web Site Internet Source:

Chicago Manual

Rosenberg, Debra. 1999. More than just a kiss: Hillary's conflicted life as first lady and candidate. *Newsweek*, November 22. http://www.newsweek.com/nw-srv/printed/us/na/a55101-1999nov14.htm (accessed November 17, 1999).

APA

Rosenberg, Debra. (1999, November 22). More than just a kiss: Hillary's conflicted life as first lady and candidate. *Newsweek*. Retrieved November 17, 1999, from http://www.newsweek.com/nw-srv/printed/us/na/a55101-1999nov14.htm

MLA

Rosenberg, Debra. "More Than Just a Kiss: Hillary's Conflicted Life as First Lady and Candidate." <u>Newsweek</u>, 22 November 1999. 17 November 1999 <http://www.newsweek.com/nw-srv/printed/us/na/a55101-1999nov14.htm>.

Government Site Internet Source:

Chicago Manual

National Labor Relations Board. 1999. National Labor Relations Board members. February 17. http://www.nlrb.gov/members.html (accessed July 14, 1999).

APA

National Labor Relations Board. (1999, February 17). *National Labor Relations Board members.* Retrieved July14, 1999, from http://www.nlrb.gov/members.html

MLA

National Labor Relations Board. <u>National Labor Relations Board Members</u>. 17 February 1999. 14 July 1999 <http://www.nlrb.gov/members.html>.

Informally Published Electronic Material Internet Source: **(Editor's Note: Include as much information as possible [author of the content, title or owner of the site, title of the page, URL]. Although** The Chicago Manual of Style *recommends against including the creation date of the Web site, it is good practice to include the creation date and the access date to inform the reader about the currency of the site and its material.)*

Chicago Manual

Brown, Jon. 1998. Homepage. October 24. http://www.polsci.swms.edu/brown/personal.htm (accessed July 8, 1999).

APA

Brown, Jon. (1998, October 24). *Homepage.* Retrieved July 8, 1999, from http://www.polsci.swms.edu/brown/personal.htm

MLA

Brown, Jon. Homepage. 24 October 1998. 8 July 1999 <http://www.polsci.swms.edu/brown/personal.htm>.

CHAPTER 9

Format and Examples for Activities to Enhance Comprehension and Synthesis of Class Materials

Enhancing Comprehension and Synthesis of Class Materials

Instructors often require special kinds of assignments to help prepare students for professional research and to develop analytical skills. Rather than simply reading the material and taking a test on the facts, or writing a descriptive term paper or essay, students are asked to process the information in some way that will help them to synthesize the material for use later on. Sometimes the assignments enhance comprehension and understanding of a particular concept or theory. In particular, the assignments are structured to help students develop research and problem-solving skills. Developing such skills encourages students to integrate and synthesize the material in a meaningful and productive way.

Although many of the standards and rules that apply to research papers and essays apply to special assignments, there are some differences. These differences are generally found in the purpose and properties of each kind of activity. The following descriptions encompass a traditional approach to each assignment. Be sure to consult your instructor for specific requirements that are additional to those described in this chapter. Each description is followed by a written example.

List of special activities described in this chapter:

> **ANALYTICAL ESSAYS**
> **ANALYTICAL MULTIPLE CHOICE QUESTIONS**
> **ESSAY EXAMS**
> **LITERATURE REVIEW PRESENTATIONS**

Writing Analytical Essays

Analytical essays are usually very limited assignments. Like essay exam answers, they are meant to be brief but well-reasoned and thorough examinations of some political theory, phenomenon, or behavior. Like a research paper, the evidence used to support an argument in an analytical essay should be source based. Most often, the instructor will provide source material in a reader or class packet. Sometimes instructors provide students with a particular question to answer or debate using course materials. The students are to take a position and support it using expert opinion. Here is a description of how to construct an analytical essay:

1. **Examine the limits and expectations stated by the instructor for the assignment**.
   - If a particular question must be answered, be sure you understand the context, limitations, and focus of the question before researching.
   - If a particular set of readings are required as sources for the essay, be sure that you have read them at least once while focusing on the issues required by the instructor.
   - Before using any materials other than those required or suggested by the instructor, ask the instructor if it is permissible to include additional sources.

2. **After reading the material, formulate an answer to the question.**
   - Use the introduction for briefly describing the context in which you are answering the question.
   - State your position clearly in a thesis statement.
   - Summarize the answer to the question in one sentence.
   - Be sure that the thesis sentence provides both an answer and a justification or reason.
   - Avoid vague or ambiguous thesis sentences.
   - Be bold, be obvious, be direct, but do not be rhetorical!

3. **Use the assigned material as evidence supporting each reason you stated in your position.**
   - Do not outline the articles or materials used as a source.
   - Assert one idea or one justification of your position per paragraph.
   - Use the assigned material to support your assertion.
   - Use the assigned material to provide examples, if necessary.
   - Avoid quoting altogether.
   - Summarize the sources' viewpoints in one or two sentences.

4. **Write a conclusion that re-asserts your position.**
   - Briefly review the main reasons why your position is valid.
   - Offer some suggestion about the value of examining the issue identified in the assignment or question given to you by the instructor.

5. **A standard two-page analytical essay should be no longer than six paragraphs**.
   - The essay should have an introduction, an explanatory paragraph for each reason given, and a conclusion.
   - Be concise and do not waste words.
   - Provide a Works Cited page for essays using assigned readings. If the readings were taken from only one source (such as a reader or packet), provide a complete reference for the source, *then* list each item referenced from that source with authors, titles, and page numbers. Provide full bibliographic references if referencing multiple sources.

"Why Should We Worry About a Judge's Ideology if Judicial Decisions Are Based on Precedent and the Constitution?"

An Analytical Essay

By
Jean M. Schuberth
Professor Schmidt
GEB 114, SEC. 3
NOVEMBER 29, 1990
(Reprinted with permission)

Judicial review has been considered a political issue since the framing of the constitution. Supreme Court Justices interpreted policy and used judicial discretion to define law and to set or overturn precedents. As a nation of people who believe in limited government and equal protection, discretion with which a judge makes decisions is at the source of concern over judicial power. In particular, if well harnessed by an ideological coalition, the act of interpreting law leaves significant opportunity for abuse of judicial power and the introduction of political bias.

Alexander Hamilton believed that the judicial system was the least powerful of the three branches of government. He argued that the court's power did not outweigh the other branches by interpreting the law because it was bound to interpretations that are consistent to the constitution. Hamilton stated that the legislative branch had controlled the money and "prescribes" the laws and rights of the community (Hamilton 1990, 567). This statement, however, was irrelevant to the power of interpreting law. Interpreting laws prescribes laws and rights to the people, as well as by ruling what can and cannot be done constitutionally. American history reflects an important change in rights and obligations when judicial decisions over-rule precedent as being unfair and unconstitutional (Marbury v. Madison 1990, 573).

A judge's ideology is significant from the standpoint that the Supreme Court makes law. Because judges are empowered to interpret the law, they have the opportunity to substitute their personal interpretation of laws. They control not only how laws are interpreted, but also when precedents apply to a case. Only when judicial self-restraint is being utilized for the sake of non-confrontation and non-intervention will a judge's views seem unbiased (Roche 1990, 577). Even then, it is questionable that precedent in this case, as interpreted by Justices, does not exist. Self-restraint allows the opportunity for a coalition of judges to interpret policy again later when a stronger case representing their ideological viewpoints can be used to overturn decisions. A passive attitude by the judiciary can reflect as much ideological input as one which is dominated by an activist court (Roche 1990, 581).

Supreme Court decisions are supposed to be reasoned by precedent and constitutionality. Unfortunately, interpretation of the constitution depends on individual Justices to put aside their individual perspectives. Justices are obliged to overcome personal needs, use authority responsibly, and at the same time reinterpret, give new definition, reword, and revise the law (Brennan 1990, 583). This is nearly impossible to do. Consequently, judicial decisions reflect a personal ideology based upon individual moral and ethical beliefs experienced as a member of society. Because the role of the Supreme Court judge involves not only interpretation, but choosing which issues to try under law (Brennan 1990, 585), the choice and processing of cases often reflect judges' community or environmental experiences. Based upon the legitimate excuse that the thousands of cases received are too many to handle, judicial discretion is necessary for managing and controlling the judicial agenda. In this process, a decision to rule on a case or not will reflect a judge's ideology, if not biases.

The American constitution, as the law of the land, is a remarkable document with elaborate checks to constrain particular interests abusing power or exhibiting political favoritism at a minority's expense. The judicial branch has no special exemption to these checks. Unfortunately, judicial decisions are as difficult to question as they are to overturn. Individual biases are masked by the aura of an interpreted constitutionality and enhanced by coalitions within the Supreme Court who set, decide, and pursue political agendas reflecting their individual, moral, and political beliefs. A judge's ideology is important to safeguarding political rights and protections because, in coalition, a judge's ideology is the mechanism that helps to define what the constitution means, as well as what principles and precedents apply to interpreting the constitution.

WORKS CITED

(All references taken from Peter Woll, ed., *American Government: Readings and Cases*, 10th ed., Glenview, IL: Scott Foresman/Little, Brown Higher Education, 1990.)

Brennan Jr., William J. "How the Supreme Court Arrives at Decisions," pp. 603–613.
Hamilton, Alexander. "Federalist 78," pp. 566–570.
"Marbury *v* Madison (1803)," pp. 571–575.
Roche, John P. "Judicial Self-Restraint," pp. 576–582.

Writing Political Editorials

Editorials, like analytical essays, are usually very limited assignments. Yet like analytical essays, editorials are meant to be brief but well-reasoned examinations of some specific phenomenon or behavior. Unlike an analytical essay or a research paper, the evidence used to support an argument in an analytical essay need not be source based. Unlike the analytical essay, the tone and language used is casual, emotive, and value laden. Most often, editorials are composed of more opinion than fact in the evidence and reasoning. In other words, they are thoughtful expressions of the author's **views** on political phenomena. The purpose of the editorial is not only to express views but also to persuade others to adopt the same views. Writing editorials, even if they are not published, helps students work on critical thinking and political argument techniques without the constraints of sources and secondary evidence. The students are to take a position and support it using reasons, logic, and, yes, even facts if necessary! Here is a description of how to construct an editorial:

Formulating an Opinion

1. **Identify and research an important salient issue.**
   - The best editorials are those that exhibit knowledge, authority, and passion about an issue.
   - Use course materials for background information.
   - Talk to people and read about the issue in a variety of sources.
   - Gather ideas and viewpoints; analyze them on the basis of credibility.
2. **Formulate a *reasoned* opinion.**
   - Students must have a reason for every assertion they make in the editorial.
   - Every assertion must have a justification.
   - Assert one idea or one justification of your position per paragraph.
   - Assertions without reasons and justifications can be easily ignored.
3. **Keep in mind most editorials are only about 300 to 600 words.**
   - Use a highly emotive, assertive, active voice with a tone of conviction.
   - Avoid jargon and formal language.
   - Keep the paragraphs and sentences short and simple.

Format for the Editorial

While there is no set format for an editorial, most editorials generally follow a pattern. The order and number of the paragraphs can be changed a bit with the exception of the first and last paragraph. Often, people read only the first and last paragraphs of editorials in the newspaper. Because of this, the first and last paragraphs contain a concise but compelling assertion about what the issue is (the first paragraph) and what should be done about it (the last paragraph). All the material between these two important paragraphs serve as justification for the assertions.

1. **First paragraph:**
   - Begin the editorial with a controversial or compelling example or comment.
   - State succinctly what is wrong or right about a decision made or action taken concerning the issue.
   - Tell what should be done.

2. **Second paragraph:**
   - Provide context or background information about the event.
   - Focus on what happened before the event.
   - State why what happened before was better or worse than the event at issue.

3. **Third paragraph:**
   - Tell how the current situation is in opposition or contrary to the previous situation.
   - Explain concisely how the current situation differs from the past practices.

4. **Fourth paragraph:**
   - Provide more contextual examples.
   - Provide more examples that are illustrative of the issue at its worst.
   - Provide a compelling anecdote.

5. **Fifth paragraph:**
   - State strongly why you believe that this situation (policy, etc.) is good or bad.
   - Provide reasons for your assertions.
   - Provide a solution to help resolve the issue.

6. **Sixth paragraph:**
   - Forecast or suggest what will happen because of this situation.
   - Tell what the future will look like if the situation is left unchanged.

7. **Seventh paragraph:**
   - Restate why the result of an unchanged situation is good or bad.
   - Provide reasons for why it is good or bad.

8. **Last paragraph:**
   - Restate the issue.
   - Restate your opinion about how to resolve the issue.
   - End with a compelling statement or rhetorical question.

Example of an Editorial

YOUNG VOICES

JUST A HOUSEWIFE? THINK ABOUT IT A BIT LONGER!

What's your impression of this ad? CEO wanted for nonprofit organization: Duties: budget planning and administration, task delegation, scheduling of activities, training and teaching, implementation of the nutrition program, plus miscellaneous duties. Prerequisites: enormous patience, organizational skills, flexibility, ability to handle emergencies efficiently, and an abundance of love and devotion. This position is voluntary, unpaid, and not highly regarded by society.

Who in their right mind would work for no pay? Believe it or not, there are millions of women out there who do this every day. Their title may not be CEO; on the contrary, they all too often refer to themselves as "just a housewife." Why is this honorable profession so terribly underrated in our society? It may just be envy.

Like so many moms on campus, we try to do it all, yet we always feel inadequate. Somehow, it is never enough. Besides, it is very unfashionable to admit that what some of us really want is an old-fashioned style family; it's almost like saying a dirty word.

Women have made great strides for equality and shouldn't face any societal barriers to reaching their full potential. But I think the scale has tipped to where we have to do it all in order to be appreciated.

Just look at the Republican-crafted Welfare Reform Bill. All it accomplishes is forcing mothers out of the home away from small kids who are still in their most impressionable years. Single mothers are mostly affected by this and are not considered in the Republican emphasis on family values.

This implies that it's more acceptable for a mother to have a career than to be a housewife and mother, regardless of marital status. This sentiment even includes men. With few, but very notable exceptions, men on the average don't want to solely provide for a family. It seems to trigger the "fight or flight response," just like the M-word. What contributed to this? Do they feel that women have expectations they can't fulfill?

Maybe we as a group portray that image by chasing after high-paying/high-prestige careers—like the one I am chasing out of pure necessity.

A satisfying career has its definite rewards, but it still falls short of the joys of full-time motherhood. I had a glimpse of that during my maternity leave.

My daughter is now 3 years old and I'm used to this rat race, but I still long for baking cookies with Santa Faces, ironing a crease into a pair of suit pants right where it belongs (I do know how to do that stuff), cooking a meal that appeals to adult taste-buds and is not yet another variety of Hamburger Helper, and asking a stressed-out, grumpy, traditional male prototype how his day went.

I'm not advocating the burning of Betty Friedan's "Feminine Mystique," nor have I just discovered that my childbearing years are down to single digits or overdosed on gender studies.

This doesn't come from an escapee from the conservative camp, but from a woman who benches 175 pounds, has fired a machine gun for a living, and hopes for the cloning of Hillary Rodham Clinton. Now that I have confessed and come out of the closet, the National Organization for Women will probably put a contract out on me.

It's just about choices. Choices subtly diminish once the maternal side kicks in, and one soon discovers that the day really has only 24 hours.

I'm far from saying that the three Ks (Kinder, Kueche, and Kirche) are for all women, but defying nature carries a cost that I'm getting tired of bearing.

Christine N. Rueda-Lynn is a columnist
for *The Southwest Standard* at Southwest
Missouri State University.
Reprinted in *Springfield News Leader*
Dec. 1, 1997, p. 8a
(Reprinted by permission)

Analytical Multiple-Choice Exams

Although taking exams is not considered a special assignment, taking an analytical multiple-choice exam is different from the average multiple-choice exam. To perform well on an analytical multiple-choice exam, students must use the same skills they use in essay writing.

- These exams require knowledge, good reading habits, and critical thinking skills.
- In analytical multiple-choice questions, there are no funny answers, no "all of the above," no "none of the above," and no questions where students must find the wrong answer in the group.
- Students must differentiate between closely related information or concepts.
- Students must understand how information, concepts, and explanations of political behavior or events are influenced by the context in which they are examined.
- The answers to analytical multiple-choice questions can rarely be guessed.
- The answers require well-reasoned responses and rarely exhibit a pattern.

Tips for Answering Analytical Multiple-Choice Questions

The questions used in an analytical multiple-choice exam are typically either factual, definitional, conceptual, or practical applications. They are best approached as essay questions! Do the following before answering the question:

1. **Determine what kind of question is being asked.**
2. **Identify the important modifiers and qualifiers in the question.**
   - If you are allowed to write on the exam question sheet, underline the key words or concepts and circle the modifiers and qualifiers.
     - Exact words, such as *always, never, none, must, necessarily*, and *without exception* mean there is no exception. If you can think of one exception, statements including these are false.
     - Indefinite words, such as *rarely, usually, seldom, some, sometimes, often*, and *frequently* suggest that the statement is true in context. How often it is true depends on the degree connoted by the indefinite word used.

- Think about how these words change or influence the meaning of the concepts or facts listed.

3. **Cover the answers or do not look at them until you think of an answer.**
    - If you are allowed to write on the exam question sheet, make a quick list of the properties of the concept, theory, document, or whatever the focus of the question is. At least visualize the answer.
    - Use critical thinking skills and logic to reason the answer if you are unsure of the correct answer to the question.
        - Do not let personal value judgments and ideology sway you.
        - Often these questions provoke biased responses and those responses are usually wrong!
        - Visualize an answer that conforms to what the instructor intended.
    - Then look at the list of responses available.
        - Match your answer with the list of responses.
        - If your answer does not match exactly with one of the choices, then find the choice that most closely approximates your answer.
        - If you are still in doubt, re-read the question and use logical reasoning to find the answer.
        - If you are still in doubt, use a process of elimination by considering the deficiencies in each choice available. Choose the one with the fewest problems.

4. **Never leave a question blank unless you will lose more points for answering that question wrong than for answering it correctly. This is generally not true of political science course exams.**

5. **Do not hurry, but do not linger too long. Answer the question and move on. Make a note to return to questions with doubtful answers after you have finished the exam.**

Examples of Analytical Multiple-Choice Test Questions

Factual

> The Constitution establishes three policy-making institutions:
> A. the House, the bureaucracy, and the presidency.
> B. Congress, the presidency, and the courts.
> C. Congress, the presidency, and the presidential cabinet.
> D. Congress, the presidency, and the bureaucracy.

This question requires both depth and breadth of understanding about what the Constitution establishes and what bodies make public policy. The important modifiers are the words "establishes" and "policy-making." A and D are incorrect because the bureaucracy was not established by the Constitution as a policy-making institution. C is incorrect because the presidency includes the cabinet. B is the answer because all three institutions make decisions that result in policy.

Definition

> _____ is a means of selecting policy makers and of organizing government so that policy represents and responds to the majority of the people's preferences.
>
> A. Populism
>
> B. Pure Democracy
>
> C. Socialism
>
> D. Representative Democracy

This question requires an understanding of theoretical concepts. The important modifiers in this question are "means of selecting," "organizing government," "represents," and "responds to." A is incorrect because populism is an ideology, not a system of government. C is incorrect because socialism is really an economic system and does not help to organize representative government. B is incorrect because pure democracy does not organize representative government. Only D is correct because, under representative democracy, policy makers answer to an electorate.

Conceptual

> In the American electorate, the majority of voters are:
>
> A. moderately liberal.
>
> B. moderates.
>
> C. moderately libertarian.
>
> D. moderately conservative.

This question taps into the reader's personal ideology, value system, and the median voter concept. The important modifier is "majority." For some students, the answer may seem to be a matter of perspective. Unfortunately, the answer, which is supported by numerous studies of the voters, is B. Answers A and D are a matter of degree. C is incorrect because libertarians are a very small portion of the electorate.

Application

> It is up to political elites in public office to actually make policy choices for the majority because American government is _____ rather than a pure democracy.
>
> A. majoritarian
>
> B. representative
>
> C. pluralist
>
> D. elitist

This question asks students to apply what they know about who makes decisions in different kinds of democracies. The important modifiers are "actually make policy choice."

The words "elites" and "majority" are not modifiers; they identify who is doing what for whom. The answer requires that the student understand the four terms well enough to apply them. C and D are incorrect because they are different theories of politics; they are not theories of the organization of government and decision-making. Although our government is majoritarian, in a majoritarian government, the majority makes the rules. In our system, representatives make decisions for the majority. This means B is the answer.

Essay Exams

Many students are uneasy about taking essay exams. Although they may write well, they are reluctant to take essay tests because it may not be clear what is expected. Essay exams are another way of synthesizing information. Here are a couple of suggestions for reading and interpreting an answer to an essay question.

1. **An essay question may contain one or more important terms.** (See Writing a Thesis for an Essay) For example, here is an essay question concerning the congressional budget process:

> "Describe and analyze the budget process. Provide reasons why each step exists."

In this case, the student must be careful to address **all** parts of the question. Just listing the information is not enough; the student must also demonstrate knowledge of why each step is important.

2. **Students must be careful, especially when answering questions that ask for criticisms or evaluations, that each assertion (or point) is supported with evidence or examples.**

3. **The question should be answered directly. Underline the key verbs and modifiers which structure or limit the scope of the question.**

4. **The thesis sentence of an answer to this essay question should repeat the key terms of the question and lay out the writer's main points.**
   - In short essays, the thesis sentence should be the first sentence.
   - In longer essays, the thesis should be in the first paragraph.

5. **Address only one idea per paragraph.**
   - Be sure to use a topic sentence, an explanatory sentence, and a summary sentence in each paragraph.
   - Use transitional words, such as *first, second, in addition*, or *thus* to organize and link ideas from paragraph to paragraph.
   - Most importantly, be obvious—do not be obtuse. Make your points clearly, simply, and directly.

6. **Time and space are usually limited during an essay exam so students must use them efficiently.**
   - If each essay contributes equally to the grade, then divide the number of essays by the number of minutes and allot equal amounts to each.
   - If each essay does not contribute equally to the grade, determine the amount of time to spend on each by the proportion of each essay's contribution to the grade.

> Group theorists argue that public policy can be defined as the equilibrium that is reached in a group struggle. Explain this theory and offer an alternative, competing explanation of how public policy can be defined. Which one is preferable? Why?

By
Edward Pettit

Pluralist theory is only one of numerous such theories about how public policy is formulated. Though pluralist theory has its strong points, it does not explain how institutional structures constrain possible policy outcomes. Institutions theory offers a competing explanation about how policy is formulated. Unfortunately, institutions theory does not explain why public policy reflects the values of groups who are not part of the policy-making institution. Because of this, institutions theory can be considered less preferable than the pluralist theory for explaining policy-making.

Pluralist theory essentially states that group struggle is the central force of politics, and that policies, including the goals, the means, and the outcomes, are directly attributable to group conflict. This theory states that individuals are important only when working in a group. Policy is defined, according to pluralist theory, as the compromise between competing groups and reflects the relative influence of each group. Although it does not account for why policy varies from institution to institution, it does explain why policy content reflects a dominant group's values.

In institutions theory, policy only results when a policy proposal is stated, adopted, implemented, and enforced by an institution. The institution provides a policy legitimacy, universality, and the coercive force necessary to enforce it equally across the populace. The structure of the policy-making institution provides both the means and constraints to formulating policy responses to public problems.

This policy definition is vastly different from the pluralist view because institutions, not people or groups, legitimize policy. It is, however, deficient because it does not state anything significant about policy content. Because policy content and institutional structure are not logically related, the institutional theory cannot explain why policy content benefits some more than others in society. In the pluralist theory, policy content represents group struggle and the dominant group's influence over the policy response and related benefits. Thus, pluralist theory explains variations in policy responses and why some groups benefit at the publics expense.

Both the pluralist and institutional models of policy formulation offer explanations of policy responses, but the pluralist model is more comprehensive because it explains, to a certain extent, not just how policy is made, but why it is made. While the institutional model explains the formal processes of public policy-making, it does not account for variations in policy content. Hence, although the process of policy making is important, pluralist theory models explain policy outcomes more directly and clearly than the institutional model.

Scholarly Literature Review Presentations

Class presentations on scholarly literature provide students the opportunity to examine different approaches and controversies not covered in the lectures or textbook. Often, the subject of the presentation is a scholarly article or book that provided a path-breaking method or conceptual examination important to building a knowledge community in political science.

Tips for Writing a Literature Review Presentation

1. **A literature review typically includes:**
   - a statement of the author's purpose.
   - an identification of the author's hypothesis.
   - a description of the issue, context, and assumptions.
   - a description of the controversy.
   - an explanation of how the controversy was examined.
   - a description of the author's findings.
   - a concluding statement about the significance of the work.

2. **A literature review presentation is generally graded with the same criteria used to grade written assignments.**
   - Students' grades usually reflect the quality and thoroughness with which they presented the material contained in the categories listed.
   - A literature review presentation is frequently graded on the degree to which the student identified the critical information provided in the scholarly book or article.
   - A solid performance by the student demonstrates depth and breadth of understanding the significance of the work related to the subfield or topic area.

3. **To write your presentation, outline the article or book using the above categories.**
   - The length and degree of detail in the presentation outline will depend on the time allotted for the presentation or the page limit set by the instructor.
   - In general, the outline should be approximately two-and-a-half pages typed in outline form.

4. **Exhibit poise and confidence (try rehearsing).**
   - Be prepared to answer questions of clarification.
   - Vary the voice level, make eye contact with other students, and use gestures.
   - Do not read word for word from the outline. Address the audience in a causal, conversational tone, but avoid rambling from point to point.

Literature Presentation Form

A literature review presentation typically includes the same material as a research presentation, except that the expectation for a clear grasp of the content is somewhat lower than it would be for a description of a student's own research findings.

Purpose: A clear statement of the purpose and focus of the article or book.

Hypothesis: A clear statement of the controversy identified by the author and the hypothesis tested. State the causal relationships clearly in terms of dependent and independent variables.

Background: A brief discussion of the context and background related to the controversy or the assumptions used to justify the model. Note any value assumptions that are controversial in nature.

Method: An explanation of the method used for testing or examining the hypothesis.

- Describe the source materials used.
- Point out any problems identified by the author related to the gathering of data.
- Be sure to relate the data and source materials to the hypothesis.

Results: A summary of the results of the examination or test.

- If data were used, reproduce illustrative charts, graphs, or tables as visual aids.
- Use a table or chart to summarize the author's main points.
- Use an overhead projector to present the material or make copies of a visual aid for everyone.

Conclusion: This statement explains how the goals of the author were accomplished. In particular, this statement summarizes how the results relate to the author's stated goals.

Significance: A statement that applies the results appropriately to an expansion of knowledge about the subject.

Example of a Scholarly Literature Presentation

AN ARTICLE REVIEW

I. **Purpose**: To review classic innovative article on voting.

   A. **Source**: Gerald Kramer. 1971. "Short-term Fluctuations in U.S. Voting Behavior 1896–1964," *American Political Science Review*, 65: 131–143.

   B. **Author's purpose**: to provide a quantitative analysis of short-term fluctuations in voting share for U.S. House of Representatives elections with respect to the impact of economic conditions, incumbency advantage, and the presidential coattails effect.

II. **Hypothesis**: Tests several competing and complementary hypotheses about influences on electoral outcomes. He argues that economic fluctuations have a greater impact on voting in House elections than political influences, such as coattail effects.

III. **Background**:

   A. Author reviews some of the literature about influence on voting behavior.

   1. Institutional advantage of the incumbent or incumbency advantage theory is problematic. Only an advantage when expectations are low for benefits. Could be a liability if expectations of voters' personal incomes are not realized.

   2. Party popularity may influence outcomes. House races come closest to Downesian model of anonymous candidates competing as members of a common team. Variations in overall popularity of the party could be a major factor in producing fluctuations in short-term voting behavior.

   3. Incumbent party is usually defined as the party of the president because the president's influence over the policy agenda is greater than that of an individual member of congress.

   4. A vote for the minor party is considered an anti-incumbent vote and is counted as part of the major opposition party vote.

   5. The coattails effect of a presidential race is reflected in the party as a team.

   B. Author makes several assumptions about behavior.

   1. An individual vote represents a choice between teams in the national election.

   2. People base their decisions on past information.

   3. People's expectations are based on the preceding year's events; they are retrospective, not prospective voters.

IV. **Method**: Uses statistical analysis to test relative impact of different influences on vote choice based on the literature review and methodological assumptions.

   A. Model: States that the Republican party's share of a two-party vote is a function of incumbency, the difference between the actual and the expected performance, and net institutional advantage.

   B. Creates a formal, testable model of voting behavior using the following variables.

   1. Dependent variable: Republican party share of votes.

       2. Independent variables: monetary income, real income, unemployment rate, time period, and coattails term.

   C. Uses data gathered from 1896–1964.

       1. Data collected from various government documents.

       2. Left out years 1912 (inability to explain progressive votes), 1918, 1942, and 1944 (wartime distortion of income and prices).

V. **Results**: Used six different forms of the model as an equation to test his hypothesis.

   A. The variables measuring expected prices and unemployment have an inverse relationship to the dependent variable.

   B. All forms of the model explain a large portion of the variance in voting behavior.

       1. Two-thirds of the variance explained by time variable.

       2. Explanatory power of the model is weaker without the time variable. Only half of the variance is explained.

       3. The income variable was significant and powerful in all the equations.

       4. The price variable was only significant with the monetary variable, but not with real income variable.

       5. The unemployment variable was not significant and the direction of influence is counter to theory. Author proposes that unemployment variable is distorted because unemployed people are disproportionately less active politically.

       6. Coattails variable was not significant. Author proposed that result was biased because the minor party vote was included in the measure because of split ticket voting. When minor party vote removed from coattail variable, it became significant.

VI. **Overall finding**: Approximately one-third of the votes gained or lost in a presidential race are carried over into congressional candidate races.

   A. Finds limits of the model. Model cannot identify or predict turning points in an election but can predict Republican vote shares.

   B. The most important determinant of vote choice is income not incumbency advantage or coattails effect. A 10 percent decrease in real income will lead to a four to five percent loss of votes for the incumbent party.

   C. Coattails effect helps only when there is a strong presidential candidate. Can increase vote share by thirty percent.

   D. The incumbent party only has an advantage when the economy is doing well.

VII. **Significance**:

   A. Economic fluctuations are important to congressional elections. An upturn helps the incumbent and a downturn helps the challenger.

   B. Found that election outcomes are more responsive to objective changes occurring under the incumbent party than to political changes.

CHAPTER 10

Format and Examples of
Assignments for Managing
and Processing Information

Assignments for Managing and Processing Information

> "We start out stupid. All we have at the beginning is the built-in wisdom
> of the body, which tells us which end to eat with…and not much more.
> But we are put here to do battle with entropy, and entropy equals stu-
> pidity. Therefore, we are obliged to learn. Our job is to process infor-
> mation and gain control of it: that is to say, to grow wiser as we go along"
> (Silverberg 1986, 225).

As suggested by this quote, the soul of investigation is to control information. It is not
enough to collect information for the sake of it. To become professionals, students must
acquire the skills necessary for managing and processing information of interest to political scientists. A paper written by someone without a method, without good research skills,
without problem-solving skills, or without the ability to synthesize the information available, is not much better than amateur journalism.

To prepare students for more complex research, instructors often require students to do
special kinds of assignments to help them organize for professional research and develop
analytical skills. Rather than simply reading the material and taking a test on the facts or
writing a descriptive term paper or essay, students are asked to process the information in
some way that will help synthesize the material for use later on or just to enhance
comprehension and understanding of a particular concept or theory. In particular, the
assignments are structured to help students develop research and problem-solving skills.
More importantly, developing such skills encourages students to integrate and synthesize
the material in a meaningful and productive way.

Although many of the standards and rules that apply to research papers and essays
also apply to special assignments, there are some differences. These differences are generally found in the purpose and properties of each kind of assignment. The following
descriptions encompass a traditional approach taken to complete each assignment. Be
sure to consult your instructor for specific requirements that are additional to those
described in this chapter. Each description is followed by a written example.

List of special assignments described in this chapter:

> **ANNOTATED BIBLIOGRAPHIES**
> **BOOK REVIEWS**
> **BRIEFING CASES**
> **OUTLINES**
> **PRESENTATIONS**
> **RESEARCH PROPOSALS**

Annotated Bibliographies

Purpose of an Annotated Bibliography

An annotated bibliography is essentially a list of sources or materials (books, articles, etc.) that have been annotated and which relate to one topic. An annotation is a description of the purpose and significance of a source. More importantly, an annotated bibliography helps the student identify the thesis and the significance of research material in political science. It is often used to help students develop pre-writing skills. The research for the assignment should reflect a balance of sources. In addition, it should include scholarly books and articles.

Four Properties of an Annotated Bibliography

Title Page: The title page must be inclusive of the topic or subject of the annotated bibliography, the name of the student, the course number, the professor's name, and the date.

Topic Paragraph: On the second page, there must be a paragraph, at least three sentences long, that states the purpose of the annotated bibliography and a general summary of the sources' ideas.

Sources: The sources or entries are constructed with the same information as a standard bibliography, reference page, or works cited page, and are listed in alphabetical order.

Annotation: An annotation is placed after the citation (skipping one line), and contains at least two full sentences stating:

- One sentence describing the purpose or thesis of the article or book.
- One sentence describing the significance of the findings and conclusions reached in the book or article.
- This assignment may be double-spaced or single-spaced. In general, the topic paragraph is single-spaced. Students should double-space between sources. The annotation to the reference should be single-spaced.

An Example of an Annotated Bibliography

AMERICANS WITH DISABILITIES ACT TITLE I: MINORITY ACKNOWLEDGED

By
Noel Adams
POLS 271a Public Policy Formation
Dr. Diane Schmidt
October 30, 2003
(Reprinted by permission)

Title I of the Americans with Disabilities Act of 1990 was enacted to eliminate discrimination in employment against individuals with disabilities. This annotated bibliography lists sources that assess the impact of Title I of the ADA and its controversial compliance costs. Overall, this literature shows that Title I of the ADA has improved conditions in employment for Americans with disabilities.

Barnart, Sharon and Richard Scotch. 2001. *Disability protests: Contentions politics 1970–1999.* Washington, DC: Gallandet University Press.
Barnartt and Scotch discuss and analyze protest concerning people who have physical and mental impairments. The authors found that many groups were involved in the passage of the ADA, mostly advocacy organizations and members of congress who were disabled or who disabled family members.

Davis, Lennard J. 2002. *Bending over backwards: Disability, dismodemism, and other difficult positions.* NY and London: New York University Press.
Davis argues for a reconsideration of the status of disability in the law, in culture, and in society. Davis presents evidence that the actual cost of ADA compliance has been exaggerated by the courts.

Environments Center, Inc. and R.S. Means Engineering Staff. 1994. *Means ADA compliance pricing guide: Cost data for 75 essential projects.* Kingston, MA: Construction Publishers & Consultants.
The authors provide a guide to the cost and building of ADA compliance modifications. The authors show that creating an accessible workplace is possible and affordable.

Hernandez, Brigida. 2000. Employer attitudes toward workers with disabilities and their ADA employment rights: A literature review. *Journal of Rehabilitation,* 66: 4–17.
Hernandez reviews 37 studies regarding the employer's attitudes toward workers with disabilities. The author finds that employers generally support the ADA as a whole, but small companies tend to be less supportive than large companies.

Johnsen, Matthew C. and Kathryn Moss. 1997. Employment discrimination and the ADA: A study of the administrative complaint process. *Psychiatric Rehabilitation Journal,* 21: 111–22.
Johnsen and Moss study the employment discrimination complaint process for the ADA. The authors found that discrimination complaints filed under the ADA improved benefit rates by 10% more than complaints filed under Section 503 of the Rehabilitation Act.

Kennedy, Jae and Majorie Olney. 2001. Job discrimination in the post-ADA era: Estimates from the 1994 and 1995 National Health Interview surveys. *Rehabilitation Counseling Bulletin,* 45: 24–31.
Using data from the Disability Supplement to the 1994 and 1995 National Health Interview Surveys, Kennedy and Majorie assess the rates of discrimination in employment against adults with disabilities. The authors found that despite the passage of the ADA, employment discrimination is still very prevalent for adults with disabilities.

Stern, Sharon M. and Judith Waldrop. Disability status: 2000. *Census 2000 Brief.* March 2003. Washington, DC: U.S. Census Bureau.
The authors report data regarding disabled persons. The authors found that disabled persons were less likely than others to be employed.

U.S. Congress. 1990. House. Committee of the Whole House on the State of the Union. *Americans with Disabilities Act of 1990.* 101st Cong., 2nd sess. http://www.lexis-nexis.com (accessed October 1, 2003).

Senator Olin and Senator Bartlett propose amendments to Title I of the ADA that deal with the accommodations employers must make for a qualified disabled person. These proposed amendments provide evidence that the cost of complying with the ADA has been controversial.

U. S. Congress, Senate. 1989. Senate Judiciary Committee. *Drugs and drug abuse.* Capitol Hill Hearing. http://www.lexis-nexis.com (accessed October 1, 2003).

Senate members discuss opposition to the inclusion of drug addicts as disabled under the ADA. Senator Walters informed the Senate that negations were underway to exclude drug addicts from characterization as disabled in the workplace under the ADA.

U. S. Congress. 1989. Senate. *Americans with Disabilities Act.* 101st Cong., 1st sess. http://www.lexis-nexis.com (accessed September 24, 2003).

Senate members discuss Title I of the ADA prior to its passage. Senator Hatch and Senator Harkin discuss the appropriate interpretation of the "reasonable accommodation" requirement and the "undue hardship" concept.

U.S. Congress. 1990. Americans with Disabilities Act of 1990. *Public Law 101–336.* 101st Cong., 2nd sess. http://www.lexis-nexis.com (accessed September 24, 2003).

Public Law 101–336 is the Americans with Disabilities Act of 1990. This Public Law presents the guidelines for qualifying disabled persons' and employers.

Book Reviews

Purpose of Book Review Assignments

- To help students develop analytical skills in reading the primary literature in the field of political science.
- To provide an opportunity for students to identify main ideas of the book and help them examine the author's reasoning and evidence.

How to Write a Book Review

1. **Provide a complete reference inclusive of name, title, place of publication, publisher, and date.**
2. **Describe the subject, scope, and purpose of the book.**
3. **Summarize the author's thesis or hypothesis.**
4. **Identify the evidence used to support the thesis.**
5. **Summarize the author's conclusion.**

6. **Critique the argument.**
   - Is it logically sound?
   - Is there a fair balance of opposing viewpoints?
7. **Critique the evidence.**
   - Is it adequate?
   - Is it factual or merely opinion?
   - Is it based on respectable authorities?
   - Is there substantive information?
8. **Critique the author's conclusion.**
   - Does it follow from the evidence presented?
   - Does it generalize beyond the evidence?
9. **Suggest how the book fits into the real world—how does the book relate to current issues or other books on the subject?**
10. **Suggest how the book relates to the material covered in the course—how does it contribute to the body of knowledge in the field?**

Tips for Writing a Book Review

1. **Most books assigned in classes for book reviews have already been reviewed by scholars. Read a review or two before reading the book and reference any ideas borrowed from the review. Look in one of these indexes to find a review:**
   - *Perspective*
   - *Social Science Citation Index*
   - *The Political Science Reviewer*
   - *Book Review Digest*
2. **Look at the Table of Contents, index, reference pages, preface, introduction, and conclusion carefully before reading the text.**
   - Note patterns in the presentation of the ideas.
   - Note the tone of the author.
3. **Read with the purpose of answering and fulfilling the requirements of a book review.**
4. **Assert your perspective or viewpoint about the book, but avoid stating your opinion with shallow words of praise or condemnation.**
5. **Do not use phrases such as "I think…" or "He thinks…". Offer only, as evidence, examples that can be identified explicitly.**
6. **Be sure to answer any questions the instructor has explicitly asked to be addressed in the book review in addition to the requirements for a book review.**
7. **For books that include edited works, summarize the focus of the work in general and use specific examples from an individual author's contributions to support particular hypotheses, theories, or arguments that embellish or explain the focus.**

A
BOOK REVIEW
OF
THE POLITICS OF CONGRESSIONAL ELECTIONS

By
Christopher Walka
Professor Schmidt
POLS 318
December 15, 1990
(Reprinted by permission)

The Politics of Congressional Elections, by Gary C. Jacobson (Boston, MA: Scott, Foresman, and Co. 1987), documents the many concerns and corresponding actions candidates undertake in order to gain political office. The book reduces these myriad factors into three sections: the historical background of the campaign process, the many elements comprising the actual campaign process, and the role of the national party in this election process. Combining statistical tables, graphs, and other informative devices with "real-life" examples candidates have employed, the book balances both parties and their importance to the candidate.

Arguably, the single most important factor to candidates is the electorate. Without their support, the candidate has little or no chance of being elected. Jacobson makes this fact poignantly clear. He provides and explains the uses of a wide range of tactics candidates use to convey their image and issue agenda to the people. Included among these as particularly effective is the use of mass media to emphasize issues important to certain demographic voting areas. Likewise, Jacobson examines incumbency and how it can factor so heavily into the campaign success. Jacobson cites and examines statistics about the re-election rates of particular candidates and corresponding campaign expenditures to show that campaign success heavily depends on incumbency status. He also illuminates efforts of incumbents to quell any challengers, via the use of advertising campaigns well in advance of the traditional election period.

Though advertising serves an important role in the campaign, news coverage is nonetheless important, providing substantive reinforcement to an incumbent's claim of constituency service, or, ammunition for a challenger's heralding claims that the office holder and the voters are not well matched. Elementary to the media's functioning is that of a watchdog over government. Media serve to help winnow out candidates before the nomination process, as well as serving as the medium by which the candidate's agenda is conveyed to the people. Why Jacobson did not address the "news side" of the media and its relation to the candidate remains unexplained.

Similarly, the issue of campaign finance is also important to the candidate. Jacobson sheds considerable light on this issue, examining funding of both parties, how political action committees factor into this, and how incumbents benefit from prior service. Funding the campaign can be a very demanding venture, both from the generation of those funds and the expenditure of those funds. Jacobson illustrates the fact that campaigns have steadily increased in expense with graphics and statistics. This fact, coupled with regulations concerning contributions to candidates, brings out why campaign finance has dramatically increased in its importance to a campaign's viability.

Jacobson also examines the respective national parties and accompanying benefits available to the candidates recognized by the parties. Party affiliation provides many benefits to the candidate, ranging from resources to constituencies, who identify and vote based on their identification with the party. Definitely not a toothless entity, the party helps lend credence to the campaign and the candidate. Similarly, facilities for the production of campaign literature, and other messages to the electorate, can be produced at substantially less cost than private firms charge. Additionally, Jacobson points out that the party helps establish a candidate to the voters: endorsements from other prominent members of the same party lending valiant support to the candidate. Ultimately, voters believe the candidate to be "for real"—worthy of their attention and worth a vote on Election Day.

Jacobson's book examines many aspects of campaigns, the scope is limited to those of congressional positions but nonetheless applicable to lesser offices too. The book balances statistics with actual, documented cases to maintain reader interest. Jacobson concludes that the road to election on the federal level is multi-faceted; these facets are as complex as the positions themselves.

**THE REAGAN ADMINISTRATION'S POLICIES
ON
SOCIAL WELFARE SPENDING: ADVANTAGEOUS OR OTHERWISE**

By
Edward M. Pettit
Professor Schmidt
POLS 324
February 22, 1990
(Reprinted by permission)

Historically, spending for social welfare programs has been the basis for controversy in the political arenas of many countries, especially in the capitalist world. American social spending, and the modern American welfare state in particular, have been no exception to this trend, serving as a solid foundation for debate in this country for decades. Since the New Deal policies of President Franklin Delano Roosevelt, the controversy surrounding the American welfare state has increased in intensity, placing welfare policies among the more crucial issues in American politics.

One can easily understand, therefore, how the welfare state has come to play such an integral role in the political platforms of many of the recent leaders of the United States. Some presidents, such as Franklin D. Roosevelt (FDR), have sought policies in support of the welfare state, while others, such as Ronald Reagan, have pursued policies to the contrary. Each of these presidents has held strong convictions regarding his stance on the issue, and each has been both praised and criticized for his position. *The Mean Season: The Attack on The Welfare State* (NY: Pantheon Books, 1987), edited by Fred Block, Richard A. Cloward, Barbara Ehrenreich, and Francis Fox Piven, offers numerous criticisms of the Reagan administration's attitude toward the welfare state. Through their individual contributions, the authors provide a variety of criticisms of arguments against the necessity of welfare policy response.

Fred Block offers an interesting perspective to one such criticism when he argues that the Reagan administration's attitude toward the welfare state rests almost predominantly on a blind acceptance of the "realist" view of American politics. Under this notion, Block explains, welfare expenditures are considered to be directly responsible for reducing economic efficiency, and thus weakening our national economy. Block disagrees with this view, claiming that "...social justice [welfare expenditures] and the pursuit of economic efficiency are compatible" (Block, 155), and that by strengthening the welfare state, the government of the United States could, in essence, "...promote equality, democracy, and a stronger economy" simultaneously (Block, 155). To Block, therefore, the policies of the Reagan administration aimed at reducing welfare spending to insure economic stability were misled and deserving of criticism.

Block's criticism certainly captures one's attention, but in many ways can be considered one dimensional. With regard to the economics in question, however, one person's dimension or perspective is as good as another's. Following from this, then, increasing the purchasing power of the disadvantaged (Block's dimension) might very well turn out to be as healthy for the national economy as providing incentives for increasing big business investment at the expense of the disadvantaged (Reagan's dimension). In this regard, Block's criticism can be considered reasonably relevant, in the abstract, and therefore worthy of further testing.

Barbara Ehrenreich adds an additional criticism of the Reagan administration's attitude toward the welfare state by uncovering what she considers to be its disguised intent. Ehrenreich discusses the Reagan administration's attempts to link the notion of "permissiveness" with the welfare state and its advocates as a means of undermining popular support for social welfare. Ehrenreich contends that by associating social welfare with the notion of "permissiveness" and its connotations of decadence and moral breakdown, the Reagan administration was essentially masking social welfare under the guise of a moral issue. In this regard, she claims the welfare state became shrouded beneath a cloud of value judgments, presenting, to a certain degree, its objective consideration by much of the American populace, and thus undermining its support.

Ehrenreich's criticism, on an ethical level, certainly warrants consideration because associating the welfare state with a moral issue could very well have denied it objective consideration. In reality, however, such clandestine intentions have come to be commonplace in political arenas worldwide, and disguising an issue in such a manner has been a trick of politicians for years. One would imagine that, under scrutinizing observation, similar tactics could most likely be found underlying many American policy issues.

Francis Fox Piven and Richard A. Cloward provide the focus of the book. They criticize the Reagan administration's attitude toward the welfare state based on its myopic perspective, particularly concerning the societal implications of relief giving. In the opinions of Piven and Cloward, the Reagan administration associated the problems of poverty and the poor directly to welfare programs, contending that welfare choices among the poor are ultimately attributable to material calculations, or the want of money. As such, the authors are quick to point out, Reagan and his subscribers openly neglected "...to consider an array of important changes in American Social institutions that ought reasonably to be investigated for their impacts on the lives of the poor" (Piven and Cloward, 83). Such changes, the authors add, might include the impact of the displacement of multitudes of southern agricultural workers during the years following WWII and the more recent impacts of rapid deindustrialization in this country.

In any event, Piven and Cloward continue by stating that by limiting its consideration of the welfare state solely to an economic agenda, the Reagan administration made "...the most basic societal processes that affect poverty and the poor seem peripheral" (Piven and Cloward, 73). As such, the Reagan administration created a model of the welfare state, and its relationship between relief giving and social behavior, which was far too simple. Certainly, as a means of criticism, this argument seems quite reasonable, since establishing a simple causal relationship within a complex social and political setting, such as that which the Reagan administration created, is virtually impossible. Therefore, by demonstrating the Reagan administration's negligence in considering numerous significant variables in the relationship between the welfare state and society, other than that of a mere economic calculus, Piven and Cloward, to a certain degree, expose a definite deficiency.

Throughout *The Mean Season: The Attack of The Welfare State*, Block, Cloward, Ehrenreich, and Piven offer numerous different criticisms of the Reagan administration's attitude toward the welfare state. These criticisms themselves, whether accepted or not, represent the long history of controversy which, in recent years, has come to play an increasingly important role in the American political arena. In their approach, these authors may very well be on the forefront of numerous changes in national opinion regarding the welfare state, especially in light of recent changes in the global economy.

Today, as will be the case in the future, the economies of the world are being fueled more and more by human talent. Therefore, investments in social welfare programs, essentially being investments in human capital, will become increasingly vital to the economic self-interests of the countries of the world and especially America. In turn, arguments in support of the welfare state, such as those of the authors of *The Mean Season: The Attack of The Welfare State*, may become increasingly influential. Despite this, however, the dispute over welfare spending will most likely continue to pepper American political discourse for many years to come.

Briefing Cases

Purpose of Briefing a Case

Preparing a case brief is a helpful way to summarize and analyze a court decision. Courts are political institutions and, therefore, decisions they make have political ramifications. Briefing a case helps students ascertain issues involved in important court cases and the justifications of the decisions.

Understanding Court Decisions

The first step to briefing a case is, obviously, to read the case. Once court Justices, such as Supreme Court members, have made a judgment in a case, they provide justifications for their determinations in documents called *decisions*. These *decisions* are bound in volumes called *reporters*. For briefing the case, students must locate specific information in these published decisions.

Name of the Case: The name of the case is distinguished by two names of participants in the case separated by a *v.* (such as Washington *v.* Davis). The first name is always the party bringing the case to the court for review; this party is generally referred to as the plaintiff or petitioner. The second name is always the target of the lawsuit; this party is generally referred to as the defendant or respondent. The plaintiff or the respondent could be an individual citizen, a representative of an organization, or a government.

Citation: The citation is the location of the *decision* in the *reporter*. For example, the Washington *v.* Davis decision is cited as 96 S.Ct. 2040 (1976). This means that the decision was published in volume 96 of *The Supreme Court Reporter* on page 2040 in 1976. Sometimes the case citation will include references to other places where the case is published.

Decision: The Justices vote on whether to support the plaintiff or the defendant in the case. Their votes will either be split between the majority (usually at least five members) and minority, or they will be unanimous. The majority vote provides the winning decision. The decision will either affirm (agree with) or overturn (disagree with) the lower appellate court decision in cases brought to the court on appeal. In the case of original jurisdiction, just the vote is recorded.

Majority Opinion: One of the Justices in the majority will write the justification for the decision.

Concurring Opinion: One of the Justices in the majority may write an alternative justification that provides additional or different reasons for the decision.

Dissenting Opinion: One of the Justices in the minority may write a rebuttal to the majority opinion that identifies the problems and weaknesses in the justification by the majority.

A case brief is essentially an extended annotated reference. It is important to identify:

- the purpose of the case.
- the significance of the case.

Students should answer the standard questions of who, what, when, where, why, and how with a particular focus on legal and political costs and benefits. They need to focus on:

- who is claiming harm or paying political costs?
- who is benefiting at the cost of someone else?
- what legal issues were involved?
- what other earlier cases (precedents) were involved?
- when did the court make the decision?
- where did the decision take place?
- why did the court make the decision it rendered?
- how did the Justice arrive at the decision?
- how much support was there for the decision among the Justices?

There is nothing difficult or mystical about writing briefs. Although written court decisions look like and sometimes are imposing prose, the justifications, written by Justices, are nothing more than analytical essays. Supreme Court decisions provide:

- a brief description of the context of the case.
- an opinion agreed to by the majority of Justices supported by evidence from previous cases, the Constitution, or legal theorists.
- dissenting opinions supported by previous cases, the Constitution, or legal theorists.

Tips for Briefing a Case

For historical, landmark Supreme Court decisions, it is often not necessary for students to brief the case from the court records to understand the purpose, reasoning, and significance of the case. A standard text on constitutional law, civil rights and liberties, or American government can provide most of the information necessary for understanding the case. Cases that are more recent are usually examined or analyzed in law journals. Nonetheless, students may need to brief less-known cases to support their arguments or assertions about the legality of an activity.

A legal brief can be a concise set of notes or an extensive set of notes depending on the reason for researching a case. Instructors of public law courses often have students briefing cases so that they may understand the more complex issues and reasoning in landmark cases. Students of public policy, however, may need to brief cases that have only been addressed by judicial decisions. In any event, a standard legal brief should be no shorter than the front side of an 8" by 5" index card. It should be no longer than it takes to fill both sides of an 8" by 5" index card. Here are some simple guidelines for briefing a case:

1. **State the name of the case.**
2. **State the full citation including the volume of the reporter, the page number, and the year.**
3. **Identify the important facts in the case—describe objectively what happened to whom.**
4. **Identify the issue—what was the problem?**

5. State the decision (holding)—find out who won.
6. List the vote margin—how many voted yes and how many voted no.
7. Identify the reasons stated why the majority of the court voted the way they did.
8. Identify particular reasons given by individual Justices for their concurring votes.
9. Identify particular reasons given by individual Justices for their dissenting votes.
10. Identify and summarize the rule of law or outcome.
11. Identify and evaluate the importance of the case to your research or public policy.

An Example of a Brief

NAME OF THE CASE: Washington *v.* Davis

CITATION: 426 U.S. 229, 96 S.Ct. 2040, 48 L.Ed. 2d 597 (1976)

FACTS:

All federal service employees, including police recruits, were required to take a standard literacy test. The number of black applicants who failed the test was four times that of white applicants. A discrimination case was filed in District Court that found no intent of discrimination. The Court of Appeals overturned that decision based on Griggs *v.* Duke Power Co. (1971) as it applied to Title VII of the Civil Rights Act of 1964. This court held that the absence of proof that the test was an adequate measure of job performance and the high number of blacks who failed the test, regardless of intent, rendered the test unconstitutional.

ISSUE:

The first issue concerned the constitutionality of a literacy test that has an unintentional but apparent adverse impact on the employment of a protected class of people. The second issue concerned whether the literacy test should be invalidated under job performance standards of Title VII of the Civil Rights Act of 1964 set forth by Congress.

DECISION:

Overturned the Court of Appeals decision.

Vote: (7 to 2), Justice White wrote the opinion.

JUSTIFICATION:

The court considered the second issue first. The Court of Appeals decision was overturned because it was based on Title VII which allows the impact, rather than the intent, to be sufficient cause for invalidating a non-job related employment test. The court said that Title VII is not a constitutional rule and invites more judicial probing and review than is justified under the constitution. Therefore, because the decision was based on Title VII, the Court did not examine the literacy test at all.

CONCURRING:

Justice Stevens concurred, but for different reasons. He argued that a literacy test was relevant to police work and, because it was given throughout the federal service without the same impact on blacks, the test met congressional standards and was not unconstitutional.

DISSENT:

Justices Brennan and Marshall argued that every district court, except the one in this case, had ruled such tests were discriminatory. The employers should have to demonstrate that the test measured skills related to performance.

RULE OF LAW:

The court stated clearly that it will not recognize impact, instead of purpose of an act, as a standard for establishing invidious racial discrimination, even though Congress established these criteria through legislation.

EVALUATION:

The court blatantly ignored congressional intent.

Constructing Outlines

Purpose

Outlines help to organize ideas, arguments, and evidence into a coherent statement. Ideas must be presented in an ordered sequence. Outlines help writers formulate a controlling pattern for presenting their ideas. Outlines help the writer to:

- order main and minor points.
- balance the introduction, body, and conclusion.
- place arguments with evidence.

Writers use several types of outlines.

Scratch Outlines: a series of ordered notes about how to proceed with the paper.

Topic Outlines: a list of ideas showing the order and relative importance of each idea in brief words or phrases.

Sentence Outlines: a list of ideas showing the order and relative importance of each idea in complete sentences.

How to Construct a Topic or Sentence Outline

1. **Topic outlines are structured to show relative importance, so before writing the outline:**
   - Write out a thesis sentence.
   - List all the ideas.
   - List all the evidence.
   - Categorize the ideas and evidence so that they form separate chunks of information relating to the points made in the thesis sentence.
   - Order the information by strength and importance.
2. **The parts of an outline are hierarchically ordered.**
   - General ideas precede specific points.
   - Each point should have corresponding evidence
3. **Each division is numbered in ascending order.**
   - General sections are ordered in Roman numerals.
   - Subsections are ordered by capital letters.
   - Supporting sections are ordered in Arabic numbers.
   - Explanatory sections are ordered by small letters.
4. **Each subsection, supporting section, and explanatory section must have at least two parts.**

Example of a Scratch Outline
(Reprinted with permission)

A POLICY FOR WELFARE REFORM

By
Thomas Mitchell

1. Issue of controlling poverty rate
2. Economic Opportunity Act of 1964
3. Employment conditions in 1964 vs. present
4. Contributing public commentary
5. Cash Support programs and controversies
6. Remedial job skill training
7. Programs for children to break poverty at an early age
8. Employment programs for the non-working poor
9. Techniques for measuring success
10. Conclusion

Example of a Topic Outline
(Reprinted with permission)

A POLICY FOR WELFARE REFORM

By
Thomas Mitchell

Thesis statement: A multi-generational program that is both curative and remedial in structure will provide training and opportunity to the working poor, the non-working poor, and their families.

I. Introduction or Executive Summary
   A. Issue
      1. Stagnant productivity of American workers
      2. Goals of remedial training and quality education

B. Recommendations
  1. Multi-generational policy
  2. Specific recommendations of analysis

II. The Issues

  A. Past Strategies
    1. Preventative, Punitive, and Alleviative
    2. Goals of each strategy

  B. History of Issue
    1. Economic Opportunity Act of 1964
    2. Employment conditions in 1964 vs. present
    3. Reasons for change in conditions

III. The Goals and Objectives

  A. Goal of Welfare Policy
    1. Security for those deemed worthy
    2. Vehicle to self-sufficiency
    3. Discourage welfare dependence

  B. Demands of the Labor Market
    1. More skills needed presently than ever before
    2. Higher levels of education for even entry-level jobs

  C. Public Commentary
    1. John Kenneth Galbraith's (1957) *The Affluent Society*
    2. Michael Harrington's (1962) *The Other America*
    3. Martin Anderson's (1978) *Welfare*
    4. George Gilder's (1981) *Wealth and Poverty*
    5. Charles Murray's (1984) *Losing Ground*

IV. Past Policy Responses

  A. Cash Support programs
    1. Examples including OASDI, AFDC, SSI, and GA
    2. Assistance in adding to income level
    3. Controversial due to loss of government authority

  B. Direct Provision of Necessities
    1. Examples including Medicare, food stamps
    2. Political feasibility of direct provision

  C. Preventive and Compensatory Efforts for Children
    1. Rationality for focusing upon education
    2. Problem of equally affordable education
    3. Creation of Upward Bound and Head Start programs

D. Employment Related Programs

    1. Explanation of the Family Support Act of 1988

    2. Focus upon JOBS program and its goals

    3. Problems of job creation, costs, and child care

V. Recommendations

A. Explain Multi-Generational Program

    1. Provide remedial training to presently impoverished

    2. Create and further educational programs for youth

B. Continuation of Employment Programs

    1. Need for programs due to welfare stigma

    2. Poor less able to compete for jobs

C. Remedial Job Skill Training Programs

    1. A means of welfare recipients acquiring skills

    2. Upon completion, recipients enter employment programs

D. Continuation of Cash Support Payments

    1. Allows millions of people to be kept off of welfare

    2. Must participate in Skill Training to receive cash

E. Curative Programs Aimed at All Youth

    1. Children of various income levels drop out of school

    2. Children drop out before the legal age

    3. Head Start, Upward Bound, and elementary programs for all high-risk youth

VI. Measuring Success

A. Time Frame

    1. Measure variables every three years

    2. Several years before remedial training can be reduced

B. Employment Programs

    1. Percentage of recipients securing employment

    2. Average duration of employment

    3. Securing of wages above welfare benefit level

C. Remedial Job Skill Training

    1. Percent completion in program

    2. Percent who enroll in employment programs

    3. Number in program should lower over time as skills of youth increase due to educational programs

D. Cash Assistance Programs

    1. Cash assistance outlays should lower as number in remedial lowers over time

    2. Cash assistance outlays should lower as number in employment programs lowers over time

      E. Curative Programs Aimed at High-Risk Children

         1. Defining high-risk youth by each school district to lower cultural and regional bias of standardized tests

         2. High school graduation rates should increase

VII. Conclusion

      A. Social Condition of Poverty

         1. New demands on labor market

         2. Resources of workers go untapped

      B. Past Poverty Strategies

         1. Past strategies have been unsuccessful

         2. Restate thesis

      C. Recommendations

         1. List the four recommendations

         2. Programs are integrated and mutually re-enforcing

         3. Need for a true welfare reform as these recommendations would provide

Example of a Sentence Outline

(Reprinted with permission)

A POLICY FOR WELFARE REFORM

By
Thomas Mitchell

Thesis statement: A multi-generational program that is both curative and remedial in structure will provide training and opportunity to the working poor, the non-working poor, and their families.

   I. The percent of the population below the poverty level has continued to increase since 1979.

      A. In order that the issue of increasing poverty rates be controlled, legislative development must be undertaken.

         1. Provide remedial training to the working and non-working poor.

         2. Ensure quality education as a curative strategy to poverty by breaking the cycle of poverty at an early age.

      B. These goals can be achieved through specific policy recommendations.

         1. Continuation of employment programs for the non-working poor.

         2. Provide remedial job skill training and education programs to provide skills to

the working and non-working poor and to induce the poor to enter the job market.

3. Continue to use Cash Support payments as a means to keep millions of individuals out of poverty.

4. Create and further curative programs aimed at high-risk children of all income and educational levels.

II. As a relative concept, poverty will always exist because inequality is a constant problem.

    A. Welfare policy has traditional taken one of four forms.

        1. Preventive strategies are designed to ensure that certain groups do not enter poverty.

        2. Alleviate strategies provide assistance to those impoverished.

        3. Punitive strategies discourage assistance to those capable of work.

        4. Curative strategies aim at controlling poverty by attacking its causes.

    B. To comprehend the issue of poverty, one must understand its history.

        1. The Economic Opportunity Act of 1964 attempted to guarantee to everyone the opportunity to live in decency and dignity.

        2. However, the employment conditions that were in existence in 1964 are no longer the same today.

        3. American businesses are now service oriented and demand more skills and education from its laborers.

III. The goals and objective of welfare policy must be considered before constructing a policy.

    A. There are three goals of welfare policy.

        1. Welfare is an attempt to provide some level of security to those deemed worthy.

        2. A lesser goal of welfare is to assist individuals in becoming self-sufficient.

        3. A third goal of welfare policy is to discourage welfare dependence.

    B. Today's labor market is demanding more of its labor force than ever before.

        1. A skilled labor force is necessary in a service sector.

        2. As the need for skilled labor increases, so does the requirement of higher levels of education.

    C. The issue of poverty gained public attention due mainly to commentary.

        1. John Kenneth Galbraith called attention to the existence of poverty amongst plenty in the United States.

        2. Michael Harrington noted the issue of regional poverty.

        3. Martin Anderson provided specific guidelines for welfare reform.

        4. George Gilder theorized that poor people remain poor because welfare benefits are greater than work incentives.

        5. Charles Murray argued that the expansion of welfare policies in the 1960's only increased poverty.

IV. Past federal programs in aid of the poor have fallen into four categories.

    A. Cash support programs provide the foundation for federal assistance to the poor.

        1. Two groups included in the Social Security Act were social insurance and public assistance programs.

        2. Because the income of the working poor is often not enough to raise them above the poverty level, Cash Support programs could add to their income.

        3. Cash Support payments are often disliked by policy makers for they have little authority in how the aid is spent.

    B. Welfare policy also includes programs that deliver goods and services directly to the needy.

        1. These programs include Medicare, public housing, and food stamps.

        2. Direct provision of necessities is more politically feasible than cash assistance.

    C. The federal government has focused on protecting children from poverty with preventive and compensatory programs.

        1. Schools play an important role in socializing and educating children for the labor market.

        2. The opportunity for an education is not equally affordable.

        3. Upward Bound was created to motivate and assist poor students early in high school.

    D. In an effort to help the non-working poor, employment programs were created to help them find work.

        1. The Family Support Act of 1988 follows the idea that training and work experience will lead to self-sufficiency.

        2. JOBS programs require states to provide comprehensive education, training, and employment services for welfare recipients.

        3. Employment programs have problems of job creation, costs, and childcare facilities.

V. To propose a welfare reform, policies must be established addressing the present economic structure of the U.S.

    A. A multi-generational program that is both curative and remedial in structure is needed.

        1. This program would provide remedial training and education to the presently impoverished.

        2. It would also create and further educational programs for the youth.

    B. In order to assist recipients in finding work, the JOBS program needs to be continued.

        1. The welfare stigma attached to recipients has handicapped them in the labor market.

        2. The poor are not equally able to compete for jobs with non-welfare recipients.

    C. A program is needed to deal with the millions of adults currently impoverished.

        1. Remedial training programs can provide a means for recipients to acquire the

skills needed by the labor market.

    2. Upon completion of remedial training, recipients can enroll in employment programs.

D. Cash assistance programs can help individuals attain an income level above the poverty line.

    1. This type of program would allow millions of persons to stay off welfare.

    2. Legislation could be enacted that would require employable recipients to participate in remedial training programs in order to attain cash assistance.

E. Curative programs should be aimed at high-risk children of all income and educational levels that are in need of additional educational support.

    1. Children of various income levels are represented in the high school dropout rate.

    2. Many students essentially drop out of school before the legal age.

    3. Programs including Head Start, Upward Bound, as well as similar elementary programs, need to be expanded for all high-risk children.

VI. To assess the success of this policy, each recommendation must be defined and evaluated.

A. The establishment of a time frame will allow for the monitoring of progress towards our established goals.

    1. The variables involved in each recommendation shall be evaluated every three years.

    2. It will require several years before remedial training funds can be lowered.

B. Since the goal of employment programs is to assist recipients in securing work, two measures of that success can be examined.

    1. The percentage of recipients attaining employment should remain high each year if the program is to be considered a success.

    2. The duration of employment should not be short or temporary.

    3. Wages secured in employment through JOBS should reflect wages above benefits from welfare assistance.

C. Remedial job skill training will eventually become less necessary because those who are participating in youth educational programs should not require the service if these programs are successful.

    1. One measure of success for remedial training programs is the percentage of recipients who enroll in as well as complete the program.

    2. The number of participants in these programs should lower over time as the skills of youth increase because of educational programs.

D. Cash assistance programs are recommended to be directly linked to the participation in job skill training or employment programs by employable recipients.

    1. Cash assistance outlays should lower over time as the number of recipients in remedial training lowers over time.

    2. Cash assistance outlays should lower over time as the number of recipients in

employment programs lowers over time.

E. To implement curative programs, high-risk must first be defined and then programs made available to all high-risk children.

1. The definition and classification of high-risk youth should be done by means of testing prepared by each individual school district to lower the cultural and regional bias associated with standardized tests.

2. These programs are successful if the graduation rates for all high-risk youth show an increase, as compared to past policies.

VII. Conclusion

A. In recent years, the poverty rate has been steadily increasing.

1. As the labor market has had to adapt to a recently established service sector, new skills and higher levels of education are being demanded.

2. However, the productivity of American labor has remained stagnant as the resources of millions of workers go untapped.

B. Past poverty strategies have proven unsuccessful in controlling the rise in poverty.

1. Therefore, this policy analysis recommends that a multi-generational program that is both curative and remedial in structure be implemented.

2. This is to provide training and opportunity to the working poor, the non-working poor, and their families.

C. This policy analysis consists of four parts:

1. Continuation of employment programs for the non-working poor accompanied by increased funding;

2. Remedial Job Skill Training and Education programs for the working and non-working poor and to induce the poor to enter the labor market;

3. Continuation of Cash Support payments to keep millions of individuals out of poverty;

4. Curative programs aimed at high-risk children at all educational levels that are in need of additional educational support.

D. These programs are integrated and mutually re-enforcing.

1. Each recommendation is to build upon each of the others, as to provide a structured and directional welfare policy.

2. The implementation of this multi-generational program will represent a true welfare reform in which major strides can be made toward reducing the social condition of growing poverty rates.

Research Presentations

Research presentations generally have two purposes. Presentations give students the opportunity to describe their research verbally to their classmates and respond to questions directly. The subject of the presentation is based on the student's research. (This outline style is very similar to the format used for research proposals.)

1. **A standard professional presentation typically includes more than a description of research. It includes:**
   - a statement of student's purpose.
   - a declaration of student's position.
   - a description of relevant background on the topic.
   - a description of the controversy.
   - an explanation of how the controversy was examined.
   - a description of the student's findings.
   - a concluding statement regarding the significance of the research project.

2. **A class presentation is generally graded with the same criteria used to grade written assignments.**
   - Students' grades usually reflect the quality and thoroughness in which they presented the material contained in the categories listed.
   - Sometimes an instructor will request a copy of your presentation, so write an outline.
   - A quick way to begin writing your presentation outline is to re-organize the topic or sentence outline for your research paper to fit into these categories.
   - The length and degree of detail in the presentation outline will depend on the time allotted for the presentation. Generally, a presentation is two-and-a-half (or less) pages typed in outline form.

3. **Class presentations are frequently graded on the degree of professionalism exhibited by the student during the presentation. A solid performance by the student demonstrates depth and breadth of subject area knowledge.**
   - Exhibit poise and confidence (try rehearsing).
   - Answer questions succinctly.
   - Vary the voice level, make eye contact with other students, and use gestures.
   - Do not read word for word from your research paper. Use an outline.

Standard Presentation Form

Purpose: A clear statement of the purpose and focus of the student's research.

Hypothesis: A clear statement of the controversy examined and hypothesis tested. If possible, try to identify the causal relationship between independent and dependent variables.

Background: A brief discussion of the context and background related to the controversy examined and assumptions behind the students' research motives.
   - Be sure to present the background so that it supports your purpose and relationships specified between the variables.

- Work from weakest to strongest assertions.

Method: An explanation of the method or how you tested your hypothesis.

- If you used quantitative data, describe how the data or source materials were collected.
- Fully disclose any problems in information gathering.
- Be sure to relate the data and source materials to the hypothesis.

Results: A summary of the results of the examination or test.

- If data were used, make charts, graphs, or tables to use as visual aids.
- Use a table or chart to summarize your main points.
- Use visual aids for complex material or highly descriptive material. For example, use maps to help the audience understand the context of boundary disputes between nations.
- Use an overhead projector to present your material or make copies of a visual aid for everyone.

Conclusion: This statement explains how the goals of the research were accomplished. In particular, this statement summarizes how the results relate to the goals of the student's research endeavor.

Significance: A statement that applies the results appropriately to an expansion of knowledge about the subject.

WELFARE REFORM PRESENTATION

By
Thomas Mitchell
Dr. Schmidt
POLS 444
July 1, 1991
(Reprinted with permission)

WELFARE REFORM PRESENTATION NOTES

I. Purpose is to examine manpower programs that are designed to increase the marketability of impoverished citizens and propose a new course of action that will help diminish the number of citizens requiring such aid in the future.

    A. Controversy:

        1. Productivity of American workers stagnant.

        2. The percent of the population below the poverty level has continued to increase since 1979.

    B. Thesis statement: A multi-generational program that is both curative and remedial in structure will provide training and opportunity to the working poor, the non-working poor, and their families.

    C. Goal: To address the issue of increasing poverty rates, legislative action must be undertaken.

        1. Provide remedial training to the working and non-working poor.

        2. Ensure quality education as a curative strategy to poverty by breaking the cycle of poverty at an early age.

    D. These goals can be achieved through specific policy recommendations.

        1. Continuation of employment programs for the non-working poor.

        2. Provide remedial job skill training and education programs to provide skills to the working and non-working poor and to induce the poor to enter the job market.

        3. Continue to use cash support payments as a means to keep millions of individuals out of poverty.

        4. Create and expand curative programs aimed at high-risk children of all income and educational levels.

II. Brief description of the context or background:

    A. Past strategies.

        1. Preventative, Punitive, and Alleviative.

        2. Goals of each strategy.

    B. History of Issue.

        1. Economic Opportunity Act of 1964.

        2. Employment conditions in 1964 vs. present.

        3. Reasons for change in conditions.

III. Explanation of research method:

    A. Analyzed explicit goals of welfare policies and employment policy.

    B. Examined and evaluated past and present programs used to address goals.

    C. Used secondary sources, primary sources, and expert opinion.

IV. Findings on Welfare Policies:

    A. Welfare policy goals.

    1. Security for those deemed worthy.

    2. Vehicle to self-sufficiency.

    3. Discourage welfare dependence.

  B. Welfare policy responses-evaluated.

    1. Cash Support programs: Examples, OASDI, AFDC, SSI.

    2. Direct Provision of Necessities: Example, Medicare.

    3. Preventive Efforts for Children: Example, Head Start.

V. Findings on Employment Programs:

  A. Goals and problems in labor market.

    1. More skills needed presently than ever before.

    2. Higher levels of education for even entry-level jobs.

  B. Employment related programs:

    1. Explanation of the Family Support Act of 1988.

    2. Focus upon JOBS program and its goals.

    3. Problems of job creation, costs, and child care.

VI. Recommendations:

  A. Explain multi-generational program.

    1. Provide remedial training to presently impoverished

    2. Create and further educational programs for youth.

  B. Continuation of employment programs.

    1. Need for programs due to welfare stigma.

    2. Poor less able to compete for jobs.

  C. Remedial job skill training programs.

    1. A means of welfare recipients acquiring skills.

    2. Upon completion, recipients enter employment programs.

  D. Continuation of cash support payments.

    1. Allows millions of people to be kept off of welfare.

    2. Must participate in skill training to receive cash.

  E. Curative programs aimed at all youth.

    1. Children of various income levels drop out of school.

    2. Children drop out before the legal age.

    3. Head Start, Upward Bound, and elementary programs for all high-risk youth.

VII. Conclusion:

  A. Social condition of poverty.

    1. New demands on labor market.

    2. Resources of workers go untapped.

  B. Past poverty strategies.

1. Past strategies have been unsuccessful.

2. Restate thesis.

VIII. Significance:

A. Summarize four-part recommendation.

B. Four parts are integrated and mutually re-enforcing.

Research Proposals

For upper-level classes, scholarships, grants, and other professional-level work, students may be asked to submit a research proposal. A research proposal is a synopsis of the main elements of a research paper. It should be brief, concise, and specific. This means that students must complete the preliminary research before writing the proposal. The length varies with the research question and design. A research proposal should be no shorter than two typed double-spaced pages and no longer than five typed, double-spaced pages. A research proposal generally includes the following:

A Title Page: Includes the title of the research project and the name of the student.

An Essay: Allocating at least one paragraph to each item, a discussion of the following:

Topic: Describe the focus of the research project, clearly, succinctly.

Purpose: Describe the purpose of the research project.

Hypothesis: Clearly express, in one or two sentences, the question or controversy you are seeking to examine. One of these sentences should be your thesis sentence. You may need to follow the thesis sentence with qualifying, explanatory sentences that clarify or propose sub-hypotheses.

Justification: Provide a discussion of the background, context, or origins of the controversy. This may take more than one paragraph. For complex research topics, include a condensed, but pertinent literature review on the subject and controversy.

Method: Describe the method and sources used to examine or test the research question.

- Be sure to specify whether qualitative or quantitative (or both) evidence will be used to support your assertions.
- If statistical tools or graphics will be used, be sure to specify the source of the data and how it will be transformed into tables and figures. If survey data are used, be sure to specify the source of the data.
- If the research is based on qualitative evidence, then identify the primary sources such as scholarly, mass publications, etc.

Expected Results: Describe, based on your preliminary research, what you believe you will find to support your hypothesis. If possible, indicate the strength of that support. Do not overstate.

Expected Significance: Describe what your research will contribute to the body of knowledge on the topic or subject. Be bold, not rhetorical. Avoid saying that your research will enlighten everyone. Keep your assertion carefully and narrowly focused on what can be understood about your subject or topic.

Example of a Research Proposal

Research Proposal

Digital Millennium Copyright Act:
Overly Restrictive or Necessary Protection?

By
Marion Harmon
POLS 300
Dr. Schmidt
September 18, 2003
(Reprinted with permission)

Topic: The topic of this research paper is Public Law 105-304, to amend Title 17, United States Code, to implement the World Intellectual Property Organization Copyright Treaty and Performances and Phonograms Treaty, also known as the Digital Millennium Copyright Act of 1998 (DMCA). The research will focus on the historical context, the legislative process, objectives of the bill, and the policy tools in the bill. It will also focus on support for and opposition to the legislation.

Purpose: The purpose of this paper is to evaluate the effectiveness of the DMCA in dealing with copyright issues related to new technologies. The broad scope of the DMCA has made it a target for criticism since its earliest days. The opposition has criticized decisions interpreting the DMCA as setting copyright law on the path toward eliminating the fair use doctrine and stifling innovation and competition. Civil liberties groups are concerned about the access of the entertainment industry to personal information on those suspected of illegally sharing copyrighted songs online. Supporters point to protecting copyright owners against the circumvention of access and copy controls used in easily copied media.

Hypothesis: The research will test the hypothesis that the DMCA is a necessary yet flawed addition to U.S. copyright law. First, I will study the legislation and legislative process leading up to the passing of the DMCA. Second, I will examine the literature surrounding its passing as well as subsequent court cases and related articles to learn about its controversies. Third, I will examine proposed bills meant to amend the DMCA for their merit in improving the act. Finally, I will determine who benefits most from the DMCA.

Justification: The DMCA sections appear to be reasonable provisions for digital copyright protections and exemptions. But study of recent news articles reveals interpretations of the DMCA that have led to 12-year-olds being sued for trading music online and librarians calling for "widespread civil disobedience" to fight for digital first sale and fair use doctrines. A bill currently before Congress, the Digital Media Consumers' Rights Act of 2002, proposes to correct some fundamental defects in the DMCA and reestablish the doctrine of fair use, which, its proponents say, has been severely diluted by the application of the DMCA. Copyright protection must be applied to the digital realm, but invading the privacy of individuals and locking up digitized educational information are serious issues deserving serious consideration.

Method: My method of examination will consist mostly of qualitative analysis. I will examine the historical context and legislative history in government documents and scholarly works. I will also study scholarly and mass publications to learn the arguments of supporters and opponents of the DMCA. I expect to use a small amount of quantitative data gathered from government documents.

Expected Results: The expected results of this research project are a clarification of the issues surrounding the DMCA and a greater understanding of what parts of the law should be amended. The diverse, complicated areas of copyright covered by the DMCA are made even more complicated by the many arguments of its supporters and opponents. I expect to find valid arguments for amending some sections of the DMCA. Finally, I do not expect to find convincing arguments to completely overturn the legislation.

Expected Significance: The expected significance of the research project is to provide a comprehensible guide to the DMCA and digital copyright issues. I hope to offer insight into whether privacy rights, fair use, and competition are truly threatened by the DMCA, and which proposed legislation makes the most sense to implement to rectify these problems. Finally, I hope to create a clearer picture of which parts of the DMCA deserve further examination and possible amendment.

CHAPTER 11

Format and Examples of
Conventional Research Papers

Formulas for Organizing Standard Research Papers

In the following pages, there are three examples of standard undergraduate research papers exhibiting a range of writing styles, topics, and research methods.

The First Paper: A Comparative Paper

"The Kennedys and the Rockefellers: Political Dynasties' Effects on the American Electorate" uses qualitative data and is a simple comparative, or case, study.

The Second Paper: An Analysis

"Youth Influence in Political Outcomes" uses a mixture of qualitative and quantitative data to examine the reasons why young people participate in politics and suggests a theory about the impact of this activity. This paper is an example of an analysis.

The Third Paper: A Position Paper

"Chief Justice Rehnquist: Does He Lead the Court?" is empirical research that tests a hypothesis using quantitative data and statistical methods. This is an example of a position paper that supports a theory about political influence and leadership in the judicial branch.

These papers exhibit the standard qualities for a research paper in political science, where students were not required to address specific criteria or questions. An explanation of the form for each type of paper precedes the examples.

Writing a Comparative Study

In many political science courses, especially in Comparative Politics or International Relations, instructors will ask students to compare government responses to issues, problems, or political phenomena. Comparison papers may use qualitative evidence, quantitative evidence, or a mixture of both. Here are three simple frameworks to organize your research and ideas (Lester 1990, 74).

Comparative Papers on Two or More Objects or People

1. **In the introduction, briefly identify and compare the items.**
   - State the central point of the comparison.

- In your thesis sentence, present your perspective on the relevance of the comparison or why the comparison is important.

2. **In the body:**
- Examine the first item's characteristics thoroughly.
- Next, examine the second item's characteristics thoroughly.
- Next, identify characteristics that are similar and offer an explanation/evidence of why they are similar.
- Next, identify characteristics that are different and offer an explanation/evidence of why they are different.

3. **Discuss the significant differences and similarities. Suggest why it was important to identify these differences and similarities.**

Comparative Papers on Two or More Ideas or Theories

1. **In the introduction, briefly identify and compare the items.**
- State the central point of the comparison.
- In your thesis sentence, present your perspective on the relevance of the comparison or why the comparison is important.

2. **In the body:**
- To start, identify characteristics that are similar and offer an explanation/evidence of why they are similar.
- Next, identify characteristics that are different and offer an explanation/evidence of why they are different.
- Next, discuss and evaluate the central issues or characteristics that differentiate the items.
- Present arguments that rank one item over the other.

3. **Reiterate the major differences and strong points of each item.**
- Suggest why it was important to identify these differences and similarities.
- Conclude by identifying and supporting the reason why one item is preferable to another.

Papers That Compare Responses to Issues by Two Subjects or Objects

1. **In the introduction, briefly identify and compare the items and the issues.**
- State the central point of the comparison.
- In your thesis sentence, present your perspective on the relevance of the comparison or why the comparison is important.

2. **In the body:**
- First, identify the first issue. Discuss the differences and similarities between the items' treatment of the issue. Present arguments about why the differences and similarities exist.

- Next, identify the second issue. Discuss the differences and similarities between the items' treatment of the issue. Present arguments about why the differences and similarities exist.
- Next, identify the third issue. Discuss the differences and similarities between the items' treatment of the issue. Present arguments about why the differences and similarities exist.
- Present arguments that rate one item's treatment over the other.

3. **Reiterate the major differences and similarities in each item's treatment of each issue.**
   - Suggest why these differences and similarities exist.
   - Conclude by identifying and supporting the reason why one item's treatment is preferable to another.

THE KENNEDYS AND THE ROCKEFELLERS:
POLITICAL DYNASTIES' EFFECTS ON THE AMERICAN ELECTORATE

By
John T. Sullivan
Professor Schmidt
POLS 318
December 1, 1988
(Reprinted with permission)

ABSTRACT

One of the most intriguing phenomena in American politics is that of the so-called "dynasty" and its effects on the voters. These political dynasties appear to create irrational tendencies in voting patterns. The dynasty also appears to be akin to a candidate-centered campaign on a greater magnitude. In particular, a political dynasty is an unpredictable anomaly on the political scene, but it is relatively easy to identify. The specific examples of the political families, the Kennedys and the Rockefellers, provide evidence that political dynasties influence the careers of family members and give them extra political influence.

INTRODUCTION

The political dynasty, in the American context, is an organization usually centered on a family which transcends traditional campaign and voter perception. By transcending these norms, the dynasty develops the image of American "royalty." The Kennedy and Rockefeller families have evolved as the most dominant examples of political dynasties in the twentieth century. The phenomena, as evidenced in these examples, appear to center around one individual and build from there. Once established, this mutation of American politics becomes its own organization, nearly independent of its respective parties in power and strategy (Salmore and Salmore 1989, 39). Even though the later elements of the dynasty benefit from their link to the overall public perception, they are, at times, mistakenly associated and credited with the dynasty's accomplishments as well (Granberg 1985, 504–16).

Each political dynasty, however, is different; each dynasty has its own dynamics that separate it from the rest of the political community. The Kennedys, for example, are a nationally recognized political family although the family center or core is in Massachusetts. The Rockefellers, while equally nationally known, have spread their political dominance over the governor's mansions in New York, Arkansas, and West Virginia (Salmore and Salmore 1989, 125). While both families exhibited a drive for dominance, the political bases of their influence span the spectrum from highly centralized to decentralized (Clinch 1973, x).

THE KENNEDY DYNASTY

The Kennedys and their episodic saga in American politics are the premier political dynasty in evidence. The roots of the Kennedy dynasty began with John F. Fitzgerald who was the mayor of Boston and a U.S. Congressman (Davis 1984, 41). The figure who is the symbol of the Kennedy mystique, however, is John F. Kennedy (JFK), 35th President of the United States. JFK's popularity and successful election have created a standard by which the Kennedy heirs were measured. Because of JFK's success and characteristic demeanor, Kennedy heirs were perceived as intellectually keen, eloquent, and youthful (Wills 1982, 153). Those virtues were even more firmly associated with the Kennedy family due to efforts by his successor, Lyndon Johnson, to immortalize Kennedy in public for political purpose to gain public support for the presidential agenda (Schuyler 1987, 503–4).

The first tests of the Kennedy dynasty's effects on the electorate came soon after JFK's assassination. In 1964, Robert F. Kennedy (RFK), brother of the former president, challenged President Johnson and the Democratic Party regulars for the presidency. RFK sought to build on the foundations of residual grief over his slain brother. In particular, RFK promised to return to the values and programs of JFK. RFK became a rallying symbol for disenfranchised party opposition to Johnson (Halberstam 1968, 5). Johnson feared, as did other Democratic party leaders, "that the country would turn to Robert Kennedy… as the successor to the throne, as the rightful heir to the Kennedy tradition…" (Schuyler 1987, 506). Even though the Kennedy campaign started late, party supporters won their first primary with the help of the Kennedy family "machine" which used its own network and popularity to sidestep the party apparatus (Halberstam 1968, 161).

The reincarnation of the Kennedy dynasty had dramatic effects, as fate again lent a hand. RFK, broadening the reformist, intellectual style of the Kennedys (Halberstam 1968, 162), contributed his final piece to the puzzle as he was assassinated following a crucial 1968 California primary. Until his death, RFK's candidacy was gaining momentum by the day. Voters, especially young people, flocked to his campaign. There is little doubt that such voting behavior was caused by the Kennedy dynasty; RFK was a late entry, a freshman senator, and opposed to the policies of his own incumbent president. These factors would destroy other contenders for the oval office.

RFK's assassination event merely further magnified the Kennedy mystique as the promises of two Kennedy family politicians would go unfulfilled (Halberstam 1968, 209). Because of this, the public looked to the last heir, apparent in Senator Edward M. Kennedy. The subsequent trials of Ted Kennedy are the best examples of the Kennedy dynasty. Because the Kennedy image had been firmly entrenched by liberals in the original Kennedy administration (Matusow 1983, 153) and enhanced by the revival of that liberalism by RFK's run in, much was expected of Ted Kennedy. Despite a divorce and a highly controversial accident in which a woman he was with died, Ted Kennedy had been easily re-elected to the Senate and was a serious candidate for the presidency. His past electoral successes and near success for president occurred in part because of the Kennedy name. In addition, he has forged an impressive senatorial record in keeping with family tradition, and he has echoed the rhetoric of his deceased brothers at two national conventions (Wills 1982, 294).

Even with the Kennedy's success, the "ghosts" of the Kennedy family's past have forced Ted Kennedy into ill fought contests for the presidency (Wills 1982, 295). The public's perception of him is still linked to the Kennedy legacies. Ted Kennedy's popularity is due in part to a public perception that he is more liberal than his record indicates (Granberg 1985, 504–16). The public has a rigid perception of the Kennedy dynasty that is evident in the emerging popularity of a new Kennedy. Joseph P. Kennedy III, oldest son of Robert, is running for his third term in Congress as he and the Kennedy machine reclaimed the seat held by his great-grandfather, uncle, and former House Speaker Tip O'Neil. Young Joseph Kennedy defeated a field of 10 candidates to win the seat ("Liberals Rebuffed" 1986, 28). Thus, the Kennedy dynasty continues with young Joe, 37 years old, maintaining and rejuvenating the family.

THE ROCKEFELLER DYNASTY

Like the Kennedy dynasty, the reign of the Rockefellers in the United States has been one of philanthropy and public service. The Rockefellers are presently in their fourth generation of public service. The Rockefeller dynasty began with the billions of dollars made by John D. Rockefeller in the late nineteenth century and early twentieth century through his success in founding Standard Oil (Ensor Harr and Johnson 1988, xiii). Unlike the Kennedys, the Rockefellers established themselves as a political dynasty more through philanthropic causes than public service (Lundberg 1975, 329). Although the Rockefellers' public image is associated with being ruthless businessmen (Collier and Horowitz 1976, 4), it is estimated that by the third generation of Rockefellers, a staggering 5 billion dollars was donated to the philanthropic causes by John D. Sr., John D. Jr., and John D. Rockefeller III (Lundberg 1975, 329).

More importantly, the Rockefeller dynasty has produced one Vice-President and former governor, a U.S. Senator and a former governor, and another governor—all from different states (Salmore and Salmore 1989, 125; Ensor Harr and Johnson 1988, 8–9). The Rockefellers first entered the political arena in 1958. Nelson Rockefeller, son of John D. Jr., ran for and won the governor's seat in New York (Collier and Horowitz 1976, 330). From there, Nelson used his reputation as a base to run for the presidency. In 1968, Nelson ran for the nomination of the Republican Party without entering the primaries (Halberstam 1968). He did this to use polls to boost his popularity and bypass any losses in primaries that would diminish his chances of success. Although Rockefeller lost to Nixon, the Rockefeller machine continued to churn.

In 1964, Winthrop Rockefeller, brother of Nelson, ran unsuccessfully for the governor of Arkansas, but he won in 1966 and 1968 (Lundberg 1975, 285). Winthrop re-shaped the new Rockefeller political mold by supporting issues important to blacks and impoverished citizens. Likewise, Nelson was very popular with black voters in his campaign for president. Winthrop became Arkansas' first Republican governor in a century (Lundberg 1975, 285). Winthrop, long regarded as the "black sheep" in the family, retired from the governor spot when his term ended in 1970 (Ensor Harr and Johnson 1988, 5).

The Rockefeller political spotlight has also shone on the nephew of Nelson and Winthrop. John (Jay) D. Rockefeller IV has gone where no Rockefeller has gone before. Though Nelson was appointed as Vice-President for the troubled Ford administration, no Rockefeller had served in Congress. Jay, following two terms as the Democratic Governor of W. Virginia, ran and won a Senate seat in 1984 ("King of the Hills and Hollers" 1984, 22–24). Although the Rockefeller dynasty has been accused of buying elections (Salmore and Salmore 1989, 125) with the election of "J.D. IV," the Rockefeller name has secured its place in the elite American political arena.

CONCLUSION

The success of the Kennedy and the Rockefeller families as two prime examples of American dynasties exemplifies the primary political dynamics that are essential to being part of American political life. These dynamics are instant name recognition for family members, instant empathy from the electorate for the family member's position on issues, nonrational voting behavior based on residual biases associated with the family, and ability to exhibit independence from party politics. The practical effects of establishing a political dynasty are political survival. The societal effect is much less noticeable; political dynasties package political change as familial continuity and thus provide for the survival of their family's influence as well as goals for society. Because of this, political dynasties built in the past shape present political life and have uncommon influence over America's destiny.

REFERENCES

Clinch, Nancy Gager. 1973. *The Kennedy neurosis.* New York: Grosset & Dunlap.
Collier, Peter and David Horowitz. 1976. *The Rockefellers: An American dynasty.* New York: Holt, Rinehart and Winston.

Davis, John H. 1984. The Kennedys: Dynasty and disaster 1848–1983. New York: McGraw-Hill Book Company.

Ensor Harr, John and Peter J. Johnson. 1988. *The Rockefeller century*. New York: Charles Scribner's Sons.

Granberg, Donald. 1985. An anomaly in political perception. *The Public Opinion Quarterly* 49 504–16.

Lundberg, Ferdinand. 1975. *The Rockefeller syndrome*. Secaucus, NJ: Lyle Stuart Inc.

King of the hills and hollers. 1984. *The Economist*, 20 October.

Halberstam, David. 1968. *The unfinished odyssey of Robert Kennedy*. New York: Random House.

Liberals rebuffed. 1986. *The Economist*, 20 September.

Matusow, Allen J. 1983. John F. Kennedy and the intellectuals. *The Wilson Quarterly* (autumn): 140–53.

Salmore, Barbara G., and Stephen A. Salmore. 1989. *Candidates, parties, and campaigns*. Washington D.C.: Congressional Quarterly Inc.

Schuyler, Michael W. 1987. Ghosts in the White House: LBJ, RFK, and the assassination of JFK. *Presidential Studies Quarterly*, 49: 503–18.

Wayne, Stephen J. 1990. *The road to the white house*. New York: St. Martin's Press.

Wills, Garry. 1982. *The Kennedy imprisonment*. Boston: Little, Brown and Co.

Writing an Analysis

In some courses in political science, instructors prefer students to examine political events or phenomena critically. Writing an analysis of an event is part descriptive, part historical, part journalistic, and part imagination! An analysis involves identifying and differentiating between relevant and irrelevant information. It is specifically focused on the causal relationship between variables. In other words, an analysis provides an examination of the causes of political events. It involves asking not just who, what, when, and where, but also who benefited politically, who paid the political costs, what were the motivation or incentives, and when was the impact of the event realized. An analysis is typically, but not always, supported with both qualitative and quantitative evidence. Here is a standard formula for political event analysis (Lester 1990, 73).

1. **Describe the event. In particular, briefly describe the context in which the event occurred.**
   - Identify specific activities that lead up to the event.
   - Identify any perceived reactions to the event or arguments about its impact.
   - State your thesis about why the event occurred.
   - Be sure your thesis sentence clearly identifies the important causal variables associated with the event.
2. **For the body, using your thesis sentence to guide you:**
   - Examine critically, all important activities preceding the event.
   - Using evidence, show how each activity is linked to the event.
   - Rank order the events by importance to the outcome. Support this ranking with evidence.

- Provide evidence that describes the political consequence of the event or outcome.

3. **Summarize the causal relationships and emphasize the important determinants of the event or outcome.**
   - Show how the evidence supported your thesis sentence.
   - Reaffirm your explanation of the event's impact on politics in society.

YOUTH INFLUENCE IN POLITICAL OUTCOMES

By
Patrick J. Brown
Professor Schmidt
POLS 318
October 9, 1990
(Reprinted with permission)

ABSTRACT

The youth in this country have had a direct influence on electoral outcomes by adding new voters to the voting block in 1972 and by taking part directly in the electoral process. Volunteering time to a candidate is the best way to get directly involved in an election. Also, if the youth vote in an election, they can add millions of votes to the outcome. In addition, if the majority of the youth movement is voting for a particular candidate, they can really make a difference in the election results. Although voter turnout of the youth has always been the lowest of the voting blocks, the youth movement can still make a difference. A good example of this occurred in the presidential election of 1968. The youth in the 1980s have identified with the Republicans and in the 1970s with the Democrats. This report will show that when the youth coalesce, they can make a difference in electoral outcome.

INTRODUCTION

According to the Twenty-sixth Amendment of the Constitution of the United States, citizens who are eighteen years of age or older have the right to vote. This Amendment was the turning point of the youth movement of the late 1960s. Now, the youth of this country can not only protest against their government, they can vote to change the representatives to govern it. Even before 1972, when the Amendment was approved, the youth (18–24) in the United States had made a difference in the electoral process and the outcomes. The youth can and have made a difference on electoral outcomes by adding a new voting block, with millions of new voters, and by taking part directly by working and volunteering for candidates.

TRENDS IN STUDENT ACTIVISM

In the 1960s, young people all over the world, particularly in the United States, seemed to develop a distinctive style of political dissent. Newspaper coverage about some youth organization holding a protest or political rally became increasingly frequent. According to Anthony Orum, there are three important conclusions that emerge from observing youth and their politics in the United States through historical perspectives. The conclusions are: the United States was not the first nation to experience vigorous political activity, it was uncommon to experience large-scale political activity by American youth until the 1960s, and most of the youth activists were well educated and wealthy.[1] A study of accredited four-year universities during the 1967–68 academic year found that only about 2 percent of the student population belonged to leftist student organizations and that an additional 8–10 percent were strongly sympathetic with the movement for social change and were capable of temporary activism, depending on the issues.[2]

The activism of the 1960s had its origins in Berkeley, California, when in 1964 student activists were banned from political activities in an area of campus where they were formerly allowed. When the American involvement in Vietnam escalated, student unrest on campuses often became violent. According to Robert K. Landers:

> Student activists, to make a distinctive mark on their time, must overcome the thinness of their ranks and assert a plausible claim to represent in essence, the future. Hence, they must somehow arouse the sympathies of—and get occasional demonstrations of support from—the mass of students. During the 1960s, activists were able to accomplish this,

but during the 1980s, they had been far less successful.[3]

The protests and the Vietnam War were both fought by young people. The unpopular war called more attention to the impact of government than any other event in this century.[4] Those who wanted to make a change had some alternatives. Some activists called for a revolution; however, others called for a non-violent means of expression.

TRENDS IN YOUTH VOTER TURNOUT

One alternative to revolution was to exercise the power of voting. Importantly, the Twenty-sixth Amendment, lowering the voting age to eighteen in 1972, created a potential new influence on the outcome of elections. In addition, the post–World War II "baby boom" also resulted in many new voters entering the electorate in the late 1960s and early 1970s. Both of these factors drastically changed the electorate in this country. There were approximately 25 million new voters.[5] Many of these voters were more inclined to be less partisan and vote more along the lines of the issues.

Disappointing Youth Voter Turnout

There was, however, a surprise to those who advocated the Twenty-sixth Amendment: the trend of a declining youth turnout. In 1972, only about 48.3 percent turned out and voted. Although voting can be a powerful force for the youth agenda, only about 45.6 percent of that same group four years later voted.[6] Further, in the 1972 election, the percentage of 18–20-year-olds who were not registered was 41.9 percent and for 21–24-year-olds who were not registered was 40.5 percent.[7]

Nonetheless, in terms of non-voters, young people tend to be more interested in politics than older Americans. Among the population as a whole, older persons are more interested than the youth. The voting turnout by age characteristics of 18–20-year-olds from the 1972 election to the 1984 election was considerably low compared with the rest of the voting classes. Since 1972, Democrats have outnumbered Republicans in terms of new voters by more than two to one.[8] The major reason was the Democrats' opposition to the war in Vietnam. Unfortunately, the Democrats, more than the Republicans, are inclined to not vote in an election. Together with youth identification from the Democratic Party, this characteristic might help explain the low youth turnout.

More importantly, the tendency of the youngest voters to identify with the Republican Party may offer the greatest hope of increasing the size of the GOP. Although youth generally identify with the political party of their parents, increasingly young voters are aligning with the Republican Party, regardless of their parent's party identification.[9] This change could help the party grow generational replacement. For example, in the 1984 election, the younger voters supported the re-election of Ronald Reagan. This was a big change since the first youth election in 1972. The cause of this shift was not a move to the right among college students, but rather a shift to the middle ground or moderate positions in 1984.[10] Further, according to a *New York Times–CBS News* poll, Ronald Reagan won the support of full-time students by a margin of 51 to 48 percent. Again in the 1988 election, George Bush defeated Michael Dukakis in the youth category 52 to 47 percent.[11]

Inducing Youth Turnout

Although young people vote less than any other category, there are opportunities to change this trend. To induce voting among youth, candidates must advocate what young people perceive as their needs. In addition, the parties must change structurally to be more appealing and inclusive of young people. Finally, voting must result in identification benefits to youths.[12] Youth need to feel something when they vote. Young people must be persuaded to find efficacy and clear reasons for participating.[13] The foremost obstacle to increasing voting participation among youth is persuading them that their votes count.

Nonetheless, students and young people participate. Many of these activists volunteer in political campaigns because they feel strongly about the issues and candidates and because they want to make a difference. In conservative terms, there is a word to describe the effort of youth activism on college campuses to participate in the electoral process. The term is referred to as the Mass-Based Youth Effort.[14] The school that a potential activist can attend is called the Morton Blackwell Leadership Institute.[15] Based in Virginia, the Institute holds training seminars in central locations throughout the U.S. During this two-day seminar, activists learn how to conduct a canvas of the university's student population. Once activists locate the strong supporters for their candidate, they remind their supporters to go to the polls and vote. These activists also learn how to identify unregistered voters who agree with their party and how to register them to vote. Youths are taught how to get active and directly involved in the electoral process, while showing young people how the election directly concerns them.

Another youth-based set of groups which mobilize students are the College Republicans and the College Democrats. Both the College Republicans National Committee and the Young College Democrats planned massive voter registration drives in the 1984 and 1988 elections. The Republicans concentrated on all fifty states, compared with the seventeen-state effort in 1980. The College Democrats, for the first time in 1984, worked in thirty states.[16] The College Republicans have a full-time staff in Washington, D.C., and they have an annual budget of $250,000. The College Democrats have only a $12,000 budget and lack any central office of staff.[17] The main reason for the difference is because Morton Blackwell used to be the Executive Director of the College Republican National Committee, and the mass-based youth effort concepts are used by the National Committee. The College Republicans now hold their own leadership training schools.

Impact of Youth Mobilization Programs

These youth movements have made a difference in electoral outcomes. In 1984, some 35,000 new student voters in Ohio helped to defeat three statewide referendums that would have raised the drinking age, and cut education funding.[18] Also, in New Orleans, at Xavier University in 1984, 98 percent of the students were registered to vote.[19] Top priority was finally placed on voter registration by youth groups in 1984. Since then, efforts are still going strong on campuses all over the country.

Students were also actively involved in Gary Hart's campaign for President in 1984. The students are credited with Hart's win in the New Hampshire primary because of the student canvassing effort. The students canvassed 90 percent of the precincts in the state.[20] The New Hampshire win placed Gary Hart in the race as a major contender. Many students joined the campaign as full-time staff for the rest of the way. About half of Gary Hart's volunteers were students, compared with a third working for Jesse Jackson, and a fourth working for Walter Mondale.[21] All of the Democratic candidates made numerous campus campaign stops in 1984, because they believed that students could make a difference in many ways.

Probably the best example of a direct youth influence on the outcome of an election happened in the presidential election of 1968. Senator Eugene McCarthy was an early Democratic candidate for President of the United States. As president, Lyndon Johnson was favored in the race. The vote predictions in the New Hampshire primary by Gallup

Polls had predicted, in January, that McCarthy had only 12 percent of the vote. When it was all over in March of 1968, McCarthy received 42.4 percent of the vote.[22] The students, most of whom could not even vote yet, came to New Hampshire from Michigan, Wisconsin, Yale, and Harvard to work for their candidate, Eugene McCarthy. McCarthy gave the students the inspiration to care about politics and the Presidency. He also promised to end the war in Vietnam. It was estimated that as many as five thousand students campaigned on weekends and two thousand were full-time.[23]

In particular, an important campaign stop for the Eugene McCarthy Campaign was in Wisconsin. Theodore H. White sums up what happened next during that visit:

> Student headquarters for McCarthy at the Wisconsin Hotel, a mile away, was explosive in contrast—eight thousand students were now roving over Wisconsin. Every town of five thousand had its student platoons, sleeping at friendly homes, in church basements, and still, on this Saturday they were pouring in, eight hundred from Michigan alone—and now the students were veterans—volunteer specialists had broken the lists down into streets, blocks, and districts—assigned eighty calls to each volunteer. By two o'clock in the morning, Sunday, student headquarters were sending back the other busloads because they could not be used.[24]

When the votes were counted, Eugene McCarthy had 56.2 percent to Lyndon Johnson's 34.6 percent and Robert Kennedy's 6.3 percent.[25] Later, President Johnson gave a speech in which he withdrew his name from the electoral process and did not seek another term. The students in Eugene McCarthy's campaign worked many tasks, from administrative to the most menial kinds of campaign work. The allure of the McCarthy campaign primarily centered on the treatment of youths in his campaign organization. His campaign staff did not distinguish between adult and the youth movement. They all worked together for a common cause.

Conclusion

The youth in this country, in terms of voting, have always had the lowest turnout. Nevertheless, youth can still make a difference in electoral outcomes. Youth groups' major influence comes because of the new voting block of 1972 and the impact of the numbers of "baby boom" votes cast in the elections. The candidates in the 1972 election had to appeal to the youth of this country. Because young people were protesting government policies, it was difficult to win over the youth vote in the late 1960s and the early 1970s. Most of those who were mobilized attached themselves to the Democratic Party. This continued to be the case until 1984, when the young people realigned to the Republican Party during the re-election of Ronald Reagan. The youth vote has been largely Republican since that time. Part of the reason was a shift to more moderate positions by the youth and because of the Republicans' youth effort to attract votes, volunteers, and registration of new young voters in this country.

Perhaps the lowering of the voting age in this country did not have the impact in terms of increasing the number of young people that actually voted. It did, however, give millions of young people an incentive to use a nonviolent means of expressing opinions about policy decisions that impact them the most. Hard-working mass-based youth movements can make a difference in this country like they did in the election for President in 1968. Theodore H. White describes that remarkable event in 1968 that best summarizes the potential impact of youth voting participation:

It was not part of the script of history that Lyndon Johnson of the Pedernales should be brought down by a poet from Watkin, Minnesota. Hard working college students, in nine weeks, had brought down not a dean, not a president of a university, but the President of the United States.[26]

NOTES

[1]Anthony M. Orum, *The Seeds of Politics* (New Jersey: Prentice-Hall, Inc., 1972), 2.

[2]Richard E. Peterson, "The Scope of Organized Student Protest," in *Protest! Student Activism in America*, eds. Julian Foster and Durward Long (New York: Morrow, 1970), 78.

[3]Robert K. Landers, "Student Politics 1980s Style," *Editorial Research Reports*, 1986, 661; see also Louis M. Seagull, *Youth and Change in American Politics* (New York: Franklin Watts Inc., 1977).

[4]William C. Mitchell, *Why Vote?* (Chicago: Markham Publishing Company, 1971), 8.

[5]Mitchell 1971, 8; see also, M. Kent Jennings and Richard G. Niemi, *The Political Character of Adolescence* (New York: Princeton University Press, 1974).

[6]David Hill and Norman Luttbeg, *Trends in American Electoral Behavior* (Itasca, Illinois: F.E. Peacock Pub, Inc, 1980).

[7]William J. Crotty, *Political Reform and the American Experiment* (New York: Thomas J. Crowell Co., 1977), 54; see also Stanley Kelly, Richard E. Ayres, and William G. Bowen, "Registration and Voting: Putting Things First," *American Political Science Review* (June 1967): 61.

[8]William H. Flanigan, *Political Behavior of the American Electorate* (Boston: Allyn and Bacon, Inc., 1972), 26.

[9]Everett Carl Ladd, "On Mandates, Realignments, and the 1984 Presidential Election," *Political Science Quarterly* (Spring 1985): 18. See also, M. Kent Jennings and Richard G. Niemi, "The Transmission of Political Values from Parent to Child," *American Political Science Review* (March 1968): 171.

[10]Landers "Student Politics 1980s Style," 613; see also Frank J. Sorauf and Paul Allen Beck, *Party Politics in America* (Glenview, IL: Scott, Foresman, 1987).

[11]Larry J. Sabato, *The 1988 Election in America* (Glenview, IL: Scott, Foresman, 1989), 32.

[12]Curtis Gans, "Why Young People Don't Vote," *Educational Digest* (February 1989): 40.

[13]Gans 1989, 43.

[14]This information is based on my field observation of the institution. See Morton Blackwell, *Leadership Source Manual*, mimeo (Springfield, VA: Morton Blackwell Leadership Institute, 1990).

[15]Blackwell 1990.

[16]Donna St. George, "Students Bone up on Art of Politics," *National Journal* (April 7, 1984): 667.

[17]Larry J. Sabato, *The Party's Just Begun* (Glenview, IL: Scott, Foresman, 1988), 81.

[18]St. George, "Students Bone up on Art of Politics," 665.

[19]Ibid.

[20]Ibid.

[21]Ibid.

[22]Eugene J. McCarthy, *The Year of the People* (New York: Doubleday and Company, Inc., 1969), 89; see also Arthur Herzog, *McCarthy for President* (New York: Viking Press, 1969).

[23]McCarthy 1969, 70.

[24]Theodore H. White, *The Making of the President 1896* (New York: Atheneum Publishers, 1969), 120.

[25]McCarthy 1969, 108.

[26]White 1969, 125.

BIBLIOGRAPHY

Blackwell, Morton. *Leadership Source Manual*. Mimeo. Springfield, VA: Morton Blackwell Leadership Institute, 1990.

Crotty, William J. *Political Reform and the American Experiment*. New York: Thomas J. Crowell Co, 1977.

Flanigan, William H. *Political Behavior of the American Electorate*. Boston: Allyn and Bacon, Inc, 1972.

Gans, Curtis. "Why Young People Don't Vote," *Educational Digest* 54 (February 1989): 40–43.

Herzog, Arthur. *McCarthy for President*. New York: Viking Press, 1969.

Hill, David and Norman R. Luttbeg. *Trends in American Electoral Behavior*. Itasca, Illinois: F.E. Peacock Publishers, Inc, 1990.

Jennings, M. Kent and Richard G. Niemi. *The Political Character of Adolescence*. New York: Princeton University Press, 1974.

_____. "The Transmission of Political Values from Parent to Child." *American Political Science Review* 62 (March 1968): 168–84.

Kelly, Stanley, Richard E. Ayres, and William G. Bowen, "Registration and Voting: Putting Things First." *American Political Science Review* 61 (June 1967): 359–79.

Ladd, Everett Carl. "On Mandates, Realignments, and the 1984 Presidential Election." *Political Science Quarterly* 100 (spring 1985): 1–25.

Landers, Robert K. "Student Politics 1980s Style," *Editorial Research Reports* 2 (1986): 609–628.

McCarthy, Eugene J. *The Year of the People*. New York: Doubleday and Company, 1969.

Mitchell, William C. *Why Vote?* Chicago: Markham Publishing Company, 1971.

Orum, Anthony M. *The Seeds of Politics*. New Jersey: Prentice-Hall, Inc., 1972.

Peterson, Richard E. "The Scope of Organized Student Protest." In *Protest! Student Activism in America,* edited by Julian Foster and Durward Long. New York: Morrow, 1970.

Sabato, Larry J. *The 1988 Elections in America*. Glenview, IL: Scott, Foresman and

Company, 1989.

_____. *The Party's Just Begun*. Glenview, IL: Scott, Foresman and Company, 1988.

Seagull, Louis M. *Youth and Change in American Politics*. New York: Franklin Watts Inc., 1977.

Sorauf, Frank J. and Paul Allen Beck. *Party Politics in America*. Glenview, IL: Scott, Foresman and Company, 1987.

St. George, Donna. "Students Bone Up to Art of Politics." *National Journal* 16 (April 7, 1984): 665–68.

White, Theodore H. *The Making of the President 1968*. New York: Anteneum Publishers, Inc., 1969.

Writing a Position Paper

Instructors in some upper-level political science classes may assign a research paper which requires the student to do more than just research what other people say about a topic or controversy. A position paper takes the research process one step further than simple comparison or analysis. In a position paper, the student is required to construct a theory or position about an event, problem, or controversy and defend that theory or position using evidence. Position papers include, at minimum, scholarly qualitative evidence. Quantitative evidence and statistical methods are often used to provide further support for the author's theory or position. Here is a standard formula for writing a position paper.

1. **Describe a problem, event, or controversy. In particular, briefly describe the significance of the item you identified.**
   - Identify alternative explanations about why the problem/controversy exists or the event occurred.
   - In your thesis sentence, state your unique perspective about why the event occurred or why the problem/controversy exists.
   - Be sure you clearly separate your perspective from the others described.
   - Be sure your thesis sentence clearly identifies the important causal variables associated with the event, controversy, or problem.

2. **Trace the evolution of the event, problem, or controversy.**
   - Describe the context in which the event, problem, or controversy occurs.
   - Analyze the details, major identifiable issues, and minor underlying issues connected with the event, problem, or controversy.

3. **Identify the arguments or different important perspectives that have been used to explain the event, problem, or controversy.**
   - Be sure to justify why these perspectives are important.
   - Differentiate between the alternative explanations. How are they different? How are they similar?
   - Criticize the alternative explanations for errors in reasoning, omissions, and/or facts.

4. **Describe your competing theory or position and justify it with evidence.**
   - State clearly how your perspective is different or corrects errors identified in other explanations.
   - Present evidence that strongly supports your theory or position.
   - Identify any evidence that appears to refute your theory or position. Explain why this evidence is not valid or how your theory must be adjusted to address the evidence, if it is valid.

5. **Restate your theory or position and provide a concluding statement.**
   - Defend your theory or position by briefly recalling the evidence that supports your explanation, and not the alternative explanations.
   - Make sure your analysis and arguments support your defense.
   - If possible, suggest a course of action on how the event, problem, or controversy could be addressed better in the future.

**CHIEF JUSTICE REHNQUIST:
DOES HE LEAD THE COURT?**

By
Chris Kozenski
POLS 435
December 7, 1989
(Reprinted with permission)

INTRODUCTION

The Chief Justice, as the head of the Supreme Court, is in both a good and bad position to lead and influence the members of the Courts. There are two limitations of power facing the Chief Justice. As Laurence Baum (1986) indicates in his book *The Supreme Court*, the first limitation is that the Chief Justice is burdened with more administrative duties than ever. As the head of the federal court system, the Chief serves both a powerful ceremonial and bureaucratic role, which keeps him very busy. According to Baum, one observer of the Court, Jeffery Morris, states that the Chief "may well stand at a relative disadvantage…" in the writing and arguing over opinions "because of the unique demands upon his time" (1986, 153).

The second limitation of the power of today's Chief Justice is that present day Justices are strong-minded, skilled individuals who are not likely to be controlled. Chief Justice John Marshall, in the early 1800s, had substantial control over his Court as seen by his writing of the Court's opinion in almost all cases. Rarely under Marshall did another Justice's views win out over the Chief Justice. Yet, Chief Justice Rehnquist would never be able to lead the Court as strongly (Baum 1986; Steamer 1986).

But the position of Chief Justice also has formal powers that strengthen his position as the leader of the Court. In particular, there are three formal powers which can be quite important: 1) presiding over oral argument and conference, 2) creating the discuss list, and 3) opinion assignment (Baum 1986). By presiding over conference, the Chief Justice opens the discussion on a case, summarizes it, and then gives his personal opinions on the case. He can also end discussion on the case. In this way, it might be possible for the Chief to "frame alternatives, thus helping to shape the outcome of the discussion" (Baum 1986, 153).

The discuss list is a set of petitions that will receive group judgment by the Court. The Chief Justice has the duty to make the first informal version of the list. By doing this, the Chief plays an important role in determining which cases will be heard and decided on by the group (Baum 1986; Chaper 1987; Cannon and O'Brien 1985).

OPINION ASSIGNMENTS IN THE REHNQUIST COURT

The Chief Justice's third power—opinion assignment—is by far his strongest leadership tool. The Chief Justice is, by position, the Justice who assigns the writer of the Court's majority opinion. If the Chief is not in the majority, then the next senior-most Justice in the majority assigns the opinion (Baum 1986; Chaper 1987). What makes this power so important is that it is in these majority opinions where the Supreme Court establishes "controlling constitutional principles" and where "broader policy objectives beyond the immediate case are fashioned" (Slotnick 1978, 219). So by assigning the opinions to the Justice of his choice, the Chief is in a good position to alter, even frame, the public policies that result from Supreme Court decisions.

Because of the importance of opinion assignment, it should be shown that certain factors do come into play when the Chief Justice makes an assignment. There are four factors, in particular, that have influence on the Chief Justice's assignment. The first is the equality of distribution. This means that the Justices should have relatively equal workloads and if the Chief assigns opinions disproportionately, he will upset those Justices who do not have an equal share of the workload, and therefore an unequal share of opinions (Slotnick 1978; 1979). Ability and expertise are also important factors the Chief takes into consideration when assigning an opinion (Brenner and Spaeth 1986; Spaeth and Michael 1985). The fourth factor is the importance of the decision. If a decision is considered important, often the Chief will self-assign the opinion. This is traditionally an unwritten norm of the court. As the "equal above equals" the Chief lends his prestige to a decision when he is the author of the opinion (Slotnick 1978).

Still, there are four other things the Chief Justice must take into consideration when making an assignment. David Danelski suggests that whomever the Chief Justice designates to speak for the court may be highly influential in:

1) determining the precedent value of a decision (because the Justice who authors the opinion often decides the grounds for the decision).

2) making the decision as publicly acceptable as possible.

3) holding a majority together when it is a close vote.

4) and minimizing the number of dissenting and concurring opinions (Danelski 1986).

Often, the assigner of the opinion will choose the Justice who stands in the middle of the voting coalitions in order to gain support for the majority decision. For example, if a particular decision has the court divided, the Chief must choose the Justice with a moderate view in order to gain votes from the dissenting side of the court (Danelski 1986).

Equality of Assignments

There are two ways in which equality of opinion assignment can be examined. The first way is through measuring absolute equality; this is simply the equality of caseloads between the Justices. Another way to examine equality is to look at it conditionally; this means that equality is based on the frequency of times a Justice is available to write the opinion (Altfeld and Spaeth 1984, 300).

To see how fairly Chief Justice Rehnquist assigned opinions, I examined majority opinion assignments from both viewpoints of equality (Altfeld and Spaeth 1984, 299–304) the same way Harold Spaeth studied court decisions.[1] Absolute equality was examined for the 1986, 1987, and 1988 terms. Table 1 displays the number of opinions that each Justice wrote per term, regardless of who made the assignment or how often the Justice was in the majority. It was measured using a mean (which is simply the average number of times a Justice wrote an opinion for that year), a standard deviation (Std. Dev.), and a coefficient of relative variation (CRV) which standardizes a set of deviations based on different means.

(TABLE 1 ABOUT HERE)

Because the Chief Justice assigns a majority of cases, it was up to Rehnquist to assign fairly and equally if he wanted a record of distributive equality in opinion assignments. Table 1 shows an impressive equal distribution of opinion writing between the Justices. Treating the terms as a whole ('86–'88) each Justice wrote an average of 15.8 opinions. The number of times a Justice varied by more than three assignments from the term average is only three (two occurring in 1986, Powell and Scalia; one occurring in 1988, Scalia). Rehnquist's CRVs are low in all three terms (1986, CRV .15; 1987, CRV .13; 1988, CRV .13).

Comparing Rehnquist to other Chief Justices only enhances his record of absolute quality. Rehnquist has an overall CRV of .12, while Burger's overall CRV is .179, and Warren's was .24. Stone, Vinson, Taft, and Hughes are all at least twice as high as Burger's, which makes Rehnquist's CRV the best of the last six Chief Justices of the Supreme Court (Spaeth 1984; Goldberg 1986).

---

[1]Opinion Assignment Ratio (OAR) was used here in order to compare with Spaeth's findings of Burger and Warren. (The overall OARs are as follows: Rehn.=14.0, Bren.=17.3, White=14.8, Mar.=16.1, Blac.=13.6, Pow.=15.8, Stev.=15.8, O'C=14.2, Sca. 11.1, Ken.=12.6.)

Rehnquist has a very good overall distribution record, but what happens when conditioned equality of assignments is looked at? To study this, opinion assignment ratios were used to see the overall picture. Again following Spaeth's study, Rehnquist's equality of assignments in "important" cases was compared to that of Burger and Warren. It is in these "important" cases where major public policy is made. To test whether Chief Justice Rehnquist is leading the Court's public policy, it is necessary to look at his opinion distribution practices in these important cases.

There have been many methods employed to define important cases. Sidney Ulmer deems a case important by the amount of times the "court cites the case within five years of the decision" (Altfeld and Spaeth 1984, 303). This cannot apply here because of the recent data being used. Another approach uses constitutional casebooks, and if the case is discussed in several of these books, then it is considered as important. But because both of these methods have come under fire for various reasons, Spaeth's method was used. Spaeth's method defined a case as important if it appears within a rectangle on the front cover of the Lawyers' Edition of *U.S. Reports*. Of these important cases (47 in all between 1986 and 1989) Rehnquist assigned 72 percent of the opinions. (He assigned 50 percent in 1986, 80 percent in 1987, and 82 percent in 1988.)

As a norm of the Court, the Chief Justice is expected to disproportionately assign important decisions to himself, being the "first above equals." Yet Rehnquist's patterns of opinion assignments in important cases show huge disparities. Using an opinion assignment ratio (OAR), each Justice was given a ratio for the '86–'88 terms. The OAR is "simply the percentage of times a given Justice is assigned the majority opinion when he is in the Court's majority" (Slotnick 1979, 63). Measuring a Justice's OAR is important because "it is more sensitive than a simple average would be when dealing with a Justice who is in dissent [or not sitting] a great deal of the time" (Altfeld and Spaeth 1984, 304).

According to their OARs, as seen in Table 2, three Justices had very high OARs and were at least 13.6 points above the mean; these Justices were Rehnquist with an OAR of 29.4, White with an OAR of 37.9, and Powell with an OAR of 42.9.

(TABLE 2 ABOUT HERE)

There were also three Justices who had OARs of zero, meaning that no time in the 1986, 1987, or 1988 term did Chief Justice Rehnquist assign them an "important" opinion to write. These Justices were Brennan, Marshall, and Stevens. Blackmun also had a relatively low OAR of 6.7. The standard deviation is 15.1 and the CRV = .96. This is a tremendously high CRV, which shows that there are great differences in the number of opinions each Justice wrote.

Comparing Rehnquist to other Chief Justices shows to what degree Rehnquist unequally assigned cases. Burger's overall CRV of important cases was .47 (Altfeld and Spaeth 1984, 304). Stone's CRV was .40, Vinson's CRV was .55, and Warren's CRV equaled .44 (Altfeld and Spaeth 1984, 304). Even if Slotnick's rule is followed, which excludes those Justices who are available in less than ten cases (Brennan and Powell), Rehnquist's CRV is still .80, while Burger's declines to .34 (Altfeld and Spaeth 1984, 304).

In sum, these results show that Rehnquist unequally assigned the opinions of important cases. In particular, he especially favored those Justices who fit his ideology. Further, according to the data reported, his distributive inequality is the largest of the last five Chief Justices.

Self-Assignment

To see if this inequity came from Rehnquist's self-assignment practices, his OARs were compared to the average OAR of the Court. Following Slotnick's (1978) study, Tables 3 and 4 show the results of the comparison.

(TABLES 3 AND 4 ABOUT HERE)

Rehnquist has a lower OAR than the Court average in the case universe, which means he writes .5 fewer opinions than does the average Justice on the court when considering all cases. When only important decisions are examined does Rehnquist's OAR exceed the Court average by 13.6.

Table 4, however, shows that it is the norm for the Chief Justice's OAR to be substantially above the Court average. This confirms Slotnick's (1978) findings. Rehnquist is only 1.5 above the total for all Justices from Taft to Burger. Thus, these findings suggest Rehnquist's unequal distribution of opinion assignments in important cases is not due to his self-assignment practices.

IDEOLOGIES ON THE REHNQUIST COURT

To further test these findings on Rehnquist's leadership practices, the Justices' judicial perspective was evaluated on an ideological spectrum. To address this same issue Harold Spaeth and David Rohde examined the conflicts between the liberal and conservative positions on the Court (Baum 1986). Rohde and Spaeth break these issues of conflict down into three categories: 1) freedom, 2) equality, 3) New Dealism. Using these categories, it is easy to rank the Justices on an ideological spectrum.

In order to say that Rehnquist is leading the Court, evidence is needed to show that he is assigning those opinions of important cases disproportionately to those who are most like him. In a study on the 1986 term, Rohde and Spaeth looked at the voting patterns on "freedom" cases in 58 non-unanimous decisions. Freedom cases are defined as involving "conflicts between individual freedoms and governmental action" (Baum 1986:138). They found that some Justices were prone to vote liberally and others were prone to vote conservatively. This comes as no surprise. By using a scalogram, Rohde and Spaeth were able to rank the Justices according to their number of liberal votes.

In 1986, according to the scalogram, Marshall, Brennan, and Stevens, in that order, had the most liberal votes. Blackmun also voted liberally more than conservatively. On the other end of the spectrum, Rehnquist, O'Connor, White, Scalia, and Powell had the most conservative votes.

Looking at the interagreement among Justices, Baum (1986) uses a table for the median percentage of cases in which pairs of Justices supported the same opinion as in the 1985 and 1986 terms. Unlike the Rohde and Spaeth study, this table includes all cases in all issue areas. Baum finds that Rehnquist agrees with Powell 87 percent of the time, and White and O'Connor 81 percent and 85 percent of the time. Rehnquist had the lowest rates of agreement with Marshall 39 percent, Brennan 42 percent, and Stevens 49 percent of the time. This interagreement, along with the findings of Spaeth and Rohde, makes a very clear picture. These findings also clearly support what I have concluded from my study— that is, Chief Justice Rehnquist assigns important opinions to Justices who will fulfill his policy objectives—these Justices often being Powell, White, and the Chief Justice himself.

DISCUSSION AND CONCLUSIONS

So far, this study has shown that Chief Justice Rehnquist has a fair overall opinion assignment rate. More importantly, this study has shown that Rehnquist has an unfair opinion assignment rate in important cases where most public policy is made. In particular, the findings show that Rehnquist favors conservatives, like himself, by giving them more politically significant opinions to write. Yet, it is important to mention that Rehnquist only assigned 73 percent of the total important cases in the three terms studied. Brennan assigned the other 27 percent of the cases, except for one assigned by Marshall. Thus, Justice Brennan appears to have assigned cases just as unfairly as Rehnquist did.

The OAR ratio should be used to examine the relative assignment behavior more closely. But because the numbers were so low, actual percentages of times Brennan assigned opinions to each Justice is an adequate and meaningful substitute for an OAR ratio. Brennan self-assigned the opinion exactly 50 percent of the time. Stevens, Marshall, and Blackmun were each assigned 10 percent. Brennan only assigned 10 important cases in all, so of the ten, he assigned 80 percent (or 8) of them to liberals on the Court.[2] Both O'Connor and Powell were assigned one opinion. From these numbers it is plain to see that Brennan uses the 27 percent of the cases he assigns to promote liberal public policies. In this way he, too, is a leader of the Court, although he is not as powerful as the Chief Justice is. Thus, this suggests that although the Chief Justice has a normal self-assignment rate, he self-assigns cases less than the average Justice overall and is similar to higher Chief Justices in self-assignment on important cases.

FINAL REMARKS

Earlier in this paper, many different factors were mentioned, each having a possible effect on opinion assignment practices. Among the more important factors mentioned were expertise and holding the majority vote together. It is true that these factors work together and produce an effect on the Chief Justice's decision. Yet, it is apparent that Chief Justices, through the use of their power of assignment, also have wide discretion in pursuing their own public policy ideals (Slotnick, 1979). Chief Justice Rehnquist is no exception; in fact, he was shown to have possibly the widest discretion of the more recent Chief Justices. It will be interesting to see if this trend continues in his future terms as Chief Justice.

---

[2]The case of K-Mart vs. Cartier was not included because of the plurality of opinions.

REFERENCES

Altfeld, M.F. and H.J. Spaeth. 1984. Measuring influence on the U.S. Supreme Court. *Jurimetrics Journal*, 24: 236–247.

Baum, L. 1986. *The Supreme Court*. 3rd ed. Washington, D.C.: Congressional Quarterly.

Brenner, S. and H.J. Spaeth. 1986. Issue specialization in majority opinion assignment on the Burger court. *Western Political Quarterly* 39: 520–527.

Cannon, M.C. and D.M. O'Brien. 1985. *Views from the bench*. Chatham, NJ: Chatham House.

Chaper, J.H. 1987. *The Supreme Court and its Justices*. Chicago: American Bar Association.

Danelski, David. 1986. The influence of the decisionmaking process. In *Courts, judges, and politics,* edited by W.F. Murphy and C.H. Pritchett. New York: Random House.

Goldberg, A.J. 1986. The Rehnquist Court. *Hastings Constitutional Law Quarterly,* 14: 21–24.

Slotnick, E.E. 1978. The Chief Justices and self-assignment on majority opinions: A research note. *Western Political Quarterly* 31: 219–25.

———. 1979. Who speaks for the Court? Majority opinion assignment from Taft to Burger. *American Journal of Political Science,* 23: 60–77.

Spaeth, H.J. 1984. Distributive Justice: Majority opinion assignments in the Burger court. *Judicature* 67: 299–304.

Spaeth, H.J. and F.A. Michael. 1985. Influence relationships within the Supreme Court: A comparison of the Warren and Burger courts. *Western Political Quarterly* 38: 70–83.

Steamer, R.J. 1986. *Chief Justice.* Columbia: University of South Carolina Press.

Table 1: Distribution of Opinions and Judgments of the Court

JUSTICE	TERM		
	1986	**1987**	**1988**
Rehnquist	17	15	16
Brennan	16	16	17
White	16	20	18
Marshall	15	15	15
Blackmun	13	15	15
Powell	20	—	—
Stevens	15	19	15
O'Connor	18	16	13
Scalia	12	16	11
Kennedy	12	7°	16
Mean	15.78	16.50	15.11
Std. Dev.	2.43	2.17	1.97
CRV	.15	.13	.13

Mean: the average number of times a Justice wrote an opinion, Std. Dev: standard deviation from the mean. CRV: a coefficient of relative variation that standardizes a set of deviations based on different means.

° Kennedy did not participate in the entire '87–'88 term, so he was excluded from the mean, std. dev., CRV. If Kennedy was included, the following data apply: mean = 15.44, std. dev. 3.44, CRV = .22.

Source: *Supreme Court Reporter* 1986, 1987, 1988.

Table 2: Rehnquist's Assignees and Their Opinion Assignment Ratios in "Important Cases"

Assignees	Number of Assignments	Times Available	OAR
Rehnquist	10	34	29.4
Brennan	0	9	0
White	11	29	37.9
Marshall	0	10	0
Blackmun	1	15	6.7
Powell	3	7	42.9
Stevens	0	14	0
O'Connor	2	18	11.1
Scalia	4	29	13.8
Kennedy	3	19	15.8

Mean (for the court) = 15.8
Std. Dev. (for the court) = 15.1
CRV (for the court) = .96
Source: Lawyers' Edition, *U.S. Reports*, 1986, 1987, 1988.

Table 3: Self-Assignment Rates v. "Other" Assignment

Unit	Rehnquist's OAR	OAR for Court
Case Universe	14	14.5
"Important" Decisions	29.4	15.8

Table 4: Self-Assignment v. "Other" Assignment

Chief Justice	Case Universe		"Important" Decisions	
	Self-Assign OAR	*Court OAR*	*Self-Assign OAR*	*Court OAR*
Taft	16.3	11.1	38.2	10.2
Hughes	15.5	11.8	34.8	10.8
Stone	16.4	13.0	19.4	13.7
Vinson	12.1	14.6	24.6	13.1
Warren	13.0	14.0	19.0	13.5
Burger	13.7	14.5	25.7	12.9
TOTAL	14.8	12.6	24.8	12.7
Rehnquist	14.0	14.5	29.4	15.8

CHAPTER 12

Format and Examples of
Assignments Requiring Special
Techniques

Assignments Requiring Special Analytical Techniques

In the following pages, there are five examples of highly specialized undergraduate research papers that exhibit a range of writing styles and topics concerning public policy and decision-making. Like standard research papers, the ideas in the papers develop from a thesis sentence and present an argument about the significance of the findings. Unlike standard research papers, these papers require a special analytical structure where to be complete, the author must include specific details and information concerning the topic. Like standard research papers, these techniques are not specific to the study of American government. The study of comparative public policy and international agreements requires the same attention to the processes and details of making and implementing public policy. These papers exhibit the standard form and degree of thoroughness necessary for studying different kinds of policy at different points in the policy life cycle. The explanation and form for each type of paper precedes the examples.

First Paper: Analytical Case Study

"Dysfunctional Behavior in the FBI," examines the organizational practices of the Federal Bureau of Investigation. As a case study of administrative behavior, the paper focuses on the historical and contemporary organizational relationships between staff, administrators, and the public.

Second Paper: Problem-Solving Case Study

"Building Inspection Expense Analysis: Building Inspection Department" is a policy memorandum that provides a highly condensed analytical summary of budget expenditures and budget recommendations.

Third Paper: An Analysis of Legislation

"Copyright Protection and Fair Use in the Digital Age: The Digital Millennium Copyright Act of 1998" uses government documents and is limited to examining the initiation phase of public policy-making.

Fourth Paper: A Policy Evaluation

"Jailbait" uses a variety of sources from political science to scientific research reports. It is limited to examining the initiation and expansion phase of public policy-making.

Fifth Paper: A Policy Recommendation

"Policy Recommendation: Needle Exchange Programs and HIV Prevention" uses a variety of literature and some statistical information to propose an evaluation and formulation of a national needle exchange program. This paper analyzes the entire policy life cycle from the initiation to the expansion to the reformulation stages.

Analytical Case Study

Analytical case studies provide students with the opportunity to apply theories learned in class to practical situations. The goal of an analytical case study is to examine behavior related to political decision-making and explain why and how that behavior influenced political outcomes. Importantly, the reason for doing case studies is to learn something about how the political *system* works by examining how a *component* of the system works.

- The usefulness of case studies is that the research provides intricate details about the structure of organizations, strategies used by decision-makers, and behavior of individuals at the individual level.
- The problem with analytical case studies is that they are not often generalizable across the political spectrum.

The best analytical case studies focus on aspects of political behavior that are applicable to the broader political spectrum, while providing a compelling story about the idiosyncratic aspects of the subject being studied. At the end, the reader should know some interesting contextual information about the subject of the case study and understand more about the effect of particular structures and behavior on political outcomes.

How to Write an Analytical Case Study

1. **Title Page**
2. **Executive Summary**
   - Use bullets to highlight the key problems.
   - Summarize the conclusions.
3. **Narrative of Historical Context**
   - Write the thesis as a statement of the specific objective of the case study (i.e., what is to be explained and how).
   - Identify when the organization was formed (cultural and political context).
   - Identify why the organization was formed (goals, mission).
   - Describe the structure of the organization.
   - Describe the external political pressures on the staff from interest groups, Congress, the president, other agencies, or courts.
   - Describe the internal political pressures on the staff from standard operation procedures, agency structure, distribution of authority, or agency missions.
4. **Problem Identification**
   - Write this section in short story form with descriptive and compelling language.
   - Identify no more than 4 problems.
   - If more than 4 problems exist, then classify or cluster the problems together into

categories.
- Rank-order the problems from most compelling to least compelling.
- Describe the most compelling problem first and then the rest in rank order.
- Provide an illustrative, compelling, descriptive example for each problem identified.
- Identify the characters involved in the problems.
- Describe how the characters are involved in controversy and/or conflict.

5. Analysis of the Problem
- Suggest how the problems identified influenced political outcomes.
- Suggest how individual behavior influences the problems and the outcomes.
- Suggest how organizational structure influences the problems and the outcomes
- Identify any attempts to solve the problems.
- Suggest why attempts to solve the problems failed.
- Identify any solutions available but untried.
- Suggest why some available solutions have not been, or cannot be, used.

6. Conclusion
- Restate the problems.
- Restate the effect of the problems on political outcomes.
- Suggest what is new knowledge about the organization.
- Suggest what is new knowledge about how the political system works.

DYSFUNCTIONAL BEHAVIOR IN THE FBI

By
Steve Goard
Professor Diane Schmidt
POL 260A
December 1, 1998
(Reprinted with permission)

EXECUTIVE SUMMARY

The primary mission of the Federal Bureau of Investigation (FBI) is to investigate federal violations, such as bankruptcy fraud, anti-trust crimes, and neutrality violations. The FBI, since the J. Edgar Hoover administration, has chosen the path of bureaucratic effectiveness over efficiency and equity. Though Congress granted authority to the FBI to investigate violations, the FBI became a bureau of corruption because of:

- unchecked personal power.
- corrupt standard operating procedures.
- legislative collusion.
- presidential collusion.

Within the context of these problems, the FBI became an effective agency in achieving more authority, creating fear, and ruining individuals. The lack of responsible oversight and accountability that was pervasive during the Hoover administration continues to taint the image of the FBI and the credibility of its agents.

ORIGINS OF THE FBI'S POWER

In July of 1907, the American born grandnephew of Napoleon I, Charles J. Bonaparte, approached Congress with the idea of creating a permanent detective force within the Department of Justice (DOJ). In July of 1908, upon authority of the United States Congress, the Federal Bureau of Investigation (FBI) was established. In 1910, Congress passed the Mann Act to help curb prostitution. The act inadvertently expanded the authority of the FBI and enabled the FBI to develop dossiers on criminals, elected officials, and wealthy socialists. During the World War I era, Congress gave the FBI the responsibility to investigate espionage, sabotage, and draft violations. At this point, the FBI demonstrated their crude tactics on monitoring and catching such violators. During this period, the FBI extended their perimeter of censorship and continued to violate more civil liberties. For example, German teachers and German music composers were prohibited from teaching and performing (Gentry 1991).

PROBLEMS IN THE FBI

In December of 1924, the young J. Edgar Hoover was appointed as the director of the FBI. Hoover's appointment was to correct the bureau's reputation as a corrupt national law enforcement agency (Turner 1970). Hoover acknowledged the orders from Congress publicly, but some historians contend that Hoover and the FBI never intended to correct, but to continue, the pre-1924 intelligence activity (Croog 1992).

Unchecked Personal Power

Faced with a corrupt FBI, Hoover publicly accepted the challenge and vowed to restore the values of the FBI. December of 1924 marked the beginning of a new era under the control of Director J. Edgar Hoover. Upon Hoover's appointment, the FBI's authority was limited to federal violations only (Charles 1997). But in 1934, FBI agents were given the power to make arrests and to carry firearms (Feinman 1991). This grant of authority prompted Hoover to create more government files on United States citizens.

Further, in 1936 the FBI was given the far-reaching authority to investigate possible Nazis. This authority, however, was quickly abused by the Hoover administration (Felt 1979). Not surprisingly, the FBI's focus centered on radical activists, organizations, and even influential personalities ranging from famous author Ernest Hemingway, civil rights activists Martin Luther King Jr. and Malcolm X, and even went so far to investigate First Lady Eleanor Roosevelt (Theoharis 1993).

Hoover, an influential and persuasive person himself, conned and convinced Congress into believing his investigations were needed in order to protect the national security. Yet, many believe that the primary motivation for the investigations was more related to controlling and containing dissent that it was to promote the public interest (Theoharis 1993).

Corrupt Standard Operation Procedures

In order for the FBI to continue such illegal investigation, Hoover and the FBI created the "secret file" system. The norm for the FBI was that agents would relay all information to the heads of the administration; they in turn would review the information and debrief the White House. The "secret file" system was a carefully calculated technique to keep some illegal investigations from being exposed (Powers 1987). All information known to be sensitive would be labeled "personal and confidential." All information that entered the FBI with that label would end up on Hoover's desk. Hoover would then review all the information and would file it away for safekeeping (Jung and Thom 1997). The "secret file" procedure kept all illegal politically motivated reports out of the FBI's central records system. This technique allowed Hoover to safely side-step the Attorney General's ban and continue to investigate and monitor political activities (Theoharis 1993).

Perhaps there was an intended coincidence in the name of the "secret files"; it is everything the name implies. The FBI investigated and kept information on influential individuals, radicals and anyone thought to be a communist. The investigative approach the FBI took involved the gathering of information using sex as a tool. The FBI used the prostitution ring and other sexual decoys to infiltrate specific groups, and sometimes individuals (Marx 1992). In New York City, for instance, the FBI financed the making of pornographic films and had policewomen direct the on-camera sex acts.

Hoover's bulging files on individuals contained information on more than just sex and other improper acts (Marx 1992). In another example, the FBI came upon information that, in Chicago, there was a link between the organized crime ring and prostitution. Federal agents took over a credit card processing company and over a four year period processed $30 million in customer payments for sexual services. These transactions were recorded on credit card receipts as food, beverages, and office supplies, which could be taken as business tax reductions. The FBI-run agency paid, out of the FBI's bank account, for sex clubs. It provided $100,000 to bribe the local police agencies in order to stay open. The investigation did not lead to any arrests, but helped the FBI collect information on high profile individuals and political leaders who received bribes (Marx 1992).

All of this was in pursuit of information. Hoover was adept at this. The information gathered implied the threat of public ruin, threat of exposure, all which was used as a political tool. But the outlandish investigations did not stop there. Sex was used as an investigative toll, as well as other inappropriate methods, in order to gather new information. The bureau investigated the sexual habits and many other elements of a person's private life. For example, the FBI investigated the Church Committee, instructing the informant to sleep with as many wives as possible (Croog 1992). The tactic here was to break up marriages and gather information.

The FBI's approach was to gather information and control that individual with the threat of public humiliation (Croog 1992). One clear example of the FBI's approach was the case involving a rather un-influential gossip columnist, Inga Arvad. Arvad became the target of an intensive FBI investigation due to her political views and employment by the *Washington Times-Herald* (Theoharis 1993). Arvad was a target due to the FBI's tainted and over expanded definition of "communist." The FBI approached Arvad's place of employment and demanded an investigative interview. For fear of the public discovering that the *Washington Times-Herald* employed a communist, the *Washington Times-Herald* complied. When the interview turned up nothing, the FBI stepped up the investigation by adding wiretaps to Arvad's personal telephone. Although the investigation turned up nothing, Hoover used his persuasive tactics to convince the Attorney General to continue the investigation. After years of harassment, the FBI discontinued the investigation. With the information gathered, the FBI discovered that Miss Arvad was a strong isolationist but held nothing that reflected pro-axis or anti-axis information.

Legislative Collusion

The FBI's jurisdiction and authority is directly granted by legislation. The president, Attorney General, and Congress all decide the authority the FBI is given. Glancing back at the events described earlier, it appears that the FBI expands its authority and jurisdiction by creating and implementing new policy within the FBI.

For example, the FBI, with this new secret policy, avoided being limited by legislation. During the 1950s, the Cold War hit its fevered pitch. Senator Joseph McCarthy and the House of Un-American Activities Committee (HUAC) alerted the nation of the serious threat of a communist take-over in the United States (Moore 1990). Congress granted the FBI the authority (known as the Responsibilities Program) to investigate communist subversives in the government. Hoover, the FBI, along with the president and Congress, used the Responsibilities Program to go after suspected communists, influential people, organizations, political opponents, and even people they plainly disliked (Jung and Thom 1997). With the Responsibilities Program safely intact, the FBI created a very broad definition of communist.

Although this was the first time that legislation gave the FBI the authority to investigate suspected communists, the truth of the matter was, the FBI had been conducting these types of investigations since the 1930s (Feinman 1992). The FBI's definition of "communist" included almost any left-wing activity that could be interpreted as subversive. The Responsibilities Program was designed to investigate possible communist subversives employed in the government and public services (Croog 1992). All information was reviewed and the FBI secretly supplied governors and high-level municipal authorities with any information about the individual being investigated. The immediate problem with the program was confidential leaks. The Responsibilities Program quickly devolved into a systematic tool of harassment providing irrelevant information on perceived subversives, which lead to many terminations of employment, particularly those in education.

To maximize total control of the new program, Hoover and the FBI insisted that FBI headquarters alone be the ones to determine the information to be divulged. This response was due to the questionable legality of the FBI's investigative techniques. The FBI established a plan in which FBI agents would see to it that those terminated from employment were not rehired somewhere else.

The fall of the Responsibilities Program came in the late 1950s. Some historians contend that the techniques employed by the FBI caused the destruction of the program. The confidential leaks to the media exposed some awful truths about the FBI's illegal investigations. There were 794 individuals investigated;. 429 who were employed in education. Hoover claimed the FBI was effective in finding and removing communists that were in the position to poison the minds of the youth of this country. Of the 429 suspected communists employed in education, 429 were terminated from educational employment (Jung and Thom 1997). The FBI made it clear that they were outraged that those individuals who leaked this information could be retained in government employment.

There was a point in the FBI's history where Hoover ignored legislation and implemented his own program of continuing his secret policies. During the Ford administration, Hoover created an execution squad. The squad's job was to cause the permanent disappearance of individuals the FBI believed would never be brought to Justice, if proper policy and procedure were followed. The squad members consisted mostly of organized crime families, but also included military personnel and local police (Marx 1992). Hoover believed the squad would be more effective if the FBI and its agents were not directly involved.

The squad was considered a special force of assassins to take out any individuals the FBI named. Although there has been no official recognition of the squad, some historians contend some of the squad's victims included KGB agents, former Japanese officers, and Nazi war criminals. Some historians claim the squad offers some insight into the relationship that the FBI had with famous organized crime families (Turner 1970). The squad gives even further insight into why the FBI was so reluctant in going after organized crime families.

Presidential Collusion

The FBI was more than just an asset to the nation's people; the FBI was a political tool for several politicians. The FBI was the mortal enemy of anyone being investigated. The FBI demonstrated its bureaucratic survival skills and capacity to manipulate the press, Congress, and the President of the United States without revealing its hand. The majority of the authority and jurisdiction the FBI was awarded can be directly contributed to the relationship the FBI had with the presidential administration. Presidents Roosevelt, Nixon, Carter, Ford, and Johnson all had a personal stake in the FBI.

With Roosevelt's election in 1932, the FBI no longer had to be so circumspect. In 1934, Roosevelt secretly ordered the FBI to investigate and monitor the activities of American Nazis and Nazi sympathizers. Between 1934 and 1936, the president requested investigative reports on all right-wingers. By 1939, Roosevelt ordered the FBI to conduct widespread surveillance on political opposition and critics of presidential policy (Jung and Thom 1997). During the Roosevelt administration, the FBI's illegal investigations primarily focused on foreign policy critics. The FBI had a favored relationship with the Roosevelt administration. Roosevelt supported the New Deal crime-control program, which gave the FBI more authority to go after "bad guys" without regard to personal and civil rights. The FBI investigated the lives and activities of political organizations, political opponents of the president, and critics of administrative policy. The FBI consistently sought potentially damaging information on individuals' personal lives (Feinman 1991). Carefully cultivated informants would relay sensitive information back to FBI headquarters (due to the FBI's secret file system, the information landed directly on Hoover's desk). Hoover would then leak this damaging information on to friendly journalists, presidents, and other politicians for the multiple purposes of destroying and discrediting those individuals.

The FBI's hit list included several members of the American Civil Liberties Union (ACLU), Charles Lindbergh, and several political opponents. Although several presidents used the FBI in their favor in order to achieve personal success, Hoover and the FBI was a feared bureaucracy (Watters and Gillers 1973). The FBI flexed its bureaucratic muscle by turning the game against those who played it. President Nixon publicly praised the FBI and Hoover for making the FBI the defender of Americans' precious right to be free from fear. But fear is what the FBI brought to President Nixon. Recorded on the White House tapes, Nixon expressed his concern about the FBI files and how the FBI had secret files on everyone, including him. Nixon feared the information the FBI collected on him. Nixon feared that the FBI could bring down the Nixon administration if Nixon ever restricted the FBI's authority.

Fear and the FBI's blackmail controlled several politicians and the way policy was enacted. While several people were successfully blackmailed, those who refused to submit were often ruined by mysterious, and sometimes false, FBI press leaks. Some historians would contend death resulted for a few who refused to comply with the FBI. With Hoover as the head of the country's Chief law enforcement agency, the president could investigate, monitor, and potentially destroy political opponents. Since 1936, the FBI catered to each of the succeeding administrations proving the FBI's political worth (Charles 1997).

EVALUATION OF PROBLEMS IN THE FBI

The secret investigations gave the FBI some persuasive power when it came to American politics. The secret files and the secret files system helped the FBI to become a powerful and experienced agency; an agency led by those committed to effectiveness. The unstoppable behavior of the FBI was directly influenced by the FBI's authority and secret power to control high profile figures, including presidents of the United States. Despite so many obvious violations of civil liberties through illegal investigations, the FBI continued to operate under a crime-control fashion.

The secret file system, in particular, proved to be an asset for the FBI and the way Hoover ran the agency. The illegal investigations included wiretaps, prostitution, physical assaults, and blatant violations of constitutional rights. These investigations even sought out the individuals who controlled the FBI (i.e. the president, Attorney General, and Congress). The FBI collected such a massive amount of damaging information on high profile figures that the threat of exposure kept the FBI's authority from being limited. The FBI became an effective agency in achieving more authority, creating fear, and ruining individuals. The FBI created several programs on its own authority and kept these programs centralized. These tactics employed by the FBI kept presidents and Attorney Generals ignorant, allowing the FBI to elude investigations into their own activity.

While the FBI initiated several of these programs on its own authority, it would be wrong to conclude that the FBI was the only factor to their creation. Hoover and the FBI took advantage of the times. The Cold War, the threat of communism, and the civil rights demonstrations created an awkward tension between political freedoms and the right to rid the United States of the communist agents. At those times Hoover led the FBI on his own personal beliefs, convincing the appropriate people and manipulating them into believing there was a need for programs (Gentry 1991).

With Hoover as the director, the FBI became the bully agency that mastered the science of manipulation and used it in its favor. While following secret orders of the president to investigate his opposition and critics, the FBI secretly investigated those giving the orders. The FBI's investigations generally uncovered damaging information, which caused fear among those expected to control the FBI. With the threat of exposure, very few would monitor the activities of the FBI. The FBI acted like a pack of hyenas, seeking out and destroying whatever they desired. Some historians have reached various conclusions that the creation of programs like the Responsibilities Program, and the Squad, were a direct result of the inadequate supervision of the FBI (Jung and Thom 1997).

The threat of communism, the civil rights demonstrations, and the subversive press were situations where the FBI manipulated the minds of members of Congress, the president, and the public. Situations described in the examples earlier demonstrate how the FBI took the opportunity to abuse and expand the FBI's power. Consequently, the FBI gained more power and authority, while the monitoring of the FBI decreased substantially. This is just what Hoover and the FBI wanted—no restriction and no limits.

CONCLUSION

Upon the authority of Congress, the United States in 1908 received its first permanent detective force, the Federal Bureau of Investigations. Charles Bonaparte succeeded with his idea and the FBI was granted the authority to investigate federal law violations. It was soon after the FBI's creation when the FBI began using illegal investigative tactics to gather information. Every time America was faced with a threatening situation, the FBI would receive greater jurisdiction and authority. The World War I era gave the FBI greater jurisdiction to investigate sabotage, espionage, and draft violators. With the insurmountable power and authority, the FBI continued to ignore the intended purpose of the FBI. The wave of corruption quickly spread through and consumed the FBI. The FBI continued to use illegal tactics that violated due process, civil liberties, and most of all, frayed the fabric of the FBI.

Faced with a corrupt law enforcement agency, the administration was pressured to make a change. With the appointment of J. Edgar Hoover, the problems became worse. Hoover publicly acknowledged the FBI's problems and vowed to restore the FBI's dignity. Privately, Hoover's plans were to ignore efficiency and equity while rebuilding the FBI's reputation. Hoover wanted an effective agency and believed the only way to achieve complete effectiveness was to attack with full force.

Using these tactics, the FBI quickly confirmed its political worth. Deception and manipulation achieved effectiveness. The FBI created the secret file system and began the onslaught of investigations. The FBI investigated a broad spectrum of individuals, including the president's wife. The secret file system allowed the FBI to continue the hundreds of illegal investigations. The system's policy required all reports that included sensitive information to be labeled "personal and confidential." Those reports fell directly on the director's desk, avoiding the FBI's central records system.

This paper clearly demonstrates, through examples, how the FBI chose bureaucratic effectiveness over efficiency and equity. The FBI currently continues to repair the reputation of a corrupt agency. Although death ended the career of the infamous Hoover, scandals like those of *Ruby Ridge* and *The Branch Dividians in Waco* continue to raise the ghost of Hoover's FBI. Some historians will contend there was a sigh of relief when Hoover's era ended. Yet, under specter of great Hoover's legacy, the FBI continues to receive more jurisdiction and authority, while still conducting investigations that remain "personal and confidential."

WORKS CITED

Charles, Douglas M. 1997. FBI political surveillance and the Charles Lindbergh investigation. *The Historian*. 59 (summer) (4): 831.

Croog, Charles. 1992. FBI political surveillance and the isolationist-interventionist debate, 1939–1941. *The Historian* 54 (3): 441–458.

Feinman, Ronald L. 1991. The rise and fall of domestic intelligence. *Presidential Studies Quarterly* 21 (1): 174.

Felt, Mark W. 1979. *The FBI pyramid: From the inside*. New York: G.P. Putman's Sons.

Gentry, Curt. 1991. *J. Edgar Hoover: The man and the secrets*. New York: Diane Publishing Co.

Jung, Patrick and Cathleen Thom. 1997. The Responsibilities program of the FBI, 1951–1955. *The Historian* 59 (2): 347–361.

Marx, Gary T. 1992. Under-the-cover undercover investigations: Some reflections on the Untied States use of sex and deception in law enforcement. *Criminal Justice Ethics* 11 (1): 13.

Moore, Richter H. Jr. 1990. United States: Politics and public policy. *Perspectives on Political Science* 23 (2): 109.

Powers, Richard G. 1987. *Secrecy and power: The life of J. Edgar Hoover*. New York: MacMillan Inc.

Theoharis, Athan. 1993. The FBI, The Roosevelt administration and the 'subversive' press. *Journalism History* 19 (1): 3.

Turner, William W. 1970. *Hoover's FBI: The men and the myth*. Los Angeles, CA: Kingsport Press, Inc.

Watters, Patty and Stephen Gillers. 1973. *Investigating the FBI: A tough fair look at the powerful bureau, its present and its future*. New York: Library of Congress.

Problem-Solving Case Studies

Unlike analytical case studies, problem-solving case studies provide students with the opportunity to go beyond problem identification to recommending a course of action. Importantly, the main reasons for doing problem-solving case studies are to identify a problem, to provide reasons for how the problem occurred, and to provide suggestions for resolving the problem most efficiently. Problem-solving case studies provide an analysis of no less than one page and no more than five pages.

- For narrowly defined problems, the case study report is a highly condensed, concise description of the problem, the causes, and recommended solutions, of approximately two pages.
- For broadly defined or complex problems, the case study report is condensed into an executive summary, with supporting material attached, of approximately five pages.

The best problem-solving case studies focus on aspects of decision-making that are internal and specific to the target of the study. External factors are only important if they are responsible for influencing the target's decisions. At the end, the reader should know what the problem is, what possibly caused the problem, and what can be done to resolve the problem.

How to Write a Problem-Solving Case Study

1. **Identify the target of the case study**
2. **Identify the objective of the case study**
   - Summarize the problem in one or two sentences
   - Write concisely, clearly, and assertively
3. **Provide a brief review of:**
   - General conditions
   - Specific conditions
4. **Identify the major problems and their causes**
   - Rank-order the problems
   - Investigate and report possible causes or causal relationships
5. **Identify possible solutions for each problem identified**
   - Rank order the solutions for each problem
   - Identify the benefits, costs, and unintended consequences of applying a solution
6. **Make a recommendation**
   - Choose a solution for each problem identified
   - Suggest how the solution can be implemented
7. **Attach any data, supporting evidence, and references for additional information**

(Reprinted with permission)

MEMORANDUM

To: City Department Manager
From: Annette Allison
Date: October 5, 1999
Re: Building Inspection Department Expense Analysis

Objective:

This report analyzes the city's Building Inspection Department Budget to identify which expenditure items are responsible for budget increases. These increases have resulted in the department being over budget for two years. The report provides a recommendation for either budget allocation increases and/or reduction of spending in discretionary budget categories. Decisions to decrease spending should be based on further investigation of the relative spending efficiency in categories showing significant increases.

1. How well did the department spend what was actually budgeted?

- FY I was under budget by 9%.
- In FY II & III the budget was within 1% of its targets.
- FY IV & V were both well over the budget targets (31% & 7% respectively).

2. Major spending categories over 5-year period:

- <u>Salaries</u> (158,712 in FY V) are the ***largest*** spending category during all five years.
- <u>Capital improvements</u> (9,795 in FY V) are the ***second largest*** spending category during all five years and show significant increases in the last two years.
- Travel expenses category show significant increases in the past two years
- Smaller spending categories are office supplies, training, and dues and subscriptions.

3. Major variances (dollar and percent changes) from year to year:

- The total spent budget increased by 31% from FY III to FY IV.
- The total spent budget increased 23% from FY IV to FY V.
- <u>Capital improvements</u>, <u>printing</u>, and <u>travel expenses</u> were major spending categories during FY V.

4. Line-item changes & changes in budget shares over time:

- <u>Salaries</u> account for the ***largest share*** of the spent budget. During the past five years, salaries have accounted for between 81%–86% of the total spent budget.
- <u>Travel expenses</u> accounted for the ***second largest share*** of the total spent budget in both FY IV & V, accounting for 9% in those years.
- <u>Capital improvement</u> was the ***third largest share*** of the spent budget.
- <u>Car allowance</u> and <u>office supplies</u> are also ***large shares*** of the spent budget.

5. **What changes are revealed when inflation is taken into account?**
   - When inflation is taken into account, the spent budget still reveals that there has been a steady increase in the total spent budget over the past five years, with a sizable increase within the past two years.
   - Although salaries have been steadily increasing over the past five years, employees are making much less over the past four years when inflation is taken into account.

6. **What else might account for the specific changes?**
   - The larger salary, training, and travel expenditures over the past five years might indicate the hiring of more staff.
   - The large amounts spent on capital improvements might indicate that the building inspection department is growing and requires new or additional facilities.

7. **Impact of spending trends on next year's budget:**
   - Since the building inspection department has been over budget the past two years, it may reflect a need for more budget allocations for the following budget year.
   - Capital improvements and travel expenses should be looked at closely when allocating the following years budget, however, because these services may not be needed.

8. **Ratio analysis:**
   - Based on the per capita ratio in FY V, each resident spends approximately $4.27 to support the building inspection department.

Recommendation:

The results of this analysis suggest that while *salaries are the largest spending item, they are not responsible* for the department being over budget in the last two years. Increases in expenses related to *capital improvements, travel, and office supplies significantly contributed the increases* in the spent budget. This report recommends scrutiny of these expenditures particularly as they relate to the purposes and necessity for continued increased spending in each of these categories. Based on the results of an evaluation of these expenditures, the city should either increase the budget allocation and/or reduce spending on capital improvements, travel, and office supplies to reduce the likelihood of the department being over budget in the future.

Attachments: Expense Analysis

Building Inspection Department
Building Inspection Expense Analysis (Excerpt)

Expense	Yr 1 Spent	Yr 1 Constant	Yr 2 Spent	Yr 1–2 $ Diff	Yr 1–2 % Change	Yr 2 Constant
Salaries	$90,340	$90,340	$99,830	$4,375	5%	$94,715
Truck & car repairs	4,286	$4,286	1,732	$(2,643)	-62%	$1,643
Travel expense	546	$546	612	$35	6%	$581
Supplies	1,092	$1,092	1,242	$86	8%	$1,178
Office supplies	3,400	$3,400	5,500	$1,818	53%	$5,218
Street lighting	208	$208	0	$(208)	-100%	$-
Telephone	146	$146	330	$167	114%	$313
Gas & oil	0	$-	0	$-		$-
Equipment repairs	0	$-	0	$-		$-
Tools & supplies	0	$-	0	$-		$-
Christmas lights	944	$944	6,662	$5,377	570%	$6,321
Real property lights	1,170	$1,170	840	$(373)	-32%	$797
Education & training	224	$224	1,190	$905	404%	$1,129
Dues & subscriptions	0	$-	0	$-		$-
Utilities	1,736	$1,736	1,400	$(408)	-23%	$1,328
Printing	236	$236	134	$(109)	-46%	$127
Capital improvements	270	$270	0	$(270)	-100%	$-
Communications	0	$-	0	$-		$-
Total	$104,598	$104,598	$119,472	$8,753	8%	$113,351

Analysis of Legislation

Purpose of an Analysis of Legislation

Analyzing a congressional bill helps the student understand more about the legislative process. Unlike other policies, which can be custom, rulings by courts, regulations written by bureaucrats, or executive orders, legislation is made in Congress. To examine the legislative process, we need to identify the context within which the legislation was introduced, the goals of the legislation, supporters, the opponents, and the problems of passing the bill. (For more information, see Robert U. Goehlert and Fenton S. Martin, *Congress and law-making: Researching the legislative process.* 2nd. ed. CA: ABC-CLIO, 1989. See the section on tracing legislation pages 53–59.)

Writing an Analysis of a Legislative Bill

1. **Choose a law that is of interest to you.**
   - Find the public law number.
   - Choose one that is at least a year old.
2. **Identify where the idea for the bill originated—Congress, bureaucracy, interest groups, or the executive office.**
   - Sometimes an idea or draft has more than one source.
   - Find out who introduced the bill.
   - Examine the hearings.
3. **Identify the objectives, targets, or goals of the bill.**
   - What was the legislation supposed to do exactly?
   - Who was supposed to benefit?
   - Does the bill expand or correct other policy action by government?
4. **Identify the means or policy instruments used to achieve the goals or objectives.**
   - How was the legislation supposed to achieve its goals?
   - Policy tools—transfers? regulation? subsidy? spending?
5. **Identify who supported and who opposed the bill.**
   - Was it a partisan bill?
   - Did support come from an ideological coalition?
6. **Examine the bill's success in passing.**
   - What constraints prevented it passing easily?
   - What kind of problems did it encounter?
7. **Using the above six steps write the paper with the following structure.**
   - Include an introduction, a description of the origins of the bill, the objectives and tools used to achieve the objectives.
   - Compare and contrast the various political arguments and forces supporting and opposing the bill.
   - Relate these political problems to any problems in passing the bill. Separate the political problems from institutional or structural problems that may exist and then provide a conclusion.

**Copyright Protection and Fair Use in the Digital Age:
The Digital Millennium Copyright Act of 1998**

By
Marion Harmon
POLS 300
Dr. Schmidt
November 11, 2003
(Reprinted with permission)

ABSTRACT

On October 28, 1998, President Bill Clinton signed into law the Digital Millennium Copyright Act of 1998, to amend Title 17, United States Code, to implement the World Intellectual Property Organization Copyright Treaty and Performances and Phonograms Treaty. The new law, also known as the DMCA, relates to copyrights of digitally transmitted and stored material. It is the first time that legislation has been enacted to regulate copyright on the Internet. This paper examines how this legislation came to be, the goals and objectives of the law, and the means used to achieve those goals and objectives. It also identifies the supporters and opposition of the bills that created the DMCA, which is the most important piece of copyright legislation in a quarter of a century.

INTRODUCTION

On October 18, 1998, President Bill Clinton signed the Digital Millennium Copyright Act into law. The most comprehensive copyright legislation in a generation, it implements provisions of two international treaties adopted by the World Intellectual Property Organization in 1996. The DMCA imposes new safeguards for music, software, movies, and written works on the Internet, and outlaws technologies that can crack copyright-protection devices. While the film, music, and software and book publishing industries are pleased with the way the law cracks down on digital piracy, many other groups, such as libraries and educational institutions, worry that it undermines fair-use rights and will lead to severe pay-per-use restrictions on content (Regan 1998).

With the increasing popularity of new technologies and the Internet, there was a serious need to address intellectual property right protection in the digital realm. After the intense negotiations in Congress and many letters and testimonies by concerned members of industry and the public, the compromise legislation that passed is a promising start in regulating copyright in the 21st century. But an outcry over the DMCA by groups concerned about fair use and other important issues is sure to continue in the coming years. Hollywood and other well-healed industries should not have the final word on copyright law.

HISTORICAL CONTEXT OF THE DMCA

U.S. copyright law is almost as old as the country itself. It has its origins in the Constitution; Article I, Section 8, Clause 8 provides Congress with the power "to promote the Progress of Science and useful Arts, by securing for limited Times to Authors and Inventors the exclusive Right to their respective Writings and Discoveries." Under this clause, in May 1790, Congress passed its first copyright statute protecting maps, charts, and books (Landesman 1998). Copyright protection and fair use, seeming contradictions, are both covered under U.S. copyright law. Title 17, Section 106 of the United States Code (USC) grants copyright owners exclusive rights to copy and distribute their work, and Title 17, Section 107 of the USC states that fair use of a copyrighted work, including for purposes of criticism, comment, new reporting, teaching, scholarship, or research is not an infringement of copyright.

An Early Balancing Act

Intellectual property, which is a subtle area of the law, has evolved in response to technological change (Lehman and Brown 1995). In the 20th century, new technologies affecting creative rights, such as the player piano roll in the first part and the VCR and cable television in the latter part, have caused increased controversy and prompted authors and users of the technologies to enlist the help of the courts, including the Supreme Court, and Congress. The Internet has brought on a whole host of new problems, one of which is how to safeguard intellectual property that can be sent across the globe with high speed and virtual accuracy. While the advent of the digital age has brought on new, more complex challenges for copyright law, it basically boils down to the centuries-old struggle between protecting copyright holders and allowing for the creative opportunities of others through fair use.

From 1790 until the latter part of the 20th century, copyright law underwent two major revisions—the Copyright Acts of 1909 and 1976—and many extensions and amendments, extending copyright protection to other formats (Landesman 1998). Congress and the courts have generally found a way to strike a balance when confronting a new technology affecting creative rights. For example, in the early 1900s, authors of sheet music charged that piano roll manufacturers were stealing their intellectual property. The Supreme Court disagreed, stating that although the pianos played content taken from sheet music, it was not a copy of the music. Congress responded by changing the law, but with a compromise that granted authors a mechanical reproduction right and copiers a compulsory licensing right. Thus, authors had the right to decide whether and on what terms their music could be recorded, but once it was recorded, others had the right, for two cents a copy, to make additional recordings without the permission of the original author (Lessig 2001).

Other examples of Congress striking a balance between compensation and control include the compulsory license for music and certain pictorial works in noncommercial television and radio broadcasts, and the compulsory licensing scheme for satellite television systems, digital audio home recorders, and digital audio transmissions. The balance lies in that copyright holders are given a guarantee of compensation without having perfect control over the use of its copyrighted material (Lessig 2001). This illustrates the special nature of the protection of copyright, giving authors a balanced right while still promoting progress.

New Technologies Call for New Legislation

With the creation of the Internet and other advanced technologies such as software encryption technology has come a cry for stricter controls from original copyright holders. Over the past two centuries, the application of copyright law to paper-based content has become relatively clear. The unique characteristics of cyberspace, though, have caused a debate over how to update copyright law to reflect its unique problems (Lessig 2001). Many individuals and organizations have had a stake in updating the law—U.S. copyright-based industries producing and promoting creative and high-technology products contribute more than $60 billion annually to U.S. trade (Clinton 1998).

The most recent major copyright legislation, the Copyright Law of 1976, was not sufficient in this new digital era where thousands of bytes of information can be downloaded at the push of a button and individual teenagers who share thousands of songs online are being sued by huge recording industry associations. Digital images can travel great distances from their originators and leave few tracks, can make excellent reproductions, and are much easier to change than hard copy (Carter 1996). Similarly, digital recordings have opened a whole new world of copying and transmitting sound.

While not evenly divided into two warring camps, there are groups of people on one side or the other of this issue depending on what is at stake. Individual copyright holders such as artists and musicians are joined by the organizations that buy their work and/or promote it. These include the music recording companies, movie studios, computer software and hardware manufacturers, and other creators of intellectual property that have called for new legislation regarding copyright law (Schmidt 2001). On the other side of the issue are those who have lobbied for exceptions to hard-line copyright restrictions—the librarians, researchers, teachers, businesses, and consumer advocates who are concerned that fair use will lose out due to overregulation (McAllester 1998). They point to the importance of the flow of new information and that we will live in a poorer society overall without the sharing of ideas and intellectual property.

Strong and sometimes extreme viewpoints can be found on both ends of the copyright spectrum. Jack Valenti, chairman of the Motion Picture Association of America, argued that copyright protects not only the financial interest of people who create intellectual property, but also the very existence of creative work. He said the Internet marauders claim that copyright is old-fashioned and a decaying relic of the non-Internet world (Nevaer 2002). Writing in *Wired* magazine, John Perry Barlow called for the death of copyright, thus ensuring that the interests of society are served through the practical values of relationship, convenience, interactivity, service, and ethics (Nevaer 2002). Both of these views show the divisiveness over the new technologies, and the reason for the hue and cry for new legislation.

FORMULATION OF THE DMCA

The process to update U.S. copyright law regarding digital transmissions began in February 1993, when President Clinton formed the Information Infrastructure Task Force (IITF). The IITF was chaired by Secretary of Commerce Ronald H. Brown and included high-level representatives of federal agencies involved in advancing information technologies (Lehman and Brown 1995). The three committees of the IITF were charged with implementing the vision of the administration for the National Information Infrastructure (NII) and worked with the private sector, public interest groups, Congress, and state and local governments. The goal of the IITF was to develop comprehensive telecommunications and information policies and programs, promoting the development of the NII, which had a budget of $2 billion for the first five years and promised to add more than $100 billion to the gross domestic product over a decade and add 500,000 new jobs (Clark 1995).

Drafting

The IITF established the Working Group on Intellectual Property Rights, chaired by Assistant Secretary of Commerce and Commissioner of Patents and Trademarks Bruce A. Lehman. The group, comprised of high-level representatives of the federal agencies that play a role in advancing the development and application of information technologies, was charged with investigating the effects of emerging digital technology on intellectual property rights and recommending appropriate changes to U.S. intellectual property law and policy in a report (U.S. Congress 1998; Lehman and Brown 1995). To prepare the report, the working group held a public hearing in November 1993, at which 30 witnesses spoke, representing the views of copyright industries, libraries, educators, and other beneficiaries of the public domain. The group also received 70 written statements during a public comment period. From its review and analysis of all the statements, the group issued a Green Paper in July 1994.

Another round of hearings was held during four days in September 1994 and, in addition, more than 1,500 pages of comments were filed by more than 150 individuals and organizations. Representing more than 425,000 members of the public, the comments came from a broad spectrum of interested parties, including electronic industries; telecommunications and information service providers; the academic, research, library, and legal communities; individual creators, copyright owners, and users; and the computer software, motion picture, music, broadcasting, publishing, and other information and entertainment industries (U.S. Patent and Trademark Office 1995). All had something to gain or lose depending on what paths future legislation in the digital copyright realm would take.

On September 5, 1995, the IITF issued *The Report of the Working Group on Intellectual Property Rights*, also known as the *White Paper*, which applied current copyright law to the NII and recommended changes to the Copyright Act of 1976 to keep current with new technology. In testimony before the Subcommittee on Courts and Intellectual Property and Committee on the Judiciary on November 15, 1995, Lehman noted that it did not provide all the answers, and maybe not all of the questions. The reason for this, he said, is that it was not known how the NII would develop (Lehman 1995). The *White Paper* itself states that the Working Group was forced to stop adjusting the text with respect to just-received news and was compelled to place the report in concrete form (Lehman and Brown 1995). The *White Paper*, which advocates strengthening the rights of copyright owners, includes a specification that the right of exclusive distribution includes electronic transmissions and the prohibition of any device or service that inhibits the effectiveness of a technological method of rights protection (Landesman 1998).

In the *White Paper*, the doctrine of fair use is called the most significant and, perhaps, murky of the limitations on exclusive rights of a copyright owner (Lehman and Brown 1995). To address the issue of fair use, the Working Group had formed a group of librarians, educators, publishers, and authors in 1993 known as the Conference on Fair Use (CONFU). Under discussion were such issues as libraries offering electronic interlibrary loans and making archival copies, and universities adapting published works for computerized long-distance learning without compensating publishers of the works (Clark 1996). More high-tech fair use issues included whether to permit electronic links from one Web site to another and the dismantling of software products to design new programs. The position of the *White Paper* makes clear that most computer transactions involve copying a copyrighted work, and under existing copyright law, a fee must be paid for use of the original work. This indicated a strong stance that leaned more toward copyright protection than fair use.

Presentation

The recommendations of the *White Paper* were introduced as identical legislation in the Senate as S. 1284 (known as the National Information Infrastructure Copyright Protection Act of 1995) by Chairman Orrin G. Hatch (R-Utah), with Senator Patrick J. Leahy (D-Vt.), and in the House of Representatives as H.R. 2441 on September 29, 1995, by Representative Carlos J. Moorhead (R-Calif.), chairman of the House Judiciary Subcommittee on Courts and Intellectual Property and original co-sponsor Patricia Schroeder (D-Colo.). Representatives Howard Coble (R-NC), Sonny Bono (R-Calif.), Richard Burr (R-NC), David Minge (D-Minn.), William Luther (D-Minn.), and Andrew Jacobs Jr. (D-Ind.) cosponsored H.R. 2441. This shows that Democrats and Republicans in both the House and

Senate would work together to advance copyright law within the digital realm, reflecting the broad reach of intellectual property rights among all private and public interests.

Exploratory Hearings. On November 15, 1995, the Senate Judiciary Committee and the Subcommittee on Courts and Intellectual Property of the House Judiciary Committee held a joint hearing to consider the NII legislation. Among those who testified were Mihaly Ficsor, assistant director general, World Intellectual Property Organization (WIPO); Marybeth Peters, register of copyrights and associate librarian for copyright services; and Bruce Lehman. Ficsor said that the two bills had chosen the right approach to the challenges of digital technology, and that while at the international level, the solution of the NII bills may not be directly applied due to the differences among various national laws, the bills may serve as useful models for establishing international norms (Ficsor 1995).

Peters argued that the Copyright Office supported the goals and basic substance of all of the proposed changes to the Copyright Act, but she also expressed a few concerns over certain technical aspects of the provisions of the bills and offered to work with Congress and affected groups to help draft minor changes to the wording (Peters 1995). In his testimony, Lehman stated that existing copyright law needed fine-tuning because of technological advances and that the administration believed the amendments proposed in H.R. 2441 and S. 1284 to the Copyright Act of 1976 would provide the necessary balance of protection of rights and limitation on those rights to promote the progress of science and the useful arts (Lehman 1995).

Issue Negotiations. Thus began a series of hearings that continued well into 1996, supplemented by a series of negotiations overseen by Representative Robert Goodlatte (R-Virg.) of the House Subcommittee on Courts and Intellectual Property. During these negotiations, representatives of copyright owners and online service providers argued over the scope of liability of service providers for the infringing acts of their users. While some issues were settled, many of the core issues remained unresolved. The information-producing industries had an overall positive response to the tighter controls over digital reproduction proposed by the *White Paper*, but the response by many library and education groups, online services, and private citizens were mostly negative—they feared that nothing could be looked at, read, used, or copied without permission or payment. Many libraries were already seeing cost increases by 10 percent or more annually for information, especially scientific books and journals (Okerson 1996).

The balance that Lehman had referred to regarding the *White Paper* did not appear to exist, leaning as it did toward strict copyright enforcement and away from fair use, according to opponents of the proposed legislation. Librarians, legal scholars, and citizens were among those that said that the suggested changes of the Lehman commission actually upset that balance. Public interest groups such as the Digital Future Coalition, which consists of 42 groups including the American Library Association, the Alliance for Public Technologies, and the Electronic Frontier Foundation, called H.R. 2441 a maximalist approach to copyright that upends the balance enjoyed by copyright owners and users. Critics in the media pointed to the paradox produced by the Clinton administration: while being the head cheerleader for the Internet as a revolutionary medium of democratic communication, the administration repeatedly accommodated the interests of lobbyists for the entertainment and other industries that would be served by strict copyright protection (Chapman 1996).

One area that prompted controversy is the statement of the *White Paper* that the memory of a computer for any length of time is fixed for purposes of copyright. This could be interpreted as making the simple act of viewing a Web page illegal without permission from the originator (Okerson 1996). This did not promote fair use and would potentially greatly inhibit use of the Internet, said critics of the proposed legislation. Another bone of contention was the statement of the *White Paper* that service providers should be held liable for the copyright infringement of their subscribers (Lehman and Brown 1995). The Working Group said it believed it was premature to reduce the liability of any service provider in the NII environment (U.S. Patent and Trademark Office 1995), but in the negotiations overseen by Goodlatte, representatives of copyright owners and online service providers were unable to reach agreement on many of the core issues regarding the scope of liability. Due to these and other unresolved issues, the collapse of negotiations between Congress and industry stalled the NII Copyright Protection Act in the 104th Congress (U.S. Congress 1998; Yoshida 1997).

International Efforts. Internationally, there were parallel efforts underway to ensure protection of copyrighted works in the digital realm. They had begun shortly after the ratification of the Berne Convention by the United States in 1989, when the WIPO was charged with forming a Committee of Experts to update the Berne Convention to reflect the challenges of the digital age and create enhanced protections for performers and producers of phonograms (U.S. Congress 1998). In December 1996, during a Diplomatic Conference in Geneva that was heavily lobbied by commercial and public interest parties, 160 countries agreed to adopt the amendments to the Berne Convention and create the WIPO Copyright Treaty and the WIPO Performances and Phonograms Treaty. A third treaty, the Sui Generis Database Treaty, which proposed setting standards for protection of databases, was tabled (Tang 2001; Lutzker 1999).

The WIPO Copyright Treaty extended copyright to the Internet, stating that protecting the rights of authors in a digital environment require legal remedies against technology used to circumvent copyright (Landesman 1998). The treaty does not, however, tell countries how to legislate this copyright protection; it is left up to the individual nations to decide how best to conform to the treaty. While many U.S. publishers of software, books, and other intellectual property supported the two treaties, many software vendors, users, and online service providers feared that the treaties might seriously hinder the free flow of information over the Internet and digital technology (Anthes and Hoffman 1996). After President Clinton submitted the WIPO treaties to the U.S. Senate on July 29, 1997, they were referred to the Foreign Relations Committee (U.S. Congress 1998).

Introduction of the Bills

In the 105th Congress, a number of bills were introduced to implement the WIPO treaties and address related intellectual property issues (Landesman 1998). The two that would eventually form the DMCA were H.R. 2281, the WIPO Copyright Treaties Implementation Act, and S. 2037, the Digital Millennium Copyright Act. Representative Howard Coble, the House Judiciary intellectual-property subcommittee chairman, introduced H.R. 2281 on July 29, 1997. Senator Hatch introduced S. 2037 on May 6, 1998, as an alternative to S. 1146, introduced in September 1997 by Senator John Ashcroft (D-Mo.). S. 2037 had incorporated S. 1121, introduced by Hatch on July 31, 1997; S. 1121 became Title I of the DMCA in the Senate Judiciary Committee (U.S. Congress 1998).

Regarding the issue of service provider liability, Representative Coble (with Representative Henry Hyde, R-Ill., as a cosponsor) introduced H.R. 2180 on July 17, 1997, and Senator Ashcroft introduced S. 1146 on September 3, 1997. The issue of the liability of online service providers was a serious legal issue; although the service providers did not place the content of their users online, they greatly facilitated widespread public access to it (Lutzker 1999). Unlike the detailed draft by Representative Goodlatte from the 104th Congress, H.R. 2180 had a minimalist approach to the problem and would later become Title II of the DMCA (Harrington 1999).

The complexity of issues relating to digital technology seems largely responsible for the diverse legislation relating to it, rather than any conflict arising from bipartisan views. Some drafts of the legislation that got bogged down included confidentiality issues, addressing the constitutional right to privacy, calling for a $1,000 fine for online service providers for unintentional violations and a $250,000 fine and up to three years in prison for willful violations (Clark 1996). Liability of online providers was of particular concern for commercial online companies and academic and public libraries, and would be an issue of continuing concern in the proposed copyright legislation, particularly among civil liberties and industry groups. For several months and under the direction of the House Judiciary Subcommittee on Copyrights, representatives of service providers, content owners, libraries, and educational institutions met to discuss and create a legal structure for online service providers (Lutzker 1999).

While S. 2037 added an exemption for libraries and educational institutions to gain access to a copyrighted work to determine whether to acquire it, it does not address fair use (Landesman 1998). This mirrors the vagueness of the *White Paper* in addressing fair use, with Congress deliberately making the fair-use language flexible to accommodate changing needs, according to Kenneth Crews, a professor of law and library sciences at the University of Indiana-Purdue University who also directs the policy group Copyright Management Center (Clark 1996). Crews participated in the CONFU talks about fair use, which issued a 1997 report concluding the first phase of CONFU, and says that in taking a middle-of-the-road position, he has been hit by both sides.

Lehman, who oversaw the *White Paper*, argued that it is unacceptable for libraries to get an exemption from copyright for such things as interlibrary loan, characterizing this as publishers giving away their wares to libraries. Lehman said that libraries and educational institutions were undergoing a right-wing political attack to take away their funding and that the Clinton administration was working overtime to get it back (Clark 1996). The partisan claws had come out regarding the seemingly nonpartisan issue of fair use, indicating at least a small amount of underlying partisanship in the passing of the DMCA.

Markup

After being introduced in July 1997 as identical legislation to S. 1121, H.R. 2281 was referred to the House Committee on the Judiciary. A week later, the bill was referred to the House Subcommittee on Courts and Intellectual Property. On September 16 and 17, 1997, the first round of hearings on H.R. 2281 took place in the House. The hearings were held to consider the issues surrounding service provider liability and implementation of the WIPO.

Supporters. Bruce Lehman and Marybeth Peters testified on behalf of the administration, and the 22 others who testified represented various organizations and associations, among them computer and software companies and associations; music organizations such as Broadcast Music Inc. and the Recording Industry Association of America (RIAA); and educational associations such as the Association of American Universities and National Association of State Universities and Land Grant Colleges. Even country music legend Johnny Cash was on the witness list, with Hilary Rosen, RIAA president and Chief executive officer, presenting a statement that urged the subcommittee to move the treaty implementing legislation without delay (Rosen 1997). The RIAA, along with other music and entertainment associations represented at the hearings as well as software associations like the Business Software Alliance, were eager to have strict protections placed on copyrighted works in the digital realm, both in the United States and internationally, and were thus quick to support H.R. 2281 with minimal changes.

Other testimony at the hearings was much more cautionary and suggested revisions to the draft. Christopher Byrne, director of intellectual property for Silicon Graphics Inc., testified on behalf of the Information Technology Industry Council (ITI). He said that while ITI applauded Chairman Coble and the efforts of the administration to draft WIPO implementation legislation that would effectively protect copyright works in the digital environment, they were concerned that section 1201 of H.R. 2281, as drafted at that time, would impede the ability of the information technology industry to continue to innovate and produce the products and services that make the information infrastructure possible. He said that ITI believed that H.R. 2281 as drafted upsets the constitutional balance between the promotion of innovation and protection of intellectual property—that it favored protection at the expense of innovation (Byrne 1997). One of the major concerns of ITI was the focus of the bill on technology rather than on behavior, which they were afraid would have a stifling effect on the ability of the information technology industry to innovate (Leopold 1997). Another major concern of ITI was the anti-circumvention provision, which would potentially prohibit the use of electronic components in the design of a computer or recorder that failed to respond to any anti-copy technology a content owner may choose (Byrne 1997).

Opposition. Whereas Byrne expressed concerns over some of the provisions of H.R. 2281 at the hearing, Earlham College President Douglas Bennett, who testified on behalf of the Digital Future Coalition, said the proposed legislation was seriously defective (Bennett 1997a). Bennett, who had served as an advisory member of the U.S. delegation to the WIPO treaty conference in December 1996, said that H.R. 2281 was both more and less than the WIPO proceedings and sound public policy require it to be. He said the proposals of the administration were anti-consumer, anti-technology, anticompetitive, and threatened personal privacy. He also said that Section 1201 stifled innovation and punished consumers, Section 1201 imposed draconian fines, and Sections 1203 and 1204 established egregious remedy provisions. Bennett concluded by saying the Digital Future Coalition submitted that any legislative package designed to implement the WIPO treaties should address the issues of service provider liability, fair use, distance learning, first sale, digital preservation, and non-negotiated license terms (Bennett 1997a).

Following the hearings, Bennett sent a letter to Representative Coble on September 24, 1997, on behalf of the Digital Future Coalition. In it, he expressed his appreciation that, in response to a question from Rick Boucher (D-Virg.), Commissioner Lehman agreed that the WIPO treaties do not require a device-oriented approach. Bennett urged him to consider the alternative formulation of Section 1201 by Boucher as a way to resolve what could be a long and contentious debate, and also to consider the other issues raised in the hearing, such as fair use, first sale, and library preservation (Bennett 1997b). The testimony and debate during the first hearing for H.R. 2281 had raised more questions than answers, and the subcommittee was working to figure out alternatives to some of its provisions.

Deliberations. For several months after the hearings, no official action was taken on H.R. 2281, although Chairman Hatch initiated intense negotiations within the Judiciary Committee among copyright owners and online service providers regarding service provider liability. The negotiations, which centered around a draft proposal put forth by Hatch, continued into April 1998 (U.S. Congress 1998). On February 26, 1998, the House Subcommittee on Courts and Intellectual Property conducted a markup of H.R. 2281 and H.R. 3209, the On-Line Copyright Infringement Liability Limitation Act (introduced on February 12, 1998, sponsored by Representative Coble and cosponsored by Representative Goodlatte). The two bills were reported favorably to the House Judiciary Committee by voice vote.

During the markup, Representative Boucher proposed that H.R. 3048 (known as the Digital Era Copyright Act and sponsored by Boucher and Representative Tom Campbell, D-Calif.) be implemented in place of H.R. 2281. Along with implementing the WIPO treaties, H.R. 3048 supported fair use provisions in existing U.S. copyright law and the use of computers for distance education. Educational and library associations, such as the American Association of Law Libraries, supported H.R. 3048 and strongly opposed H.R. 2281 because it failed to maintain balance between creators, owners, and users in the digital age, jeopardizing public access to electronic information (Meadows and Oakley 1998).

The American Civil Liberties Union and the Electronic Frontier Foundation also strongly supported H.R. 3048 (Steinhardt and Murphy 1998). The Boucher substitute bill, however, was defeated 11–2 by the House Judiciary Committee. On April 1, in an effort to clarify online service provider liability, Representative Goodlatte announced a compromise agreement among all interested parties, and H.R. 3209 was merged into H.R. 2281 as an OSP liability amendment (FARNET 1998a). Other than the addition of the amendment, H.R. 2281 had undergone no significant changes at this stage.

Senate Consideration. On May 6, in the Senate, Chairman Hatch introduced S. 2037 to the Committee on the Judiciary as companion legislation to H.R. 2281. Hatch had renamed it the Digital Millennium Copyright Act, which stressed its importance as U.S. copyright policy (Lutzker 1999). On May 11, Hatch filed Senate Report 105-190. The Senate considered S. 2037 on May 14, and passed the bill, amended, by a roll call vote of 99 yeas to 0 nays, with Senator Gregg not voting. A significant amendment to S. 2037 was the provision for limiting the criminal liability of online service providers for copyright-infringing activity by their customers. The bill contained a "safe harbor" provision, whereby the service provider is not liable absent knowledge of the infringement. The bill also prohibited the manufacture or sale of technologies used to circumvent technical copyright protection measures (FARNET 1998b).

Opponents of S. 2037, such as Adam Eisgrau representing the American Library Association, feared that a legal infrastructure was being created that would lead to a strict pay-per-use information environment. Eisgrau said that, in practical terms, the new right to control access to information gutted the principle of fair use (Schwartz 1998). Proponents of the bill such as publishers and movie studios maintained that strong copyright protection must be instituted to prevent digital piracy.

Referral. On May 22, 1998, H.R. 2281 was referred to the House Commerce Committee and the House Ways and Means Committee for consideration. On June 5, the House Commerce Subcommittee on Telecommunications, Trade, and Consumer Protection held hearings on the bill. In a letter to Representative Tom Bliley, the

American Civil Liberties Union and the Electronic Frontier Foundation urged him to reject H.R. 2281 because it posed a direct threat to the free speech and privacy rights of online users. They noted that while proponents of the bill described it as a compromise measure, the only thing being compromised was the well-established balance between content owners and content users in the digital world. They called it a dangerous bill and specifically objected to three sections: Section 1201, which made the use, manufacture, or sale of any technology used to circumvent copyright protections illegal; Section 1202, which allowed for the collection of personally identifiable information; and Section 201, which encouraged system operators to violate the privacy and protected speech right of their users (Steinhardt and Murphy 1998).

Professor Peter Jaszi, spokesperson for the Digital Future Coalition, said the coalition hoped that the deliberations of the committee would begin the process of converting H.R. 2281 from a serious setback to an important opportunity for American companies and individuals who use electronic information networks. The coalition stated that the bill would give sweeping and unprecedented new legal powers to a few large content-owning companies (Digital Future Coalition 1998). The American Civil Liberties Union, Electronic Frontier Foundation, and Digital Future Coalition all advocated substituting H.R. 3048 for H.R. 2281 because it did a better job of striking a balance between content owners and information users (Steinhardt and Murphy 1998; Digital Future Coalition 1998).

Other testimony at the June 5 hearing, such as that by a representative for the Digital Media Association, said that H.R. 2281 was an important first step, but that their basic concern was that the bill did not accommodate the needs of those who build the technologies and the Web sites that use those technologies. The Digital Media Association called the bill unbalanced and anti-technology as it was written at that time, and proposed working with the committee to make it a more fair and balanced bill (Greenstein 1998). Proponents of the bill, such as the RIAA and the Motion Picture Association of America (MPAA), expressed strong continued support for H.R. 2281. The MPAA representative urged the House to approve the legislation speedily, even though the association noted that 11 additional amendments had served to narrow the anti-circumvention provisions of the bill, causing it to no longer be a pristine piece of minimalist legislation (Metalitz 1998).

Committee Deliberations. Two weeks after the hearing, the subcommittee met in open markup session, making substantial changes to improve the legislation and favorably recommending it to the full House Commerce Committee. New language clarified that consumer electronics, and computer and telecommunications products would not be required to respond to any and all technological measures used by program providers (Home Recording Rights Coalition 2003). A pro-privacy amendment was tentatively approved, with details to be worked out later (FARNET 1998c). Due to the serious concerns raised at the hearing and in recognition of the complexity of the issues posed by the legislation, the chairman of the Commerce Committee requested that the referral of the Committee be extended (U.S. Congress 1999).

The referral received three extensions: to June 26, then to July 21, and finally to July 22. The legislators were struggling to come up with a compromise acceptable to movie studios, music and book publishers, and the software industry that still preserved the fair use of copyright works. Libraries and others feared that new high-tech safeguards would create pay-per-use works that could no longer be lent to patrons for free. The compromise amendment, sponsored by Representative Scott Klug (R-Wisc.), delayed the anti-circumvention rule for two years while the Secretary of Commerce reviewed the problem. After two years, the anti-circumvention rule would go into effect, but the secretary could waive the rules every two years for certain classes of works. The committee approved two other amendments, allowing cryptography researchers to crack anti-piracy safeguards and Internet users to disable such measures to prevent collection of personal information (Reuters 1998). On July 17, after the full Commerce Committee met in open markup session, H.R. 2281 was reported to the House, amended, by a roll call vote of 41 yeas to 0 nays.

On September 17, the Senate, by unanimous consent, took H.R. 2281 from the Senate calendar and passed the bill, amended with the text of S. 2037 as passed by the Senate. Thus ensued a series of disagreements between the Senate and the House, resulting in conferences between the two legislative bodies. After the Senate insisted on its amendment to H.R. 2281 and met with the House, it vitiated passage of S. 2037 and indefinitely postponed further consideration of the bill on September 17 (U.S. Congress 1999).

Conference

Deliberations on H.R. 2281 in the House/Senate Conference Committee then began. One issue was that the House bill allowed the Commerce Department to create exceptions to the anti-piracy provisions; the Senate bill did not (Samuelson 1998). Another issue was the controversial database provision, which would be created by embedding H.R. 2652 into H.R. 2281, that would give database owners the right to prevent bulk use of their databases (Chambers et al. 1998; PR Newswire 1998). The conference committee deleted the provision at the request of the White House and after receiving a letter from the presidents of the leading U.S. science and engineering societies opposing the provision (Chambers et al. 1998). The letter pointed out two problematic sections of the bill: one that would create new civil penalties for misappropriation of data, and one that would criminalize circumventing a copyright protection system (Business/Technology Editors 1998).

With the database provision gone and compromises reached, H.R. 2281 was ready to be passed and a conference report was filed in the House on October 8. The Senate agreed to the conference report by unanimous consent. In what appeared to be partisan politics, the House delayed its voice vote of the bill. Democratic Senator Patrick Leahy accused the House Republican leadership of holding the legislation hostage to petty partisan politics, saying that according to reports in roll call, *Reuters*, and the *Washington Post*, House Republicans were mad that one of their colleagues was not hired to head the Electronic Industries Alliance (Leahy 1998). On October 12, the House agreed by voice vote to adopt the conference report on H.R. 2281. On October 20, the bill was presented to President Clinton, who signed it into law on October 28, creating Public Law No. 105-304, also known as the Digital Millennium Copyright Act.

The final version of the DMCA is divided into five titles. Title I implements the WIPO treaties; Title II creates limitations on the liability of online service providers for copyright infringement when engaging in certain types of activities; Title III creates an exemption for making a copy of a computer program by activating a computer for purposes of maintenance and repair; Title IV contains six miscellaneous provisions relating to the functions of the U.S. Copyright Office, distance education, exceptions for libraries and for making ephemeral recordings, webcasting of sound recordings on the Internet, and collective bargaining agreement obligations regarding transfers of rights in motion pictures; Title V creates a new form of protection for the design of vessel hulls (U.S. Copyright Office 1998).

In signing the bill, the president said the act carefully balances the interests of both copyright owners and users. In the last paragraph of his statement, he notes that the Department of Justice advised him that certain provisions of H.R. 2281 and the accompanying conference report regarding the Register of Copyrights raise serious constitutional concerns. He said that he would construe the sections in question to require the Register to perform duties only as they are consistent with constitutional principles (Clinton 1998). It appeared the complexity and the controversy was not ended by the signing of the Digital Millennium Copyright Act.

CONCLUSION

The highly controversial Digital Millennium Copyright Act took years to win approval and was the subject of intense lobbying efforts by the film, music, and software industries. After months of debate and negotiation, a final compromise has created new safeguards for music, film, written works, and software on the Internet and outlaws technologies that can crack copyright-protection devices. While the businesses that supported and stand to gain protection under the new law have made a giant first step in that direction, the critics of the DMCA warn against the restrictions it places on such organizations as libraries and research and educational institutions, and the privacy rights it endangers.

The broad scope of the DMCA has made it a target for criticism since its earliest days. The opposition has criticized decisions interpreting the DMCA as setting copyright law on the path toward eliminating the fair use doctrine and stifling innovation and competition. Civil liberties groups are up in arms over the access of the entertainment industry to personal information on those suspected of illegally sharing copyrighted songs online. Supporters point to protecting copyright owners against the circumvention of access and copy controls used in easily copied media. These criticisms and support are both valid; the DMCA is a necessary yet flawed addition to U.S. copyright law that deserves careful analysis and possibly even revision. Time will tell whether the legislation holds up, or whether new revisions or laws will try to strike a better balance between copyright protection and fair use in the digital age.

REFERENCES

Anthes, Gary H. and Thomas Hoffman. 1996. U.S. digital copyright proposals trigger debate. *Computerworld*. http://web.lexis-nexis.com/ (accessed December 9, 2003).

Bennett, Douglas. 1997a. Capitol Hill hearing testimony before the Subcommittee on Courts and Intellectual Property of the Committee on the Judiciary, U.S. House of Representatives. http://web.lexis-nexis.com/ (accessed September 17, 2003).

Bennett, Douglas. 1997b. DFC Letter to Representative Coble. http://www.dfc.org/dfc1/Archives/wipo/benny.html (accessed September 24, 2003).

Business/Technology Editors. 1998. Leading science and engineering societies oppose pending copyright legislation. *Business Wire*. http://proquest.umi.com/pqdweb?index=419&did=000000034134535&SrchMode +1&sid=3&Fmt...client1d+17840 (accessed September 18, 2003).

Byrne, Chris. 1997. Statement before the Subcommittee on Courts and Intellectual Property of the Committee on the Judiciary, U.S. House of Representatives. http://www.house.gov/judiciary/4023.htm (accessed September 17, 2003).

Carter, Mary E. 1996. *Electronic highway robbery*. Berkeley: Peach Pit Press.

Chambers, Chad R., Lewis W. Kono, Stuart E. Pollack, and Linda Wong. 1998. Digital millennium copyright act is enacted. *The Journal of Proprietary Rights* 10, no. 11: 24.

Chapman, Gary. 1996. Copyright bill would infringe on the Internet's real promise. *The Los Angeles Times*, May 20, http://www.eff.org/IP/NII_copyright_bill/chapman_copyr_bill_960520.article (accessed September 17, 2003).

Clark, Charles S. 1995. Regulating the Internet. *CQ Researcher*, June 30, http://library.cqpress.com/cqresearcher/document.php?id=cqresrre1995063000&type=hitlist&num=2& (accessed September 17, 2003).

Clark, Charles S. 1996. Clashing over copyright. *CQ Researcher*, November 8, http://library.cqpress.com/cqresearcher/document.php?id=cqresrre1996110800&type=hitlist&num=0& (accessed September 18, 2003).

Clinton, Bill. 1998. Statement on signing the Digital Millennium Copyright Act. *Public Papers of the Presidents of the United States*. http://www.gpo.gov/nara/pubpaps/photoidx.html (accessed October 28, 2003).

Clinton, Bill. 1998. Weekly compilation of presidential documents. http://frwais.access.gpo.gov (accessed December 7, 2003).

Digital Future Coalition. 1998. June 5 Commerce Committee Hearing to showcase controversial, fast-tracked bill that threatens competition, innovation, education, privacy and public information access. *PR Newswire*, June 4, http://proquest.umi.com/pqdweb?index=10&sid=1&srchmode=1&vinst...FULL&ts=1068 (accessed October 28, 2003).

FARNET. 1998a. House Judiciary Committee approves WIPO Copyright Treaties Implementation Act—Adds last-minute OSP Liability Provisions. *FARNET's Washington Update*. http://www.educause.edu/pub/wu/1998/19980410.html#1 (accessed April 10, 2003).

FARNET. 1998b. Senate overwhelmingly passes WIPO Copyright Legislation. *FARNET's Washington Update*. http://www.educause.edu/pub/wu/1998/19980591.html#0 (accessed May 19, 2003).

FARNET. 1998c. House Commerce Subcommittee approves WIPO legislation with amendments. *FARNET's Washington Update*. http://www.educause.edu/pub/wu/1998/19980623.html#0 (accessed June 23, 2003).

Ficsor, Mihaly. 1995. Capitol Hill hearing testimony before the Subcommittee on Courts and Intellectual Property of the Committee on the Judiciary, U.S. House of Representatives, http://web.lexis-nexis.com/congcomp/document?_m=5844a4cb6500771a309...ebe9c563e1 (accessed November 15, 2003).

Greenstein, Seth. 1998. Capitol Hill hearing testimony before the Subcommittee on Telecommunications, Trade, and Consumer Protection of the Commerce Committee, U.S. House of Representatives, http://web.lexis-nexis.com/congcomp/document?_m+ada1c46790aa89...e891288 (accessed June 5, 2003).

Harrington, Mark E. 1999. On-line copyright infringement liability for Internet Service Providers: Context, cases and recently enacted legislation. For Intellectual Property Law class. http://infoeagle.bc.edu/bc_org/avp/law/st_org/iptf/articles/content/1999060401.html (accessed June 4, 2003).

Home Recording Rights Coalition. 2003. Home recording rights coalition: History. http://www.hrrc.org/history/chronology.asp (accessed November 9, 2003).

Landesman, Betty. 1998. Copyright and the Internet. *Problems of Post-Communism* 45: 63.

Leahy, Patrick J. 1998. House delay in passage of the Digital Millennium Copyright Act, H.R. 2281. *Congressional Record Online*, http://cyber.law.harvard.edu/openlaw/DVD/dmca/cr20oc98s.txt (accessed October 20, 2003).

Lehman, Bruce A. 1995. Statement of Bruce A. Lehman, Assistant Secretary of Commerce and Commissioner of Patents and Trademarks on S. 1284 and H.R. 2441, before the Subcommittee on Courts and Intellectual Property of the Committee on the Judiciary, U.S. House of Representatives, http://www.uspto.gov/web/offices/com/doc/ipnii/nii-hill.html (accessed November 15, 2003).

Lehman, Bruce A., and Ronald H. Brown. 1995. *Intellectual property and the national information infrastructure: The report of the Working Group on Intellectual Property Rights.* Washington, DC: U.S. Patent and Trademark Office.

Leopold, George. 1997. Digital-copyright bill sparks computing rift. *Electronic Engineering Times*, 01921541, no. 966, http://web17.epnet.com/citation.asp?tb=1&_...=1&fn=1&rn=1& (accessed November 15, 2003).

Lessig, Lawrence. 2001. *The future of ideas.* New York: Random House.

Lutzker, Arnold P. 1999. *Primer on the digital millennium.* Washington, DC: American Library Association.

McAllester, Matthew. 1998. Putting the brakes on highway robbery. *Newsday,* October 28, http://www.proquest.umi.com (accessed November 15, 2003).

Meadows, Judy and Bob Oakley. 1998. Join AALL President Judy Meadow's lead on post-card campaign! AALL Washington Affairs: Postcard Alert, http://www.ll.georgetown.edu/aallwash/postcard.html (accessed October 15, 2003).

Metalitz, Steven J. 1998. Capitol Hill hearing testimony before the Subcommittee on Telecommunications, Trade, and Consumer Protection of the Commerce Committee, U.S. House of Representatives, http://web.lexis-nexis.com/congcomp/document?_m+ada1c46790aa89...a434d6476 (accessed June 5, 2003).

Nevaer, Louis E.V. 2002. *The dot-com debacle and the return to reason.* Westport, Connecticut: Quorum Books. 152.

Okerson, Ann. 1996. Who owns digital works? *Scientific American*, 275, no. 1. http://search.epnet.com/ (accessed June 5, 2003).

Peters, Marybeth. 1995. Capitol Hill hearing testimony before the Subcommittee on Courts and Intellectual Property of the Committee on the Judiciary, U.S. House of Representatives, http://www.copyright.gov/docs/niitest.html (accessed November 15, 2003).

PR Newswire. 1998. 1998 Pulitzer prize winning historian urges speaker to decouple and defer dangerous 'Database' Legislation. *PR Newswire*, http://proquest.umi.com/pqdweb?index=604&sid=1&srchmode=1&vinst...FULL&ts=1067735498 (accessed October 2, 2003).

Regan, Tom. 1998. Internet access and new copyright law head for a collision. *Christian Science Monitor*, November 12, http://www.proquest.umi.com/pqdweb?index=585&sid=1&srchmode=1&vinst...scaling=FULL&ts=106 (accessed October 2, 3003).

Reuters. 1998. House panel backs new digital copyright law. *Reuters*, July 20, http://cyber.law.harvard.edu/openlaw/DVD/dmca/wipo-hit2.htm (accessed November 15, 2003).

Rosen, Hilary. 1997. Statement before the Subcommittee on Courts and Intellectual Property of the Committee on the Judiciary, U.S. House of Representatives. http://www.copyright.gov/docs/niitest.html (accessed September 17, 2003).

Samuelson, Robert J. 1998. Meanwhile, back on the Hill. *The Washington Post*, September 17, http://gateway.proquest.com/openurl?ctx_ver+z39.88…pq_clntid=17840 (accessed November 15, 2003).

Schmidt, Diane. 2001. Protecting intellectual property and regulating MP3: A first amendment trojan horse? Paper presented at the annual meeting of the American Political Science Association, San Francisco.

Schwartz, John. 1998. The net impact of the new copyright bill. *The Washington Post*, May 18, http://proquest.umi.com/pqdweb?index=426&sid…FULL&tx=106 (accessed October 2, 2003).

Steinhardt, Barry and Laura Murphy. 1998. Letter regarding H.R. 2281. American Civil Liberties Union Freedom Network, http://archive.aclu.org/congress/1060498b.html (accessed June 4, 2003).

Tang, Puay. 2001. How electronic publishers are protecting against piracy: Doubts about technical systems of protection. *Information Society* 14, no. 1: 22.

U.S. Congress. Senate. 1998. Committee on the Judiciary. *Senate Report 105-190—The Digital Millennium Copyright Act of 1998.* 105th Cong. 2d sess. Washington, D.C.: Government Printing Office.

U.S. Congress. Senate. 1999. Committee on the Judiciary. *Senate Report 105-846.* 105th Cong. 2d sess. Washington, D.C.: Government Printing Office.

U.S. Copyright Office. 1998. *Pub L. No. 105-304—The Digital Millennium Copyright Act of 1998: U.S. copyright office summary.* December. Washington, D.C.: Government Printing Office.

U.S. Patent and Trademark Office. 1995. Executive summary. *Intellectual property and the national information infrastructure: The report of the working group on intellectual property rights*, http://www.uspto.gov/web/offices/com/doc/ipnii/execsum.html (accessed November 15, 2003).

Yoshida, Junko. 1997. Copy-protection questions delay digital rollouts. *Electronic Engineering Times*, 01921541, no. 939, http://web17.epnet.com/ (accessed October 2, 2003).

y Analysis: Evaluation or Recommendation

Purpose of a Policy Analysis

The purpose of a policy analysis is to examine a public policy's impact on the political environment in which it was or is to be implemented.

- Not all public policies are made by Congress.
- Policies can be custom, rulings by courts, regulations written by bureaucrats, or executive orders.
- When examining a public policy, we want to identify the goals, the tools, and the outcomes so that we can assess whether it was or is a successful and worthwhile intervention by government.

Formats of a Policy Analysis

Policy analysis is usually found in one of two formats:

Policy evaluation is limited to evaluation of past or present policies. This type of policy analysis entails examining the characteristics of a current or past policy. To do this, we must identify and analyze the policy's origins, the policy's goals, who benefits, the instruments used to implement the goals of the policy, and its perceived or actual impact.

Policy recommendation involves proposing a new solution to a new or existing problem. This type of policy analysis may or may not involve an analysis of a current policy. To produce a policy recommendation, we must first evaluate current policy responses to the problem or similar to the problem identified. A policy recommendation, however, takes the analysis one step further. After evaluating past policy responses to similar problems, a policy recommendation then argues for the adoption of a new solution to the current problem. It provides both the rationale for the solution and a description of how it would be implemented, who it would benefit, who is likely to oppose it, and how we would evaluate its progress toward solving the problem.

Researching and Writing a Policy Evaluation

1. **Identify a social problem or social condition.**
   - Look in the newspaper for ideas.
   - Choose something of particular interest to you.
   - State clearly why you are interested the problem.
2. **Identify indicators of the social condition.**
   - Find one relevant quantitative indicator from each of the following:
     - An almanac.
     - A statistical yearbook.
     - American Statistics Index.
   - Locate sources related to the topic or problem using a computer search system, the library catalog, abstracts, and indexes.
   - Obtain two books on your subject.

- Locate five scholarly journal articles.
- Locate two articles from quality publications.
- Locate two articles from mass publications.
◆ Locate one government publication related to your topic or problem from each of the following:
  - Congressional Information Service Index.
  - Monthly Catalog of U.S. Publications.
  - Congressional Record.

3. **Identify the nature of the problem.**
   ◆ Describe the problem.
     - Explain clearly what the problem is.
     - Explain clearly why the problem is public concern.
   ◆ Present evidence of the existence of the problem.
     - Quantitative (statistical or numerical) evidence.
     - Qualitative (expert opinion, examples) evidence.
   ◆ List the factors underlying the problem.
     - Identify the broad underlying factors.
     - Identify the specific underlying factors.

4. **Find the public policy, if there is one, dealing with the problem.**
   ◆ Describe the different solutions proposed or available and the solution adopted.
   ◆ Identify where the public policy originated—custom, Congress, bureaucracy, judicial, or executive policy.
     - Examine how and where the policy was initiated.
     - Sometimes a policy has more than one source.
   ◆ Identify five important political actors or players who either supported or opposed the solution adopted.
     - State the issue position of each player.
     - State the power of each player.
     - Identify at least two reasons why you included each player.
     - Rank order the players by importance to implementing the solution.
   ◆ Identify whether the policy been expanded or adjusted over time.
     - State the conditions for the change.
     - State the reasons for the change.

5. **Identify the objectives, targets, or goals of the policy.**
   ◆ What was the policy supposed to do exactly?
     - What target population was supposed to benefit?
     - Is the solution curative? preventative? remedial?
   ◆ What were the means or policy instruments used to achieve the goals or objectives?
     - How was the policy supposed to achieve its goals?
     - Policy tools—transfers? regulation? subsidy? tax?

6. **Analyze who or what benefited and who or what was hurt by the policy.**
   - ◆ Who seems better off, who is worse off?
   - ◆ Who paid the cost, who benefited?

7. **Evaluate the success of the policy by examining whether the goals or objectives were achieved.**
   - ◆ Match the goals with the outcomes.
   - ◆ How can you tell the policy is working?
   - ◆ Did the targets benefit as expected?
   - ◆ What constraints prevented it from working well?
   - ◆ What do the experts say about the policy?

8. **When writing your evaluation, include a discussion, in order, of the following:**
   - ◆ An introduction which includes:
     - • A brief description of the social problem.
     - • The context.
     - • Solution adopted to solve the problem.
     - • A statement which assesses the usefulness of the solution for solving the problem.
   - ◆ Subheadings identifying the discussion of:
     - • The issue.
     - • The historical context or background.
     - • The objectives of the solution with justification.
     - • The critique of the policy response in meeting the objectives with justification.
     - • An assessment with a cost-benefit analysis.
   - ◆ A conclusion which restates briefly the context of the social problem and the justification of your critique of the solution.
   - ◆ Do not forget to include a list of sources for all borrowed ideas, arguments, and data. Use tables, charts, and graphs to illustrate data where necessary.

Policy Evaluation Guide and Check-Off Sheet

Brief Description
- • Identify the policy.
- • Summarize its implied and/or expressed goals in concise detail.

Problems & Issues Identified
- • Describe the social problem thoroughly.
- • Describe how the problems were identified.
- • Describe how the problems became issues.

Historical Context
- • Identify and explain, chronologically, the who, what, where, when, how, and why (politics) related to getting the problem/issue on to the governmental/decision agenda.

- Describe the process and circumstances of the formulation of the policy decision.
- Describe the legitimization of the policy decision.
- What kind of policy process was involved in passing this policy?
- Specifically, what types of individuals supported or did not support the proposed response to the problem/issue?
- Describe how information was use in formulating a solution.

Objectives of the Solution

- Describe the purpose of the tools or instruments used as policy responses to the problems/issues.
- Do the goals of the policy solution directly relate to the identified problems/issues? Why or why not?
- Specifically, what goals, problems, and/or issues are these tools supposed to address, remedy, fix, or resolve?
- Particularly, who are the targets of these tools?
- Explain why these tools were chosen over others.

Critique of Policy Response in Meeting Objectives

- Based on your research, do the policy responses adequately address the identified problems? Why or why not?
- Are there unresolved problems or issues that have been identified but not addressed by the policy response?
- Specifically, what criteria and/or data are supposed to measure the policy's success?

Assessment/Cost-benefit Analysis

- Based on your research, was the policy outcome worth the costs associated with the policy response?
- What are the barriers to measuring whether the policy outcomes reflect success or not?
- What intervening events or unexpected circumstances influenced the policy outcomes positively or negatively?
- Were there budget or implementation problems that constrained policy success?
- Did pluralist forces help or hinder the implementation process?

Conclusions About the Problem and Critique of Solution

- Identify important findings from the evaluation.
- Was the policy proposal a good proposal with carefully built structures of support?
- What is the value of this evaluation to understanding public policy formation related to the policy domain?

Example of a Policy Evaluation

**Jailbait:
Has California's Statutory Rape Law
Deterred Teen Pregnancy?**

By
Meredith Reynolds
271B-Schmidt
5/23/02
(Reprinted with permission)

INTRODUCTION

Few if any societies exhibit a more perverse combination of permissiveness and prudishness in their treatment of sexual issues than California (Rhode 1994). Many adults have difficulty acknowledging *adolescent* sexuality, particularly when it involves sexual relationships between adolescents and adults. As a response, California statutory rape laws are based on the premise that until a person reaches a certain age, that minor is legally incapable of consenting to sexual intercourse (Donovan 1997).

In California, adolescent sexuality has lead to an overwhelming amount of teen pregnancies. The "crisis" of teenage pregnancy in California has increased substantially, which enabled California policymakers to draft Assembly Bill 1490 as statutory rape legislation. A growing number of these policymakers in California claimed that teenage pregnancy and birth rates could be reduced if states passed and enforced statutory rape laws. Former Governor Wilson of California predicted that "the increased ability to more aggressively prosecute statutory rape offenders will send a loud message that there will be serious consequences for adult men who impregnate minors, thereby creating a significant deterrent effect" (Donovan 1997, 31).

The intent of the California legislation, entitled the Teenage Pregnancy Prevention Act of 1995, is to have district attorneys vigorously investigate and prosecute adults guilty of having unlawful sexual intercourse with minors, especially in cases where that unlawful sexual intercourse results in pregnancy (AB 1490 1995). Another purpose of the legislation is to create civil liability for adults who engage in unlawful sexual intercourse with minors, the money from which can help fund future efforts to prevent teenage pregnancy and help deter adult sexual predators from victimizing minor females (Governor's Office of Criminal Justice Planning 1999).

The primary goal of this legislation is to send a clear message to adults who have unlawful sexual intercourse with minors that they are committing a crime and will be very seriously prosecuted and fined. Former California Governor Pete Wilson stated, "This bill sends a strong message to adult men who think they can pursue and impregnate minors without consequences" (Bailey 1996, 2). Other goals of the legislation include reducing teenage pregnancy and child sexual abuse through prosecution and heightened public awareness.

The purpose of this paper is to determine if the Teenage Pregnancy Prevention Act of 1995 actually deters the problem of teenage pregnancy in California, or does the law have unexpected and unforeseen outcomes? Does California's statutory rape law, the Teenage Pregnancy Prevention Act of 1995, have a deterrent effect on teen pregnancy in California and has this law functioned as a successful pregnancy prevention measure? I argue that the California statutory rape law, the Teenage Pregnancy Prevention Act of 1995, not only ignores contributing factors to adolescent sexual behavior, but it overestimates the impact on deterring relationships between minors and adults that result in unlawful sexual activity.

FROM PROBLEM TO ISSUE

Beginning in the late 1960s and early 1970s, a serious recognition of teen pregnancy as a social problem occurred (Rhode 1994). Teen sexual activity and unmarried parenthood became a more prominent and socially disturbing trend; the total number of births to unmarried teens more than doubled between 1960 and 1970 (Furstenberg 1991; Alvarez 1995). The problem of teen pregnancy became an issue, not only because of its frequent occurrences, but also because of other issues connected with it, such as sexuality, abortion, family values, and welfare policy. The problem of teen pregnancy began when single parenthood was associated with disrupted education, reduced employment opportunities, and a higher poverty rate for the mothers, along with increased medical risks and developmental difficulties for the children. Adolescent sex is also closely related to the incidence of sexually transmitted diseases. Many teens greatly underestimate the risk of unprotected sexual activity, such as unwanted pregnancies, but also AIDS and other sexually transmitted diseases (Rhode 1994).

Teen pregnancy became a much more significant issue when the United States had the highest teen pregnancy rate in the developed world in the late 1980s (Wood 1996). Close to 45 percent of adolescent females were sexually active before marriage, which resulted in 1,000,000 teen pregnancies each year (Rhode 1994). California has the nation's highest rate of per capita teen pregnancy to date (Grad and Warren 1997). On an average California day 76 teenage girls, 17 and younger, will give birth (Statutory Rape Prosecution Unit 2001).

California, however, has seen changes in its teen pregnancy rates. Statistics from the National Center for Health Statistics (NCHS) and the U.S. Department of Health and Human Services show that the national teen pregnancy and birthrate peaked in 1991. The age group 15 to 17 had a 38.7 percent birthrate and a 73.2 percent teen pregnancy rate in 1991 (Henshaw 2001). From 1992–1996 the teen pregnancy rate in California dropped 22 percent, ranking them ninth among all states (Teen Pregnancy and Childbearing in California 2000). From 1991 to 1999 there has also been a national decrease in teen pregnancy rates and teen birthrates. In the age group 15–17, birthrates went from 38.7 percent to 28.7 percent, while the national teen pregnancy rate went down from 73.2 percent to 57.7 percent (Henshaw 2001). Currently, California's teen birthrate is ranked fourteenth among the nation as a whole. This significant drop has been attributed by the Centers for Disease Control (CDC) to an increase in condom use, increased use of implanted and injectable contraceptives, and a leveling-off of teen sexual activity (Centers for Disease Control 1997).

HISTORICAL CONTEXT

There are many steps to policy development for a statutory rape law. The initial step is to study the past and current trends in sexual activity in order to find ways to predict future sexual activity. Such a study, like the one conducted by Elo and King (1999), provides society with up-to-date information regarding the state of teen pregnancy and the policies that attempt to reduce its incidence. This study also concludes that sexual activity involving teens must be viewed from a long-term perspective because focusing on short-term information can lead to incorrect conclusions (Elo and King 1999).

Recently, in President Clinton's 1995 State of the Union Address, he challenged leaders and parents across the nation to join together in a national campaign against teen pregnancy (Rhode 1993). The National Campaign to Prevent Teen Pregnancy reports that more than 40 percent of American females become pregnant by the age of 20 (Brown 1996). The idea behind this campaign was that teen pregnancy contributes highly to many other societal problems. The goal of this campaign is to reduce the teen pregnancy rate in the United States by one third by 2005. The strategy that this campaign is enlisting coalitions on the local level to organize and confront the problem.

New to most public policy discussion, is the realization that part of the strategy for reducing teen pregnancy should be a discussion of religious, cultural, and public values. There is also some debate that the perception of the "crisis" of teen pregnancy has been provoked by the political agendas of certain interest groups. When revisiting the claims of a coalition including social scientists, policymakers, and family planning advocates, it seems that they may have organized information in such a way that suggested the rise of teen pregnancy when, in fact, the rates had been dropping (Furstenberg 1991). These coalitions had misused information to convince politicians that by preventing teen pregnancy, the social and economic costs of poverty would be combated. This gave both liberals who wanted to expand services and conservatives who wanted to control welfare costs a middle ground of compromise (Furstenberg 1991).

OBJECTIVES OF THE TEEN PREGNANCY PREVENTION ACT OF 1995

The Teenage Pregnancy Prevention Act of 1995 makes it a crime in California for an adult to have sexual intercourse with a minor or for two minors to have sexual intercourse unless the couple is married. This act also makes unlawful sexual intercourse with a minor three years older or younger than the perpetrator a crime with a penalty of a misdemeanor or a felony, depending upon the circumstances. Finally, this law calls for civil penalties to be used to repay the costs of pursuing the action with any remaining monies to be put into the Underage Pregnancy Prevention Fund, which is used for purposes that prevent teenage pregnancy upon appropriation by the state legislature (CA Assembly Bill 1490 1995).

Adult Targets

Given that other liberals and conservatives were seeking a compromise between services and controlling costs, the objective of the Teen Pregnancy Prevention Act was broadened to include both minors and adults as targets. Policymakers feel that this law would regulate the way that adults interact with minors, as well as holding both minors and adults accountable for their actions. Recently, policymakers have examined the law focusing on punishing male adults for taking advantage of underage females. The law is written as though there is a consensus that teenage girls are not mature enough to make major decisions because they are vulnerable to coercion and exploitation (Oberman and Delgado 1996).

Yet, adult targets of these objectives are an often overlooked component to teen pregnancy. Findings from the 1995 National Survey of Family Growth revealed that most underage females have older sexual partners. Forty-three to 50 percent of teen pregnancies were born to males who were at least three years older than their female partners (Elo and King 1999). At least half of all babies born to minors are fathered by adult males (Donovan 1997). This shows that adult males are committing the crime of statutory rape. Statistics show high rates of teen pregnancies from adult males, yet males who are minors lack protection from adult females under the statutory rape law in California.

There is also the problem of the reverse stereotype, older females/women and underage males, which has been overlooked for a long time (Age Differences... 2001). Males are seen as perpetrators, and most of the literature on teen pregnancy reveals a bias against males. More recently, statutory rape legislation was passed into law broadening the definition of statutory rape to include women as perpetrators and make statutory rape a gender-neutral crime (Gladstone and Weintraub 1993).

Criminalizing Sexual Behavior

One tool of the Teen Pregnancy Prevention Act of 1995 is the Statutory Rape Vertical Prosecution Program (SRVP), created by this legislation to vertically prosecute adults who engage in unlawful sexual intercourse with a minor (Governor's Office of Criminal Justice Planning 1999, 3). The SRVP hopes that it will provide information on the nature of the problem as well as the accomplishments of the program. Prosecution within this legislation is divided into two different categories: civil and criminal prosecution with corresponding penalties. Civil penalties include fines ranging from $2,000 to $25,000 for statutory rape (Vertical Prosecution Report 1999). Criminal penalties include misdemeanor or felony convictions and jail or prison sentences ranging from one to four years (Vertical Prosecution Report 1999).

Supporters of Assembly Bill 1490/The Teen Pregnancy Prevention Act of 1995 argue that the current statutory rape laws are not effective and are seldom enforced. The bill provides prosecutors with a powerful tool for punishing adult males who prey on minor females. Critics of this bill, however, argue that the approach of singling out statutory rapes that result in pregnancy could backfire and hurt the victims. Pregnant minors who do not want to see the father prosecuted or fined might refuse to come forward to receive child support or medical treatment (Bee 1996).

The new focus on statutory rape law has inspired debate over the effectiveness of this method as a potential answer for the ongoing problem of teen pregnancy and since the passing of the Teen Pregnancy Prevention Act of 1995, much has been raised regarding the effectiveness of this law to deter people from unlawful sexual intercourse. However, some opponents to this law believe that this approach is the wrong way to go about punishing adults who engage in sex with minors. Opponents of the statutory rape laws distrust using the criminal code as a form of social control.

Advocates of diligent enforcement assert that adult men who "prey" on minor females will avoid these sexual relationships with them if they believe that prosecution and severe punishment will follow violation of the law (Donovan 1997). The incarceration of men who are convicted of the crime of statutory rape will by itself have an impact on teenage pregnancy and birthrates. Adult men will be deterred from getting involved with minor females in the first place if a state makes clear its intention to vigorously prosecute statutory rape and follows through on the threat with some highly publicized cases (Donovan 1997). The result, these advocates predict, will be fewer adolescent pregnancies and births because of the deterrent effect of the statutory rape law.

Increasing Access to Contraceptives

Some other tools used in preventing teen pregnancy that should be mentioned include direct access to women's health care and insurance coverage of contraceptive services. The President's Advisory Commission on Consumer Protection and Quality in the Health Care Industry issued the Consumer Bill of Rights and Responsibilities. This Bill of Rights called for managed care plans to provide "direct access" to women's health care (Donovan 1997). The states that had preexisting laws on the books amended their policies to make direct access services more available to women, while states who had passed this law for the first time expanded the options for direct access services. The passing of the direct access law in these states provided a safe, confidential, and convenient way for women to obtain health care if they become pregnant.

Insurance coverage for contraceptive care is a very significant issue because it requires that insurance companies cover contraceptive services and supplies as a standard benefit (Donovan 1997). Such measures have been introduced in 20 states and seriously considered in 12. In California, state lawmakers passed contraceptive coverage legislation twice, but both times it was vetoed by Governor Wilson. The reasons for his veto were that if the state mandated that contraceptives be covered, then employers could drop medical coverage altogether, and he objected to a provision that would allow employees who could not obtain contraceptive benefits as a result of their employers exemption to receive state-subsidized services (Bailey 1996).

Education

The solution to the issue of teen pregnancy has been multifaceted, but includes educating teenagers regarding the laws. The information packet distributed by the Teen Parents Organization informs the public about the law on statutory rape (2001). It includes frequently asked questions and the answers in order to help those who need to know the law regarding statutory rape. The Teen Parents Organization packet is just one of the ways that information is used to educate teens about the statutory rape laws in California. Another educational tool for teenagers regarding the statutory rape laws in California is a pamphlet distributed by the Public Council Law Center of Los Angeles. This pamphlet informs the public about the laws on statutory rape, including age requirements, fines, jail and prison sentences, and helpful contact numbers (Public Council Law Center 2001).

The Teenage Pregnancy Prevention Act of 1995 is California's statutory rape law. California's Penal Code section 261.5 states that "In California, females under the age of 18 years gave birth to 28,065 children in 1994." The Teenage Pregnancy Prevention Act of 1995 defines a minor as a person under the age of 18 (Public Council Law Center 2001). Sixty-six percent of the fathers of those children were adult males, and 10,768 of those fathers were between the ages of 20 and 29 years (California Assembly Bill 1490 1995). This prompted legislation to deter teenage pregnancy by making it a crime for a minor to consent to sexual intercourse if a person is under the age of 18. On February 24, 1995, California Assembly Bill 1490, called the Teenage Pregnancy Prevention Act of 1995, was passed into law.

CRITIQUE OF THE TEENAGE PREGNANCY PREVENTION ACT

The recognition of the decline of teen pregnancy rates in California and the nation since 1992 has prompted some debate over the need for such a law. Some opponents to the statutory rape law see no apparent need for such a law since the teen pregnancy rates in California have been on the decline since 1991. The teen pregnancy rate had already hit a peak in 1991, and naturally took a dive without the intervention of the law. By 1995, the consistent decline of the teen pregnancy rates questioned the need for an intervention law.

Teen Pregnancy Declining

When looking at the years previous to the Teen Pregnancy Prevention Act of 1995, the national average of teen pregnancy was on the decline (California experiences...1999). Between 1991, which was the highest national average since 1972, and 1995, teen pregnancy decreased from 73.2 percent to 65.0 percent (Henshaw 2001). This shows that it decreased 8.2 percent and this questions whether or not teen pregnancy was such the political crisis it was made out to be. Even from 1995, when the Teen Pregnancy Prevention Act was passed in California, to 1996, when it was put into practice, the national average birthrate went down 2.2 percent from 36.0 percent in 1995 to 33.8 percent in 1996 (Henshaw 2001).

In California, the same trend has been happening. The California Health and Human Services Agency released a report showing that for the sixth consecutive year the teen birthrate had decreased significantly in California. Births to teenagers age 15–19 dropped 8 percent from 1995 to the present (California Health and Human Services Agency 2001). This decrease is close to three times larger than the decrease reported by the nation as a whole. Birthrates of adolescents age 10–14 have also dropped by 15.4 percent. This trend is part of a consistent decline since 1992. This also shows that the teen pregnancy and birth rates had been decreasing, and continued to decrease regardless of legislation, or the lack thereof.

Difficult to Enforce

The goals of the Teenage Pregnancy Prevention Act of 1995 relate to the problem of teen pregnancy in that they provide civil and criminal penalties to hold perpetrators responsible for their acts of unlawful sexual intercourse. It also establishes the Statutory Rape Vertical Prosecution Program, which provides counties with a way to track down and prosecute these perpetrators. The Vertical Prosecution Program is constrained in that it only has the ability to catch those certain circumstances in which two people engage in unlawful sexual intercourse and they are either reported, or their acts result in pregnancy. It can be noted, however, that making unlawful sexual intercourse a crime may not be the most accurate goal in relation to the problem. When examining the Statutory Rape Vertical Prosecution Report, it shows how cases were referred, how many cases were filed, and how many convictions were gained. The report then goes on to suggest that the Vertical Prosecution Program be continued based on the high amount of convictions to cases referred. Not once is there a mention of this program actually deterring unlawful sexual intercourse, or creating a decline in those who engage in unlawful sexual activity. Therefore, this program and its goals only accomplish punishing those people it actually catches, and neglects to address all of the other people who engage in unlawful sexual intercourse and are never caught.

Poor Enforcement

Based on the statistics from the Statutory Rape Vertical Prosecution Report, the Office of Criminal Justice Planning (1999) would like the public to think that the program is working properly. When questioning experts in the fields of reproductive health, women's rights, policy analysis, and law enforcement, most experts do not believe that greater enforcement of the statutory rape laws in California can significantly reduce teen pregnancy. There is also some criticism of the impact of this law when national rates of teenage pregnancy are declining.

The problem of teen pregnancy is much more complicated than simply older males preying on younger females. Adolescent childbearing is the outcome of an extensive web of factors that include limited opportunity, poverty, low self-esteem, and many other issues that statutory rape laws do not address (Donovan 1997). The intent of the law is that the imprisonment of men who are convicted of the crime will by itself have an impact on teenage pregnancy and birth rates. It is believed that men will be deterred from getting involved with teenage females with the state vigorously prosecuting statutory rape and enforcing the law. Any deterrent effect will only occur if those whom it targets are educated about the statutory rape laws.

EVALUATING THE COSTS AND BENEFITS OF THE ACT

Over the past five years the California Department of Health Services has implemented many inventive strategies which intended to prevent teen pregnancy, such as pregnancy prevention programs like the vertical prosecution of statutory rape. The statistics show that these programs have some advantages, however, the controversy lies in the measure of their success. The teen pregnancy rate and the teen birthrate have been on the decline since 1991, before these programs were enacted to stop the "crisis" of teen pregnancy in California.

Measurement Problems

To measure the success of the Teen Pregnancy Prevention Act of 1995, statistics from the Statutory Rape Vertical Prosecution Program are used. For example, statutory rape cases in Orange County have more than doubled with 110 people being charged with statutory rape in 1996, compared with 55 cases in 1995. Out of the 110 cases from Orange County in 1996, 69 have resulted in convictions (Grad and Warren 1997). During the fourth year of the SRVP, 6,016 cases were referred for prosecution, 2,862 cases were filed in court, and 2,110 cases were completed with convictions and sentences (Office of Criminal Justice Planning 1999). This report concludes that the steady increase of cases over the last four years is evidence that the program outreach efforts within their communities have accomplished positive results. This report assumes that an increase in the number of cases brought by district attorneys across California demonstrates that the program is valid and effective.

In addition, this report may show an increased number of statutory rape cases, but it does not reflect that these cases are having any positive effect on deterring the teenage population regarding pregnancy. This method of using the number of convictions to assess the deterrence of crime does not correctly correlate. This method neglects to count all those minors and adults who are engaging in unlawful sexual intercourse, but who are never caught. The correct correlation would be to examine the number of those minors and adults who engage in unlawful sexual intercourse but who are never caught and then compare it to those who are convicted of the same act. If the conviction number is a high percentage of the number of people who engage in unlawful sexual intercourse, then the comparison would be valid.

MEASUREMENT ERROR

There are many barriers to measuring the costs and benefits of the Teenage Pregnancy Prevention Act of 1995. First, there is a number of evidence that statistics showing the large numbers of births in California due to older "predatory" adult males have been misleading. Some say that Governor Wilson misused this information to pursue his own agendas, while others ignore the reason but work to refute the misleading statistic: two-thirds of all teen pregnancies are caused by men over 20 (Rendon 1997). This misused statistic was a contrived unprincipled action by Governor Wilson in which he violated the standard classification of a minor in relation to teen pregnancy and statutory rape, which made teen pregnancy in California a bigger issue than it really was.

The misused statistic was originally from a study by the Guttmacher Institute in "Family Planning Perspectives," which studied teen pregnancy in general (State legislators…1999). The group studied teenagers up through age 19 who gave birth. They discovered that most teen pregnancies were the result of sex with a man over age 20, but the majority of these teens who gave birth were between 18 and 19 years old (Rendon 1997). This study also did not look at age differences between the men and girls, which is usually a requirement for prosecution. By the time the statistic was misused, however, the disturbance regarding statutory rape was soon out of control. The Guttmacher Institute then went to work on a second study using the same data as the first, but removed the 18 and 19 year olds, and only looked at unmarried couples where the males were five or more years older that the girls. The findings were sensationally different; the researchers found that prosecutable statutory rape by this criteria was responsible for only 8 percent of teenage births (Rendon 1997).

Unexpected Circumstances Affect Policy

Research suggests that existing laws do not deter young females from getting romantically involved with older males because the teen culture has taken up a set of justifications which make the relationships legitimate (Higginson 1999; Donovan 1997). This suggests that the statutory rape laws need to be modified or eliminated. If modified, the laws would need to be more stringently enforced to show that not everybody has sex, and there are consequences to one's actions even as a minor. To take this route, however, would be costly and time-consuming because it would be attempting to change an entire culture of teenagers. If the statutory rape laws were to be eliminated, this would release money to be used in sex education programs and contraception for adolescents rather than enforcing ineffective laws. This move would further liberate minor females from their historically disadvantaged position of needing protection from their own irrational desires (Higginson 1999). Also, punishing an adult father by fining him and sentencing him to imprisonment leaves the mother without his financial support and may necessitate her entry into the realm of the welfare system.

Budget Restraints

If and when success is determined by how many people are convicted of statutory rape under the Vertical Prosecution Program, then this program can only survive on the civil penalties that are brought in by convictions. In short, the more people that are convicted and given a civil penalty, the more money the Statutory Rape Vertical Prosecution Program has to turn around and convict more people of unlawful sexual intercourse. The more people who are convicted and given a civil penalty, the stronger the program becomes in its ability to continue prosecuting people of unlawful sexual intercourse. This program only perpetuated the SRVP program and encourages convictions for money.

CONCLUSION

The study of the statutory rape laws in California is very important because not many policymakers want to regulate sex. Sex is a taboo issue in American society for religious and moral reasons and policymakers always come into conflict when it comes to making laws about sex because it is difficult to regulate a personal belief or value. Most policymakers will stay as far away from the issue of sex as possible, but in California there is an attempt to curb sexual behaviors of minors.

The most important thing that was found in the evaluation of the Teen Pregnancy Prevention Act of 1995 was something that was missing or possibly excluded from all of the government based research. This important missing piece of information was that there was lack of attention paid to the fact that this policy has no legitimate way of measuring success. Measuring success based on prosecution statistics is not a legitimate way of determining that the Teenage Pregnancy Prevention Act of 1995 works. In fact, statutory rape convictions do not measure deterrence, but do measure the failure to deter. There is no solid connection between increased conviction rates of statutory rapists and the decrease in unlawful sexual intercourse. The problem definition is not logically followed because the actual outcome based on the tools is extremely limited.

The analysis of the Teenage Pregnancy Prevention Act of 1995 shows that government can not deter teen pregnancy by mandating morality. This policy is incomplete, not comprehensively effective, and the law did not look deep enough into the circumstances influencing unlawful sexual intercourse to solve the problem of teen pregnancy in California.

A Good Policy Intervention?

The possible positive effects of this legislation do not outweigh the negative consequences. The one positive effect that could result from this policy is decline of the teenage pregnancy birthrate. The teenage pregnancy birthrate, however, has been declining in the past five years, and there is no sure way of measuring the actual effect the Teenage

Pregnancy Prevention Act may have had on it. Also, the negative outcomes of this policy seem to outweigh the positive effect. Teens may refuse to seek medical care for themselves or their unborn babies for fear of involvement with law enforcement and loss of financial support. Teen fathers who accept responsibility for their actions are discouraged from doing so and from taking part in their child's life for fear of being prosecuted, fined, and imprisoned.

This legislation is a quick fix and too simple a solution for a complex problem. The Teenage Pregnancy Prevention Act of 1995 does not address or relieve societal problems or influences that relate to adolescent sexuality and pregnancy. It also does not establish that a law is not the only answer to the problem of teen pregnancy. Finally, this law lacks a plan for education, which would, in this case, help inform the target populations.

The Value of Regulating Morality

The evaluation of the Teenage Pregnancy Prevention Act of 1995 shows that government can not mandate morality. This policy is incomplete and not comprehensively effective. The law did not solve the problem of teen pregnancy in California. Policymakers always face conflict when it comes to making laws about sex because it is difficult to regulate a personal belief or value. Most policymakers will stay as far away from the issue of sex as possible, but in California some organizations and policymakers have attempted to curb the sexual behavior of minors. It is for these reasons that this legislation was passed and it is for these reasons that this legislation has been ineffective.

REFERENCES

Age differences between sexual partners in the United States. 1999. *Family Planning Perspectives 31, no.5*, http://www.agiusa.org/pubs/journals/3116099.html (accessed September 16, 2001).

Alvarez, Fred. 1995. Program to battle teen pregnancy targets men; Crime: The County vows vigorous prosecution of statutory rape cases. The pilot project is part of an effort to make fathers responsible. *The Los Angeles Times*, November 20, 4.

Bailey, Eric. 1996. New law levies sizable fines for intercourse with minors; Crime: Bill signed Monday by Governor Wilson establishes a legislative fund for anti-teenage pregnancy programs. *The Los Angeles Times*, September 24, 2.

Bee, John Matthews. 1996. Bill is tougher on statutory rape: Measure would mean prison, fines for men who get minors pregnant. *The Fresno Bee*, May 15, 2.

Brown, Sarah. 1996. Targeting teen pregnancy. *Policy Review* 79: 60.

California experiences another significant drop in births to teens. 1999. *California Department of Health Services*, http://www.dhs.ca.gov (accessed November 15, 2001)

Donovan, Patricia. 1997. Can statutory rape laws be effective in preventing adolescent pregnancy. *Family Planning Perspectives* 29:30–36.

Elo, Irma and Rosalind King. 1999. Adolescent females: Their sexual partners and the fathers of their children. *Journal of Marriage and the Family* 61: 74–94.

Furstenberg, F F. 1991. As the pendulum swings: Teenage childbearing and social concern. *Family Relations* 40: 127–44.

Gladstone, Mark and Daniel Weintraub. 1993. New law broadens the provisions of statutory rape legislation: The gender-neutral statute provides stronger punishment for women who have sex with underage boys. *The Los Angeles Times*, October 2, 2.

Governor's Office of Criminal Justice Planning. 1999. *Statutory rape vertical prosecution report*, June 30, http//www.ocip.ca.gov/publications/pub_srvprpt4.htm (accessed

September 27, 2001).

Grad, Shelby and Peter Warren. 1997. Statutory rape prosecutions surging in Orange County. *The Los Angeles Times*, August 13, 3.

Henshaw, Stanley. 2001. Teenage pregnancy statistics. *Alan Guttmacher Institute*, http://www.agi-usa.org (accessed November 15, 2001).

Higginson, Joanna. 1999. Defining, excusing, and justifying deviance: Teen mothers' accounts for statutory rape. *Symbolic Interaction* 22:25–46.

Oberman, Michelle and Richard Delgado. 1996. Statutory rape law: Does it make sense to enforce them in an increasingly permissive society? *American Bar Association*, 82:86–90.

Official California Legislative Information. 1995. *Assembly Bill 1490*. February 24, http://www.leginfo.ca.gov/pub/95-96/bill/asm/ab_1451-1500/ab_1490_bill_960923_chaptered.html (accessed September 16, 2001).

Public Counsel Law Center. 2001. *Statutory rape: What you should know*. February 2001, http://www.publiccounsel.org (accessed September 16, 2001).

Rendon, Jim. 1997. Jail baited. *Metroactive*, December, http://www.metroactive.com/papers/metro/12.18.97/cover/teensex-9751.html (accessed September 16, 2003).

Rhode, Deborah. 1993. Adolescent pregnancy and public policy. *Political Science Quarterly* 108:635–70.

State legislators in 1998: On two roads to goal of prevention. 1999. *The Guttmacher Report on Public Policy*, 2, no. 1, http://www.agi-usa.org/pubs/journals/gr020108.html (accessed September 16, 2001).

Teen Parents Organization. 2001. *Unlawful sexual intercourse: Statutory rape*. September 7, http://www.teenparents.org/usi.html (accessed September 16, 2001).

Wood, Daniel. 1996. States are rushing to curb sex crimes. *Christian Science Monitor* 88: 4–5.

Researching and Writing a Policy Recommendation

1. **Identify a social problem by examining newspapers or observing yo.. civi-ronment.**
   - Choose a new problem (aids).
   - Or choose an old problem (homelessness).

2. **Conduct a policy evaluation of a policy addressing problems like or similar to the problem identified.**
   - For new problems, examine policies closely related to the problem or which indirectly address the problem identified.
   - For old problems, examine policies currently enforced which directly or indirectly address the problem.
   - Be sure to identify the inadequacies of existing government policies you examined.
     - This step will aid in preventing you from proposing a policy solution that is already in force.
     - This step provides you with the depth and breadth necessary to recommend policy solutions.

3. **Identify the goals or objectives to be achieved in an ideal solution to the problem you identified.**
   - What do you want to do about the problem?
   - What do experts say should be done about it?
   - Rank the objectives by order of importance.
   - What desired outcome is most important?

4. **Identify alternative solutions proposed to solve the problem.**
   - What public actions do experts propose to deal with the problem?
     - Identify at least three alternatives.
     - Be sure you know the position and qualifications of each source.
   - Identify which alternatives address the objectives and outcomes you stated as being most important.
     - Clearly distinguish between each alternative's objectives.
     - Be sure to identify undesirable objectives stated by the experts who are supplemental or complementary to those which are desirable.
   - What are the proposed outcomes of the alternative solutions?
     - Identify the expected outcomes of each alternative.
     - Clearly distinguish between outcomes which are desirable and undesirable.
     - Match up the objectives you stated with the outcomes from each alternative.
   - Rank order the alternatives by preferred objective and outcome.
     - Be able to justify which alternative best fits the objectives and outcomes you prefer.
     - Clearly distinguish between objectives and expected outcomes.

5. Who do experts say should perform the actions?

- ◆ Identify the level of government that will be responsible for the policy.
- ◆ Identify the government agency that will implement the policy.

6. Identify the costs and benefits of each alternative.

- ◆ Examine all the real and implied costs.
  - Describe how you would measure the costs.
  - Identify the data source used to measure costs.
  - Identify and justify three real costs.
  - Identify and justify three implied costs.
- ◆ Examine all the real and implied benefits.
  - Describe how you measure the benefits.
  - Identify the data source used to measure benefits.
  - Identify and justify three real benefits.
  - Identify and justify three implied benefits.

7. Recommend the alternative that provides the greatest benefit for the least cost.

- ◆ Decide which benefits are necessary.
- ◆ Be able to justify all acceptable costs to achieve the benefits.

8. Identify at least five important political actors or players who are likely to either support or oppose your solution.

- ◆ Be sure you identify some players that are supporters and some that are part of the opposition.
- ◆ Identify the issue position, the power, and priority of each player listed.

9. When writing your recommendation, include a discussion, in order, of the following:

- ◆ An executive summary which includes:
  - A brief description of the social problem.
  - The context.
  - Previous attempts to solve the problem.
  - Your recommendation.
- ◆ Subheadings identifying the discussion of:
  - The issue.
  - The historical context/previous or current policy responses.
  - Evaluation (critique and assessment) of previous policy responses
  - The objectives of the ideal solution with justification.
  - The critique of available alternatives with comparative cost-benefit analysis.
  - Your complete recommendation with justification.
- ◆ A conclusion which restates briefly the context of the social problem and justification of your solution.
- ◆ Do not forget to include a list of sources for all borrowed ideas, arguments, and data. Use tables, charts, and graphs to illustrate data where necessary.

Policy Recommendation Guide and Check-Off Sheet

Brief Description
- Identify the policy problem.
- Summarize previous attempts to remedy the problem.
- Summarize your recommendations.

Problems & Issues Identified
- Describe the social problem thoroughly.
- Describe how the problems were identified.
- Describe how the problems became issues.

Historical Context/Previous Policy Responses
- Identify and explain, chronologically, the who, what, where, when, how, and why (politics) related to getting the problem/issue on to the governmental/decision agenda.
- Specifically, what types of individuals supported or did not support a response to the problem/issue?
- Describe the purpose of the tools or instruments used as policy responses to the problems/issues.
- Do the goals of the policy solution directly relate to the identified problems/issues? Why or why not?
- Specifically, what goals, problems, and/or issues are these tools supposed to address, remedy, fix, or resolve?
- Particularly, who are the targets of these tools?
- Explain why these tools were chosen over others.

Evaluation (critique and assessment) of Previous Policy Responses
- Based on your research, do the policy responses adequately address the identified problems? Why or why not?
- Are there unresolved problems or issues that have been identified but not addressed by the policy response?
- Based on your research, was the policy outcome worth the costs associated with the policy response?

Ideal Solution
- What problems or issues still need remedial action?
- What do experts or targets say is the most desired outcome?

Cost/Benefit Analysis of Available Alternative Solutions
- How does each alternative solution address (or not) the unresolved problems or issues you identified?
- Compare the expected benefits of each proposed solution to the ideal solution.
- Compare the costs of each proposed solution to the ideal solution.

Recommendations

- State specifically what actions you recommend.
- Identify which problem/issue is resolved by each action.
- Provide a justification for each action you chose.
- Provide a cost-benefit analysis with suggestions for how success will be measured.

Conclusions About the Problem and Justification of Your Proposed Solution

- Identify important inadequacies of the past or current policy responses.
- Restate why these inadequacies must be addressed.
- Summarize the reasons why your recommendations are the best way to address these inadequacies.

**POLICY RECOMMENDATION:
NEEDLE EXCHANGE PROGRAMS
AND HIV PREVENTION**

By
April Alexander
POLS 271A Public Policy Analysis
May 2, 2000
(Reprinted with permission)

EXECUTIVE SUMMARY

Intravenous drug use (IDU) has become the second leading cause of Human Immunodeficiency virus (HIV) transmission in America (US Census Bureau 1999). The rates of HIV transmission through IDU have soared, while rates for other transmission categories have steadily declined (National Research Council 1995). HIV in drug users and their children accounts for a large proportion of new infections. Intravenous drug uses of heroin and cocaine are both against the law and a social stigma. Many states in America have anti-drug paraphernalia laws that prohibit people from supplying or possessing drug use equipment (Gostin et al. 1997). In addition, many states include a provision regarding the sale of syringes without a prescription. Because of theses laws, many needle users cannot obtain sterile needles for drug use and they end up sharing equipment. Sharing drug equipment between users results in the following problems:

- As drug users share needles, the likelihood of transmitting a virus like HIV or Hepatitis becomes very high.
- Contaminated needles have become a major factor in transmitting these viruses.

Many concerned individuals and groups have been trying to find an effective solution to this problem, especially in high-risk areas like New York City and San Francisco. Some have organized counseling groups to offer immediate and long-term drug and disease counseling. Other groups have started bleach distribution programs (San Francisco AIDS Foundation 2000). Still others have implemented and operated both legal and illegal needle exchange programs. Currently there is a congressional ban on federal funding for the operation of needle exchange programs (NEPs) (42USCS §300ee-5 2000).

Implementing a national needle exchange program is the best alternative for HIV prevention in IDUs. A national needle exchange program best addresses the problems of preventing cross-contamination between drug users. Because there is currently a congressional ban on federal funding for the operation of NEPs and because state and local programs are not consistent across the United States, this policy analysis specifically recommends:

1. The federal government should lift its ban on supplying federal funds to local needle exchange programs.
2. State and local governments should reexamine their current laws regarding drugs and paraphernalia and make exceptions for needle exchange programs in high-risk areas.
3. Local public heath departments should assist in currently established needle exchange programs, as well as implement new programs where they are needed.

PROBLEMS AND ISSUES INVOLVING IDU

In the years between 1985 and 1998, intravenous drug use has directly or indirectly caused 180,287 cases of AIDS in America (World Almanac 1999). There are an estimated 1.5 million Intravenous drug users (IDU) in America (Gostin et al. 1997). This means that intravenous drug use has become the second most prevalent cause of AIDS transmission, second only to make homosexual intercourse. While the rates of AIDS transmitted through male homosexual contact have declined significantly, the rates of AIDS from intravenous drug use transmission have soared (US Census Bureau 1999). In 1981, 12 percent of new AIDS cases were attributed to intravenous drug use. By 1993, 28 percent could be traced back to IDU. Homosexual contact between males in 1981 caused 74 percent of new AIDS cases, while in 1993, the number had fallen to 47 percent (National

Research Council 1995). These numbers show that the AIDS epidemic is changing and preventing efforts must be addressed accordingly.

The primary way IDUs transmit the AIDS virus is through contaminated drug use equipment. There are a number of different ways the virus is transmitted through contaminated equipment. These processes can be broken into two main categories, direct and indirect (National Research Council 1995).

Direct Needle Sharing

The AIDS virus can be transmitted using a variety of methods where the syringe comes in contact with a user's blood. These methods are known as registering, booting, and shooting galleries. Through these methods transmit disease by using each others contaminated equipment.

Registering. The first direct way of transmission is through a practice called "registering." Registering occurs when a user draws blood into the syringe before he or she injects the drug, simply to be sure there is contact with a viable vein. This results in a contaminated needle, barrel, hub, and plunger. IDUs typically rinse out the needle after they use it; however, the virus can still adhere to the equipment, and be passed on to the next user (National Research Council 1995).

Booting. The second way of direct transmission is a practice called "booting" (National Research Council 1995). In addition to registering, the user draws blood into the barrel after the drug has been injected. He or she often repeats this practice a number of times. Drug users claim that this enhances the euphoric effect of the drug, as well as increases the economy by increasing the chance that the user used the full amount of drug available (National Research Council 1995).

Shooting Galleries. Another harmful way drug users increase their chances of obtaining a contaminated needle is through a "shooting gallery." Shooting galleries are secret locations where drug users can go to rent needles, which results in anonymous needle sharing (Des Jarlais et al. 1994). A study done on a Miami shooting gallery showed that 20 percent of the syringes that had visible blood residue were HIV positive. A follow-up study done two years later showed that 52 percent of the needles with blood were HIV positive (National Research Council 1995).

Indirect Needle Sharing

Indirect needle sharing is usually defined by the sharing of drug-use equipment like cookers, cotton, and rinse water (National Research Council 1995). Unlike direct needle sharing, the transmission of disease through indirect methods involves the handling of contaminated equipment. Importantly, the contamination occurs either before or after the equipment is used.

Cookers. Cookers are small containers in which a drug user mixes the powder form of the drug with water to make it liquid for injection. The needle is then dipped in and the liquid is drawn into the syringe. When users share cookers, it is possible that viruses are left from the needles touching the container.

Cotton Balls. Drug users often soak a ball of cotton in the liquid form of a drug and draw the drug into the syringe through the cotton as well. This acts as a filter and removes the particulate matter. These cotton balls are stored and saved for later use when drug supplies are limited. It is possible that at a later time someone else will use the contaminated cotton (National Research Council 1995).

Rinse Water. Rinse water is another way drug users can spread viruses (National Research Council 1995). IDUs usually rinse needles after use and before they pass the equipment to the next person. This involves drawing up water into the barrel of the syringe, releasing it and repeating. Often the water is not thrown out after each rinsing, thus increasing the chances that viruses will be released and passed on.

These direct and indirect methods of sharing drug use equipment pose a threat to a drug user because they are the most common ways HIV is spread among IDUs. With an estimated 1,000 injections of illicit drugs every year, an IDU has a disturbingly high chance of contracting a life-threatening disease every day (Gostin and Webber 1998). The most troubling aspect of this problem is that the spread of HIV through IDU is entirely from contaminated equipment and could be more easily controlled by addressing the way in which HIV is contracted.

CONTEXT OF IDU AND HIV PREVENTION

There are a number of important concerns when considering adopting an HIV prevention program. Examining how well IDUs understand their risk in sharing equipment sheds some light on how well any prevention effort might work. Finally, dissecting public opinion constraints also leads to understanding the public's acceptance of various HIV prevention efforts.

Understanding Risk

Studies report varied results on whether or not drug users understand their risk in sharing needles and equipment. A study done in 1994 by Koester and Hoffer showed that only 7 percent of the drug users they surveyed understood that sharing practices presented any threat to their health (National Research Council 1995). The American Medical Association, however, states that most IDUs understand the risks, and many times are simply unable to protect themselves by obtaining new equipment and sterile needles (American Medical Association 1998).

Public Opinion Constraints

While many health professionals and people who work with drug users believe that measures should be taken to prevent further HIV infection, many people believe that the prevention programs encourage drug use (American Medical Association 1998). People believe that by deregulating the sale of syringes and needles, there will be a boom in the numbers of drug users. People are concerned about the moral issues of providing drug users access to their destructive habit. Repealing drug paraphernalia and prescription laws would condone drug lifestyles. The current congressional ban on federal funding for needle exchange programs reflects the perception that Americans do not support deregulation of drug paraphernalia and syringe prescription laws. A survey conducted by the Kaiser Family Foundation, however, showed that two-thirds of those polled favor providing clean needles to slow the spread of AIDS (San Francisco AIDS Foundation 1999).

Drug users understanding their risks and public opinion constraints are all serious matters that surround the problem of HIV in IDUs. Misconceptions by both IDU and the general public have prevented them from understanding the value of providing clean, unused drug equipment. Because of these misconceptions, needle exchange programs have had problems with public support.

STATE AND LOCAL POLICIES CREATE PROBLEMS

Most state and local policies focus on preventing the acquisition of drug equipment as a way of addressing the cross-contamination through equipment sharing. Given that a needle exchange program is prohibited at the national level, state and local policies have created some additional problems. Even though the medical community and research support shows a direct reduction in cross-contamination when new equipment is available, most state and local communities attempt to prevent the sale of such equipment.

Failures. State laws inhibit access to clean equipment by criminalizing the sale, supply, and possession of drug paraphernalia (Gostin et al. 1997; Lurie and Drucker 1997). These policies create a needle shortage, and IDUs often use each other's needles rather than safer, sterile needles. In addition, such laws put public health officials and other activists at risk of arrest and prosecution for providing clean drug equipment to IDUs (Gostin and Webber 1998). A study done by a panel of medical doctors and health law attorneys surveyed the various drug laws across the country. They found that forty-seven states have enacted broad drug paraphernalia laws; the exceptions are Alaska, Iowa, and South Carolina. Most states classify a possession violation of these laws as a misdemeanor, while delivery is considered a felony. Some states assess both civil and criminal penalties for violations of these statutes (Gostin et al. 1997).

Further, syringe prescription statutes prohibit distribution of syringes without a prescription. This puts pharmacists at risk of violating laws if they allow a person to buy syringes without a prescription, regardless of whether the pharmacist knows that providing the syringes might prevent sharing contaminated needles. Only eight states specifically mandate prescriptions for syringe sales, but ten more restrict by local ordinances (Gostin et al. 1997). Other states have laws putting a maximum number of needles purchased at one time, and three states specifically exempt needles under their prescription laws (Gostin et al. 1997).

Successes. Research continually shows that IDUs will use sterile needles if they are available (Watters et al. 1997). For instance, diabetic IDUs typically have lower HIV rates. This is attributed to the easy access to needles they have (Gostin et al. 1997). In addition, a Connecticut law passed in 1992 allowing the purchase of ten syringes without a prescription led to lower rates of needle sharing and a shift from street purchase to pharmacy purchase (American Medical Association 1998).

Currently there are estimated 113 NEPs operating in the country (From the Centers... 1988). One of the first successful programs implemented was the San Francisco AIDS Foundation's Prevention Point project (San Francisco AIDS Foundation 2000). Politicians, community members, drug users, and operators of the program agree that their program has been effective in combating the AIDS epidemic in San Francisco's drug-user population (Moore and Wenger 1995).

Furthermore, the U.S. Surgeon General David Satcher acknowledges that NEPs are effective means to prevent HIV transmission. In an interview for the journal *Lancet*, Mr. Satcher said that the science is difficult to deny. The only concerns he has relate to public relations and support. As head of the Centers for Disease Control, Mr. Satcher recommended to the Department of Health that they publicly report that NEPs reduce the spread of HIV and do not increase drug use in communities (Frankel and Rovner 1998).

SEEKING THE IDEAL SOLUTION

IDUs must have access to clean needles so they do not continue to spread the diseases. The ideal situation would be to eradicate the problem of AIDS transmission through needle and equipment sharing. If an IDU never had direct or indirect access to a contaminated needle, his or her risk of contracting HIV through contamination would be zero. While this ideal situation seems impossible, studies have shown that providing sterile needles for IDUs decreased the AIDS spread by 33 percent (Coming clean...1995). The U.S. General Accounting Office furthermore concluded that 33 percent is an "understatement" in a New Haven, Connecticut, HIV prevention project. If the option of using sterile equipment is available to drug users, the chances of them choosing to use contaminated needles is unlikely

Making IDUs Aware of the Risk

The first goal to achieve is to help IDUs become aware of the risks they are taking by sharing needles. This would require some level of outreach to drug users and continual interaction so they can make educated decisions about drug equipment. While this would require some public tolerance of such an outreach program, an education program would be an essential first step to reducing cross-contamination and disease.

Decriminalizing Access to Clean Needles

The second goal to eradicate the problem of HIV in IDUs is to make it easier for IDUs to access clean needles. This easy access could virtually eliminate the need to share needles. The American Medical Association (1998) states that the ideal situation would be to provide sterile equipment to drug users, while getting IDUs into treatment for their drug problems. They understand that many drug users are not ready or willing to stop using drugs, while many drug treatment centers are currently overfilled. Until all drug users can be in treatment centers, the only thing to do currently is deal with the transmission problems.

COST BENEFIT OF AVAILABLE ALTERNATIVES

There are three viable alternatives in addressing the problem of HIV in IDUs, as seen in Table 1: counseling and education services, bleach distribution programs, and needle exchange programs (Kahn 1998). Each one addresses education and access to clean needles in different ways. Importantly, each addresses the problem of cross-contamination direct intervention rather than to indirect intervention through prohibiting the sale and/or use of equipment.

(Table 1 About Here)

Counseling and Education

Counseling and education services revolve around outreach to IDUs in high-risk areas (Kahn 1998). These services help IDUs make decisions about treatment for their drug problems and often assist them in seeking treatment. They also provide education to IDUs on how to lower their risk of contracting diseases. This includes education on drug use, drug equipment sharing, condom use, and education about sexually transmitted diseases. While these programs are relatively low cost, studies show that they induce limited behavioral change. Extended counseling programs are usually more effective, but are likewise more costly.

A counseling and education program meets only one of the stated goals. This kind of outreach helps IDUs understand the risks they take in sharing needles. Although this alternative is effective in reaching this objective, it fails to physically change the situation of the drug user because it assumes the drug user will apply the education obtained to his or her daily life. This alternative relies on the responsibility of the drug user. In the stage of drug addiction the user might be, this is demanding unreasonable behavior.

Bleach Distribution

Bleach distribution programs are another effective and relatively low-cost alternative. These programs typically distribute household-strength bleach in which drug users can rinse their drug equipment. They also typically provide education and counseling along with the actual distribution of bleach (National Research Council 1995). Bleach distribution programs can work because bleach has proven to be effective in combating diseases that exist on inanimate objects like needles and other drug equipment. Bleach even less concentrated than household bleach has shown to inactivate many viruses in less than ten minutes. Other factors, however, can decrease the effectiveness of bleach (Kahn 1998).

First, disinfection is only achieved by first cleaning the equipment with water (National Research Council 1995). If this is not done, bleach is virtually useless. Second, if bleach is used multiple times, the concentration of the virus-killing chlorine goes down. As the content of chlorine decreases, so does its efficacy in fighting contamination. Furthermore, if bleach is exposed to prolonged sunlight, oxygen, or heat, the chlorine content goes down as well. When used appropriately, however, there is a strong indication that bleach can be an effective means of killing viruses on inanimate objects. Whether or not IDUs can maintain their bleach cleansing systems to attain maximum effectiveness is another issue. The effectiveness of this program, like the counseling and education, relies on the responsibility of the user. Although bleach distribution programs take the epidemiological risks away, the user is still responsible for understanding how to use the bleach correctly, which may be too much to expect.

Needle Exchange

The final alternative to alleviating this problem is implementing a needle exchange program (NEP). Needle exchanges have been operating in the United States for a number of years, both legally and illegally. IDUs, nonprofit agencies, local governments, and state governments have run NEPs. They are offered in both steady physical and mobile locations (Moore and Wenger 1995). In areas that present a high risk for IDUs, many different organizations have attempted to ease the problem by providing sterile syringes to IDUs. Most NEPs also provide some level of drug counseling and often referral to treatment programs. In a study of eighty-one cities performed from June 1992 through December 1996, researchers discovered that the rates of HIV in cities with NEPs went down 5.8 percent on average. Cities with no NEP saw HIV rates jump 5.9 percent on average (American Medical Association 1998). This is a clear indication of the efficacy of NEPs.

NEPs with drug counseling and education provide the most comprehensive approach to achieving the goal of HIV prevention. Not only does it provide the base education that can be effective, it takes the responsibility away from the drug user to make a life-threatening decision. Placing a clean syringe in the hand of a drug user is eliminating the chance that he or she shares a needle at that moment. The NEP attacks the problem of HIV and IDUs at the core by taking away the immediate health risk (From the Centers... 1998).

RECOMMENDATIONS

Needle exchange programs have shown to be an effective means to the greater goal of HIV prevention. The benefits largely outweigh any other alternative. A national needle exchange program addresses the health risk problem at the core, and prevents the mass spread of HIV in IDUs. No other alternative more effectively eradicates the problem of transmission through contaminated equipment.

To implement this solution, a number of legalities must be reexamined. First of all, the federal government should repeal its ban on allowing federal funds for operating needle exchange programs. As shown in previous studies, the cost-effectiveness of an NEP relies heavily on the concentration of drug users in an area. America has pockets of high-risk areas but the need for a nationwide program is not present at this time. Exchange programs should, however, have the access to federal funds so they can provide greater relief to the IDU population in highly concentrated areas. The administration must allow the Surgeon General to officially and publicly announce the benefits to needle exchange programs so Congress can end their sanction on federally-funded NEPs.

States should likewise examine their current drug paraphernalia and prescription laws to include a provision exempting needle exchange programs. This would allow NEPs to operate within full legal capacity. States can follow Hawaii's example and implement a statewide needle exchange program or simply amend their drug laws to allow for safe operation of NEPs (HRS §325-113 1999).

On a local level, public health departments should work with existing successful needle exchange programs and continue their efforts. The public health department should also implement new exchange sites where they are most needed. The public health department should also conduct a public awareness education program to provide drug users with information about the risks of sharing drug equipment and to provide the general public with information about the public benefits of preventing the spread of AIDS through reducing contamination.

Justification

There are many different levels on which an NEP can work, and its cost-effectiveness depends on how highly concentrated the IDUs are in the area (Kahn 1998). NEPs typically run by offering a 1:1 exchange ratio to clients. Although NEPs have been found to be effective in fighting HIV in IDUs, researchers have discovered that the cost-effectiveness of an NEP depends largely on the concentration of IDUs in one area (Kahn 1998). The higher the concentration of the drug users in the area, the more risk there is to reduce. This tends to result in greater economic benefits than implementing a large program with more dispersed need (Kahn 1998).

Costs. The estimated annual cost of running an NEP in a city with a high concentration of drug users is $169,000 (American Medical Association 1998). This includes all costs intrinsic in operation like supplies and personnel. When broken down on an individual level, the American Medical Association estimates that the cost of each infection averted is $9,400. Considering that the lifetime cost of treating a patient with AIDS is $195,188, this is a savings of $185,788 per person. The amending of drug paraphernalia and prescription laws might also result in a savings on law enforcement costs. Not only do monetary benefits result, the state of public health will rise for adults and children. Furthermore, the price of human life saved is immeasurable.

Benefits. There are many people who will benefit from a national needle exchange program. Drug users will have access to information and clean equipment. Community members in areas surrounding NEPs also have a stake in the policy. The reduction in the spread of HIV from IDUs improves the health and safety of the community. Public health specialists and officials also have a stake in the policy because they will be providing the services to the drug users legally. Medical providers will also be responsible for all follow-up care or rehabilitation efforts. Finally, law enforcement officers also have a stake in the policy because they are primarily responsible for taking care of safety problems that arise from illicit drug use.

In addition to the direct benefits, there are those who will indirectly benefit from a national needle exchange program. Supporters of implementing an NEP, such as U.S. Surgeon General David Satcher, the American Medical Association, and various other smaller grassroots organizations will have a legitimate basis to argue for funding these programs. Researchers in the National Institute of Health and the Institute of Medicine will have more public support for studying the problem of contamination.

Monitoring and Evaluating Policy

Success of the program can be measured in a number of ways. First, two years after a needle exchange program is implemented, the program success can be measured by finding the rate at which HIV levels dropped or raised in the communities where a needle exchange program has been implemented and compare that rate to communities where there is no needle exchange program. If the program is a success, the HIV levels should be lower in communities with needle exchange programs.

Second, the public education aspect of the policy should be examined by using a public opinion poll of the community residents where a needle exchange program has been implemented. The public opinion poll should identify how well the public understands and supports the needle exchange program. If the public education aspect of the policy has been effective, public opinion polls should reflect positive public support for the program.

Finally, the success of the IDU outreach aspect of the program should reflect both an increase in awareness of the dangers of sharing equipment as well as a willingness of drug users to request and use drug equipment through the needle exchange program. A survey of drug equipment requesters should indicate how much IDUs understand about the risks of sharing equipment. In addition, the number of requests and the frequency of requests by the same person should increase over the first two years of the program if the outreach is effective.

CONCLUSION

Current policies dealing with the problem of HIV and IDUs are inadequate while the federal government prohibits needle exchange and state policies generally prohibit the sale of drug equipment for non-medical use. Although some local communities and organizations have successfully conducted needle exchange and outreach programs, most do so illegally due to federal and state restrictions.

Yet, there is significant consensus in the science and medical fields that needle exchange programs are very effective ways of combating HIV infection in IDUs. Although federal studies have shown that NEPs reduce the prevalence of HIV in IDUs, none of these studies has resulted in the federal government changing its strict stance on the funding of NEPs, regardless how strongly the statistics supported the programs. Based on extensive evidence from both legal and illegally conducted NEPs across the United States, a needle exchange is the best solution for reducing the rates of HIV infection from contaminated equipment. Other solutions, while less costly and more politically acceptable, do not address the spread of HIV through cross-contamination between IDU. A national NEP would provide the funding and standardization necessary to remove the obstacles to preventing cross-contamination from sharing drug equipment. In addition, outreach programs provide opportunities to educate both IDU and the general public about the public and personal risks involved in sharing drug equipment. Such an outreach program should also help create public support for needle exchange programs. A national needle exchange program should address the issue of drug users understanding their risks and they should inform the public about the efficacy of NEPs. In the long run, allowing and funding NEPs should be successful in bringing down the rates of HIV in IDUs.

REFERENCES

American Medical Association. 1998. Prevention: Does needle exchange work? December, http://www.ama-assn.org/special/hiv/preventn/prevent3.html (accessed April 8, 2000).

Coming clean about needle exchange. 1995. *Lancet*, 346:1377.

Des Jarlais et al. 1994. Continuity and change within and HIV epidemic. *JAMA*, 271:121–27.

Frankel, David H. and Julie Rovner. 1998. Heading up the American dream of health. *Lancet*, 352:978–82.

From the Centers for Disease Control and Prevention. 1988. *JAMA*, 280:1217–18.

Gostin, Lawrence O. and David W. Webber. 1998 HIV infection and AIDS in the public health and health care systems. *JAMA*, 279:1108–13.

Gostin, Lawrence O. and Zita Lazzarini. 1997. Prevention of HIV/AIDS and other bloodborne diseases among injection drug users. *JAMA*, 277: 53–62.

HRS §325–113. 1999.

Kahn, James G. 1988. Economic evaluation of primary HIV prevention in injection drug users. In *Handbook of economic evaluation of HIV prevention programs*. Edited by David R. Holtgrave. New York: Plenum Press.

Lurie, Peter and Ernest Drucker. 1997. An opportunity lost: HIV infections associated with lack of a national needle exchange programme in the USA. *Lancet*, 349:604–09.

Moore, Lisa D. and Lynn Wenger. 1995. The social context of needle exchange and user self-organization in San Francisco: Possibilities and pitfalls. *Journal of Drug Issues*, 25: 583–99.

National Research Council. 1999. *Preventing HIV transmission. The role of sterile needles and bleach*. Washington D.C.: National Academy Press 1995.

San Francisco AIDS Foundation. 2000. *SFAF HIV Prevention project (needle exchange)*, December 17, http://www.sfaf.org/prevention/needleexchange/index.html (accessed April 13, 2000).

U.S. Census Bureau. 1999. *Statistical abstract of the United States, 119th ed*. Government Printing Office: Washington D.C.

US 42 USCS §300EE-5. 2000.

Watters, John K., Michelle J. Estillo, George L. Clark, and Jennifer Lorvick. 1994. Syringe and needle exchange as HIV? AIDS prevention for injection drug users. *JAMA*, 271: 115–20.

World Almanac and Book of Facts 2000. 1999. Mahwah, NJ: PRIMEDIA Reference.

Table 1: HIV Prevention Methods & Efficacy

	Description	Strengths	Weaknesses
Education & Counseling	Short & Long Term drug counseling	Low Cost: no need to amend existing drug laws	High Turnover; does not eliminate immediate health risk
Bleach Distribution Program	Household Strength bleach & education on cleaning drug equipment	Low Cost; no need to amend existing drug laws	Street use does not result in optimum efficacy of bleach
Needle Exchange Program	1:1 needle exchange, optional referral to treatment, education	Eliminates immediate health risk; can offer comprehensive care	Public opinion constraints; must amend many existing drug laws

National Research Council. 1999. *Preventing HIV transmission. The role of sterile needles and bleach.* Washington, D.C.: National Academy Press

CHAPTER 13

Format and Examples of
Assignments and Exercises in
Applied Political Science

Assignments and Exercises in Applied Political Science

In the following pages there are three examples of writing assignments that require students to apply concepts, theories, and accepted wisdom in political science to real life experiences. These papers build on the student's training and knowledge in a subfield. Such assignments provide students with the opportunity to collect information, manage it, and make it useful by writing about it. These assignments build not only on the class materials, but offer students the opportunity to use their critical thinking and writing skills on topics and information in a nonacademic, unstructured environment. Such assignments test skills as well as mastery of subfield knowledge. The paper examples exhibit a variety of backgrounds and writing styles. These papers are personal reports of students' experiences in applying what they learned to what they observed. An explanation of the form for each type of paper precedes the examples.

First Paper: Event Analysis/Clipping Thesis

"Policy Formation: Before and After September 11, 2001" follows current events regarding a particular set of related topics covered by the media. The student follows the issues over a specified time, usually a semester, and then writes an analytical essay using the course material and the media reports as supporting evidence.

Second Paper: Participant Observer/Internship Report

"Internship Report: Campaign Volunteers: VIP's or Peons?" provides an introspective view of the relevance of fieldwork accomplished to theoretical constructs learned previously in the classroom. This assignment requires the student to identify where theory and practice conflict or agree. The work is performed outside the classroom setting.

Third Paper: Event Observation, Participation/Journal Essay

"Campaign '88: Against All Odds" combines the skills applied in event analysis with the goals of participant observer assignments. In this type of assignment, the student becomes a participant observer during a timely event, such as a campaign, while writing in a journal, maintaining a clipping file, and attending class. It combines all necessary elements for synthesis and learning. In these assignments, while students are learning about theories, they are conducting a small amount of fieldwork and observing the larger context of the event examined.

Event Analysis and Clipping Thesis

Purpose

A clipping thesis is a file of clippings from various newspapers and magazines that have been collected over time concerning a particular issue or event. Students use these clippings to write an analysis of the event or issue. A clipping thesis has many of the properties of a journal.

- Like a journal, a clipping thesis or clipping file helps students keep track of information and reactions to current events related to a broad subject area.
- A clipping thesis, however, is focused on a particular topic or subject rather than on the broad array of daily experiences.

How to Construct a Clipping Thesis

1. **Choose an issue related to the course material. Check with the instructor for ideas or direction for choices.**
2. **If possible, use at least two newspapers and one news weekly magazine as your sources. Some sources are online.**
    - One of the newspapers should be a national paper such as the *New York Times*.
    - Read or skim various sources regularly.
3. **For paper-based articles, clip or photocopy articles, cartoons, and commentary that are related to your topic. Be sure to clip, photocopy, or print all of the item.**
    - Be sure to put the source, date, and page number on each paper-based item.
    - Be sure to put the source, date, and access date on each item from an online source.
4. **Attach the paper clipping or photocopy to a piece of 8" by 11" white bond paper with glue.**
    - Cut and paste the clipping to fit the page.
    - Do not leave any part of the clipping hanging off the paper.
    - Place only one item per page.
5. **Place the clipping page into a notebook or folder.**
6. **On the clipping page, summarize the information in the item and write your reaction to the item.**
7. **Based on the body of clippings, write an analysis of the issue or event including:**
    - An explanation of the origin.
    - A description of the development over the time period covered.
    - The degree of government intervention.
    - The current status of the issue.
    - A projection about future developments.
8. **Use additional sources for background on the issue or event if necessary. For large clipping files, include an index by topic when using a variety of background materials.**
9. **Write an analytical essay using some of the clippings as references. Be sure to fully reference all materials used to construct the essay and to observe all standard format guidelines for typing and writing an analytical essay. Do not forget to number the all pages including those containing the clippings.**

Example of an Event Analysis/Clipping Thesis

**Policy Formation:
Before and After September 11, 2001**

By
Meredith Reynolds
POLS 199 X- Schmidt
12/13/01
(Reprinted with permission)

INTRODUCTION

There are many types of events that shape the formation of issues in today's political society. Since September 11, 2001, the nation has been turned upside down and the people are the political system need to learn how to cope and recover. The articles relating to business, labor, health, and the economy that were collected for this assignment are evidence that the US is attempting to recover, rebuild, and protect itself after the terrorist attacks on the World Trade Center and the Pentagon on September 11, 2001.

PRIOR TO SEPTEMBER 11

Before September 11, 2001 there were many routine issues that were being addressed by the national government. Routine issues are things that happen every year, like the budget for example. Some routine issues that Congress worked on prior to September 11 were Social Security and antitrust laws. For example, Republicans and Democrats were in agreement when it came to upholding their promise not to spend Social Security money on other programs to revive the economy (Stevenson, 2001c). Democrats blamed the economic slowdown on President Bush, while Republicans blamed former President Clinton.

Another issue, which was not routine, but instead based on technology, was the Microsoft case of violating antitrust laws. New technology brings up new issues and in the case of Microsoft, lawmakers must be prepared to deal with this new technology. For instance, the Bush administration is no longer seeking a break-up of the Microsoft business, yet they are willing to seek less severe fines to move this case quickly through the legal system (Labaton 2001b). The Microsoft antitrust case is an issue that has risen from the increased ability of man to technologically innovate. This issue, however, and all other issues get put aside in the midst of a crisis. This is exactly what happened immediately following the terrorist attacks on September 11, 2001.

THE CRISIS OF SEPTEMBER 11

During a crisis, emergency issues become urgent and are top priority of policy-makers. A crisis normally justifies any money that is spent by the government. A new crisis that arose after September 11 was the Anthrax scare. Major figures such as Senate Majority Leader Tom Daschle, and NBC news anchor Tom Brokaw were sent Anthrax-infested letters through the US postal service. This new threat had the potential to sicken and kill many people, especially those who worked in US Postal Service sorting facilities. These workers came into close contact with many pieces of mail daily and were at high risk for Anthrax.

Tom Ridge, the new Domestic Security Chief who began his job on October 8, came forward to make an effort to calm the public. There had been only six actual cases of Anthrax and there had been a $1 million reward for information leading to the conviction of anyone responsible for Anthrax attacks (Purdum & Becker 2001: A1). There were more confirmed cases of Anthrax exposure and the Bush administration told the public of an expansion of a program to deal with this threat by purchasing mass quantities of antibiotics (Shenon 2001). The White House would ask Congress for an additional $1.5 billion to buy antibiotics to help 12 million people (Shenon 2001: A1).

In response to the crisis created by the terrorist attacks, a campaign, to convince Congress to help aid the airline industry so they can survive, wanted a cash payment and loan guarantees (Wayne & Moss 2001). This is not only an example of the power of the airline industry and its lobbyists, but Congress justifies bailing out the airline industry because of the national crisis. Airline executives told the House that their companies need $17.5 billion in cash, loan guarantees, and protection from liability from damages and deaths on the ground in order not to file for bankruptcy (Alvarez & Holston 2001: C1). The White House sent Congress a proposal to give an immediate $5 billion in cash to the airlines and legislators from both parties were in favor of giving the airlines an immediate financial assistance (Alvarez & Holston 2001: C1).

The bailout for the airline industry has other business industries like the insurance industry, travel agents, pilots, and restaurant workers lining up for federal aid (Wayne 2001). Republicans want to help business with a stimulus package of tax cuts, and Democrats want to offer laid-off workers extended unemployment benefits. The US Postal Service has also lost $500 million in revenue, which is a drop of 10 percent, because of the terrorist attacks (DePalma & Deutsch 2001: B1). Officials are concerned that the Postal Service will increase its charges on the public in order to get its financial situation under control. The Postal Service has already got $175 million in federal money to buy things like 88 million pairs of industrial gloves and 4.8 million respirator masks for quick precautions (DePalma & Deutsch 2001: B1). Congress voted to extend billions of dollars in loans to the insurance industry if there are terrorist attacks next year, which would allow loans to the industry to cover 90 percent of terrorism costs greater than $1 billion (Labaton 2001a, B7). The bill would also protect smaller insurers that have big claims and it would give the insurance industry tax breaks to encourage it to plan reserves for terrorist coverage.

Along with crisis issues come active issues, which are issues that are taken up right away. In order to calm the public's fear about unsafe airports, the government must take action right away. President Bush announced that the federal government would take a role in airport security by creating a new agency that would take over supervision of the 28,000 workers who screen passengers and baggage, stating that this new approach would give more control to government over training, performance standards, wages, and benefits (Bumiller 2001: A1). Currently, President Bush has called troops from the National Guard to be stationed at airport metal detectors and carry-on luggage checks.

Democrats in the House and Senate stated that they are in favor of a federal takeover of airport security because it is important to restore the public's confidence in airport security and that federal control is the best solution (Wald 2001). The FAA said that the takeover of screening passengers at the 700 checkpoints could cost the government $1.8 billion a year (Wald 2001: B6). The Senate passed a bill 100–0 that would create 28,000 new federal workers, the largest increase in the federal payroll since the presidency of LBJ (Alvarez, 2001a: B8). House Republicans prefer a bill that would have the federal government in charge of supervising and training security workers. Conservatives say, however, that the creation of federal labor would lead to less flexibility in dismissing bad workers.

President Bush wants a defeat of the plan to make 28,000 airport security workers federal employees under the Department of Justice (Alvarez 2001a). The President believes that this undesired growth would expand the federal government. President Bush supports having these workers be under private contracts, but still under strict government supervision and held to stricter standards.

There are, however, trade offs between crises and routines. There is a displacement effect where all routine issues become ignored during a crisis. Because of September 11, issues addressed before like Social Security and antitrust cases are put aside. Since September 11, not until recently has Social Security been back on the national agenda, and only because now Congress can not use the surplus money to fix Social Security, it must spend it on the national crisis. President Bush's Social Security Commission looked at three options which would let workers establish investment accounts and said that benefit cuts and other steps would have to take place in order to avoid a long-term financial crisis (Stevenson 2001a). All three of the proposals allowed but did not require workers to invest part of their Social Security payroll taxes in stocks and bonds; these workers would have to give up some of their scheduled benefits.

Trade and labor issues are now back on the national agenda after being set aside for more pertinent issues. The Bush administration has made the trade bill, which allows for the president to negotiate fast track deals that cannot be amended by Congress, a top economic priority (Greenhouse 2001). Union leaders say that this trade bill would push American jobs to low-wage countries overseas creating more unemployed laborers in the US. Labor leaders say that they would support this bill if the president included that other countries enforced their labor and environmental laws and honored the right to form unions, bans on child labor, bans on forced labor, and bans on discrimination.

REASONS FOR POLICY

There is always a reason that policies are what they are. Time, place, and political culture are both players in how US policy is shaped. The United States is facing a declining economy, many big businesses are struggling, and the unemployment rate is on the rise. Seeing figures that a recession has begun, Congress has explored new spending and tax cuts and the Federal Reserve has continued to put money into the system to assure people that the economy is stable (Stevenson and Kaufman 2001). Republicans are making plans for a fiscal stimulus of tax breaks to businesses, and have said that their promise not to touch Social Security funds should be put on hold because of the state of the economy. While Democrats support a fiscal stimulus, they are wary of the Republican's plans.

In looking at the current political culture, the government is presently trying to combat unemployment, economic recession, and business failure. The reason for legislation regarding issues like business bailout, unemployment insurance, and economic stimulus plans is because the fallout from the terrorist attacks on September 11 have left many people without jobs, has intensified the economic slowdown, and has depleted many industries of millions of dollars. In particular, unemployment is rising, the stock market is falling, many big businesses are hurting, and Congress is looking at new plans to help rescue the economy without promoting a fiscally irresponsible free-for-all (Stevenson 2001c).

More importantly, while many in Congress are considering a tax cut for only those who pay taxes as an economic stimulus, some Democrats want to cover people who pay taxes and low income households as well. Conservatives are also interested in reduction of the tax on capital gains to make investment more attractive. The Senate stopped a $73 billion Democratic economic plan that emphasized aid to the unemployed (Clymer 2001b). Republicans want a plan that includes tax cuts and so they dropped the Democrats plan in favor of other alternatives. The Bush administration expects to run budget deficits for at least the next three years because the recession and the cost of fighting terrorism have both used the surpluses (Stevenson 2001f). Republicans continue to fight for tax cuts and Democrats fight for financial assistance for low-income workers and the unemployed. Both Republicans and Democrats were in agreement to run budget deficits for the next three years to combat terrorism and to revive the economy (Stevenson 2001f).

TYPES OF POLICY

To more closely examine the policies that came from the US government after September 11, it is important to define and exemplify the types of public policy. There are three types of policy: regulatory, distributive, and redistributive. A distributive policy is when costs and benefits are distributed broadly, and regulatory restricts behavior. For instance, the House of Representatives passed the antiterrorism legislation, which attacks money laundering (Clymer 2001c). President Bush supports the bill and made it clear to congressional leaders that he expects to have the bill ready to sign by that Friday. The Senate then passed the antiterrorism legislation, which would expand the powers of the federal government to be able to penetrate money-laundering banks (Clymer 2001a). In the Bush administration's economic policy, a freeze was put on all assets in the US suspected of helping terrorist groups and individuals and also gave the treasury department broad discretion to impose sanctions (Sanger & Kahn 2001). Foreign banks that harbor terrorists can now be economically cut off from business in the US. US officials have also found that Osama bin Laden has been taking advantage of the financial system of the United Arab Emirates (Gerth & Miller 2001). US and UAE officials met to discuss detecting and deterring the movement of money of terrorist groups. The outcome seems to be an alliance between the US and the UAE. The Bush administration said that it was going to shut down the financial institutions that harbor terrorists. The Al Barakaat and Al Taqwa moved cash, provided communications, and was a network to transmit intelligence to the Al Qaeda organization (Sanger & Eichenwald 2001). All of these articles portray a policy that is deemed good for the whole population. Taxpayers will be paying for defense against terrorism through the disruption of their finances, and taxpayers will be reaping the benefits of this lack of financial support for terrorism and increased safety.

A redistributive policy is when taxes are paid to help someone else. To illustrate, unemployment is on the rise and the government will assist those people who have lost their jobs after the terrorist attacks. Over 100,000 workers in NY are likely to be unemployed because of the terrorist attacks, and 10,800 people have already filed for unemployment (Pristin & Eaton 2001: B8). Nearly 75,000 people will file for unemployment insurance, 37,500 will receive benefits under the Disaster Employment Assistance Program, and a total of 700,000 jobs have been affected by September 11 (Pristin & Eaton, 2001: B8). The implication that laborers are likely to be laid off is high and unions have fought vigorously to protect workers from layoffs. Unemployment insurance will be extended and President Bush pressures states to use federal money allocated for job and welfare programs (Stevenson 2001b). Also, Democrats put their recovery plan through the Senate Finance Committee which includes programs to help the unemployed, a tax rebate for low-income people, and tax breaks for some businesses (Stevenson 2001: B1).

CONCLUSION

In policy formation, there are three components to policy decisions: the goals, the means, and the outcomes. The goals are what the government wants to do, such as recover, rebuild, and protect the US after the terrorist attacks on September 11. The means are the tools such as taxing, spending, and regulating that government uses when the nation is in a state of crisis. The outcomes are yet to be seen because of the magnitude of the terrorist act. Policy-makers expect the outcomes to accomplish the set goals, however, only time will tell if the nation has the resilience to protect itself from another terrorist attack, rebuild its buildings and economy, and to recover individually and nationally after the great losses the US suffered.

REFERENCES

Alvarez, Lizette. (2001a). Bush seeking house allies on airport security plan. *New York Times*, November 1.

Alvarez, Lizette. (2001b). The antiterror pill that house republicans refuse to swallow. *New York Times*, October 16.

Alvarez, Lizette & Laura Holson. (2001). Airlines ask for rescue plan worth $17.5 billion from US. *New York Times*, September 20.

Bumiller, Elisabeth. (2001). Bush to increase federal role in security at airports. *New York Times*, September 28.

Clymer, Adam. (2001a). Bush set to sign. *New York Times*, October 26.

Clymer, Adam. (2001b). Democrats' stimulus plan for economy dies in senate. *New York Times*, November 15.

Clymer, Adam. (2001c). Terror bill clears house: Moves to senate. *New York Times*, October 25.

DePalma, Anthony and Claudia Deutsch. (2001). Postal service is expected to ask US for bailout. *New York Times*, November 7.

Gerth, Jeff and Judith Miller. (2001). US gains ground in isolating funds of terror groups. *New York Times*, November 5.

Greenhouse, Steven. (2001). Labor leaders oppose a trade bill. *New York Times*, October 17.

Labaton, Stephen. (2001a). House committee approves measure to aid insurance industry in terrorist attacks. *New York Times*, November 8.

Labaton, Stephen. (2001b). US abandoning its effort to break apart Microsoft, saying it seeks resolution. *New York Times*, September 7.

Pristin, Terry and Leslie Eaton. (2001). Disaster's aftershocks: number of workers out of a job is continually rising. *New York Times*, September 26.

Purdum, Todd and Elizabeth Becker. (2001). Bush officials step out in force in effort to calm anthrax fears. *New York Times*, October 19.

Sanger, David and Joseph Kahn. (2001). Banks On Notice. *New York Times*, September 25.

Sanger, David and Kurt Eichenwald. (2001). US moves to cut 2 financial links for terror group. *New York Times*, November 14.

Shenon, Phillip. (2001). US is stepping up plan for handling anthrax threat. *New York Times*, October 15.

Stevenson, Richard. (2001a). Bush panel outlines 3 plans for social security overhaul. *New York Times*, November 30.

Stevenson, Richard. (2001b). Bush proposes extending aid to the jobless. *New York Times*, October 5.

Stevenson, Richard. (2001c). Debating politics of the surplus. *New York Times*, September 5.

Stevenson, Richard. (2001d). Democrats' recovery plan moves forward in senate. *New York Times*, November 9.

Stevenson, Richard. (2001e). Many stimulus options weighed. *New York Times*, September 27.

Stevenson, Richard. (2001f). White House says it expects at least 3 years of deficits. *New York Times*, November 29.

Stevenson, Richard and Leslie Kaufman. (2001). Some see recession as eminent after terrorist assaults. *New York Times*, September 14.

Wald, Matthew. (2001). Democratic leaders say they back a government takeover of security. *New York Times*, September 24.

Wayne, Leslie. (2001). Airline bailout encourages other industries to lobby for government assistance. *New York Times,* September 27.

Wayne, Leslie and Michael Moss. (2001). Bailout for airlines showed the weight of a mighty lobby. *New York Times,* October 10.

ANNOTATED CHRONOLOGICAL LIST OF NEWSPAPER CLIPPINGS

Stevenson, Richard. (2001c). Debating politics of the surplus. *New York Times*, September 6.
Republicans and Democrats are in agreement when it comes to sticking to their promise not to spend Social Security money on other programs. Democrats are trying to blame President Bush, while Republicans blame the slowdown on former President Clinton. This article is valuable because it questions whether to continue with an economic policy that was developed for a prosperous nation.

Labaton, Stephen. (2001b). US abandoning its effort to break apart Microsoft, saying it seeks resolution. *New York Times*, September 7.
The Bush administration is no longer seeking a break-up of the business Microsoft, yet they are willing to seek less severe fines to move this case quickly through the legal system. This article shows that the Bush administration is paying less attention to the actual anti-trust cases themselves and pushing for a quick run through the legal system.

Stevenson, Richard and Leslie Kaufman. (2001). Some see recession as eminent after terrorist assaults. *New York Times*, September 14.
Seeing figures that a recession has begun, Congress has begun to explore new spending and tax cuts and the Federal Reserve has continued to put money into the system to assure people that there is plenty of money and the economy is stable. Republicans are making plans for a fiscal stimulus of tax breaks to business, and have said that their promise not to touch Social Security funds should be put on hold because of the state of the economy. While Democrats support a fiscal stimulus, they are wary of the Republicans' plans.

Alvarez, Lizette & Laura Holson. (2001). Airlines ask for rescue plan worth $17.5 billion from US. *New York Times*, September 20.
Airline executives told the House that their companies need $17.5 billion in cash, loan guarantees, and protection from liability from damages and deaths on the ground in order to not file for bankruptcy. The White House sent Congress a proposal to give an immediate $5 billion in cash to the airlines, and legislators from both parties were in favor of giving the airlines this immediate cash.

Wald, Matthew. (2001). Democratic leaders say they back a government takeover of security. *New York Times*, September 24.
Democrats in the House and Senate stated that they are in favor of a federal takeover of airport security because it is important to restore the public's confidence in airport security and that federal control is the best way to do this. The head of the FAA said that this takeover of screening passengers at the 700 checkpoints could cost the government $1.8 billion a year.

Sanger, David and Joseph Kahn. (2001). Banks "On Notice." *New York Times*, September 25.
The Bush administration put a freeze on all assets in the US suspected of helping Islamic terrorist groups and individuals and also gave the treasury department broad discretion to impose sanctions. Foreign banks that harbor terrorists can now be cut off from doing business within the US. This article shows that the President will treat banks that do not cooperate as hostile entities.

Pristin, Terry and Leslie Eaton. (2001). Disaster's aftershocks: number of workers out of a job is continually rising. *New York Times*, September 26.

Over 100,000 workers in NY are likely to be unemployed because of the terrorist attacks, and 10,800 people have already filed for unemployment. Nearly 75,000 people will file for unemployment insurance, 37,500 will receive benefits under the Disaster Employment Assistance Program, and a total of 700,000 jobs have been affected by September 11. The implication that laborers are likely to be laid off is high and unions have fought vigorously to protect workers from layoffs.

Stevenson, Richard. (2001e). Many stimulus options weighed. *New York Times,* September 27.

Unemployment is rising, the stock market is falling, and many big businesses are hurting, and Congress is looking at new plans to help rescue the economy without promoting a fiscally irresponsible free-for-all. The idea behind the plans is that Congress is considering a tax cut, but Democrats want to cover people who pay taxes and low-income households as well. Conservatives are also interested in reduction of the tax on capital gains to make investment more attractive.

Wayne, Leslie. (2001). Airline bailout encourages other industries to lobby for government assistance. *New York Times,* September 27.

The bailout for the airline industry of $15 billion has other industries like the insurance industry, travel agents, pilots, and restaurant workers lining up for federal tax aid. Republicans want to help business with a stimulus package of tax cuts, and Democrats want to offer laid-off workers extended unemployment benefits.

Bumiller, Elisabeth. (2001). Bush to increase federal role in security at airports. *New York Times,* September 28.

President Bush announced that the federal government would take a role in airport security by a new agency that would take over supervision of the 28,000 workers who screen passengers and baggage, stating that this new approach would give more control to government over training, performance standards, wages, and benefits. Currently, President Bush has called troops from the National Guard to be stationed at airport metal detectors and carry-on luggage checks.

Stevenson, Richard. (2001b). Bush proposes extending aid to the jobless. *New York Times,* October 5.

Unemployment in on the rise and the government will assist those people who have lost their jobs after the terrorist attacks to revive the economy. Unemployment insurance for workers will be extended and Bush pressures states to use federal money that has been allocated for job and welfare programs.

Wayne, Leslie and Michael Moss. (2001). Bailout for airlines showed the weight of a mighty lobby. *New York Times,* October 10.

A campaign, to convince Congress to help aid the airline industry so they can survive, wanted a cash payment and loan guarantees. This is an example of the power of the airline industry and its lobbyists.

Shenon, Phillip. (2001). US is stepping up plan for handling anthrax threat. *New York Times,* October 15.

There were more confirmed cases of anthrax exposure and the Bush administration told the public of an expanded program to deal with this threat. The White House would ask Congress for an additional $1.5 billion to buy antibiotics for reserve to help 12 million people.

Alvarez, Lizette. (2001b). The antiterror pill that house republicans refuse to swallow. *New York Times,* October 16.

The Senate voted 100–0 to pass a bill that would create 28,000 new federal workers, the largest increase in the federal payroll since the presidency of LBJ. House Republicans prefer a bill that would have the federal government in charge of supervising and training security workers with high standards. However, conservatives say that the creation of federal labor would lead to less flexibility in dismissing bad workers.

Greenhouse, Steven. (2001). Labor leaders oppose a trade bill. *New York Times*, October 17.
The Bush administration has made the trade bill, which allows the president to negotiate fast track trade deals that can not be amended by Congress, a top economic priority. Union leaders say that this trade bill would push American jobs to low-wage countries overseas. Labor leaders say that they would support this bill if the president included that other countries enforced their labor and environmental laws and honored four basic labor rights: right to form unions, bans on child labor, bans on forced labor, and bans on discrimination.

Purdum, Todd and Elizabeth Becker. (2001). Bush officials step out in force in effort to calm anthrax fears. *New York Times*, October 19.
Tom Ridge, the new domestic security Chief who began his job on October 8th, came forward to attempt to calm the public. There had been only 6 actual cases of anthrax and there had been a $1 million reward for information leading to the conviction of anyone responsible for anthrax attacks. This article is important because it's the first time the public has heard an authoritative source.

Clymer, Adam. (2001c). Terror bill clears house: Moves to senate. *New York Times*, October 25.
The House passed the antiterrorism legislation which had attacks on money laundering. President Bush supports the bill and made it clear to congressional leaders that he expects to have the bill ready to sign by that Friday.

Clymer, Adam. (2001a). Bush set to sign. *New York Times*, October 26.
The Senate passed the antiterrorism legislation, which would expand the powers of the federal government to be able to penetrate money-laundering banks. This legislation also allows for the sharing of intelligence to thwart terrorism and allow judges to authorize intelligence wiretaps.

Alvarez, Lizette. (2001a). Bush seeking house allies on airport security plan. *New York Times*, November 1.
President Bush and his allies want a defeat of a plan to make 28,000 airport security workers federal employees under the Department of Justice. The President believes that this undesired growth would expand the federal government. Bush is in support of having these workers be under private contracts, but still under strict government supervision and held up to stricter standards.

Gerth, Jeff and Judith Miller. (2001). US gains ground in isolating funds of terror groups. *New York Times*, November 5.
US officials have suspected and warranted that Osama bin Laden has been taking advantage of the free-wheeling financial system of the United Arab Emirates. US and UAE officials met to discuss detecting and deterring the movement of money of this terrorist group. The outcome seems to be a new alliance between the US and the UAE.

DePalma, Anthony and Claudia Deutsch. (2001). Postal service is expected to ask US for bailout. *New York Times*, November 7.

The US Postal Service has lost $500 million in revenue, which is a drop of 10 percent, because of the terrorist attacks. Officials are concerned that the Postal Service will increase its charges on the public in order to get its financial situation under control. The Postal Service has already got $175 million in federal money to buy things like 88 million pairs of industrial gloves and 4.8 million respirator masks for quick precautions.

Labaton, Stephen. (2001a). House committee approves measure to aid insurance industry in terrorist attacks. *New York Times,* November 8.
Congress voted to extend billions of dollars in loans if there are any terrorist attacks next year, which would allow loans to the industry to cover 90 percent of terrorism costs greater than $1 billion. The bill would also protect smaller insurers that have big claims and it would give the insurance industry tax breaks to encourage it to plan reserves for terrorist coverage.

Stevenson, Richard. (2001d). Democrats' recovery plan moves forward in senate. *New York Times,* November 9.
Democrats put their recovery plan through the Senate Finance Committee, which is a $66.4 billion plan which has an expansion of programs to help the unemployed, a tax rebate for low income people, and tax breaks for some businesses. This is an important article because it shows how the Congress can sometimes come together to make important advances in helping the people of this country.

Sanger, David and Kurt Eichenwald. (2001). US moves to cut 2 financial links for terror group. *New York Times,* November 14.
The Bush administration said that it was going to shut down financial institutions that harbor terrorists. The Al Barakaat and Al Taqwa moved cash, provided communications, and were a network to transmit intelligence to the Al Qaeda organization.

Clymer, Adam. (2001b). Democrats' stimulus plan for economy dies in senate. *New York Times,* November 15.
The Senate stopped a $73 billion Democratic economic plan that emphasized aid to the unemployed. Republicans want a plan that includes tax cuts and shot down the Democrats' plan in favor of other alternatives.

Stevenson, Richard. (2001f). White House says it expects at least 3 years of deficits. *New York Times,* November 29.
The Bush administration expects to run budget deficits for at least the next three years because the recession and the cost of fighting terrorism have both used the surpluses. Republicans continue to fight for tax cuts and Democrats fight for financial assistance for low-income workers and the unemployed. Both Republicans and Democrats were in agreement to run budget deficits for the next three years to combat terrorism and to revive the economy.

Stevenson, Richard. (2001a). Bush panel outlines 3 plans for social security overhaul. *New York Times,* November 30.
President Bush's Social Security Commission looked at three options which would allow workers to establish investment accounts and said that benefit cuts and other steps would have to take place in order to avoid a long-term financial crisis. All three of the proposals allowed, but did not require workers to invest part of their Social Security payroll taxes in stocks and bonds, however in return these workers would have to give up some of their scheduled benefits.

Example of a newspaper clipping that has been pasted on a page.

THURSDAY, NOVEMBER 8, 2001

House Committee Approves Measure to Aid Insurance Industry in Terrorist Attacks

By STEPHEN LABATON

WASHINGTON, Nov. 7 — Congress edged closer to aiding the insurance industry tonight when a House committee voted to promise insurers billions of dollars in loans in the event of any large terrorist attacks next year.

The measure, approved by a voice vote of the Finance Services Committee, would generally provide loans to the industry to cover 90 percent of terrorism costs greater than $1 billion. For attacks causing more than $20 billion in losses, the bill would impose a special assessment on insurance policyholders to help defray the costs. House Republicans said they had decided to adopt a one-year measure now and advance a longer-term plan next year.

Democrats on the committee failed in efforts to raise the amount of money the insurance industry would have to pay before the government offered any assistance. The Democrats said tonight that they would continue trying to raise this amount in the full House. A measure being prepared in the Senate would offer assistance only after the insurance industry paid the first $10 billion in claims from any terrorist attack next year.

The bill the committee approved this evening would protect smaller insurers that face big claims and would give the industry tax breaks to encourage it to build up reserves for terrorism coverage. It also protects

REMEMBER THE NEEDIEST!

An industry says an economic crisis is imminent if Congress does not act.

the insurers from punitive damages in any lawsuits arising from terrorist attacks.

Bush administration officials and industry executives say that to avert an economic crisis Congress must adopt the legislation before adjourning shortly.

The world's leading reinsurance companies, which provide insurance to primary insurers, have said they intend to stop covering losses from terrorist attacks as 70 percent of insurance contracts come up for renewal at the end of the year. Without adequate coverage, banks and other lenders say they will stop providing credit for major construction projects and corporate equipment purchases.

Though a consensus has emerged in Congress that quick action must be taken, there is wide disagreement about the details. Although competing measures provide different kinds of federal relief, they all take the first step of putting the federal government into a new supervisory role over the insurance industry.

The House legislation sidestepped some lawmakers' concern about a Senate plan endorsed by the Bush administration. That proposal would rely on the federal treasury to bear the costs of any large-scale attack.

"Unlike other approaches that have been suggested by the Senate and the administration, the bill that I and 30 other bipartisan members introduced is clearly a backstop, not a bailout," said Representative Michael G. Oxley, the Ohio Republican who heads the House Financial Services Committee. "We are providing a helping hand-up, by creating immediate federal assistance in the aftermath of another terrorist attack, but not a hand-out, by demanding that every dollar of American taxpayer assistance ultimately be repaid."

But Democrats and industry experts say the House plan will not do enough to keep insurance premium rates down in the same way the Senate plan might. Some lawmakers were also critical of the tax breaks that the House bill would give the industry.

"While the proposal purports to recover money from industry, it also provides the industry with a long-term subsidy which could well exceed what it pays," said Representative John J. LaFalce of New York, the ranking Democrat on the Financial Services Committee. He said the proposal "could actually impede the re-emergence of the private market" for terrorism insurance.

Prospects remain uncertain for the completion of a bill before Congress adjourns. The Senate measure has stalled over a jurisdictional squabble among three committees.

The Senate bill, being prepared by senior Democrats and Republicans on the Senate banking committee, would require the industry to pay for $10 billion in insurance claims before the government intervened. The government would pay 90 percent of losses that exceeded $10 billion.

But the legislation has been bogged down in a dispute over its limitations on the civil liability of insurers. Senator Ernest F. Hollings, the South Carolina Democrat who heads the Commerce Committee, has indicated his interest in possibly introducing a rival measure.

None of the measures under consideration would provide money for any losses from the attacks of Sept. 11. Experts estimate those attacks could cost the industry more than $40 billion. *p. B7*

Participant Observation and Internship Reports

An internship is a special course that many political science departments offer. Internships usually involve fieldwork in a governmental agency, a political party, an interest group, or some other public agency. The purpose of an internship is to give students the opportunity to combine their academic and fieldwork experiences. Usually, internship students are required to have a faculty and a fieldwork supervisor who will be responsible for co-directing the internship. In most cases, the student is responsible for producing a field report that relates a set of theoretical concepts particular to a subdiscipline of political science to what the student has observed, participated in, and experienced in the field.

Guidelines for an Internship Report

1. **Get a detailed job description of your duties and your faculty and field supervisors' expectations for your fieldwork.**
   - Make sure that you are achieving the goals set for you by both your faculty and field supervisors.
   - Make sure you conduct your work in a responsible and professional manner.
2. **Keep a detailed log of your day's activities.**
   - Be sure that you differentiate between significant and insignificant details in your log.
   - Describe your experiences in detail and include facts and measurements.
   - Be sure to get permission from your field supervisor to record any data that might be considered classified or personal.
   - Depending on the work assigned, keep a tally or list of the number of times the same type of duty was assigned or task was repeated.
   - Put the date and time worked on each new entry.
3. **Annotate each entry, writing for at least 10 minutes. If necessary, use a "stream of consciousness" writing style. Freewrite as much as possible.**
   - Pose questions about why some condition exists or what purpose a particular task served.
   - Draw some conclusions about the significance of the observations and experiences.
   - How did you feel about what you observed, experienced, or participated in when it was happening?
   - How do you feel about what you observed, experienced, or participated in right now?
   - Make some connections between what you know from your academic training and what you observed, experienced, or participated in.
4. **At the close of the internship, conduct a content analysis of your log.**
   - To conduct a content analysis on your log, create a typology of the types of phenomena you observed, types of situations you experienced, and types of activities you participated in, which are listed in your log.

- ◆ A typology is a set of distinct categories of information.
- ◆ In this case, one category would be observation, one category would be experiences, and one category would be activities.
- Label each item in each category by some ranking method. Try the following, but be prepared to justify the designation you give each item:
  - ◆ Significant or Insignificant.
  - ◆ Conforms or does not conform to theory.
- Identify the frequency (how many times or how often) of which each item in the typology occurred.
  - ◆ Was there any pattern in the time, place, or context in which an event occurred?
  - ◆ How many times did the same type of event occur?

5. **Using your typology, prepare a report that compares theories about political phenomena or behavior with the events you observed, experienced, or participated in during your internship.**
  - The format for the report should be similar to an analytical essay.
    - ◆ The report should not be purely descriptive.
    - ◆ Describe the goals and expectations associated with the fieldwork.
    - ◆ Describe the context of the fieldwork.
  - Assert in your thesis statement whether your observations, experiences, or activities support or cast doubt on these theories.
    - ◆ Identify a theory or parts of theories about political phenomena or behavior that are the focus of your report.
    - ◆ Suggest whether they are valid or not valid based on your fieldwork.
  - Compare and contrast theory and practice.
    - ◆ Begin your comparison by briefly describing the theory or theories in question.
    - ◆ Use the events which occurred during your fieldwork as evidence to support or cast doubt on the theory or theories.
    - ◆ Clearly separate what you observed from what you experienced, and from what you actually participated in.

6. **After comparing and contrasting theories with the field events, write a conclusion.**
  - Summarize the goals of the fieldwork.
  - Review briefly the incidences where the theory was confirmed by the fieldwork.
  - Review briefly any discrepancies between theory and practice.
  - Suggest how the fieldwork expanded your knowledge or awareness of political phenomena or behavior. Did you benefit from this experience? How?

7. **Include in an appendix of your report a copy of a letter or internship evaluation form that is signed by the field supervisor. The letter should contain an assessment of the quality of your performance related to the following:**
  - Dependability.
  - Initiative.
  - Cooperation.

- Thoroughness.
- Professional attitude.
- Assertiveness.
- Professional strengths.
- Professional weaknesses.
- Overall quality of fieldwork completed.
- Number of hours worked.

Example of a Letter for Assessing a Field Intern

(Be sure to ask for an evaluation of your work. It is best, even if you must use an evaluation sheet similar to the one on the following page, to ask for a letter, on the organizational stationary anyway. This letter, if you have done a good job in your internship, can be placed in your professional portfolio and sent with your career file for job interviews. This example is a fictional letter.)

December 1, 1988

Dr. Redd Coetsacumin
Political Science Department
Wonifby Land College
Tue Efbyse, Virginia 17762

Dear Dr. Coetsacumin,

Thank you for allowing Betsy Ross to conduct an internship with my organization. Betsy was a competent worker during our revolutionary campaign. She was courteous, dependable, and cooperative. Betsy's main strengths were her positive attitude and willingness to learn new skills. In particular, she became especially skilled in flagging discrepancies and sewing them up before the place fell apart. Her only weakness was her inexperience. She soon addressed that through hard work. Betsy completed more than her required 13 hours, and I would give her a gold star for each week she worked as a member of our staff. Given her drive and ambition, she will place her stamp on national politics someday.

Sincerely,

Imayank Quedu-Duldande
Volunteer Supervisor
Dumptha Kingsway PAC

Cc: Betsy Ross

Example of an Evaluation Form for an Internship

Many internship programs have evaluation forms for assessing an intern's work in the field. In the event that your program does not, ask your faculty advisor what is necessary for evaluation. Then, ask your field supervisor for a letter assessing your work and a more detailed evaluation according to the standards set by your faculty advisor. Use the one below as a guide. This evaluation, together with a letter and good fieldwork, will provide credentials for future employment.

(A SAMPLE COVER LETTER)

_____

July 4, 1996

Imayank Quedu-Duldande
Volunteer Supervisor
Dumptha Kingsway PAC
1776 Patriots Way
Revo Loosion, MA 11776

Dear Mr. Quedu-Duldande,

Thank you for having me as an intern in your organization. I appreciate your willingness to include me among your staff. As you know, I will receive a grade based on the work I completed for your organization. Please take a moment to evaluate the work I performed. I have enclosed an evaluation form for your convenience. Please return the attached form, with your signature, to:

Dr. Redd Coetsacumin
Political Science Department
Wonifby Land College
Tue Efbyse, Virginia 17762

Again, thank you for your cooperation. I enjoyed working with you and your staff.

Sincerely,

Betsy Ross
13 Starsnstripes
Fohr Ehver, MA 11776

Sample Intern Evaluation Form

A. On the following scale, please rank your intern's performance:

5 = Excellent 4 = Good 3 = Average 2 = Poor 1 = Unacceptable

a. _____ Dependability

b. _____ Initiative

c. _____ Cooperation

d. _____ Thoroughness

e. _____ Professional attitude

f. _____ Assertiveness

g. _____ Professional strengths

h. _____ Professional weaknesses

i. _____ Overall quality of fieldwork completed

j. _____ Number of hours worked

B. What were the intern's major strengths?

C. In what ways could the intern improve?

D. What is your overall assessment of the intern's performance?

E. Were the number of hours worked equivalent to the number agreed on at the beginning of the internship?

Please sign your name to verify this assessment.

(Name)_____ (Title)_____ (Date)_____

An Example of a Participant Observation/Internship Report

INTERNSHIP REPORT

CAMPAIGN VOLUNTEERS: VIP'S OR PEONS

By\
Caryn M. Cieplak
Professor Diane Schimdt
POLS 395
November 23, 1988
(Reprinted with permission)

INTERNSHIP REPORT

I have had the unique opportunity to work for a politician that has served in a vast and diverse number of elected positions. Harry "Bus" Yourell has been in public office for close to 35 years. Harry "Bus" Yourell is a very well-known political figure in Cook County. His experience ranges from local trustee positions, to his newly elected position of Commissioner of the Metropolitan Sanitary District-Cook County. His recent exit from his position as Cook County Recorder of Deeds was to give him the County experience needed to run for this new position. The new position will take him out of the limelight because he will be sharing it with two other people newly elected to the position. This will give him the incentive to adopt necessary changes within the scope of this office.

In his new position, Bus will be dealing with issues such as building dams, water pollution, and air pollution. My fieldwork was conducted during Bus' campaign for Commissioner. I was expected to help in the election activities. I was particularly interested in studying the role of campaign volunteers and constituency targeting election techniques. My experiences as a volunteer in Bus' campaign support the theories of incumbency advantage through constituency service, name recognition, and local party support. In particular, my experiences in working with him have inspired me to run for a local office someday.

Before my internship, my knowledge of politics was limited to what I could understand from the conversations around me and what I learned from class. Because of my inexperience, one of my main duties was to help with his election to Commissioner by being an envelope stuffer. Stuffing envelopes, though tedious, is something that every campaign headquarters must engage in and is probably one of the most effective ways to reach constituents. Through periodic mailings, constituents are given the opportunity to "get to know the candidates" by reading about their backgrounds and past records in politics. Not only does it clearly define the stances that the particular candidate takes, it provides some humor when the candidate's literature criticizes the opponent(s). Further, mailings are vital in order to effectively and efficiently reach the entire area (on a local level). Walking the precincts can be effective, but it is much easier to reach people through the mail.

One interesting finding from my fieldwork relates directly to the source of the mailings. None of the mail was sent out for Bus' personal benefit. The Cook County Democratic Headquarters covered the county candidates through their mass mailings. The mail sent from Bus' office consisted mainly of literature that promoted the township candidates, the State Representative, and United States Representative. The literature, i.e., personal bibliographies, sample ballots, etc., were all signed by Bus because he is the Committeeman of Worth Township. It was apparent from this literature that Bus was closely aligned with his party.

Not only did I stuff envelopes, but I answered the telephone as well. An important part of a volunteer's job in a township office is manning the telephones when constituents call to question a candidate's position on certain issues. Again, this is not a glamorous job, but it is a very important one. When constituents call to clarify a candidate's position, it is a chance to capitalize on the possibility that the person does not know enough about the candidate. If this is true, then it may be possible to convince the person to vote for your candidate.

For example, it is very common for one out of every two telephone calls to Bus' office to be from a senior citizen. They need to be dealt with very lightly and very carefully.

Senior citizens are very powerful people in Worth Township and although Bus never uses his age as a way to relate to this segment, they realize that he is 69 and has been in local politics for almost 35 years. Anyone who is going to answer these types of phone calls needs to be well versed in not only the candidate's position but in what certain segments of the constituency want to hear.

Past records of the candidate play a very important role when trying to convince undecided voters to vote for a candidate. For instance, one day while I was manning the telephones, a constituent called and asked me exactly what Bus had done for them in the past that should make them vote for him in a new position. Taxes at the local level are always a major concern to taxpayers. Knowing this, I was able to tell the voter something that he did not know. Bus, as the Cook County Recorder of Deeds, was able to computerize his entire office at absolutely no cost to the taxpayer and therefore enable more efficient work output to the public. Bus also managed to increase his budget by less than 1 percent over the four years he was in office. Success like this can only come from years of experience. The voter on the other link of the telephone was very pleased to hear this and thanked me repeatedly for my time.

This leads me to another point that is important—experience. When it came time for Bus to run for the Commissioner of the Metropolitan Sanitary District, it was clear that the position was something new to him. As a representative serving in the Illinois State Legislature for nine terms, Bus has dealt with local pollution topics before, whereas the other nine candidates in the running for this position had minimal exposure to this subject. His experience qualified him for this position.

Knowing of his experience, however, I was able to address many of the questions people had, but not all of them. Because I was ignorant of the duties he would take over as Commissioner, I could not adequately answer some questions at first. I was uncomfortable about not knowing the answers so I read everything I could find about the Sanitary District. After researching the Commissioner's role in the Sanitary District, I felt much more confident in my discussions with constituents and candidates.

In a way, volunteering can create loyal party members and can serve as a recruiting device. For example, it is clear that as a volunteer, feeling ignorant and ineffective in helping constituents provided me with incentives to become more educated about the issues in local politics. Once I became informed, I experienced a great sense of efficacy. Researching the commissioner's role in the Sanitary District gave me more confidence in what I know about local political offices. More importantly, it has provided me with a foundation to collect information and the confidence to effectively address public problems with confidence when I run for office.

Not only do the personal contacts with volunteers help a candidate secure a loyal inner circle of trusted campaign workers, another great asset that an experienced politician can use to his advantage is the personal contacts that he has made over his years of public service. These personal contacts include both Democrats and Republicans. While in the State Legislature, Bus established some long-term relationships with members from both parties as well as with many business professionals. These relationships turn into very credible endorsements when it comes time to run for office. Further, these endorsements turn into votes when constituents are unsure of Bus' qualifications, but feel strongly about one of the public figures that endorsed him.

Through working in a campaign and meeting important people, volunteers can also make important political contacts and, perhaps, even establish their own network of potential supporters. By being part of Bus' campaign staff, I have had the unique opportunity to get to know several of these politicians, some more than others have. I plan to develop these relationships so that when I am ready to run for public office, I too can reap the advantages of such long-standing relationships.

I have realized several things in my tenure as an intern. First, a volunteer's job is extremely important to the success of an election. At first, when given very tedious responsibilities, I questioned my overall usefulness. But as I became more interested in politics I have come to the realization that the only way to learn is through being in the arena in some capacity. I have experienced many things, thanks to the responsibilities Bus has given me, as well as the dedication I have to Worth Township politics.

Moreover, as a volunteer, I have acquired a great deal of knowledge that I otherwise would not have learned. The knowledge I have gained about politics at the local, state, and national level is something that will forever be useful to me no matter what career I enter. I have a greater appreciation of the value of constituency service, candidate credibility, name recognition, and of volunteers in winning campaigns. In particular, I have a deeper appreciation of the value of political connections, political participation, and political education.

All this became very clear to me when I was talking to a top executive at Chrysler Corporation. He said, "Caryn, although your knowledge of the Chrysler Corporation is not near to what mine is, your knowledge of politics is far beyond that of mine. We can teach each other something." In light of this executive's comment, I feel extremely grateful for having this internship experience. Working for Bus has not only made me realize my importance as a volunteer, but also has broadened my appreciation for the knowledge I have gained both in the classroom and in the field. More importantly, it appears to have enhanced my potential for a career in politics.

An Abridged Example of a Log for Internship Field Work

LOG OF INTERNSHIP FIELD WORK

By

Caryn M. Cieplak
(Reprinted with permission)

October 9, 1988
2pm – 5pm
Worth Township Democratic Headquarters (WTDH)

Today was an interesting day at the office. Harry "Bus" Yourell (Bus) was his usual witty self, asking me why I was home for the weekend and not at school studying. So, I told him that I had to come home because, without my help, he might lose the election in November for Commissioner of the Metropolitan Sanitary District of Cook County. After our usual exchange of personal stories we (his staff consisting of Mary, Mary Ann, and Ray) decided to do some work. The first thing that needed to be done was telephone calls. One of the things I think I hate the most, but one of the things that clearly emerges as one of the most important parts of any campaign. This campaign's success almost totally relied upon calling constituents to make sure that they were aware of the fact that "Bus" was running for a position that would make him less visible but more powerful. Many of his supporters have been backing him for 30+ years now and helping him remain in the limelight. We needed to explain to people the importance of putting Bus on the County ticket in this position in order to be sure that all the candidates were elected.

The only exciting thing about today's work was the fact that, through the use of an automatic dialing system hooked up to the phone, no one could fight over not wanting to talk to those well-known citizens who will give you a three hour dissertation.

It was interesting to see how truly uneducated the voters are, and how well known Bus really is.

October 10, 1988
5pm – 7pm
Condesa DelMar

Last night was a great night; I almost didn't mind volunteering my time at Marty Russo's cocktail party. Marty is running for his 8th election into the House of Representatives of the United States and I had the opportunity to serve as an intern in his Washington, D.C., office this past summer. I was given the responsibility of handing out literature on the candidates running for the local election, while watching all the big-shots walk around playing important. Little did they know that there would be a private party for all Marty's past "staffers" (never use the word employee when speaking of those who work on Capitol Hill). Anyway, after the dignitaries all got their chance to speak and everyone drank their money's worth. The cocktail party ended and we (the "staffers") got to enjoy a D.J. while mingling with the local candidates and Marty's special guests, which included twelve Congressmen from around the country. It was a great opportunity for me to see what these people are like outside of their public appearance. They're great.

Anyway, the night ended around 1 a.m. but not until I was invited back to Washington to interview with several different offices after graduation. I guess that doing the piddly work for a while really does pay off. I'm actually considering interviewing with the offices that offered me the opportunity, but only because someday I plan to run for office.

November 4, 1988
10am – 2pm
WTDH

With the election only four days away, it is very difficult for me to outline what I did today. The morning started out with breakfast with Bus and his staff discussing what will be going on the next couple of days. And because I was only going to be there for two of those four days, my duties were limited to more phone calls, walking the precincts with precinct captains, as well as driving Bus to and from some political functions. The day concluded with dropping of literature and money for the judges for Tuesday's election.

November 5, 1988
12pm – 2pm
6pm – 11pm
WTDH

Saturday started out with breakfast at 8am with the staff. The usual topics of discussion were addressed, including who has to go to the rally where Jesse Jackson was going to endorse the county ticket. Naturally, being the youngest member of the staff, I was chosen to stay at the office and take any last minute reservations for Bus's dinner that night. So, here I was for a couple hours bored to tears, reading the same literature over and over and getting to know the candidates like they were family.

Unfortunately, this was the most exciting part of the weekend as far as Saturday morning and early afternoon go, but then it led to something a little more exciting....I received a telephone call that Senator Lloyd Bentsen was planning to make an appearance at Bus' dinner that evening. This put the rest of the afternoon at high-speed trying to find a company that could produce a sign to welcome the Senator and going to the restaurant where the dinner was to be held to meet with the Secret Service to determine whether or not it would pass security. Obviously, this put the other duties that Bus had assigned to us (by this time I had found another staffer that was working the precincts) on hold for a while, but instead we were given responsibilities that we never thought could happen. The afternoon proceeded when the Dukakis headquarters called with the very disappointing news that the restaurant did not pass security inspection. This shattered my entire day. We had done so much preparation in such a short time period that I thought I would never vote for the Democratic ticket in just three days.

Well, the dinner went on without Senator Bentsen and was a huge success, nonetheless. Everyone enjoyed him- or herself and was very thankful for the opportunity to interact with the local candidates. However, it wouldn't be a political function without Caryn working at some point in the night. I began the night by arriving with the rest of the staff to make sure that everything was set up: table numbers, the VIP lounge, and other formalities that only staff could ever worry about. Ticket taking is probably the worst part of the night, especially when people arrive to a sit-down dinner without reservations. We had 800 seats and close to 925 people wanting to eat. Needless to say, some quick action needed to be taken to find these (rude) people a place to eat. Luckily, management liked the organization and was able to do some quick moving and added the extra tables that we needed. The entire night was a great success despite the misfortune of Senator Bensten not showing up and the lack of responsibility on the part of 125 people.

Event Observation, Participation, and Keeping a Journal

Purpose

Journals are useful for many reasons.

1. **Journals help students organize their thoughts about current political events and social problems occurring in their community, as well as in the world.**
2. **Journals are ways of raising students' consciousness about what they are learning and observing.**
3. **Journals contain information as well as personal reactions to current events and course lectures.**
4. **Journals can be used to keep track of thoughts or ideas in the discovery phase of a research project.**
5. **Journals can be used to document students' activities in an internship.**
6. **Journals are part personal diary, part scrapbook, and part intellectual inquiry.**

What to Write in a Journal

Reference: Using a notebook, put the date and time on each entry.

Observation: Write informally about whatever you have observed that day. Describe experiences in detail and include facts and measurements.

Speculations: Write down all speculative thoughts about why something exists or occurred.

Questions: Use critical thinking skills to pose questions about why some condition exists or doubts about reasons given for a political outcome.

Conclusions: Write down any conclusions made based on observations and experiences.

Connections: Write about how experiences and observations relate to personal life and to other political phenomena.

Information: Use the journal as a scrapbook for interesting material and information. Clip and paste the information into the journal, if possible, and then write a reaction to it.

Synthesis: Use the journal to put together what has been learned in class, what has been experienced in the field, and how both relate to the larger context of politics.

Tips on Keeping a Journal

1. **Use a ring-bound notebook.**
2. **Do not use the notebook for any other purpose.**
3. **Always put the date and time on each page and each entry in the journal.**
4. **Write every day for at least 10 minutes.**
5. **Use a new page for each day.**
6. **Do not be afraid to use a "stream of consciousness" style if stumped for something to say.**

Writing a Journal Essay

Sometimes an instructor will require students to write an essay based on their journals. The format for the essay depends on the type of essay required and the material to be included in the journal.

1. **If fieldwork was done, use the format for an internship report included in this text.**
2. **If an essay uses some event or issues described in the log entries, collected clippings, and other materials in your journal, then use the format for a clipping thesis included in this text.**
3. **If the instructor requires a simple essay, use the format for an analytical essay included in this text.**
4. **Whatever the case, do not write your essay in a "Dear Diary" form.**
5. **Examine your log and materials closely.**
   - Draw conclusions about patterns in behavior.
   - Find patterns that confirm (or not) those you learned about in class.
6. **Decide what general statement can be made and write directly concerning that statement.**
7. **Avoid rambling aimlessly about feelings and events. Make a point.**
8. **Make an important, meaningful statement about:**
   - Political observation.
   - Political theory.
   - Political life.

CAMPAIGN '88:
AGAINST ALL ODDS

By
Jenna Herhold
Professor Schmidt
POLS 318
December 1, 1988
(Reprinted with permission)

CAMPAIGN '88: AGAINST ALL ODDS

Campaigns for congressional seats make interesting study material on American election behavior. Voting theorists disagree about what motivates voter participation in elections and what determines their vote choice. Are voters irrational, emotional, party identifiers who vote based on how candidates deliver their messages as described by the American Voter model? Or do they vote as rational actors who weigh, when possible, the candidates' positions on important issues as described by rational choice models of voting? My observations of the recent congressional election in the twenty-second district suggest that people, for the most part, are best described by the American Voter mode.

My assignment in this course was to participate in the upcoming elections in the 22nd Congressional District. So, starting from square one, I went to the College Republican's first campaign kick-off meeting, motivated by the requirements. I decided to go to the College Republican meeting simply because the Democrats' meeting time did not fit my schedule. The idea to call my parents up and ask them which party I should support crossed my mind a couple times. Nevertheless, I decided to make my own observations and then make my decisions. Reflecting back now, I think my lack of knowledge of politics and pressing issues was a blessing in disguise. I was not predisposed to support one candidate over the other. I was lucky enough to start with a clear slate and base my decisions on what was to come.

I went to the Republican meeting and listened attentively to what the panel of Republican candidates had to say. I was hardly impressed. I left the meeting still quite unsure of my political bias. I wanted to know more about the other party and what its candidates were like. What stance did they take?

The perfect opportunity came on September 14 at their first debate. The debate would clear up many of my concerns and point out the differences between Poshard and Kelley. This was the first opportunity the people had to hear them speak out against one another publicly (D.E. Sept. 14:1). This was also a debut public appearance for Kelley. Unlike his opponent, Poshard's stance on the issues had already been heard by many from Poshard's past position on the Illinois State Senate for the 59th District. Kelley had his work cut out for him.

The debate touched quite a few issues, starting with the economy and the budget. Poshard came out saying he wanted to give smaller businesses chances to compete and that we hardly needed to bother spending our money to get "two of every weapon!" Naturally, Kelley addressed the defense issue by saying that there is no way we could be in negotiations with other countries unless we were the stronger forces. An issue was raised by one of the questioners on what projects they would have voted down if they had been our congressional representatives. Kelley said he would have voted down a railroad project in Southern Illinois. This comment caused quite a disturbance from the other side. I paid close attention to this type of controversy and to what induced cheers and support from each side.

From my observations, I concluded that this was very much a candidate-centered campaign. Poshard won his audience because of his enthusiasm and his ability to speak well. The other side, as a whole, did not appear educated enough about the issues to fully understand the stance Poshard was taking. Poshard, like most Democratic candidates, took the party position on many issues. But, of course, the audience was much more receptive to Poshard because he is a good, effective speaker whereas Kelley is a rather passive, reserved speaker.

This was one of the major problems costing Kelley the election. It became very clear at this debate that what the candidate says is as important as how he says it. It all falls back to the incredible influence the IMAGE projected has on the outcome of the election. Kelley was a poor speaker. He failed to motivate the audience the way Poshard did. He did not fulfill the image that people have programmed into their ideals of what and how a candidate should act.

Even so, I supported Kelley because I liked his stance on the issues the best. In order to make a rational vote, the voter needs to first identify the issues that are of most importance to himself and then find the candidate to suit his own needs. People need to base their votes on the issues at hand and how the candidate stands on them. Unfortunately, most of the public does not know or even care enough about the issues. They too often base their decisions on what they see. The campaign strategy often becomes a game of building illusions for the candidates, whether it is through the media, or by reconstructing character to meet the image ideals set in the public's mind.

Ultimately, I came out of this debate thinking that, although Kelley is not the stronger of the two candidates when it comes to saying what he wants to say effectively in front of hundreds of people that mostly oppose him, what really matters is how he would vote in Congress, because that is what is going to affect me. If elections were about whom the better speaker is, who can captivate a crowd, and who is better at public appearances, I would support Poshard one hundred percent of the way. Nonetheless, I made my decision finally; I chose to support Kelley because of his position on the issues that interested me the most.

After the debate, I talked to some Republican students who had decided to vote for Poshard. I cannot see any logic to their way of thinking. If they support the Republican ticket, how could they rationalize supporting Poshard? Easy, they "like" Poshard. Simply because they "like" a candidate better than the other, is no reason to overlook that candidate's beliefs. Such inconsistencies exemplify irrational voting behavior. The voters are no longer taking into consideration what is good for them or Southern Illinois from a political standpoint, but rather considering what appeals to their emotions.

Thus, the candidate's image remains a key to a successful campaign. That is why Poshard's campaign strategy was to stress personal issues such as his leadership qualities and his experience in Illinois politics. Furthermore, Kelley was the "defending" candidate. The twenty-second district has long since been a Democratic safe seat held by politically powerful people, such as Paul Simon and Ken Grey.

In other words, Kelley, as the Republican challenger, was the candidate who had the burden of proving himself worthy. He had to counter-attack. One major point the Kelley campaign emphasized was his stance on the issues. He was consistently pushing the issues; Poshard would talk about being a strong leader and Kelley would try to get Poshard to go back to addressing the issues. He constantly attacked the issues of government waste and regional development. He tried to convince people his stance was the one to support. For example, Scott Perry reported in the Daily Egyptian, "Kelley has made an issue of Poshard's stances on such issues as abortion, gun control, and gay rights" (D.E. Oct. 6:5). Kelley's objective may have been to give people an alternative or a better choice, so that people would concentrate on the issues and put aside Poshard's good leadership qualities. As he said, "leadership takes place in context" (D.E. Oct. 5:7).

Unfortunately, this was an almost impossible goal to attain because, at the same time as he was trying to convince people that his positions were best, Kelley had to try to overcome Poshard's popularity and distinguish himself on the issues. In addition, Kelley had to get as much public exposure as possible. Kelley was hardly a recognizable public figure to Southern Illinoisans and he did not have a political record. To address these problems, getting out and meeting the public in one-on-one situations became a priority for Kelley.

Ultimately, Kelley's biggest obstacle and hardest to overcome was the heavy Democratic district he was competing in. He was the underdog from the start and Kelly knew he was going against the odds (D.E. Nov. 4:3). When Kelley entered into a debate he knew the odds were that the crowd would predominantly be Democratic and his supporters would be outnumbered. Poshard was able to go into his public appearances knowing that he was the people's choice candidate.

Even with the odds in his favor, I found it very interesting that Poshard shied away from a public appearance with Kelley on the SIU-C campus. It is known that a high percentage of the students at SIU are from Northern Illinois where there is much more of a Republican stronghold. As reported in the D.E. on October 12, 1988, "the Poshard campaign has been reluctant to meet with the Republican candidate at the University saying it gives an unfair advantage to Kelley." When Poshard stepped on his own territory he seemed to lose many of those leadership qualities he holds when he feels confident. Poshard became nervous and reluctant.

In the end, the forum on the SIU-C campus did happen between Kelley and Poshard. This was not a debate. Nevertheless, it did give the candidates a chance to offer information to the public and show their differences. This was hardly a threat to Poshard. "I never dreamed this would happen," Poshard said when he found out he had won, late on election night (D.E. Nov. 8:1). It was hard to believe that Poshard did not expect to win this race. Of course he did.

I am glad I got so involved in this election. I supported the candidate that I thought would best fight for my needs. Although, I must admit Poshard had good leadership qualities, I think the most important thing remains the issues. Kelley tried to convince voters that the issues should be what influences peoples' vote the most. I agree. I listened to the issues and backed Kelley for what he and the Republican Party stood for, not how he stood for it.

MATERIALS REFERENCED FOR SCRAPBOOK CLIPPINGS

Perry, Scott. "Government's role debated," *Daily Egyptian* (September 14, 1988): 1, 5.

_____. "Kelly criticizes Poshard's TV ad," *Daily Egyptian* (September 14, 1988): 1.

_____. "Kelly: Government should play leading role in housing," *Daily Egyptian* (September 14, 1988): 9.

_____. "Kelly, Poshard defend VP choice," *Daily Egyptian* (September 14, 1988): 1, 5.

_____. "Kelly, Poshard make stances clear," *Daily Egyptian* (September 14, 1988): 1.

_____. "Kelly, Poshard set to debate tonight," *Daily Egyptian* (September 14, 1988): 1.

_____. "Kelly, Poshard to debate on campus," *Daily Egyptian* (September 14, 1988): 1, 7.

_____. "Poshard, Kelly show differences," *Daily Egyptian* (September 14, 1988): 1.

_____. "Poshard says constituents get the credit for his victory," *Daily Egyptian* (September 14, 1988): 1, 5.

CAMPAIGN '88

JOURNAL/SCRAPBOOK

By
Jenna Herhold

(Author's Note: The following material is an abridged campaign journal and scrapbook. The assignment was to spend 10 hours working in a campaign, keep a journal, construct a clipping file/scrapbook, and write an analytical essay about the 1988 Congressional Campaign. Students were to use their journals and references to the scrapbook materials. Not all of the scrapbook or journal is reproduced here for the sake of parsimony and copyright prohibitions. The student did, however, include copies of campaign literature, buttons, stickers, and other election media in her scrapbook. Nothing is irrelevant in a journal/scrapbook. Include anything that strikes your fancy!)

CAMPAIGN JOURNAL

Wednesday, September 7, 1988
7:00P–8:45 P
College Republican Meeting/Speakers:

It was obvious that the College Republicans did not expect so many people at this kick-off meeting. There were hardly enough accommodations for the students. Several of the Republican campaigners from our area were at the meeting and lined up to give speeches. They, too, were not prepared for such a large group. I listened to what they had to say and asked questions. The speakers were thrilled to see people like myself, there to show their support.

Of the speakers, I think the one that I was impressed by most was Mike Maurizio. He was able to speak effectively and he knew the audience was young and not very educated. He addressed his issues to the audience and the audience was able to relate because of it. The other speakers were very poor speakers and I found it hard to pay attention. Even so, I showed my support and interest.

SATURDAY, SEPTEMBER 10, 1988
8:30A–12:30P
CARTERVILLE PARADE:

It was a beautiful morning for a parade! We all met at Kelley's headquarters and waited for the others to join. I helped make a few telephone calls to make sure people were able to get out of bed. Once the group had organized, we caravanned to the parade sight. "You might run across some unfriendly people 'cause Carterville is really a Democratic," one said while the others laughed. They told horror stories the whole way out there about unfriendly encounters with Democrats. I was scared. I did not know what to expect. They handed me their green campaign shirt and some literature. Kelley warned us not to put any stickers on children unless we asked them or their parents first. This is so that we did not offend anyone. The parade started and we went through the town of Carterville. I had no rude people say nasty things to me or treat me poorly. In fact, most people were very polite and receptive to all of the people helping Kelley pass out information. I enjoyed handing out the information and stickers!

WEDNESDAY, SEPTEMBER 14, 1988
6:00P–10:30P
POSHARD/KELLEY DEBATE SHAWNEE COLLEGE:

Before this, I had never been to a debate. The Shawnee gymnasium was filled with Poshard supporters. I was with the group of about ten people from Southern. It was obvious to me that Poshard was already perceived as the strongest candidate in this election. I cheered Kelley on, holding up signs and rallying for him. I was disappointed in Kelley's ability to speak. He seemed too intimidated by his opponent.

WEDNESDAY, OCTOBER 12, 1988
7:30P–9:30P
POSHARD/KELLEY FORUM:

Because I work on the Student Programming Council, I was able to help a co-chair with the set-up of the program. We had the Student Center Auditorium set aside and ordered a podium through scheduling and catering. We also ordered some refreshments for after the forum. We had to make sure that Student Center Security was aware and present at the event. Kelley was not in a good mood that night. Perhaps he was nervous about the forum, but he was certainly less than friendly. The forum started a little past the target time of 7:30 p.m. but all was going smoothly. Then, the side door leading from private back halls in the Student Center opened and two men carrying a coffin walked out on stage to everyone's surprise. The coffin was covered with "EDUCATION" and when the two guys got on stage, one of them said, "Vince makes sense!" They hurried out of the room before anybody realized what was going on. It was an obvious slam on Kelley for his stance on education. I was shocked. After the event, I talked with people and they felt that the forum lacked any real content. I even got a chance to voice my opinions on local television as they interviewed me. I think the forum was a good event to have but one can never be too careful with security!

MONDAY OCTOBER 24, 1988
8:00P–9:00P
COLLEGE REP. V. COLLEGE DEMOCRAT (DEBATE):

The College Republican representative took on a representative from the Democratic College organization. The debate was not structured like most debates. The audience asked the questions and the debaters took turns answering them. It simply gave them the opportunity to take a stance on the issue. There was hardly any disputing. Andy Leighton was there, but he was sitting in the audience. He was the only one that really fired up a dispute. He argued that the Republicans are ignorant to the Greenhouse Effect issues. I, again, was there to support the Republican Party and help as the need arose.

FRIDAY, NOVEMBER 4, 1988
12:00NOON–1:00P
SOLICITATION TABLES:

I worked the information tables on the first floor of the Student Center. I handed out information and was available to answer questions for those people with questions. Most people who stopped by were friends of the co-worker's or mine. No one came up to the table and asked serious questions.

MONDAY, NOVEMBER 7, 1988
12:00NOON–1:00P
SOLICITATION TABLES:

(Same as Above.)

VERIFICATION OF CAMPAIGN WORK

1) COLLEGE REPUBLICAN MEETING: WEDNESDAY, SEPTEMBER 7, 1988 7:00P–8:45P
2) CARTERVILLE PARADE: SATURDAY, SEPTEMBER 10, 1988 8:30A–12:30P
3) POSHARD/KELLEY DEBATE: WEDNESDAY, SEPTEMBER 14, 1988 6:00P–10:30P
4) POSHARD/KELLEY FORUM: WEDNESDAY, OCTOBER 12, 1988 7:30P–9:30P
5) COLLEGE PARTY'S DEBATE: MONDAY, OCTOBER 24, 1988 8:00P–9:00P
6) SOLICITATION TABLES: FRIDAY, NOVEMBER 4, 1988 12:00NOON–1:00P
7) SOLICITATION TABLES: MONDAY, NOVEMBER 7, 1988 12:00NOON–1:00P

TOTAL HOURS: 15.25

VERIFICATION: (Signed by the campaign supervisor)

Kelley, Poshard set to debate tonight

By Scott Perry
Staff Writer

Voters in the 22nd Congressional District have the opportunity tonight to see congressional candidates Patrick Kelley and Glenn Poshard discuss the issues in the first of three public debates.

Kelley and Poshard will meet face to face, taking questions from a four-member panel and the public at 7:30 p.m. at Shawnee College in Ullin.

Both candidates are seeking the seat to be vacated by Rep. Kenneth Gray (D-West Frankfort), who is retiring because of health problems. Gray has held the position from 1955 to 1975 and again from 1984 to the present.

Both have been campaigning for the congressional spot since late last year.

Republican candidate Patrick Kelley said the debate will be a good opportunity for the public to get involved and hear how each candidate stands on issues that concern the region and the na-

tion, and to show the differences between the candidates.

"It's important to find the differences," Kelley said.

People haven't had the opportunity to hear both candidates speak at the same time and to see how they differ on particular issues, he said.

Kelley said he wants to present an alternative to the approach taken by those who have represented the area in the past.

"The policies of the past haven't worked," he said.

Democratic candidate Glenn Poshard said he was ready to debate but said no special preparations have been made.

"I think there is such a thing as over-preparation," Poshard said.

Poshard, who has represented the 59th District in the Illinois Senate, said his stance on the issues are clear.

"I've had the same stance on the issues for several years and I don't think it would do me a whole lot of good to go back now and try to struggle with that

(changing his stance)."

Kelley, on the other hand, only has become known throughout the district since beginning his bid for Congress. His "grassroots" campaign relies heavily on getting out and meeting people.

Among the issues expected to be debated are the economy of Southern Illinois, ways of creating jobs for the region, education, taxes, defense spending, abortion, drug policies and the deficit.

The panelists for tonight's debate are: Tim Landis, Southern Illinoisian, respresenting newspaper; Bill Cromer, WEBQ, representing radio; Bonnie Wheeler, WSIL, respresenting television; and Jason Edwards, of the Shawnee College newspaper TEMPO, representing the hosting school. Barry Gowin, president of Shawnee College, will moderate the activities.

The public will be invited to ask questions of the candidates after the formal discussion is through.

Daily Egyptian, September 14, 1988.
Reprinted with permission.

Poshard, Kelly Show Differences

By Scott Perry
Staff Writer

In an atmosphere resembling a high school basketball game, congressional candidates Patrick Kelley and Glenn Poshard debated the issues Wednesday night that one of the will face in January.

About 1,000 spectators packed into the gym at Shawnee Community College, carrying the banners of their favorite candidate.

Taking questions from a four-member panel, the candidates outlined their stances on such issues as the depressed Southern Illinois economy, taxes, national defense, the war on drugs and education.

Both agreed that higher education is in trouble and that something should be done about it.

Kelley proposed a follow-up on a George Bush proposal to create a savings plan to help meet the cost of higher education.

The savings bond system is being tried in Illinois and has been very sucessful, according to a representative of the Illinios Bureau of the Budget.

"The needs to be a commitment to promote higher education," Kelley said.

Poshard agreed, saying "better education will mean a stronger nation."

Poshard said he is in favor of federal policies to assist anyone that wishers to go to college as long as the policies were cost savings and efficient.

Both candidates said they thought the debate was a success. Kelley said the debate was successful in bringing out the differences between the candidates, which was a pre-debate goal.

Poshard said the voters can clearly see the distinction between the candidates.

Daily Egyptian, September 15, 1988.
Reprinted with permission.

Kelley, Poshard make stances clear

By Scott Perry
Staff Writer

INA — Leadership was the "message of the day" during the second debate between Congressional candidates Patrick Kelley and Glenn Poshard.

Both men began the evening outlining the problems facing the 22nd Congressional District, giving reasons why they are best suited to take the long-held position of Rep. Ken Gray, D-West Frankfort, in the U.S. House of Representatives.

"Who can best lead this district is the question of this election," Poshard said.

Poshard, D-Carterville, made reference to his past two years as a state senator representing the 59th District.

Kelley, a faculty member of the SIU-C law school, believes his background will allow him to create common-sense solutions to the districts problems. He said his work as an educator, city con-cilman and member of an anti-drug group will aid him if elected.

Kelley, who has been condemmed for his stance on gay rights legislation, insists "the power should not be put in the hands of the government, but in the hands of the individual."

"The government should help protect the rights of those who have characteristics they can't help -- sex, race — but not those that are determined by conduct," Kelley said.

Poshard agreed with Kelley despite the Democratic platform's stance on the rights of gays.

Kelley used Poshard's stance on the issue to again attack him for straying from the party's platform. He said Poshard would be obligated to vote with the Democrats in Washington.

"Sending someone to congress that will vote for (Speaker of the House) Jim Wright is like pouring gasoline on a fire," Kelley said.

Poshard said he votes based on "the best facts brought to bear and the dictates of my conscience."

On the issue of minimum wage, Kelley and Poshard took opposing stances.

Kelley said raising the minimum wage would "throw people out of work and not help those who need it."

Poshard disagreed, saying because of minmum wage people are becoming dependent on welfare.

Daily Egyptian, September 29, 1988.
Reprinted with permission.

Staff Photo by Cameron Chin

Political animals

Donald Durham of Elco shows his support for Glenn Poshard amid a field of Patrick Kelley backers at Wednesday's debate at Rend Lake College.

Daily Egyptian, September 29, 1988.
Reprinted with permission.

Kelley, Poshard defend VP choice

By Scott Perry
Staff Writer

CENTRALIA — While the vice-presidential candidates were debating the issues, the congressional candidates were debating over the vice presidential candidates.

"I think Lloyd Bensten will be a great vice president," Glenn Poshard, Democratic candidate for Congress said during a debate with Patrick Kelley Wednesday night.

The debate was the third between the candidates vying for the position being vacated by long-time seat holder Kenneth Gray, D-West Frankfort.

"I'm glad Michael Dukakis has the courage to choose someone that dosen't align with him on all the issues," Poshard said.

He used this time to defend prior allegations by Kelley that Poshard would be ineffective in Washington because of his differences with the Democratic platform.

Kelley has made several references to Poshard's views on abortion, gun control and gay rights, which stray from the Democratic platform.

Kelley continued his attack on the Democratic party saying that choosing Bensten for vice president was an attempt by Dukakis to rid himself of the liberal label the Bush campaign has placed on him.

Poshard defended Dukakis' choice by attacking Bush's choice of Dan Quayle for vice president, saying at least he didn't choose him for good looks and youth.

"What a nice way to choose a candidate," Poshard said.

Poshard also questioned Kelley's alignment with the Repubichan party.

"Do you intend to go along with our leadership? Do you?" he said.

Kelly said that he and Bush agree on all the issues and their is no reason to stary from them.

Poshard then questioned how Kelley could vote on Reagan administration issues such as acid rain legislation, social security and college grants and loans.

But the battle didn't end there.

The war on drugs also brought a heated confrontation between the candidates.

Poshard supports use of the military in ending the drug problem in America, saying it is "a national security issue."

Defending his stance, Poshard reminisced about his days in the Army. When he returned from Korea, Poshard wen to New York City to ease racial tensions.

"I was trained in the city of New York to deal with domestic affairs. This isn't a game, it's a war. It's a war on drugs."

Kelley quoted a defense official as saying, "We don't train our men to give Miranda warnings. We train them to shoot and kill."

Kelley also blamed the Democrat-controlled Congress for cutting $75,000 out of the federal budget that would aid the National Guard in efforts to control the influx of drugs into America.

Both candidates agreed that education is one of the keys to ending the drug problem.

Daily Egyptian, October 6, 1988.
Reprinted with permission.

Kelley, Poshard to debate on campus

By Scott Perry
Staff Writer

The debate that isn't a debate between Congressional candidates Patrick Kelley and Glenn Poshard will be 7:30 tonight in the Student Center auditorium.

The Congressional Candidate forum, as it is officially called, is sponsored by the Jackson County League of Women Voters with the cooperation of several local orgainizations.

Kelley and Poshard are seeking the position in the U.S. House of Representatives being vacated by long-time seat holder Kenneth Gray, D-West Frankfort.

The forum's format is similar to that of a debate in that the candidates will answer written questions from the audience. Each candidate will have four minutes to answer the question. Each candidate also is given five minutes for their opening

statements and seven minutes for their closing statements.

In a late-August interview, Jim Wilson, Poshard's campaign manager, said the Poshard campaign was being "more than generous" in organizing the three debates, which have already been held throughout the 22nd district.

The sites for the three debates were Shawnee College in Ullin, Rend Lake College in Ina and Kaskaskia College in Centralia.

Linda Helstern, president of the Jackson County League of Women Voters, said not holding a debate in Jackson County "is an insult to the community."

"There are many intelligent and informed voters in the area," Helstern said.

"SIU is the centerpoint of life in Carbondale as well as being the focal point on Southern Illinois," she said.

The Poshard campaign has

been reluctant to meet with the Republican candidate at the University, saying it "gives an unfair advantage to Kelley."

Kelley is a professor at the Law School.

Wilson, using the same logic, said a gathering at John A. Logan would give the same unfair advantage to his candidate.

"Logan is in Glenn's backyard," Wilson said.

But Gail Klam, organizer of the forum, said she was able to convince Wilson there was no other site in Carbondale as suitable as the University.

The forum is open to the public, but tickerts must be obtained, Klam said.

Free Tickerts can be picked up at the Student Programming Council office on the third floor of the Student Center.

Daily Egyptian, October 12, 1988.
Reprinted with permission.

Government's role debated

By Scott Perry
Staff Writer

The foundation of America, and what needs to done to keep it strong, was the issue at hand during the Congressional Candidate Forum Wednesday night.

Glenn Poshard, Democratic candidate for the 22nd District's Congressional seat, used the analogy of his grandfather's barn to stress the importance of a strong foundation in the nation.

Poshard said his grandfather paid $150 to have the tine roof of the barn painted. At first, he said, the roof was so shiny that it could be seen for miles. But with the first hard Southern Illinois rain, the paint came off.

"And when the termites began to eat away at the foundation of the barn, he had no money with which to save it," Poshard said.

Poshard used this analogy to stage an attack on the Reagan-proposed Strategic Defense Initiative and the United States' large national debt.

Poshard said the federal government should "invest in the foundation of this country and not ina space defense system."

Republican candidate Patrick Kelley disagreed, saying the job of the national government is to provide leadership and a strong national defense.

Kelley said SDI is needed to combat the uneven balance between U.S. and Soviet nuclear weapons.

Kelley stood strong on the Republican ideal of limited government control on the affairs of the states.

Kelley said the federal government should have a limited part in the lives of Americans.

"We should encourage people to do things on their own," Kelley said. "But when people really need help, we need to be sure there will be a compassionate government and people there to help them."

The question of legislation to ensure job security for women who take maternity leaves, led to an attack by Poshard over Kelley's summer sabbatical, which he took to write a book.

Poshard praised Kelley for writing the book but said women don't have the same security as he had when they decide to have a baby.

"And you did it with pay. We're not even talking pay for them," Poshard said.

Kelley's sabbatical was questioned since he used the time to campaign for Congress

Rennard Strickland, former dean of the Law School, defended Kelley's sabbatical saying he accomplished more on his book than he had originally planned and used only free time to work on his campaign.

Daily Egyptian, October 13, 1988
Reprinted by permission

Kelley criticizes Poshard's TV ad

By Scott Perry
Staff Writer

Congressional candidate Patrick Kelley said his opponent's "self-confessed ignorance" on defense issues should be a deciding factor in electing the next congressman to represent the 22nd district.

Speaking at his final press conference prior to the Tuesday election, was referring to a television advertisement where State Sen. Glenn Poshard, running against Kelley, says he

knows little about the complicated national defense issues, but says he does know a lot about the problems of Main Street.

Kelley said the people of Southern Illinois "deserve a congressman who knows enough about defense to keep America strong."

Poshard was unavailable for comment.

Poshard and Kelley have received much praise for a "clean" campaign, but Poshard campaign manager Jim Wilson

said he was unhappy with the recent attack on Poshard by Kelley in his advertisements.

Wilson said the Poshard camp has been running a very positive campaign with no reference to Kelley in any of their advertisements.

Kelley, however, has been using his commercials to attack Poshard, Wilson said.

In one commercial, Kelley takes issue with House Speaker Jim Wright, and Poshard's connection with him.

Kelley said as a representative

the first vote one will have to make is for speaker.

Kelley disagrees with the naming of Wright to the position of speaker because of the recent accusations that Wright has been unethical in the way does business

"Jim Wright runs the House like the dictator of a banana boat," Kelley said during his press conference.

Among the leading differences Kelley says there is between the two candidates is the way each of them hopes to bring jobs to Southern Illinois.

Kelley wants to continue with many of Reagan ideals such as low taxes, tax incentives and less government regulations.

Kelley is against the raising of the minimum wage, something Poshard is for, saying it would throw many Americans, including Southern Illinoisans, out of work.

Kelley said he was pleased with the campaign and that he felt the momemtum was there to take him to Washington on election day.

Daily Egyptian, October 13, 1988.
Reprinted with premission.

Kelley: Government should play leading role in housing homeless

By Scott Perry
Staff Writer

The role the government should play in providing housing for the homeless is one of leadership, Patrick Kelley, Republican candidate for Congress, said.

Kelley, during a press conference Wednesday, said the government should encourage and assist the private sector in meeting our housing needs. He also said the government should not bear the entire financial burden.

"I don't agree with those who assume all we need to do is spend more government money to solve our housing problem," he said.

Kelley said he disagreed with the plan proposed by Michael Dukakis that would tax developers and use union pension funds to provide for the nation's

"I don't agree with those who assume all we need to do is spend more government money to solve our housing problems."

— Patrick Kelley

housing needs.

"I'm not for a raid on private pensions," Kelley said.

Kelley said the tax would discourage development and raise the housing cost.

He said the key to creating a good housing policy was to install a policy that allows home ownership to be possible.

"The best housing policy is a sound economic policy," he said.

Kelley said strengthening the savings and loan institutions is a must if the government hopes to provide the proper environment for individual home ownership.

"We need to let people know they don't need to worry about the safety of their investment,"

he said.

Kelley used this opportunity to attack House Speaker Jim Wright.

Wright is presently being investigated for allegedly interferring with the closing of several Texas institutions.

Kelley strongly supported a voucher system which allows low-income families to live in privately owned rental propery.

Daily Egyptian, October 20, 1988
Reprinted with permission

Poshard says constituents get the credit for his victory

By Scott Perry
Staff Writer

With his wife and two children at his side, an excited Glenn Poshard raised his hand in the air, gave a big thumbs up and claimed victory in the race for the 22nd Congressional District.

"I never dreamed this would be able to happen," Poshard told a crowded room of supporters at the Marion Holiday Inn Tuesday.

"If this victory belongs to anyone, it belongs to you," Poshard said, thanking those made his dream a reality.

"No one has worked harder, no one has gone out and knocked on more doors and mailed more letters than you have. From the bottom of our hearts my family thanks all of you for this victory you have given us."

Poshard's announcement came at 10:10 p.m., three hours after the Illinois polls closed Tuesday.

In his speech, Poshard made a promise to the people of the district.

"I want to go there (Washington) and be a good congressman. I want to do what's right. I want to work hard for Southern Illinois and I want to be honest and truthful to the people. As long as we can do that we will win again, because we are going to do the best job a congressman can do. I promise you that and I thank you for it."

Poshard also used the opportunity to thank his opponent, Patrick J. Kelley, for being a "gentleman" and running "a fine campaign."

Poshard said he wished the kind of campaign run in the 22nd Congressional District could be run in every district throughout the State.

He praised Kelley, saying he has "some very deep beliefs and he's serious about those beliefs."

Poshard showed some compassion for his opponent telling the crowd he knew what it was like to lose.

Kelley called the Poshard headquarters immediately after the victory announcement was made. The two candidates spoke for about five minutes about the campaign and congratulated one another.

"I consider you my friend," Poshard told Kelley. "We'll have to get together sometime."

Kelley told Poshard, "You ran a really good campaign. I think the people of the district were pleased with the campaign."

Poshard said he planned to sleep until noon today and wake-up to a late breakfast and spend some time with his family.

After that he said he was going to get caught up on his state Senate business and prepare to go back to session next month.

Poshard said there are still a few things he would like to accomplish before heading for Washington.

Daily Egyptian, November 9, 1988. Reprinted with permission.

President

No. of states	Candidate	votes
35	George Bush	34,980,444
8	Michael Dukakis	29,609,469
7	Unknown	

U.S. House

District	Candidate	votes
22	Patrick Kelley	46,870
	Glenn Poshard	78,631

State House

District	Candidate	votes
116	Frankie Eggemeyer	5,617
	Bruce Richmond	14,906
	Other	0
117	Jim Rea	9,842
	Other	0
118	Bob Winchester	16,981
	David Phelps	25,828
	Other	0

State Senate

District	Candidate	votes
58	L. Gene Clarke	16,048
	Ralph Dunn	26,165

State Constitution

Constitutional Convention	votes
Yes	188,613
No	613,378

Voting Age Amendment	votes
Yes	294,787
No	265,646

Delinquent Tax Scales Amendment	votes
Yes	294,787
No	215,237

State's Annorney

Candidate	votes
Michael Maurizio	8,243
W. Charles Grace	12,409
Other	0

Circuit Clerk

Candidate	votes
Bill Grob	7,774
Jennie Crawshaw	12,602
Other	0

Note: Information for table taken at 1 a.m. this moring. Story information may differ.

Daily Egyptian November 9, 1988
Reprinted with permission

CHAPTER 14

Assignments for Organizing
and Documenting
Achievements for Research

Organizing and Documenting Achievements Using Project Folders

This chapter is dedicated to helping students organize and present their classwork professionally. It contains formats and examples for organizing students' research and for organizing students' work. Project folders are a set of files specifically related to a research project. Rather than leaving heaps of material all over a desk or room or keeping the material in a stack inside a notebook, a project folder contains only the materials related to the research project. The materials are summaries of information and checklists to remind students of the nature and scope of the assignment. Students should be able to write their papers directly from the sources contained in the project folder.

Constructing a Project Folder

Every research project should begin with a project file. Each item listed below should have its own section dividers:

- a copy of the professor's explicit instructions
- a writing schedule
- a draft checklist
- a copy of the standard criteria for evaluation
- an outline
- a journal/scrapbook
- notes and references
- photocopies of information
- a draft of the paper
- a backup disk of your draft and final manuscript

Professor's Explicit Instructions

Identify the professor's instructions from the handout, syllabus, or lecture for the paper assignment and write them down.

- Check them off as you complete them.
- Recheck them as you revise your draft.
- Keep in mind the standard criteria for grading.
- Keep the writing schedule handy.

Writing Schedules

Students should set a reasonable schedule to follow for their research projects. Examine your syllabus and note any explicit dates set by the professor as the assignments' due dates. Pace yourself so that you are not researching, writing, and typing a week or less before the assignment is due. Use the schedule outline below. (Adapted with permission from Corder and Ruszkiewicz, p. 703.)

<u>Date</u>	<u>Activity</u>
_____	Choose a topic.
_____	Do exploratory reading for discovery of ideas.
_____	Construct working thesis sentence and scratch outline.
_____	Begin search for references, materials, and data.
_____	Complete research and note-taking.
_____	Refine thesis and construct a topic outline.
_____	Write first draft.
_____	Revise draft.
_____	Type final copy; proofread and make a photocopy of it.
_____	Give the finished paper to the professor.

Draft Checklist for a Research Paper

__ Page limit of the assignment _____   Date due:_____
__ Specific information required:

__ _____

__ _____

__ _____

__ Title page includes the title of the paper, your name, professor's name, course number, course name, and date.

__ The paper is stapled and pages numbered.

__ You included an abstract.

__ Each paragraph is at least three sentences long.

__ You have presented evidence or examples for each point made in each paragraph and referenced each one.

__ Each paragraph in the body of the paper has at least two references, except for your original information.

__ No more than three quotes are included in the text.

   __ The quotes are absolutely necessary (delete if not).

   __ Long quotes (over three lines) are indented.

__ You have used at least three articles from professional political science journals as sources.

__ Your references are parenthetical citations, footnotes, or endnotes and are in proper form according to a stylebook.

__ Tables, figures, and appendices are clearly marked, referenced in the text, and placed after the last page.

__ You have included a complete bibliography (works cited).

   __ It is in standard bibliographic form.

   __ It is typed as a hanging paragraph.

   __ It has full reference information for each entry.

   __ It is alphabetized by the last name of the authors.

__ You have checked your text carefully for typographical and spelling errors.

__ You have removed all first person references (such as I think, I believe, my opinion, I know)

__ You have removed all contractions (such as don't, it's, won't, can't)

__ You have removed all forms of linguistic bias.

   __ You have used gender neutral language.

   __ You have used culturally sensitive descriptions.

Criteria for Grading a Research Paper

Minimum Requirements for Receiving Credit for the Paper

__ Did the student do the paper as assigned?

__ Did the student do his/her own work—no plagiarism?

__ Did the student meet the deadline for the paper?

Point Assignment for the Evaluation Criteria

Excellent = 5 Good = 4 Adequate = 3 Inadequate = 2 Unacceptable = 1

An A paper will accumulate a range of points from 100 to 90.

A B paper will accumulate a range of points from 89 to 80.

A C paper will accumulate a range of points from 79 to 70.

A D paper will accumulate a range of points from 69 to 60.

An F paper will accumulate a range of points from 59 to 20.

Criteria of Evaluation

__ Format of the manuscript conforms to the instructor's criteria.

__ Manuscript is well organized and well written.

__ Complete and thorough description of the background or context of the research topic.

__ A clear, well-developed thesis statement.

__ Presents a unique or interesting perspective on the topic.

__ Logical development of student's argument.

__ Identifies important supporting evidence, arguments, and perspectives concerning research topic.

__ Identifies important evidence, arguments, and perspectives concerning research topic that does not support student's view.

__ Explains all evidence, arguments, and perspectives presented concerning research topic.

__ Critiques all evidence, arguments, and perspectives presented concerning research topic.

__ Analysis reflects thorough understanding of the topic.

__ Student addressed all issues raised in the analysis.

__ No apparent factual errors.

__ Very few spelling or grammatical errors.

__ Evidence, arguments, and ideas are well documented. If quotes are used, they are used correctly and sparingly.

__ Reference page is complete.

__ References and sources used were clearly relevant.

__ References and sources used were of high quality.

__ References and sources used exhibit depth and breadth.

__ References and sources used exhibit variety.

Storing Notes and References

The most common way of storing notes and references is on index cards. Cards are handy, but they are only useful if you can put a complete thought or summary of an argument on them. Try the following:

1. **Use 4" by 6" or 5" by 7" index cards.**
   - information is stored easier on them.
   - both are wide enough to punch holes in so that they can be put into a ring binder.
2. **On the reference card, put the full bibliographic information on the card.**
   - write the last name first.
   - write the library call number on the card for easy retrieval in case you must return to the source.
   - annotate it with at least one sentence about the purpose of the source and one sentence about the significance of the source.
   - keep the cards in alphabetical order.
3. **On the note cards put the following:**
   - put the author's name and page numbers in the left-hand corner.
   - put the subject in the right-hand corner.
   - write the summary, paraphrase, or quote on the card.
   - on the bottom line of the card, write a note to yourself about where this fits into your paper.

Example of a Reference Card

303.380973
L767c
1987

Lipset, Seymour Martin and William Schneider. 1987. <u>The confidence gap: Business, labor, and government in the public mind</u>. Rev. Ed. MD: Johns Hopkins University Press.

These authors conduct an extensive examination of influences on public confidence in business, labor, and government. They also present evidence that news coverage shapes people's attitudes about these important political actors as well as people's perspectives on political events. They conclude that people have lost confidence in big government, big business, and big labor because of negative coverage.

Example of a Note Card

Lipset and Schneider: 403–406   Evidence/P.0.

Media is the major source of political information. Studies show direct links between political cynicism and negative news reporting. "The special impact of television is that it delivers the news to a much larger and 'inadvertent' audience than was the case before television, when only a limited segment of the population chose to follow news about politics and government. When people read newspapers and magazines, they edit the information by skipping over articles about subjects they are not interested in. Television watchers, however, are exposed to everything." p. 405

(supports the argument that media is a strong influence on public attitudes)

Photocopies and Printouts of Information

Do not waste your time photocopying and printing all the sources you think you need to write the paper.
- Photocopy and print only what you believe is essential to your research.
- For Web site sources, print out the entire source—it may be gone the next time you try to access it.
- Write all bibliographic information on the photocopy or printout.
- For Web site sources, make sure that the full Web address is on the printout.
- For all sources, write the key words, search engines, indexes, or databases used to find the source of the copies
- Cut and paste essential data or critical information from the photocopy or printout onto an index card.
- Put material that is too large for an index card into a separate section in your folder entitled "photocopies and printouts." Summarize the material on an index card.

An Outline

Keep your scratch outline, topic outline, and sentence outline handy in your notebook as you write them for easy reference as you do your research.

- Keep all revisions of your thesis sentence.
- Add to the outlines as you continue your discovery of information and ideas.

A Project Journal/Scrapbook

In addition to your outlines, keep a journal of thoughts and ideas, tidbits of information gathered, names of good reference people, phone numbers of the library, and bits of data which do not quite fit into your project...yet!

- Be sure to date the journal entry.
- Be sure to fully identify the source of any information.

A Draft of the Paper

Keep a working draft in your folder at all times.

- Once you have the final copy, make a photocopy of it (or print another copy of the paper) and place it in the folder as well.
- Never destroy your draft before you have turned in the assignment and received a grade.
  - Instructors are becoming increasingly vigilant in the fight against plagiarism.
  - A draft can help document your efforts. See http://www.plagiarism.com.

CHAPTER 15

Assignments for Organizing
and Documenting
Achievements for Career
Development

Organizing and Documenting Achievements Using a Professional Portfolio

This chapter is dedicated to helping students organize and present themselves professionally. It contains formats and examples for organizing students' best works to use as examples of work for the job market. Students often complain that what they do in class is not related to what they want to do for a career. This is just not true. Every activity and every skill contributes to the value of that student in the job market.

Students will eventually need to compile a set of documents to show prospective employers. Compiling a portfolio is just like putting together a project folder. In fact, a portfolio is a project folder for a job search or for advanced training. It is meant to be self-contained. All addresses and relevant professional material should be placed in this folder. The materials in a professional folder provide a template for all communication with a prospective employer or graduate school admissions committee. Students should be able to compile documents and information necessary for applications, to just about anything, from this portfolio.

Professional Portfolio or Dossier

Many colleges and universities are introducing capstone or senior professional courses into their curriculums. Sometimes the purpose of these capstone courses is to polish students' skills, as well as prepare them for the job market or graduate school. Sometimes these capstone courses are part of an educational assessment program designed to examine the enrichment of students from their major areas of study.

Whatever the case, one of the important instruments for evaluating the quality of students' work and potential is through an examination of their personal writing portfolios. Artists, designers, architects, and other professionals keep portfolios of their best work for examination by prospective employers. A comprehensive file containing prepared work for each class is equally valuable for a political science student as a job marketing strategy, or to select items as evidence of the student's accomplishments to send along with graduate school applications.

Compiling a good portfolio requires students to practice almost all the techniques and skills described in this book. It requires data gathering, organization of materials to support a statement, analysis, problem-solving skills, and good writing skills for presenting or communicating to evaluators the degree and nature of the value added to the student's professional development through education. The materials in student portfolios provide material evidence that they are worth considering for advanced training or professional positions in an organization.

Students should be keeping a professional portfolio from the first day they attend classes in their college or university. In particular, they should keep a portfolio for both their major and minor areas of study. If the student uses personal computer word processing, it is best if the student stores the computer disks containing the files for each paper and for any personal reference information in the portfolio.

The portfolio should contain, at minimum, the following items separated by dividers with a scratch copy and a finished copy:

- CURRICULUM VITAE
- RESUME
- AUTOBIOGRAPHICAL ESSAY/OUTLINE
- COPY OF AN OFFICIAL TRANSCRIPT OF CLASSES
- LIST OF COURSES CATEGORIZED BY SUBFIELD
- REPRESENTATIVE COPIES OF WRITTEN WORK AND TESTS
- LIST OF PROSPECTIVE EMPLOYERS
- SAMPLE COVER LETTER
- COPIES OF LETTERS OF RECOMMENDATION OR INTRODUCTION

Compiling a Curriculum Vitae

A curriculum vitae is a professional document primarily used in academics. For the most part, the purpose of a curriculum vitae is to present, document, and communicate to an evaluator the scope, nature, and degree of the student's professional and academic training and accomplishments. It makes a first impression on an evaluator and often determines whether the student will be interviewed or accepted into a program.

The student should put as much time and thought into preparing the student's curriculum vitae as the student would put into any paper. The curriculum vitae contains information about the student's personal history, professional accomplishments, level of education achieved, and professional work experience which qualifies the student for a particular job or advanced training program. It should present the student's work in its best light.

The curriculum vitae must be concise, but not brief. It is similar to a resume but its focus is on academic achievements. There is no recommended length for a curriculum vitae. It must be presented in a professional and organized manner. There must no typographical errors, erasures, or any other marks on the document. If a curriculum vitae is typed on a word processor, it should be printed professionally on a laser printer on good high cloth content paper. The organization's or institution's address should be typed on a mailing label to be attached to a manila envelope. Do not fold the materials. The envelope should contain enough postage to get it to the organization.

Format for Curriculum Vitae Items

Curriculum vitae should include the following items where applicable and use the headings and subheadings in the order in which they are presented here:

Personal information:

- Name
- Present address
- Present status (senior, student assistant, etc.)

Education: List each institution attended, starting with the most recent to high school. For each entry:

- Name of university or college
- City, state, and country if not in the U.S.
- Major and minor or focus of the work
- Highest level achieved or degree granted
- Month and year degree awarded
- Beginning and ending month and year attended if no degree awarded

Publications: This includes any of the student's work that has been published. It is rare, except for journalism students, for undergraduate students to have publications. In the event that they do, it should be on their vitae. Even editorials in the school newspaper count as publications.

- List the full reference citation of your work. List the title of the manuscript first, the name of the publication, and then the date it was published.
- List these in descending order from the most recent to the first one published.
- If you have a publication that is pending, list it first, designating it as either pending or in review.

Professional Presentations: This includes any of the student's work that has been presented at a professional meeting. It is rare, except for students in Phi Sigma Alpha or other honors societies, for undergraduate students to have presented material professionally. In the event that they do, it should be on their vitae.

- List the title of the presentation first, your role (presenter or discussant), the name of the conference, the city, state, and country (if not in the U.S.) and then the dates of the conference.
- List these in descending order from the most recent to the first one presented.
- If you have a presentation that is upcoming, list it first, designating it as upcoming.

Professional Associations: List any political science, social science, or other professional or honors societies to which you belong.

- List the title of the association, your role (member, president, etc.), and dates of the membership.
- List these in descending order from the most recent to the first one joined.
- If you have an official appointment to an administrative position that is upcoming, list it first, designating the appointment dates.

Private Associations: You may, with caution, want to list private associations such as the Young Republicans, ACLU, NRA, NOW, Animal Defense League, etc., if you held official positions in them. List only those activities you feel enrich your profile. Be careful not to reveal any private activities that you do not wish to prejudice your file. Use the same format as that presented for professional associations.

Grants: List any grants which you received during your academic career.

- List the title of the grant and your role or award, the name of the granting institution, the location of the institution (city, state, and country, if not in the U.S.), and then the dates of the grant.
- List these in descending order from the most recent to the first one received.
- If you have a grant proposal outstanding or a grant that is upcoming, list it first, designating it as upcoming or pending.

Honors and Awards: List any scholarships, fellowships, citations of special recognition, honorable mentions in competitions, or nominations for awards.

- List the title of the honor or award, the purpose of the honor or award, your role (winner, nominee, etc.), the name of the source of the honor or award (the country, if not in the U.S.), and then the date the honor or award was given.
- List these in descending order from the most recent to the first one received.
- If you have an honor or award that is outstanding, do not list it unless you were nominated. Then be sure to designate it as a nomination until it is resolved.

Professional Experience: This is any work accomplished that is pertinent to political science. List all employment in political or social other organizations, research assistance provided to professors and other professionals, all volunteer work, and all consulting work.

- Specify your title first, such as student assistant or manager, the name of the organization or institution, the name of your supervisor, a brief one to two line annotation of what services you performed, and the dates of service.
- List these in order from the most recent to the first one worked.
- Be sure to use assertive words connoting activity, not passivity. Use words such as aiding, advising, consulting, managing, writing, assisting, preparing, and researching.

Areas of Study: List the subfield courses which best describe your preparation and training.

References: List three references each from professors, employers, and/or associates from the activities listed under professional activities.

- Put the referee's name first, the referee's association or institution and official title, the referee's full institutional or association address, and the referee's business telephone number.
- Be sure to ask for the referee's permission to use them as a reference. Ask them to write you a broadly framed letter of recommendation that you may keep on file at the University or College Placement Office (if there is one).
- Ask for a letter of recommendation shortly before or after you finish a course or

leave a job. Do not wait until you need a recommendation. You can always request another, more specific letter later. By getting letters on file, the referees can use them to refresh their memories about the accomplishments later.

- Some people will let you keep a copy on file in your portfolio. Ask permission to have a copy for your files.
- When requesting a second letter of recommendation from someone you have not seen in a while, be sure to provide them with a copy of the old letter, if have written one before.

CAITLIN MAGGIE SCHMIDT
100 Ezee Street
Somwherin, Illinois 62345
(393) 733-2020

EDUCATION:

1987–1991	Southern Illinois University, Carbondale, IL. B.A. Summa Cum Laude. January 1991.
	Major in Political Science, minor in Economics.
	Emphasis on policy, interest groups, and Congress.
1986–1987	Longway Community College, Frome Aniwher, IL. General Studies.
1984–1986	Podunke High School, Podunke, IL. Graduated with honors.

PUBLICATIONS:

"Students are Key to Environmental Policy Change," *Community News* (April 1, 1990).

PAPERS:

"Student Participation in Government," Illinois Political Science Association Annual Meeting, Springfield, IL, August 1990.

PROFESSIONAL ACTIVITIES:

Reviewed *Expository Writing in Political Science* by Diane Schmidt for HarperCollins Publishers, January 1990.

PROFESSIONAL ASSOCIATION AND SOCIETY MEMBERSHIP:

Illinois Political Science Association

Phi Kappa Phi (National Honors Society)

Pi Sigma Alpha (Political Science Honors Society)

GRANTS:

Political Student Activities Grant, Undergraduate Student Activities Board, American Student Activities Association, "Mobilizing and Activating Student Participation in Government," January 1990.

HONORS AND AWARDS:

Nominated for the Best Student Paper Award for paper delivered at the 1990 Annual Meeting of the Illinois Political Science Association.

Illinois College Newspaper Award 1990

Student Activities Award 1989, 1990

Who's Who Among Women in American College and University Students. 1989.

EXPERIENCE:

Research Assistant to Ms. Boryn Phree, Clean and Healthy Agency, Carbondale, Illinois (1991–present).

Student Assistant to Dr. Gaia Green, Southern Illinois University. Survival of Humanity. (1990–91).

Student Worker for Mr. Chip Bites, Southern Illinois University, Faner Computing Lab (1988–1990).

Sierra Club, Local Chapter Vice President, Marion, Illinois (1990–91).

AREAS OF STUDY:

Major	*Minor*
American Government	Environmental Policy
Interest Groups	Economic Regulation
Legislative Process	Regulation/Public Administration

REFERENCES:

Gaia Green, Southern Illinois University, Political Science Department, Carbondale, Illinois 62901, (618) 628-1234. (Senior Thesis Director)

Boryn Phree, Clean and Healthy Agency, 1289 Main St., Carbondale, Illinois, 62901, (618) 628-6781

Chip Bites, Faner Computing Lab, Southern Illinois University,(1988–1990), (618) 628-1678.

Gud D. Tooshus, Southern Illinois University, Political Science Department, Carbondale, Illinois 62901, 618-628-2340.

What to Do with Official Transcripts

Obtain an official copy of your transcripts from each school you attended. Keep an updated copy in your files at all times. Annotate each entry.

1. If not provided, write the names of the courses next to the course identification and the names of the instructor who taught the course.
   - This will allow you to remember what courses you took and who taught them to you.
   - Use this as a beginning of your professional network of associations.
2. For each course, list the skills required and reason for the grade you received.
   - Be honest with yourself.
   - For good grades, identify your best work and why it was good. For poor grades, identify what you did wrong or could not do well.
   - List any extenuating circumstances which contributed to the poor performance such as family crisis, accident, illness, etc.
   - This is the beginning of an accounting of your professional assets and liabilities.

Constructing a List of Coursework

Categorize your university or college coursework by subfields and skills that adequately represent your training and preparation. Be sure to include any related courses in other disciplines and courses that provided you with technical training of any kind.

1. List the courses that support the areas of interest specified above.
2. List the courses that required word processing, data management, or computing skills.
3. List the name of the courses and professors' name, and the name of the institution if you attended more than one.
4. End the page with the following statement:

Official Transcripts Available Upon Request.

Example of an Abridged List of Coursework

CAITLIN SCHMIDT

PROFESSIONAL COURSEWORK

American Politics

Institutions – Professor Gud D. Tooshus
Pluralism and Its Critics – Mobe I. Lization
Bureaucratic Politics – Professor Ess. O. Pea

Public Policy/Political Economy

Public Policy – Dr. Menie Thengs
Politics of Environmental Policy – Professor Gaia Green
Survival of Humanity – Professor Gaia Green

Methods

Micro Computing – P.C. Mac*
Introduction to Mainframe Computing – Aski Epsidik

*All coursework completed at Southern Illinois University except where indicated.

Official Transcripts Available Upon Request.

Preparing a Resume

The purpose of a resume is to present to a potential employer, in as concise a form as possible, information about students' personal history, education, and work experience which qualifies them for a particular job. A well-prepared, professional looking resume is essential for anyone seeking employment, because it makes a first impression on an employer which determines whether they will be interviewed. Students should put as much time and thought into preparing their resumes as they would any other writing assignment.

The resume must be concise. In general, the recommended length for a resume is one page. A resume is a professional document and must be presented in a professional manner. There must no typographical errors, erasures, or any other marks on the document. If the resume is typed on a word processor, it should be printed professionally on a laser printer on good high-cloth content paper. The organization's or institution's address should be typed on a mailing label or the envelope itself. The envelope should contain enough postage to get the materials to the organization.

Resume Items

Like any well-written document, a resume can be divided into parts. A resume should contain the items as they are listed below. All of these items can be found in your curriculum vitae, and list of courses, except the statement of your employment goals. This statement may come from your autobiographical essay.

Personal Information:

- List your full name and place it in a bold font with a 16–24 point type
- Address, and telephone number of your current and permanent address (if they are different)
- Fax, email, and/or Web page addresses if you have them

Employment Goals:

- This is optional
- At the beginning of your resume, state the specific position for which you are applying
- State how it relates to your career goals

Education:

- List institutions you attended beginning with the most recent where you received a degree
- Include dates, institutions, cities, and degrees earned
- Include major, minors, certificates, and/or licensing
- Include your GPA if it is fairly high
- List fluency in a foreign language
- List computer or technical skills
- List relevant coursework and class projects only if they highlight important skills and training

Employment History:

- List all the positions you have held, beginning with the most recent, which qualify you for the job being offered
- List any internships or volunteer work that are related to your career field
- List your job title first, then the employer's name, city, and date
- Describe your experience, duties, and accomplishments briefly and in an assertive, active voice using words such as *conducted, planned, designed, administered, implemented, analyzed, organized, trained,* and *completed* to describe each activity

Personal Background Information: In this section, list any other information that you want the potential employer to know about. Be careful that you do not provide any material that may prejudice your file. Employers may not legally ask your age, gender, or race. Depending on the position and the aggressiveness of the organization in pursuing equal opportunity or affirmative action goals, you may want to list any membership in an organization that suggests your demographic characteristics or ideological perspective.

- List any honors, scholarships, or prizes you won for work you performed, which you have received
- List activities you engaged in such as clubs, fraternities/sororities, professional associations, etc.
- List your title first, then what you won

References:

- Do not list references on your resume
- Have a list of them with names, addresses, and telephone numbers/email/fax numbers at your interview in case someone wants to see them

Example of a Resume

Caitlin Schmidt
100 Ezee Street
Somwherin, Illinois 62345
(393) 733-2020

OBJECTIVE: Research analyst for a midsize consulting firm with a special emphasis on energy and environmental policy.

EDUCATION: Southern Illinois University, Carbondale, IL.
- B.A. *Summa Cum Laude*. January 1991. GPA 3.95.
- Major in Political Science, minor in Economics.
- Emphasis on policy, interest groups, and Congress.

Longway Community College, Frome Aniwher, IL. 1986–1988
- Information Management.

Computer Literacy: Microsoft Word, Excel, SPSS, LexisNexis, and Internet

RELEVANT EXPERIENCE: **Research Assistant**: For Ms. Boryn Phree, Clean and Healthy Agency, Carbondale, Illinois (1991–present). Researched sources and co-authored grants. Coordinated and trained volunteers.

Student Assistant: For Dr. Gaia Green, Southern Illinois University. Survival of Humanity. (1990–91). Assisted in developing and administering coursework. Graded and recorded course assignments.

Computing Assistant: For Mr. Chip Bites, Southern Illinois University, Faner Computing Lab (1988–1990). Assisted in developing services for computing facilities clientele. Assisted with developing educational programs and modification of materials for clientele.

PERSONAL INFORMATION: **Vice President**, Sierra Club, Local Chapter, Marion, Illinois, 1990–1991

Nominated, Best Student Paper Award for paper delivered at the 1990 Annual Meeting of the Illinois Political Science Association, 1990

Recipient, Illinois College Newspaper Award 1990

Recipient, Student Activities Award 1989, 1990

Recipient, Who's Who Among Women in American College and University Students. 1989.

References available upon request.

Writing a Cover Letter

In addition to the information contained on a resume page or curriculum vitae, students should include a cover letter written specifically to the potential employer.

- The cover letter may be used to reinforce the resume or curriculum information, but not to elaborate on it.
- Use the cover letter to induce support for your application by accentuating your accomplishments and skills as they relate to the position you are seeking or program you wish to enter.
- Ask for clarification when the job descriptions or program descriptions are vague or ambiguous.
- The cover letter should be brief and less formal in tone than the resume or curriculum vitae.

Format for the Cover Letter

- Write this like an executive summary.
- Use standard or block format.
- Single space your letter and double space between paragraphs.
- Keep the paragraphs at about 4–5 sentences at the most and 3 sentences at the least.
- Use a laser printer and bond paper.
- Tailor the letter to the position—show how your experiences and qualifications match the job duties and company goals.
- PROOFREAD!

Cover Letter Contents

Addressing the Letter

- Put your name and address first.
- Space down two lines and add the date.
- Space down two lines and put the company address, beginning with the person's name who is responsible for personnel decisions.
- Space down two lines and put the salutation in the form of Dear Mr. or Ms. It is your responsibility to find out the name of the person in charge of hiring. If you cannot find out the name of that person, then address it to Dear Personnel Director.

First Paragraph

- Open the paragraph with a grabber. If you know someone or were recommended by someone who works at the place you are applying or is known to the personnel director, drop the name in the first line.
- State your career objective and/or relevant training and experience.
- Mention how you know about the company, especially any research you did to find out about the company—relate that research to why you think your qualifications fit

the company goals/image.

- Refer to the content of the ad you are answering and relate your skills and qualifications to each item in the ad.
- State how you can help the company achieve its goals and mission.

Next Paragraphs

- Develop your approach taken in the first paragraph.
- List the skills and qualifications you have that illustrate your strong points.
- It is your job to match the job with your skills—use active words.
- Use bullets to highlight exactly how you fulfill the requirements of the ad.

Closing Paragraph

- Encourage action—ask for an interview or say you will call for an appointment.
- Restate how well you fit the job description.
- Thank the person for their time.

Sign Off

- End the letter with the word *Sincerely*.
- Space down four spaces.
- Put your name—be sure to sign the letter!

Example of a Cover Letter

April 1, 1994

Ms. Caitlin Schmidt
100 Ezee Street
Somwherin, IL 62345

Ms. Cleen Itup
Personal Director
Environmental Lobbyist Inc.
1 Millyondoller Place
Washington, DC, 20001

Dear Ms. Itup,

Please accept my application for the research analyst position you advertised in the spring issue of the Sierra Club newsletter. The position you listed sounds interesting to me because of my background in environmental politics. I have recently graduated with a bachelor's degree in Political Science and am looking for a research position in a consulting firm specializing in energy and environmental problems.

Your ad states that applicants must have public relations and research skills. I am especially qualified for this position.

- I have been active for many years in local environmental movements.
- I have written several manuscripts, one of which was published, on mobilizing young people for environmental policy change.
- I have been working as a research assistant for a local environmental agency devoted to cleaning and preserving the community parks and natural areas.

If you would like to see a copy of my work on environmental policy, please feel free to contact me at (393) 733-2020. I also have letters of reference on file in the Southern Illinois University Placement Office. I look forward to hearing from you in the future.

Sincerely,

Caitlin Schmidt

Autobiographical Essay/Outline

Students should write a brief, one page autobiographical essay describing and highlighting their personal and professional achievements. This amounts to a "brag sheet" where students systematically describe how they developed their strengths and overcame their weaknesses. Why is this necessary? Employers and graduate school admission committees often evaluate the student based on a verbal and/or personal statement. This statement must be clear and concise; it must leave the evaluator with a positive image of the student as a potential employee or applicant. Here are a few pointers:

1. **Use a personal computer word processing program to write the essay. Then revise the essay periodically. Keep the disk in your portfolio.**
   - Use a topic or sentence outline to structure your essay.
   - Keep the outline and the essay.
   - Use the outline to prepare for a personal interview.
   - Use the essay as a way to prepare a cover letter or personal statement on an application, where required.

2. **Basically, the form for an autobiographical sketch is similar to an argument. It should focus on a concise characterization of your credentials, supported by examples that accent your positive, marketable assets and explain or minimize your academic, professional, or personal liabilities**

3. **The essay should have an introduction, body, and conclusion which all achieve the final goal of creating a positive image of your skills and preparation. In particular, emphasize your problem solving, writing, research, and technical skills. Accentuate, but do not exaggerate or distort your achievements or liabilities.**

4. **Use concise examples of how you maintained and improved upon your previous accomplishments and overcame obstacles. Use whatever information available that could give a prospective employer or graduate school a reason to accept your application over others. Here are some examples:**
   - You maintained a high grade-point average while working two jobs.
   - How, despite your earlier problems in mathematics, you were able to master simple regression in your political methods course.

5. **This essay will be central to any competitive activities you choose to address. When you must prepare a personal statement for a grant, scholarship, fellowship applications, or any other competitive activity (including job hunting), revise your outline and essay examples and statement of goals to accent where your credentials and goals converge with those outlined in each job or grant description. Your essay will be a skeleton on which you will flesh out how your credentials fit with the evaluators' goals and purposes.**

Example of an Autobiographical Essay

Cleaning up the environment has been a passion for me since I was very young. My mother used to sing me to sleep with Pete Seeger's "The Garden Song" and Woody Guthrie's "This Land Is Your Land." As a youth, I worked with local scouting groups to clean up parks and natural areas. I felt a great sense of satisfaction after working and contributing to a safer, cleaner environment. As a college student, I pursued a political science degree and specialized in environmental policy because I felt that there was no substitute for a disciplined study of the problems and constraints involved in environmental protection.

The study of political science was interesting to me because of my background in environmental politics. I have been active for many years in local environmental movements and have written several manuscripts, one of which was published, on mobilizing young people for environmental policy change. In addition, I have been working as a research assistant for a local environmental agency devoted to cleaning and preserving the community parks and natural areas.

The courses I took in college have prepared me for doing research in regulatory policy and politics. I chose courses that would help me develop research and writing skills. Although my experience in my English composition course was not very rewarding, I have worked to maintain straight A's in my political science courses. Most of my political science courses required research papers in them, so I was able to improve and practice my research and writing skills. Many of the class papers I wrote received high grades.

Although I would prefer to work in the environmental policy field, I am trained to do research in a variety of areas. I believe that I can best use my problem solving, writing, and technical skills by working in a consulting firm. I have taken courses in data processing and management and would like to work with data. While my coursework in mathematics was not rewarding for me, I was intrigued with my computing courses. With some practice, I believe I could become quite good with computers.

In sum, although my life-long interests have revolved around environmental politics, I am dedicated to general policy research. I have focused my university training on acquiring problem solving, writing, and technical skills. My goal is to obtain a position in a consulting firm and to pursue a career as a research analyst.

Copies of Written Work

Students should include copies of the best work they have produced during their academic training and professional activities in their dossier. These copies should be kept in two forms. A graded or evaluated copy should be kept with a clean, unmarked copy of the work. If it was produced with word processing, the disk should be kept with the item.

1. **If using a word processor, you should keep a disk with the manuscripts files on them, with, or near the work. Revise handwritten material and type them into a file as well.**
2. **If the paper was good, but not near perfect, use the instructor's comments to correct the problems.**
3. **Then rank order your papers according to skill level and quality of writing.**
4. **Use these unmarked copies of papers as evidence of your skills and preparation.**
5. **Keep copies of any achievement scores from any standardized tests taken such as the LSAT, SAT, and GRE.**

List of Prospective Employers

Students should create an open-ended list of employers or graduate schools of the people they admire. These people could be school faculty, authors, or other professionals they were influenced by or impressed by their skills or credentials. The institutions or entities where these people work should be the first places they send applications.

1. **Use your research skills to locate the mission statements, either implied or expressed, of institutions or entities. Intellectually, and in terms of matching your skills with the job market or graduate school, these places are the student's best opportunities for receiving a sympathetic review of your application.**
2. **If you know any one of these people personally:**
   - Ask for a letter of recommendation or a letter of introduction that you can keep on file. A letter of introduction need not be confidential and is often a good way of networking.
   - Ask their advice about where to apply.

Methods of Submitting Resumes or Vitae

There are a variety of ways to submit resumes and vitas for consideration.

Paper Submission

- Always include a cover letter that is personalized to the person in charge of hiring. If necessary, call the organization and ask for the name of the person. Never send a "To whom it may concern" letter. Those kinds of letters usually end up in the trash along with the resume/vitae.

- In the first line of the resume, specify position for which you are applying.
- Format the document using bold and all capitals for major headings, bold and capitals of the first letter of each word for secondary headings, and italics for third level headings.
- Laser print the document on high quality paper. Avoid colors other than white or light beige, tan, or grey.
- Send it in a manila envelope. Do not fold the cover letter or resume/vitae.

Email Submission as an Attachment

- Use the attachment function for your email to attach your resume to an email message.
- If the organization specifies a word processing program, such as MSWORD, then attach the file in the specified program.
- If the organization does specify a preferred word processing program, then the file will need to be attached as a text file. To create a text file, simply save the resume/vitae file with the extension .txt. That will remove all the formatting and recreate a machine readable file. Once it is saved as a text file, open the file and move all the headings to the left-hand side of the page. Line up every item so that it is flush with the left side of the page. Put major heading in all capital letters. Double space between major items. Do not add any other formatting.

Email Submission Inserted in the Message or Posted to an Internet Site

- Many organizations prefer a resume/vitae that is imbedded in the email message or have Internet sites where applicants can post their materials. To do this, the file must be a text file.
- To create a text file, simply save the resume/vitae file with the extension .txt. That will remove all the formatting and recreate a machine readable file. Once it is saved as a text file, open the file and move all the headings to the left-hand side of the page. Line up every item so that it is flush with the left side of the page. Put major headings in all capital letters. Double space between major items. Do not add any other formatting.
- Select the entire document.
- Paste the document into the email message or paste the document to the Internet site.
- For email submissions, be sure to identify the job listing or position in the message line.

Scannable Submissions

- Some organizations require resumes/vitas that are machine readable by scanners. While some scanners are able to maintain a fairly high accuracy rate, some still have trouble interpreting script, italics, or variable size fonts. Keep the document simple.
- Use one font size and do not vary the font. The font size for the document should be

at least 12 point and use a common font such as Ariel, Times Roman, or Courier.

- The document may be formatted using a minimum of bold font and capital letters to separate the categories.
- Keep sentences short—usually one line if possible.
- The text should be aligned to the left-hand side of the page.
- The first line should include keywords related to the job title, skills, and abilities related to the job listing.

Resource Manuals and On-Line Help for Career Management and Organization

Ask the headhunter: The insider's edge on job search and hiring.
   http://www.asktheheadhunter.com.

Careerbuilder.com. http://www.careerbuilder.com.

Careers and the study of political science: A guide for undergraduates. 2001. 6th ed.
   Washington, DC: American Political Science Association.

Corcodilos, Nick. 1997. *Ask the headhunter: Reinventing the interview to win the job.*
   NY: Penguin/Plume.

Earning a Ph.D. in political science. 1999. Rev. ed. Washington, DC: American Political
   Science Association.

Jobstar central: Job search guide. http://www.jobstar.org.

Jobweb: Your online complement to the job choices magazine series. http://www.jobweb.com.

Monster: Career advice. http://content.monster.com.

Reed, Jean. 2002. *Resumes that get jobs, 10th ed.* New York: Arco Publishing.

Wetfeet: Helping you make smarter career decisions. http://www.wetfeet.com.

What you need to know about job searching: Technical. http://jobsearchtech.about.com.

APPENDICES

Glossary

Text Acknowledgments

References

Glossary

Abridged List of Political Science Terms for Writing and Talking Politics

The following is a list of political science terms that are common to most classes. While there are plenty of terms not represented here, those that are listed represent the discourse found in political discussions from the newspaper to cocktail parties to campaign literature.

Abstract topics: are those involving values, problems, or a process.

Accountability: answering for one's actions.

Ad hominem: personalizing the issue by concentrating on the real or imagined negative characteristics of those who hold different or opposing views.

Affirmative Action: removal of artificial barriers to employment for women and minorities.

Agenda: a list of goals to achieve rank ordered by preference and importance. The presidential agenda often reflects the party platform.

Amendment: change a prior law or bill by adding to it.

Amicus curiae brief: a brief filed by a third party to inform the court.

Analysis assignments: these assignments usually ask students to examine the relationships between the parts of a political document or some political events. Typically, these assignments require the student to provide a perspective or reasoned opinion about the significance of an event or a document. Students may be required to assert and defend an opinion about what are the most important features in the constitution.

Analyze: give main divisions or elements.

Anarchism: belief that government is corrupt and should be abolished.

Antifederalists: those against the new constitution in 1780s who wanted strong states rights and weak central government.

Appeal: request to higher body for a review of lower body's decision.

Apportionment: a system that determines how legislative seats are allotted to states.

Appropriation: funding for programs and policies.

Argumentation assignments: these assignments often require the student to prove or debate a point. Typically, these assignments ask for normative assertions followed up with evidence and examples to support these assertions. For instance, instructors may ask students to provide an argument supporting (or not) automatic voter registration, random drug testing, or a constitutional amendment protecting the flag.

Aristocracy: a system of government where power to rule is held by a few people based on wealth or social factors.

Authoritarianism: rule by an individual whose power derives from the ability to coerce compliance.

Authority: power to compel others to obey.

Beliefs: These each are a state of mind related to a conviction or unconscious trust in a statement which is not fact-based or based on objective evidence. They are often associated with faith or custom. Natural rights, liberty, Justice, freedom, and self-sufficiency are examples of beliefs. Like facts, they cannot be disproved and are not subject to argument.

Bicameralism: a two-chambered legislature.

Brief: a written statement by an attorney to a party in a court case summarizing the facts and issues in the case.

Bureaucracy: an administrative organization.

Calendar: legislative agenda.

Capitalism: an economic system where supply and demand determine the quantity produced and price of a good.

Caucus: a closed meeting by party officials.

Cause and effect assignments: these assignments typically require the student to speculate about the reasons some political event has occurred. For example, students may be asked why people vote, why do members of Congress worry about their images, what caused the civil war, or why some people are disillusioned with government.

Censure: method of discipline in legislatures.

Census: a method of taking an inventory of the population, done every ten years in the U.S.

Centralization: the concept of placing authority and power of government at the national level.

Checks and balances: a mechanism to grant a limited set of powers to each branch of government over the other.

Civil rights: rights of citizenship that guarantees non-discrimination by government.

Civil servants: government employees, bureaucrats.

Classification assignments: these assignments usually ask the student to identify the pattern or system of classification such as types of voters, types of political systems, or types of committees in congress.

Classify: arrange into main divisions.

Closed primary: election to select party nominee that is open only to registered party members.

Cloture: a three-fifths vote by the Senate to end a filibuster or debate.

Coalition: a group of people or a set of groups with different interests working together for a common cause. Unions and education groups work together for more education funding from government.

Coattail effect: the effect of one candidate's popularity on other candidates of the party.

Collectivism: community centered rather than individual centered perspective.

Commerce clause: gave Congress the power to regulate commerce in Article I, Section 8.

Communism: an economic theory where the ownership of the means of production is held and shared equally by the people.

Compare: point out the likenesses.

Comparison or contrast assignments: these assignments usually ask the student to identify the differences and similarities between political roles, political systems, or political events.

Concepts: things that are felt, acknowledged such as dilemmas, processes, values, beliefs, principles, ideologies, and theories.

Conclusions: are assertions made by the author concerning the relationship between the hypothesis and the evidence.

Concurrent powers: power held by both national and state governments.

Confederacy: a system of government where states delegate power to the national government.

Conflict: a disagreement between opposing parties. Group conflict results from one set of people opposing the activities of another.

Consciousness: a feeling among people that they share something or have something in common. The war protests of the 1960s had the effect of raising people's consciousness about the undesirability of the war.

Consensus: a general agreement among a group of people. There is a consensus among citizens that voting is good.

Conservatives: in the U.S., people who prefer limited government in economic affairs but not necessarily social affairs. Outside the U.S., those who believe in a hierarchically ordered society.

Constituent: a citizen in a public official's area of authority.

Constitutionalism: the notion that government should be limited and its authority is derived through the consent of the governed, often with a written contract or constitution.

Constraint: a barrier, something that prevents some action. The fluctuations of the business cycle acts as a constraint for addressing problems of unemployment.

Contrast: point out the differences.

Criticize: give your perspective on good and bad features.

Deductive reasoning: applying generalizations or conclusions that are accepted as true to slightly different but similar situations or issues.

Definition assignments: these assignments usually ask the student to define a political concept, term, or phrases such as democracy, socialism, or capitalism. Students must provide examples of distinguishing features and differentiate the topic from others in its functional class.

Demagogue: a leader who appeals to the prejudices of others to gain popularity.

Democracy: theory of government in which the people hold power to rule.

Describe: name the features in chronological order.

Dilemmas: are undesirable situations or problems that seem to be difficult to resolve. They are often associated with unwanted and unsatisfactory conditions. They can also be related to a difficulty in achieving some preferred outcome. Political apathy, political intolerance, providing for social welfare during a recession, providing for cleaner air without devastating the coal industry, and reconciling individual liberties with the public good are examples of dilemmas.

Discuss: examine in detail.

Disincentive: an inducement not to perform some action. Policy makers place taxes on activities that are undesirable.

Divine right: the belief that power to rule is granted by a Supreme Being.

Due process: fair and equal treatment in government processes.

Efficacy: a feeling of usefulness, of purpose, of empowerment. People who vote because they believe it will change policy have a sense of political efficacy.

Electoral College: electors who meet to determine the president and vice-presidential elections.

Elite theory: a belief that power should and is controlled by a small number of people.

Equity: relating to being equal but not necessarily identical. Sometimes related to fairness and compensation. As long as the Supreme Court accepted that segregation did not deny blacks equity, it was upheld.

Evaluate: give your perspective on the value or validity.

Events: these are events that led to political outcomes or consequences or are political outcomes. The Kent State Massacre, political assassinations, campaigns, and the Nixon resignation are examples of concrete topics.

Evidence: is data. There are two kinds of data. See quantitative and qualitative evidence.

Examples: are specific references or instances of the point being made and are typically referred to as anecdotal evidence. The strength of anecdotal evidence is found in its generalizability and representativeness.

Expert opinions: are judgments made by authorities based on their experience with evidence and assessment of the facts. When facts are unavailable, expert opinions are the next strongest evidence a writer can supply to support an argument. Expert opinions and facts are the very strongest kinds of evidence a writer can use.

Explain: make clear, give reasons for.

Faction: a club, a smaller group within a group of people working for benefits for the few and not the many. The conservative faction of the Republican Party has pushed for anti-abortion legislation as part of the party platform.

Facts: are statements that can be verified. They are the strongest proof or evidence a writer can supply to support an assertion. They are also the most difficult kind of evidence to obtain.

False analogy: assuming that things that are alike in one respect are alike in other respects.

False dilemma: stating that a complex question has only two answers that are both good, both bad, or one good and one bad.

Fascism: a nationalistic, totalitarian system where power is vested in a dictator.

Federal: a system of government where power is divided between state and national governments.

Filibuster: unlimited debate in the Senate.

Fragmentation of powers: a division of powers within government to achieve the goal of limited government; implemented in the U.S. by federalism, separation of powers, and checks and balances.

Gerrymandering: redrawing district lines so that they favor a particular party, race, or ethnicity.

Grand jury: citizens selected to hear evidence to determine if charges should be issued.

Grants-in-aid: grants of money given to state and local governments to implement national goals.

Habeas corpus: a court order to inform a person in custody of the reason for detention.

Hasty generalizations: a generalization that is based on very little evidence or which overstates.

Hypothesis: is a generalization that can be tested.

Ideologies: each has an integrated body of ideas, values, beliefs, and aspirations that constitute a socio-political program. They are associated with a desire, a need, a moral obligation, or a utopian vision. The ideas, beliefs, or values need not be socially acceptable; all that is needed is that the ideas, beliefs, and values are linked coherently. Liberalism, Conservatism, anarchism, authoritarianism, pacifism, imperialism, Marxism, fascism, Nazism, Libertarianism, nationalism are examples of ideologies.

Illustrate: give one or more examples of.

Impeachment: the first part of a process by which an official can be removed from office; in the U.S., it is done by the House of Representatives. Once impeachment is voted, the Senate then conducts a trial to remove the official from office.

Implied powers: powers of the government that are implied by other stated powers.

Incentive: an inducement to perform some action. Policy makers provide subsidies for activities that are desirable.

Incrementalist: a cautious, step-by-step movement toward a direction or change. The American social system is incrementalist because change occurs very slowly.

Incumbent: an official in office.

Independent: no party affiliation.

Indictment: an accusation charging a person with a crime.

Individualism: individual-centered rather than community-centered perspective.

Inductive reasoning: generalizing from observations or attributing a cause to a set of observed circumstances.

Inference: a conclusion based on evidence. This is based on inductive reasoning.

Inherent powers: powers not specified.

Initiative: a proposal for legislation submitted by members of the public to the public.

Institution: these are any body that engages in routinized interaction. Affiliations, association, alliances, and political organizations such as Congress, bureaucracies, political parties, interest groups, and even families are institutions.

Institutionalize: some behavior or activity that has become part of an institution, part of a pattern of behavior.

Interest group: a set of individuals with shared interests that is organized to influence policy.

Interpret: give the significance.

Iron triangle: the symbiotic relationship between bureaucracy, congressional committees, and clientele.

Justify: defend, show to be right.

Knowledge: is what we have learned from political inquiry. The true goal of all political inquiry is to contribute to a universal body of knowledge. As scholars, we are obliged to learn, to contribute to this body of knowledge.

Laissez-faire: "hands off" the economy; a belief that government should not interfere in economic affairs.

Left wing: change-oriented outlook favoring policies that help the masses.

Legitimacy: a belief that something is right, correct, and proper to do. It does not mean legal. Some laws like the 55 mile an hour speed limit are routinely ignored because they lack legitimacy among those who like to drive fast cars; perceived right to make binding decisions.

Libel: discrediting someone's reputation in writing.

Liberals: in the U.S., people who prefer limited government in social affairs but not necessarily economic affairs. Outside the U.S., those who believe limited government in both economic and social affairs.

Libertarians: a belief in minimal government intervention in citizen's lives.

Linkage: connecting one concept or entity with another. Political parties and interest groups provide different kinds of linkages between people and government.

Lobbyists: people, usually hired, to influence public institutions for the benefit of their group or clients.

Logrolling: reciprocity, vote trading between decision makers.

Majoritarian: of the majority, used in context with majoritarian principles. The Bill of Rights was adopted to prevent the majoritarian ideas of what is politically correct from infringing on minority rights granted in the constitution.

Majority rule: majority decisions win.

Mean: an average.

Monarchy: a political system where the power to rule is granted by divine right.

Natural Law: a concept that human behavior is governed by laws of nature.

Naturalization: a process of becoming a citizen in a land other than that of one's birth.

Nepotism: providing political favors to family members.

New Left: a 1960s liberal movement spawned in the U.S. promoting civil rights and social Justice.

New Right: a conservative movement with an evangelical and intolerant perspective promoting traditional moral virtues.

Non sequitur: when two ideas are presented with no logical connection.

Norm: an expected behavior or pattern of behavior. Specialization in subject areas related to a committee assignment is a norm in Congress.

Objects: things that can be seen physically such as players, institutions, events, and policies.

Oligarchy: a political system where power is concentrated in the hands of a few, elite individuals.

Open primary: an election for selecting a party candidate where the voters do not have to disclose their party identification or membership but may only vote in one primary.

Opinions: are judgments based on facts. A thesis sentence of an argument is an opinion. Opinions are testable and arguable because they are viewpoints arrived at through the examination of facts and evidence. Opinions are not arguments—arguments with supporting evidence are used to support opinions.

Oversimplification: stating that one event caused another when there is either no relationship or where other causes exist.

Patronage: providing a job or government benefits in return for political favors or support.

Platform: a party's agenda.

Players: these are people who have been politically important in the past or the present. Presidents, members of congress, interest group leaders, bureaucrats, judges, and are examples of political players.

Pluralism: bargaining among groups to influence political decisions. Pluralism describes group conflict in the political arena.

Plurality: the most, not but not a majority, of the votes.

Pocket veto: a way to veto a bill by not signing it within ten days following the end of a legislative session.

Police power: power to establish order.

Policies: these are or can be any decision made by any public official in any branch of government which has the force of law. Policies also include custom as well as non-decisions on problems. Congressional legislation, bureaucratic regulations, presidential orders, judicial decisions, or common law are policies.

Political action committees (PACs): a legal entity designed to legally provide money to campaigns.

Political correctness: is a term used to denote the socially accepted phrasing or perspective on an issue.

Political machine: a well-connected, widely networked party organization

Political party: an organization explicitly designed to get their candidate elected to office.

Poll: survey of opinions.

Poll sample: a subset of the population.

Populism: a political philosophy promoting the interests of lower income citizens over the interests of the upper income classes.

Pork barrel legislation: a bill that promotes the interests of a particular subset of a legislator's constituency.

Post hoc fallacy: jumping to the conclusion that event A caused event B just because event A occurred earlier.

Precedent: an earlier decision used to structure a present decision. Judges use precedents to decide current cases.

Prejudices: are opinions that have been formed on insufficient or unexamined evidence. They are often thoughtless oversimplifications and typically reflect a narrow-minded view of the world. They are testable and easily refutable by the presentation of facts and evidence.

Primary election: an election within the party to determine which candidate will be the party's candidate in the general election.

Principles: these are doctrines or codes of conduct that are usually held in high esteem. Self-determination, limited government, constitutionalism, rule of law, and legitimacy are examples of principles.

Problems: are concepts or ideas that connote undesirability. They are associated with unwanted and unsatisfactory conditions. Political apathy or racism are two examples of abstract topics.

Process assignments: these assignments usually ask the student to describe how some political phenomena relate functionally to other political phenomena. For example, students may be asked to describe how media influence voting behavior or how decisions are made in committees.

Processes: refers to observable patterns of political behavior in people and groups. They are associated with procedures and mechanisms for using, acquiring and distributing political power. The methods and structure of congressional, judicial, and bureaucratic decision-making are examples of processes. Democracy, Federalism, Confederation, oligarchy, monarchy, feudalism, socialism, communism are all different processes for organizing government.

Promulgate: to make known to everyone. Laws must be promulgated so that everyone has the opportunity to know them.

Qualitative evidence: subjective or authoritative data usually from interviews, firsthand observations, inference, or expert opinions.

Quantitative evidence: objective or numerical data usually from a survey, poll, tests, or experiments.

Quorum: minimum number of members to conduct legislative business.

Ratification: a process by which states decide to accept or reject an amendment to the constitution.

Reactionary: a person who wishes to return to a previous status quo in response to progressive change.

Referendum: a procedure through which legislatures submit laws or amendments to the voters for approval.

Republic: a form of government where power resides in the people who elect agents to represent them in decision-making.

Reserved powers: powers delegated expressly to state governments.

Review: examine on a broad scale.

Right wing: a conservative, reactionary outlook favoring policies that favor the promotion of capitalism, the military, and cultural conservatism.

Saliency: something that is important with connotations of being immediate, pertinent, something that is of acute interest. Media coverage of political protests heighten the saliency of the events; this often causes the right to protest to become a salient issue.

Separation of powers: dividing powers between branches of government.

Single-member district: legislators represent only one distinct set of constituents determined through apportionment of legislative seats.

Slander: a verbal disparagement against someone's character.

Socialism: in practice, system of government where the government owns the means of production and provides for the public welfare.

Sovereignty: government is supreme in power, rank, and authority and is free from external interference.

Split ticket: voting for candidates in different parties for different offices.

Spoils system: providing benefits to loyal supporters.

Statistics: are often called probabilistic evidence because they are based on probabilities of correctness and depend on strict adherence to representative sampling technique. Statistics are not facts; they are the next best things to facts when facts are unavailable. Unfortunately, statistics alone provide weak support for an argument. Together with expert opinion and examples, statistics can provide powerful support for arguments.

Statute: a law passed by a legislative body.

Straight ticket: voting for candidates only in one party for different offices.

Summarize: briefly go over the essentials.

Theocracy: a political system where the leader claims to be guided by a Supreme Being.

Theories: are sets of plausible statements or general principles offered to explain phenomena or events. Theories offer testable hypotheses or speculations about the causes of political outcomes. Theories are often modified or constrained by ideological perspectives. Democratic Theory, corporatism, the Downesian model of party competition, egalitarianism, the American Voter Model, the Domino Theory, feminism, elitism, and pluralism are all theories.

Thesis sentence: sums up the main ideas that the writer wants to make.

Totalitarianism: a political system where all aspects of social and economic life are strictly controlled by the government.

Unicameralism: a one-chambered legislature.

Unitary: a political system where power is centralized in the national government, which then delegates power to state and/or local governments.

Utility: having use for something, used with the connotation that whatever has utility is fruitful. The many poor people have not understood the utility of voting for changing their economic or political status.

Values: these are outlooks, perspectives, and subjective or biased opinions. Values are often associated with irrational, moral, or ethical judgments. A value is a sentiment that may or may not be socially acceptable. For example, support for a political party or for racial supremacy are values which sustain vastly different levels of public support. Patriotism, individualism, collectivism, racism, and loyalty are examples of values.

Veto: a process where the president does not sign the bill but sends it back to Congress whereby each chamber must vote to pass the legislation by a two-thirds majority. If the votes do not yield a two-thirds majority, the bill is not enacted into law.

Welfare state: a governing system where the focus of policy is to maximizing the economic and social benefits to each citizen.

Text Acknowledgments

Reprinted by Permission from the Following Books

Coplin, William D. and Michael K. O'Leary. *Policy Skills Workbook*. Croton-on-Hudson, NY. Copyright 1988, William D. Coplin and Michael K. O'Leary. Adaption of policy analysis.

Corder, Jim. and John Ruszkiewicz. *Handbook of Current English*, 8th edition, IL. Copyright 1989, Scott Foresman Publishers. Adaption from pages 631, 731.

Fowler, H. Ramsey and Jane Aaron. *The Little, Brown Handbook*, 4th edition, IL. Copyright 1989, Scott Foresman Publishers. Adaption of pages 95–96, 115, 117, 118, 119.

Kalvelage, Carl, Albert Melone, and Morely Segal. *Bridges to Knowledge in Political Science: A Handbook for Research*, Pacific Palisades, and CA. Copyright 1984, Palisades Publishers. Adaption of pages 118–119.

Reprinted by Permission from the Following Newspapers

Labaton, Stephen. House committee approves measure to aid insurance industry in terrorist attacks, *New York Times* (November 8, 2001): B7. Copyright 2001.

Perry, Scott, "Government's role debated," *Daily Egyptian* (September 14, 1988): 1, 5. Copyright 1988.

_____. "Kelly criticizes Poshard's TV ad," *Daily Egyptian* (September 14, 1988): 1. Copyright 1988

_____. "Kelly: Government should play leading role in housing," *Daily Egyptian* (September 14, 1988): 9. Copyright 1988.

_____. "Kelly, Poshard defend VP choice," *Daily Egyptian* (September 14, 1988): 1, 5. Copyright 1988.

_____. "Kelly, Poshard make stances clear," *Daily Egyptian* (September 14, 1988): 1. Copyright 1988.

_____. "Kelly, Poshard set to debate tonight," *Daily Egyptian* (September 14, 1988): 1. Copyright 1988.

_____. "Kelly, Poshard to debate on campus," *Daily Egyptian* (September 14, 1988): 1, 7. Copyright 1988.

_____. "Poshard, Kelly show differences," *Daily Egyptian* (September 14, 1988): 1. Copyright 1988.

_____. "Poshard says constituents get the credit for his victory," *Daily Egyptian* (September 14, 1988): 1, 5. Copyright 1988.

Rueda-Lynn, Christine N. "Just a housewife? Think about it a bit longer," *Springfield News-Leader* (Dec 1, 1997): 8a. Copyright 1997.

Student Manuscripts Reprinted by Permission

Adams, Noel. Annotated bibliography. Unpublished manuscript.

Alexander, April. Policy recommendation: Needle exchange programs and HIV prevention. Unpublished manuscript.

Allison, Annette. Building inspection expense analysis: Building inspection department. Unpublished manuscript.

Brown, Patrick. Youth influence in political outcomes. Unpublished manuscript.

Cieplak, Caryn. Campaign volunteers: VIPs or peons? Unpublished manuscript.

Dueñas, Gilbert Peña. 2003. Policy implementation and the collaborative management process. Chico, CA: California State University, Chico.

Goard, Steve. Dysfunctional behavior in the FBI. Unpublished manuscript.

Harmon, Marion. Copyright protection and fair use in the digital age: The Digital Millennium Copyright Act of 1998. Unpublished manuscript.

_____. Research proposal: Copyright protection and fair use in the digital age. Unpublished manuscript.

Herhold, Jenna. Kelly for Congress: Campaign '88. Unpublished manuscript.

Kosenski, Christine. Chief Justice Rehnquist. Unpublished manuscript.

Mitchell, Thomas. Outlines. Unpublished manuscript.

Pettit, Edward. The Reagan administration policies on social welfare spending. Unpublished manuscript.

_____. Midterm Exam: Question 5. Unpublished manuscript.

_____. NEPA: America's Policy Responses to Environmental Crisis. Unpublished manuscript.

Reynolds, Meredith. Jailbait. Unpublished manuscript.

_____. Policy formation: Before and after September 11, 2001. Unpublished manuscript.

Schmidt, Alan. Federal funding for NEA. Unpublished manuscript.

Schuberth, Jean M. Why should we worry about a judge's ideology if judicial decisions are based on precedent? Unpublished manuscript.

Sullivan, John T. The Kennedys and the Rockefellers: Political dynasties' effect on the American electorate. Unpublished manuscript.

Walka, Christopher. A review of the *Politics of Congressional Elections*. Unpublished manuscript.

References

Association of College and Research Libraries. 2000. *Information literacy competency standards for higher education*. Chicago, IL: Association of College and Research Libraries.

Association of Research Libraries. 2002. *Timeline: A history of copyright in the United States*. http://www.arl.org/info/frn/copy/timeline.html (accessed April 14, 2004).

Babbie, Earl. 1998. *Plagiarism*. Social Science Research and Instructional Council Teaching Resources Depository: Other Teaching Tools. http://www.csubak.edu/ssric/Modules/Other/plagiarism.html (accessed March 28, 2004).

Chicago manual of style. 2003. Revised and Expanded. 15th ed. Chicago: Univ. of Chicago Press.

Coplin, William D. and Michael K. O'Leary. 1988. *Policy skills workbook*. Croton-on-Hudson, NY: Policy Studies Associates.

Corder, Jim. and John Ruszkiewicz. 1989. *Handbook of current English*. 8th ed. Chicago, IL: Scott Foresman.

Fowler, H. Ramsey and Jane Aaron. 1989. *The Little, Brown handbook*. 4th ed. Chicago, IL: Scott Foresman.

Harnack, Andrew and Eugene Kleppinger. 1998. *Online!: A reference guide to using Internet sources*. NY: St. Martin's Press.

Gibaldi, Joseph. *MLA handbook for writers of research papers*. 6th ed. NY: Modern Language Assoc. of America. 2003.

Goehlert, Robert U. and Fenton S. Martin. 1989. *Congress and law-making: Researching the legislative process*. 2nd ed. CA: ABC-CLIO.

History of congressional elections. http://clerweb.house.gov/histrecs.../elections/political/divisions.html (accessed March 10, 1999).

Indiana University, Bloomington. 2004. *How to recognize plagiarism*. School of Education. http://www.indiana.edu/~istd/examples.htm (accessed March 28, 2004).

Johnson, Kristin and Sarah Blakselee. 2004. *The information timeline*. Chico, CA: Meriam Library's Information Literacy/Instruction Program.

Kalvelage, Carl, Albert Melone, and Morely Segal. 1984. *Bridges to knowledge in political science: A handbook for research*. Pacific Palisades, CA: Palisades Publishers.

Kurian, George. 1994. *Datapedia of the United States, 1790–2000*. Lanham, MD: Bernian Press.

Leahy, Richard. Spring 1990. "What the college writing center is—and isn't." *College Teaching*, 38: 43–48.

Lester, James D. 1990. *Writing research papers: A complete guide*. Chicago, IL: Scott, Foresman.

Mackenzie, G.C. 1996. The presidential appointment process: Historical development, contemporary operations, current issues. In *Obstacle course: The report of the twentieth century fund task force on the presidential appointment process*. Edited by G.C. Mackenzie and Robert Shogan. New York: The Twentieth Century Fund Press.

Melone, Albert P. 1990. *Researching constitutional law*. Chicago, IL: Scott, Foresman.

OWL. 1995–2004. *Avoiding plagiarism*. Purdue University Online Writing Lab. Purdue

University. http://owl.english.purdue.edu./handouts/print/research/r_plagiar.html (accessed March 28, 2004).

Publication manual of the American psychological association. 2001. 5th ed. Washington, DC: American Psychological Assoc.

Ruggiero, Vincent Ryan. 1991. *The art of thinking: A guide to critical and creative thought.* 3rd ed. New York: Harper-Collins.

Salisbury, Robert. H. 1968. The analysis of public policy: A search for theories and roles. In *Political science and public policy*, ed. Austin Ranney. Chicago, IL: Markham Pub.

Schmidt, Steffen, Mack Shelley II, and Barbara Bardes. 1989. *An introduction to critical thinking in American politics.* New York: West Publishing Co.

Silverberg, Robert. 1986. *Star of the gypsies.* New York: Warner Bros.

Standler, Ronald. 2000. *Plagiarism in colleges in USA.* http://rbs2.com/plag.htm (accessed March 28, 2004).

Stanley, Harold W. and Richard G. Niemi. 1998. *Vital statistics on American politics.* Washington, D.C.: Congressional Quarterly Press.

Strunk, William Jr. and E.B. White. 1979. *The elements of style.* New York: MacMillan Pub. Co.

Twain, Mark. 1961. *Wit and wisecracks.* Selected by Doris Bernardete. White Plains, NY: Peter Pauper Press, Inc.

University of California, Davis. 2001. *Avoiding plagiarism.* Student Judicial Affairs. http://sja.ucdavis.edu/avoid.html (accessed March 28, 2004).

Ward, Kathryn. 1990. *Curriculum integration workbook.* Manuscript. Southern Illinois University, Carbondale.

Written word II. 1983. Boston: Houghton Mifflin.

Index